GLOBAL NETWORKS

LINKED CITIES

D0165724

The United Nations University

UNU/IAS

Institute of Advanced Studies

In April 1996, the United Nations General Secretary inaugurated the United Nations University/Institute of Advanced Studies (UNU/IAS) as a community of scholars vigorously pursuing knowledge at the intersection of social and natural systems. The programmatic agenda of UNU/IAS was created to be dynamic and flexible, focusing on finding creative solutions to pressing global issues arising at this nexus. As an overarching theme, UNU/IAS adopted the concept of *eco-structuring*, an approach to sustainable development that envisions shifting technological and societal systems towards greater equity between developing and developed countries, between humankind and the envi.ronment, and between current and future generations.

An integral component of UNU/IAS research involves the examination of urbanization. This volume reflects the work of UNU/IAS and is part of a series of research projects dedicated to furthering knowledge on contemporary forces underpinning urban development.

GLOBAL NETWORKS

LINKED CITIES

EDITED BY **Saskia Sassen**

ROUTLEDGE
NEW YORK • LONDON

Published in 2002 by
Routledge
29 West 35th Street
New York, NY 10001

Published in Great Britain by
Routledge
11 New Fetter Lane
London EC4P 4EE

Routledge is an imprint of the Taylor & Francis Group.

Printed on acid-free, 250-year-life paper.
Manufactured in the United States of America.

10 9 8 7 6 5 4 3 2 1

Library of Congress Cataloging-in-Publication Data

Global networks, linked cities / edited by Saskia Sassen.
    p. cm.
  Includes bibliographical references and index.
  ISBN 0-415-93162-2 (alk. paper) — ISBN 0-415-93613-0 (pbk.: alk. paper)
    Urban economics—Case studies. 2. Globalization—Case studies. 3. Computers and civilization—Case Studies. 4. Information technology—Economic aspects—Case studies. 5. Business enterprises—Computer networks—Case studies. I. Sassen, Saskia.

HT321 .G55 2002
303.48'34'—dc21

                                                              2001041831

Contents

SASKIA SASSEN

Acknowledgments

This book is the last stage of a project that began in 1996. It involved setting up a network of researchers working on the new information technologies and on midrange global cities, mostly in the global south.

The project was generously supported by the Institute of Advanced Studies of the United Nations University (Tokyo). It could not have been done without the institute's support throughout all of these years. I am deeply grateful to Dr. Fu-Chen Lo, former Deputy Director and Urban Programme Senior Manager, Tarcisio Della Senta, former Director UNU/IAS, and Dr. Peter Marcotullio, also of the Institute. I would also like to thank J. A. van Ginkel, Rector of the UNU, who has been a great supporter of urban research at the university, and the Center for Advanced Studies in the Behavioral Sciences (Palo Alto, California) for hosting one of our work meetings. Above all, I am grateful for the excellent work and commitment of the nineteen authors who took part in this project. As with all such projects, the hard work of my research assistants was indispensable. My single largest debt is to Ajay Chanayil of the London School of Economics. All-night work sessions and 5 A.M. meetings were not beyond him. I also want to thank Sara Shousha, Faysal Ahmad, Rosita Blashu, and Harel Shapira. Finally, I thank my editor at Routledge, David McBride, and the assistant editor, Vik Mukhija, who were exceptionally helpful and effective in managing the process of producing the book.

LOCATING CITIES ON GLOBAL CIRCUITS

Saskia Sassen

Cross-border economic processes—flows of capital, labor, goods, raw materials, travelers—have long existed. And over the centuries enormous fluctuations have occured in the degree of openness or closure of the organizational forms within which these flows took place. In the last hundred years, the political interstate system came to provide the dominant oganizational form for cross-border flows, with national states as its key actors. It is this condition that has changed dramatically since the 1980s as a result of privatization, deregulation, the opening up of national economies to foreign firms, and the growing participation of national economic actors in global markets.

In this context we see a rescaling of what are the strategic territories that articulate the new system. With the partial unbundling or at least weakening of the nation as a spatial unit come conditions for the ascendance of other spatial units and scales. Among these are the subnational, notably cities and regions; cross-border regions encompassing two or more subnational entities; and supranational entities, such as global electronic markets and free trade blocs. The dynamics and processes that get terrritorialized or are sited at these diverse scales can in principle be regional, national, and global. There is a proliferation of specialized global circuits for economic activities that both contribute to and constitute these new scales. (See generally, Taylor 1995; Storper 1997; Scott 2001; Veltz 1996; Gravesteijn, van Griensven, and de Smidt 1998; Jessop 1999; Brenner 1998; Sum 1999).

The organizational architecture for cross-border flows that emerges from these rescalings and articulations increasingly diverges from that of the interstate system. The key agents now include not only national states but also firms and markets whose global operations have been facilitated by new policies and cross-border standards produced by willing or not-so-willing states. Among the empirical referents for these non-state forms of articulation are the growing number of cross-border mergers and acquisitions, the expanding networks of foreign affiliates, and the growing numbers of financial centers that are becoming incorporated into global financial markets. Increasingly NGOs (non-governmental organizations), government regulators, mayors, professional associations, and others, operate transnationally and thereby constitute a variety of cross-border networks. As a result of these and other processes to be addressed in this essay, a growing number of cities today play an increasingly important role in directly linking their national economies with global circuits. As cross-border transactions of all kinds grow, so do the networks binding particular configurations of cities (Yeung 2000; Warf and Erickson 1996; Santos, Souze, and Silveiro 1994). This in turn contributes to the formation of new geographies of centrality in which cities are the key articulators.

A central feature of this organizational architecture is that it contains not only the capabilities for enormous geographic dispersal and mobility but also pronounced territorial concentrations of resources necessary for the management and servicing of that dispersal and mobility. The management and servicing of much of the global economic system takes place in a growing network of global cities and cities that might best be described as having global city functions. The growth of global management and servicing activities has brought with it a massive upgrading and expansion of central urban areas, even as large portions of these cities fall into deeper poverty and infrastructural decay (Marcuse and Van Kempen 2000; Peraldi and Perrin 1996; Pozos Ponce 1996). While this role involves only certain components of urban economies, it has contributed to a repositioning of cities nationally and globally.

Further, the fact that strategic global processes are at least partly embedded in national territories via the concentration of specialized global management and servicing functions in cities, introduces new variables in current conceptions about the relation of economic globalization and the state. That is to say, the geography for major new global economic processes partly overrides the duality global/national presupposed in much analysis of the relation between the global economy and state authority. National states have had to participate in creating the enabling institutional and legal environments that contribute to the formation of this cross-border geography for crucial functions largely embedded in the network of global cities. Thereby particular components of national states become denationalized (Sassen 2003).

The central effort in this book is to contribute to the empirical and theoretical specification of this organizational architecture and its consequences for cities. It does so by focusing on how cities in the global south which are mostly in the mid-range of the global hierarchy become articulated with cross-border economic circuits. Secondly, it examines the implications of the new information and communication technologies for both heightening and reducing inequality in this hierarchy. Thirdly, it examines the socio-spatial reorganization inside these cities. The factors involved are many, including state policy, the capabilities brought on by telecommunications and the new networking technologies, older histories of economic advantage enjoyed by some cities, location in specialized global circuits, and the spatial and social restructuring required for the development of global city functions. The fact that these cities are in the global south and in the mid-range of the global hierarchy provides a somewhat distinct cast to the operation of these variables and fills a gap in the scholarship on this subject. But perhaps more important for purposes of research and theorization, it allows us to capture a dynamic in formation, unlike what is the case with global cities already well established.

In examining how cities become part of global circuits there are several possible units of analysis. The chapters in this book focus in part on current global and local architectures of technical connectivity, transport networks, firms and their overseas offices, cross-border transactions such as investment and trade, alliances among financial markets, and growth of transnational labor markets for professionals and specialized service workers. But there are, in principle, many other units of analysis that one might have considered, such as illegal trafficking networks in people, drugs, stolen goods; immigrant personal and business networks; art biennales; the art market; tourism patterns (for instance, stops for major cruise lines); and activists' networks, from environmentalists and human rights efforts to poor people's advocacy organizations. It is impossible to cover such a diverse range of units of analysis in one book.

In this introduction I focus on some of the key features of the global economic system to provide a larger framework for the ensuing chapters. Among these features are the combination of centralization and dispersal trends, the disproportionate concentration of value and transactions in the North Atlantic, the role of cities in an increasingly digitized global economy, especially as illustrated by the growth of finance and specialized services, and the impact of the new networking technologies on urban economies.

WORLDWIDE NETWORKS AND CENTRAL COMMAND FUNCTIONS

The geography of globalization contains dynamics of both dispersal and centralization. The massive trends toward the spatial dispersal of economic activities at the metropolitan, national, and global levels that we associate with globalization have contributed to a demand for new forms of territorial centralization of top-level management and control functions. Insofar as these functions benefit from agglomeration economies even in the face of telematic integration of a firm's globally dispersed manufacturing and service operations, they tend to locate in cities. This raises a question as to why they should benefit from agglomeration economies, especially since globalized economic sectors tend to be intensive users of the new telecommunications and computer technologies and increasingly produce a partly dematerialized output, such as financial instruments and specialized services. D. Linda Garcia (this volume) examines the extent to which business networks are a crucial variable that is to be distinguished from technical networks. Such business networks have been crucial since long before the current networking technologies were developed. Business networks benefit from agglomeration economies and hence thrive in cities even today when instantaneous global communication is possible. Elsewhere (2001: chap. 2 and 5) I examine this issue and find that the key variable contributing to the spatial concentration of central functions and associated agglomeration economies is the extent to which this dispersal occurs under conditions of concentration in control, ownership, and profit appropriation. This dynamic of simultaneous geographic dispersal and concentration is one of the key elements of the organizational architecture of the global economic system. Let me first give several empirical referents and then examine some of the implications for theorizing the impacts of globalization and the new technologies on cities.

The rapid growth of affiliates illustrates the dynamic of simultaneous geographic dispersal and concentration of a firm's operations (table 1). By 1999 companies had well over half a million affiliates outside their home countries accounting for U.S. $11 trillion in sales, a very significant figure if we consider that global trade stood at U.S. $8 trillion. Peter Taylor, D. R. F. Walker, and J. V. Beaverstock (this volume) examine a specific instance by showing the global geography of offices for leading London firms in finance, accounting, law, and advertising. Firms with large numbers of geographically dispersed factories and service outlets face massive new needs for central coordination and servicing, especially when their affiliates involve foreign countries with different legal and accounting systems. The extent of geographic dispersal is well captured in tables 2 and 3 which show the global network of affiliates for Chicago-based firms in two of these four sectors, accounting and advertising.

Another instance today of this negotiation between a global cross-border dynamic and territorially specific sites is that of the global financial markets. The orders of magnitude of cross-border financial transactions have risen sharply, as illustrated by the 1999 U.S. $68 trillion in the value of internationally traded derivatives, a major component of the global economy. These transactions are partly embedded in electronic systems that make possible the instantaneous transmission of money and information around the globe. Much attention has gone to this capacity for instantaneous transmission. But the other half of the story is the extent to which the global financial markets are actually located in cities.

TABLE 1

FOREIGN AFFILIATES, 1996–1998 (BN USD AND PERCENT)

Item	Value at Current Prices (bn USD)		
	1996	1997	1998
Sales to foreign affiliates	9,372	9,728	11,427
Gross product of foreign affiliates	2,026	2,286	2,677
Total assets of foreign affiliates	11,246	12,211	14,620
Exports of foreign affiliates	1,841	2,035	2,338
Employment of foreign affiliates	30,941	31,630	35,074

Source: UNCTAD, World Investment Report 1999: Foreign Direct Investment and the Challenge of Development, p. 9

TABLE 2A

TOP CHICAGO ADVERTISING FIRMS, 1999

Rank	Name	Fee Income 1998 (US$ Millions)	No. Affiliates in other Cities
1	Starcom Worldwide	3,700	40
2	Leo Burnett Worldwide	3,100	38
3	FCB Chicago	1,310	44
4	DDB Chicago	1,200	5
5	DraftWorldwide	859	24
6	Ogilvy & Mather	446	47
7	BBDO Chicago	349	47
8	Publicis & Hal Riney	203	5
9	Abelsom-Taylor	202	1
10	GSP Marketing	199	1

Source: Fee income rankings downloaded from Crain's Chicago Business, http://www.chicagobusiness.com/cgi-bin/mag/article.pl?static_id=4 on Dec 20, 2000; number of affiliates based on individual firm's website listings

TABLE 2B

GEOGRAPHIES OF AFFILIATES, TOP TEN CHICAGO ADVERTISING FIRMS, 1999

No. of Firms with Offices in City	City
7	Paris
6	Amsterdam, Bangkok, Brussels, Frankfurt, Hong Kong, Kuala Lumpur, London, Milan, Montreal, Moscow, New York, San Francisco, Seoul, Singapore, Stockholm Sydney, Tokyo, Toronto, Zurich
5	Beijing, Budapest, Buenos Aires, Caracas, Copenhagen, Istanbul, Jakarta, Madrid, Melbourne, Mexico City, Prague, Santiago, Shanghai, Taipei
4	Barcelona, Johannesburg, Los Angeles, Miami, São Paulo
3	Atlanta, Dallas, Hamburg, Manila, Rome
2	Berlin, Dusseldorf, Minneapolis, Munich, Washington, DC

TABLE 3A

TOP CHICAGO ACCOUNTING FIRMS, 2000

Rank	Name	Fee Income 1998 (US$ Millions)	No. Affiliates in Other Cities
1	Pricewaterhouse Coopers	15,300	55
2	Andersen Worldwide	13,900	55
3	Ernst & Young international	10,900	51
4	KPMG International	10,400	53
5	Deloitte Touche Tohmatsu	9,000	25
6	BDO International	1,601	6
7	Grant Thorton International	1,506	1
8	Horwath International	1,185	10
9	RSM International	1,182	9
10	Moores Rowland International	1,141	7

Source: Fee income rankings downloaded from Crain's Chicago Business, http://www.chicagobusiness.com/cgi-bin/mag/article.pl?static_id=4 on Dec 20, 2000; number of affiliates based on individual firm's website listings

TABLE 3B

GEOGRAPHIES OF AFFILIATES TEN TOP CHICAGO ADVERTISING FIRMS, 2000

No. of Firms with Offices in City	City
9	Minneapolis
8	New York, Washington, DC
7	Dallas, Los Angeles
6	Atlanta, Boston, London, Miami, Paris
5	Berlin, Budapest, Buenos Aires, Caracas, Frankfurt, Hamburg, Hong Kong, Houston, Istanbul, Jakarta, Johannesburg, Melbourne, Milan, Moscow, Munich, Prague, Rome, São Paulo, Santiago, Seoul, Shanghai, Singapore, Stockholm, Sydney, Taipei, Tokyo, Toronto, Warsaw
4	Amsterdam, Bangkok, Barcelona, Beijing, Brussels, Copenhagen, Geneva, Kuala Lumpur, Madrid, Manila, Mexico City, Zurich
3	Osaka
2	Dusseldorf

Expansion in these markets is partly a function of the expanding number of cities that become part of the global network. Yet even as the volume of the industry has risen sharply there has not been a significant reduction in the disproportionate concentration of assets in cities of the global North. Indeed, the degrees of concentration internationally and within countries are unexpectedly high for what is an increasingly globalized and electronic economic sector. Inside countries the leading financial centers have come to concentrate a greater share of national financial activity over the last fifteen years, and internationally, cities in the global North concentrate well over half of the global capital market. (I discuss this subject empirically in a later section).

Stock markets constitute one of the components of the global capital market. The late 1980s and early 1990s saw the addition of markets such as Buenos Aires, São Paulo, Mexico City, Bangkok, Taipei, Moscow, and growing numbers of non-national firms listed in many of these markets. This growing number of financial centers incorporated in the global capital market has contributed to raise the capital that can be mobilized through the global network, reflected in the sharp worldwide growth of stock market capitalization which reached more than U.S. $30 trillion in 2000. This globally integrated stock market system, which makes possible the circulation of publicly listed shares around the globe in seconds, is embedded in a grid of very material, physical, strategic places.

The specific forms assumed by globalization over the last decade have created particular organizational requirements (see, e.g., Amin and Thrift 1995; Aspen Institute 1998; Castells and Hall 1994). The emergence of global markets for finance and specialized services and the growth of investment as a major type of international transaction have contributed to the expansion in central functions and in the demand for specialized services for firms.

By central functions I do not only mean headquarters functions; I am referring to all the top-level financial, legal, accounting, managerial, executive, and planning functions necessary to run a corporate organization operating in multiple countries. These central functions are partly embedded in headquarters, but also in good part in what has been called the corporate services complex, that is, the network of financial, legal, accounting, and advertising firms that handle the complexities of operating in more than one national legal system, national accounting system, advertising culture, and so forth and do so under conditions of rapid innovations in all these fields.[1] Such services have become so specialized and complex that headquarters increasingly buy them from specialized firms rather than produce them in-house. These agglomerations of firms producing central functions for the management and coordination of global economic systems are disproportionately concentrated in an expanding network of global cities. This network represents a strategic factor in the organization of the global economy.

It is important analytically to unbundle the fact of strategic functions for the global economy or for global operation, and the overall corporate economy of a country. These global control and command functions are partly embedded in national corporate structures but also constitute a distinct corporate subsector. This subsector in each city can be conceived of as part of a network that connects global cities across the globe through firms' affiliates or other representative offices, and through the specialized servicing and management of cross-border transactions.[2] For the purposes of certain kinds of inquiry this distinction may not matter; for the purposes of understanding the global economy, it does.[3]

National and global markets as well as globally integrated organizations require central places where the work of globalization gets done. Finance and advanced corporate services are industries producing the organizational commodities necessary for the implementation and management of global economic systems. Cities are preferred sites for the production of these services, particularly the most innovative, speculative, internationalized service sectors. Further, leading firms in information industries require a vast physical infrastructure containing strategic nodes with hyperconcentration of facilities; we need to distinguish between the capacity for global transmission/communication and the material conditions that make this possible. Finally, even the most advanced information industries have a production process that is at least partly place-bound because of the combination of resources it requires even when the outputs are hypermobile.

Theoretically this addresses two key issues in current debates and scholarship. One of these is the complex articulation beween capital fixity and capital mobility, and the other, the position of cities in a global economy (See, e.g., Castells 1996; Allen et al. 1999; Kostinsky 1997; Cohen et al. 1996; Ascher 1995). Elsewhere (2001: chap. 2) I have developed the thesis that capital mobility cannot be reduced simply to that which moves or to the technologies that facilitate movement. Rather, multiple components of what we keep thinking of as capital fixity are actually components of capital mobility. This conceptualization allows us to reposition the role of cities in an increasingly globalizing world, in that they contain the resources (including fixed capital) that enable firms and markets to have global operations.[4] The mobility of capital, whether in the form of investments, trade, or overseas affiliates, needs to be managed, serviced, coordinated. These tasks are often rather place-bound, yet are key components of capital mobility. Finally, states—place-bound institutional orders—have played an often crucial role in producing regulatory environments that facilitate the implementation of cross-border operations for national as well as foreign firms, investors, and markets (Sassen 2003).

In brief, a focus on cities makes it possible to recognize the anchoring of multiple cross-border dynamics in a network of places, prominent among which are cities, particularly global cities or those with global city functions. This in turn anchors various features of globalization in the specific conditions and histories of these cities and in their variable insertions in their national economies and in various world economies across time and place. The chapters on Mexico City (Parnreiter, this volume), Beirut (Huybrechts, this volume), Shanghai (Gu and Tang, this volume), and Buenos Aires (Ciccolella and Mignaqui, this volume), all explore the specific trajectories through which these cities are becoming part of global circuits in the current period. This type of conceptualization about globalization contributes to identifying a complex organizational architecture that cuts across borders and is both deterritorialized and concentrated in cities. Further, it creates an enormous research agenda in that every particular national or urban economy has its specific and inherited modes of absorbing change and linking up with current global circuits. The chapter by Taylor, Walker, and Beaverstock in this volume begins to develop a new methodology for this type of research. Once we have more information about variance across countries and cities we may also be able to establish whether position in the global hierarchy makes a difference and the various ways in which it might do so.

THE GEOGRAPHY OF CROSS-BORDER CAPITAL FLOWS

This type of analysis of globalization, which seeks to map the strategic sites with hyperconcentration of resources as well as the cross-border networks that link these sites and others, helps us understand to what extent there is a specific geography of globalization and the fact that it is not a planetary event encompassing all of the world.[5] It is, furthermore, a changing geography, one that has undergone multiple, often specialized transformations over the last few centuries and over the last two decades,[6] and most recently has come to include electronic space.

A first step in capturing this geography of globalization is to examine some of the patterns of cross-border capital flows. These flows are often used as (partial) indicators of economic globalization. The empirical patterns of foreign direct investment and global finance show both a sharp concentration in certain areas of the world and a growing incorporation of particular sites in the less developed world. The evidence makes it clear that the center of gravity lies in the North Atlantic region. The northern transatlantic economic system (particularly the links among the European Union [EU], the United States, and Canada) represents the major concentration of processes of economic globalization in the world today. This holds whether one looks at foreign direct investment flows generally, at cross-border mergers and acquisitions in particular, at overall financial flows, or at the new strategic alliances among financial centers. At the end of 1999, the North Atlantic accounted for two-thirds of worldwide stock market capitalization, 60 percent of inward foreign investment stock and 76 percent of outward stock, 60 percent of worldwide sales in mergers and acquisitions (M&As), and 80 percent of purchases in M&As. There are other major regions in the global economy receiving capital flows (table 4)—Japan, Southeast Asia, Latin America—but they are dwarfed by the weight of the northern transatlantic system (See table 5; see also Schiffer, table A, this volume). A second major pattern is the significant growth in the absolute level of flows going to other parts of the world, even though they do not compare with the North Atlantic region. Disaggregating these patterns makes clear that most of the the capital is going to a limited number of sites. Flows in Latin America reflect these two patterns well: a massive increase in foreign investment but mostly concentrated in Brazil, Mexico, and Argentina (see table 5; see also Schiffer table A, this volume).

Cross-border M&As today dominate global foreign direct investment (FDI) flows. M&As are heavily concentrated in Organization for Economic Cooperation and Development countries, which account for 89 percent of purchases and 72 percent of sales. A growing number of companies opt for mergers as a mode of overseas expansion or consolidation. For instance, acquisitions represented 90 percent of total FDI in the United States in 1996. In 1998

TABLE 4

AVERAGE ANNUAL GROWTH RATE OF DIRECT FOREIGN INVESTMENT FROM DEVELOPED TO DEVELOPING COUNTIRES, 1960–1998 (PERCENT)

Period	Growth Rate
1960–1968	7.0
1968–1973	9.2
1973–1978	19.4
1980–1987	1.9
1988–1996	16.8
1997–1998	−4.0

Source: 1960–1978: OECD, *Recent International Direct Investment Trends* (1981); 1980–1987: World Bank, *World Development* (1988); 1988–1998, OECD, *Survey of OECD Work on International Investment* (1998).

TABLE 5

FOREIGN DIRECT INVESTMENT FLOWS BY REGION, 1986 TO 1997, SELECTED YEARS (MN USD AND PERCENT)

Region	FDI Inflows			FDI Outflows		
	1986–1991 (annual average)	1997	% of world totals in 1997	1986–1991 (annual average)	1997	% of world totals in 1997
North Atlantic[1]	121,144	213,852	53.4	131,646	323,111	81.8
Latin America and the Carribean[2]	9,460	56,138	14.0	1,305	9,097	2.3
South, East and Southeast Asia[3]	15,135	82,411	20.6	8,315	50,157	12.7
Subtotal	145,739	352,401	88.0	141,266	382,365	96.7
World total	159,331	400,486		180,510	395,236	

Source: UNCTAD, *World Investment Report 1998,* Annex B, 361–371.

Notes: [1] North Atlantic region includes all countries in the European Union, Iceland, Norway, Switzerland, Gibraltar, Canada, and the United States [2,3] Please refer to source for detailed listing of all countries included.

M&As in the North Atlantic reached US$256.5 billion, up from U.S. $69.4 billion in 1995. The average transnationality index for the EU is 56.7 percent compared to 38.5 percent for the United States (but 79.2 for Canada). This index is an average based on ratios of the share that foreign sales, assets, and employment represent in a firm's total of each. The index has grown for the 100 largest TNCs in the world since it was first used in 1990. Most of the United States and EU TNCs in this top 100 list have very high levels of foreign assets as a percentage of total assets: for instance, 51 percent for IBM, 55 percent for Volkswagen Group, 91 percent for Nestle, 96 percent for Asea Brown Boveri, and so on. The United States, the United Kingdom, France, Germany, and Japan together accounted for three-fourths of these 100 firms in 1997; this has been roughly so since 1990.

We are seeing the consolidation of a transnational economic system that has its center of gravity in the North Atlantic both in terms of the intensity and value of transactions, and in terms of the emerging body of rules and standards. This system is articulated with a growing network of sites for investment, trade, and financial transactions in the rest of the world. It is, however, a complex geography. There is also a strengthening of cross-border regions at various levels of the global hierarchy. The cases of Mercosur and the Iran-Dubai corridor described in this volume are two such instances. (See Schiffer, this volume; Parsa and Keivani, this volume). Globalization does indeed entail dispersal, but the combination of concentration and network expansion makes for a strongly hierarchical distribution.

The weight of the North Atlantic system in the global economy raises a number of questions. One concerns the extent to which this growing interdependence is moving toward the formation of a cross-border economic system.[7] The weight of these transatlantic links needs to be considered against the weight of established zones of influence for each of the major powers—particularly, the Western Hemisphere in the case of the United States, and Africa, central and eastern Europe for the European Union. Elsewhere I have argued that incorporation in a hierachical global network centered in the North Atlantic now increasingly shapes the economic relations of the United States and major European countries with their zones of influence. Thus, while the United States is still a dominant force in Latin America, several European countries have become major investors in Latin America on a scale far surpassing past trends (see chapters on Mexico City, São Paulo, and Buenos Aires, this volume). And while several European Union countries have become leading investors in central and eastern Europe, U.S. firms are playing a role they never played before. This contributes to shape a new grid of economic transactions superimposed on the old geoeconomic patterns. The latter persist in variable extents, but they are increasingly submerged under this new cross-border grid.

IMPACTS OF NEW INFORMATION AND COMMUNICATIONS
TECHNOLOGIES ON CENTRALITY

Cities have historically provided national economies, polities, and societies with something we can think of as centrality. In terms of their economic function, cities provide agglomeration economies, massive concentrations of information on the latest developments, and a marketplace. How do the new technologies alter the role of centrality and hence of cities and metro areas as economic entities particularly for those sectors that can benefit from these new information and communications technologies (ICTs)? And, further, how do they alter the spatial organization inside cities and metro areas as they alter the meaning of centrality?

Centrality remains a key feature of today's global economy. But there is no longer a simple straightforward relation between centrality and such geographic entities as the downtown, or the central business district (CBD) (Veltz 1996; Scott 2001; Santos et al. 1994). In the past, and up to quite recently in fact, the center was synonymous with the downtown or the CBD. Today, partly as a result of the new technologies, the spatial correlates of the center can assume several geographic forms, ranging from the CBD to a new global grid of cities. Simplifying one could identify three forms of centrality today.[8]

First, while there is no longer a direct relation between centrality and geographic entities such as the downtown, the CBD remains a key form of centrality. But the CBD in major international business centers is one profoundly reconfigured by technological and economic change (Abu-Lughod 1999; Souza 1994; Beauregard 1991). Stephen Graham (this volume) examines the variety of impacts of the new technologies on this reconfiguration, and the chapters on Mexico City (Parnreiter, this volume), Beirut (Huybrechts, this volume), Shanghai (Rose Gu and Tang, this volume), and Buenos Aires (Ciccolella and Mignaqui, this volume; see also Pirez 1994) describe the multiple ways in which this can occur. (See also Orum and Chen 2000).

Second, the center can extend into a metropolitan area in the form of a grid of nodes of intense business activity (Veltz 1996; Marcuse and van Kempen 2000). This is a case well illustrated by recent developments in Buenos Aires (Ciccolella and Mignaqui, this volume). One might ask whether a spatial organization characterized by dense strategic nodes spread over a broader region does or does not constitute a new form of organizing the territory of the "center," rather than, as in the more conventional view, an instance of suburbanization or geographic dispersal. Insofar as these various nodes are articulated through cyberroutes or digital highways, they form a grid that is a geographic correlate of the most advanced type of "center." The places that fall outside this new grid of digital highways, however, are peripheralized. This grid of nodes represents, in my analysis, a reconstitution of the concept of region. Far from neutralizing geography, the grid is likely to be embedded in conventional forms of transport infrastructure, notably rapid rail and highways connecting to airports. Ironically perhaps, conventional infrastructure can to maximize the economic benefits derived from telematics. I think this is an important issue that has been lost somewhat in discussions about the neutralization of geography through telematics.

Third, we are seeing the formation of a transterritorial "center" constituted via telematics and intense economic transactions. It consists of the multiple and diversifying inter-city links that take place partly in electronic markets and transactions and partly through the intensifying circulation of goods, information, firms, and workers. In this regard this is both a territorialized and deterritorialized space of centrality. It requires both a specific logic for territorial development and the infrastucture for global networking technologies (Graham, this volume). The work of developing a city's capability for "housing" global city functions is well described in all the chapters focused on specific cities and regions in this book (See Parts Two and Three, this volume). These chapters show us how the development of global city functions entails a whole new logic for territorial development; to achieve this takes enormous resources, both private and governmental, and it takes re-regulation of crucial sectors by governments. The chapters in Part One show us the formation of cross-border networks that connect cities through technology, business transactions, firms' affiliates, and airline travel. The most powerful of these new geographies of centrality at the interurban level binds the major international financial and business centers: New York, London, Tokyo, Paris, Frankfurt, Zurich, Amsterdam, Chicago, Los Angeles, Sydney, and Hong Kong, among others.[9] But this geography now also includes cities such as São Paulo and Mexico City. The intensity of transactions within this geography, particularly through the financial markets, trade in services, and investment, has increased sharply, and so have the orders of magnitude involved. We are also seeing emergent regional geographies of centrality, as is illustrated by the case of São Paulo in the Mercosur free-trade area (Schiffer, this volume) and by the relation between the participating entities in the Iran-Dubai corridor (Parsa and Keivani, this volume).

The specific processes through which new spaces of centrality are constituted can also be expected to have an impact on inequality between cities and inside cities. We would expect these processes to reorganize particular features of space inside each city and region and to reorganize their articulation with national and global economic circuits (For a broad range of perspectives see, e.g., Tardanico and Lungo 1995; Keil 1993; Sum 1999; Persky and Wievel 1994; Nijman 1996; Landrieu et al. 1998). There is an expectation in much of the literature about ICTs that they will override older hierarchies and spatial inequalities through the universalizing of connectivity that they represent. The chapters in this book suggest that this is not quite the case. Whether it is the network of financial centers and foreign direct investment patterns discussed in this chapter, or the more specific examinations of the spatial organization in particular cities, the new technologies have not reduced hierarchy nor spatial inequalities even as they restructure space. Nor have socioeconomic inequalities been reduced in the cities examined here. (For other cities, see, e.g., Baum 1997; Elliott 1999; Fincher and Jacobs 1998; King 1995; Abbott 1996; Gugler 2002). And this is so even in the face of massive upgradings and state-of-the-art infrastructure in all of the cities examined in this book.

There is little doubt that connecting to global circuits has brought with it a significant level of development and expansion of central urban areas and metropolitan grids of business nodes, and considerable economic dynamism. But various forms of spatial unevenness have not been reduced; on the contrary, all these chapters show growing spatial fragmentation even as economic dynamism and spatial upgrading of expanding areas inside these cities and regions have also occurred. Further, the pronounced and sharpened orientation to the world markets evident in high-growth economic sectors in these cities suggest a diminished, or at least changed, integration with their national economies, their regions, and the larger economic and social structure inside these cities. Cities have typically been deeply embedded in the economies of their immediate region, indeed often reflecting the characteristics of the latter; and they still do. But cities that are strategic sites in the global economy tend, in part, to disconnect from their region.[10] This conflicts with a key proposition in traditional scholarship about urban systems, namely, that these systems promote the territorial integration of regional and national economies. There has been a sharpening inequality in the concentration of strategic resources and activities between each of these cities and others in the same country, though this tends to be evident only at fairly disaggregated levels of evidence. For example, Mexico City today concentrates a higher share of some types of economic activity and value production than it did in the past, but to see this requires a very particularized set of analyses, as Christof Parnreiter (this volume) shows us.[11] Though with different modalities, this also holds for Buenos Aires (Ciccolella and Mignaqui, this volume) and São Paulo (Schiffer, this volume)

THE INTERSECTION OF SERVICE INTENSITY AND GLOBALIZATION

To understand the new or sharply expanded role of a particular kind of city in the world economy since the early 1980s, we need to focus on the intersection of two major processes. The first is the sharp growth in the globalization of economic activity; this has raised the scale and the complexity of transactions, thereby feeding the growth of top-level multinational headquarter functions and the growth of advanced corporate services. With qualifications, this also holds for multisite firms that operate only nationally. Thus while these firms need not negotiate the complexities of international borders and the regulations of different countries, they are still faced with a territorially dispersed network of operations that requires centralized control and servicing.

The second process we need to consider is the growing service intensity in the organization of all industries. By this term I mean that today firms in all sectors of the economy—from mining and manufacturing to finance and consumer services—buy more intermediate service inputs. This has contributed to a massive overall growth in the demand for producer services, including financial, accounting, insurance, communications, and maintenance services.[12] The key process from the perspective of the urban economy derived from this growing demand for services by firms in all industries is the fact that cities are preferred production sites for such services, whether at the global, national, or regional level. Hence the increase in service intensity in the organization of all industries has had a significant growth effect on cities beginning in the 1980s in the North Atlantic and in the 1990s in Latin America and Asia. The chapters on Mexico and São Paulo examine these issues in great detail (see this volume). As a result we see in cities the formation of a new urban economic core of financial and service activities that comes to replace the older, typically manufacturing-oriented core. Some of these cities cater to regional or subnational markets; others cater to national markets, and yet others cater to global markets. Seen analytically, globalization changes the scale and adds complexity to these patterns of urban growth.

In the case of cities that are major international business centers, the scale, power, and profit levels of this new core suggest that we are seeing the formation of a new urban economy. This is so in at least two regards. First, even though these cities have long been centers for business and finance, since the late 1970s there have been dramatic changes in the structure of the business and financial sectors as well as sharp increases in the overall magnitude of these sectors and their weight in the urban economy. (See, generally, Graham and Spence 1997; Harris and Fabricius 1996; Moulaert and Scott 1997). Second, the ascendance of the new finance and services complex, particularly international finance, engenders what may be regarded as a new economic regime (Sassen 2001: chapters 1 and 10). That is, although this sector may account for only a fraction of the economy of a city, it imposes itself on that larger economy. Most notably, the possibility for superprofits in finance has the effect of devalorizing manufacturing insofar as the latter cannot generate the superprofits typical in much financial activity.

But not everything in the economy of these cities has changed. There are continuities and many similarities with cities that are not global nodes. Rather, the implantation of global processes and markets has meant that the interna-

SASKIA SASSEN

tionalized sector of the economy has expanded sharply and has imposed a new valorization dynamic—that is, a new set of criteria for valuing or pricing various economic activities and outcomes. This has had devastating effects on large sectors of the urban economy. High prices and profit levels in the internationalized sector and its ancillary activities, such as top-of-the-line restaurants and hotels, have made it increasingly difficult for other sectors to compete for space and investments. Many of these other sectors have experienced considerable downgrading and/or displacement, as, for example, neighborhood shops tailored to local needs are replaced by upscale boutiques and restaurants catering to new high-income urban elites.

These trends became evident in the late 1980s in the global cities of the North and in the early 1990s in a number of major cities in the developing world that have become integrated into various world markets: São Paulo (Schiffer, this volume), Buenos Aires (Ciccolella and Mignaqui, this volume), Bangkok, Taipei, and Shanghai (Rose Gu and Tang, this volume), Beirut (Huybrechts, this volume), and Mexico City (Parnreiter, this volume) are only a few examples. As in the North, also here the new urban core was fed by the deregulation of various economic sectors, ascendance of finance and specialized services, and integration into the world markets. The opening of stock markets to foreign investors and the privatization of what were once public sector firms have been crucial institutional arenas for this articulation. Given the vast size of some of these cities, the impact of this new core on the broader city is not always as evident as in central London or Frankfurt, but the transformation is still very real.

It is important to recognize that manufacturing remains a crucial sector in all these economies, even when it may have ceased to be a dominant sector in major cities. The interaction between manufacturing and the producer services is complex and the subject of disagreement.[13] In my research (2001) I have found that even when manufacturing—and mining and agriculture, for that matter—feeds growth in the demand for producer services, its actual location is of secondary importance in the case of global level service firms. Thus whether manufacturing plants are located offshore or within a country may be quite irrelevant as long as these plants are part of a multinational corporation likely to buy the services from those top-level firms. Moreover, a key proposition in my global city model (2001: Preface to the New Edition) is that the territorial dispersal of plants, especially if international, actually raises the demand for producer services. This is yet another meaning, or consequence, of globalization: the growth of producer service firms based in New York or London or Paris can be fed by manufacturing located anywhere in the world as long as it is part of a multinational corporate network. Third, a good part of the producer services sector is fed by financial and business transactions that either have nothing to do with manufacturing, as is the case in many of the global financial markets, or for which manufacturing is incidental, as in much merger and acquisition activity centered as it is on buying and selling firms rather than the buying of manufacturing firms as such.

THE LOCATIONAL AND INSTITUTIONAL EMBEDDEDNESS OF GLOBAL FINANCE

Several of the issues discussed thus far assume particularly sharp forms in the emerging global network of financial centers. The global financial system has reached levels of complexity that require the existence of a cross-border network of financial centers to service the operations of global capital.[14] This network of financial centers increasingly differs from earlier versions of the international financial system. In a world of largely closed national financial systems, each country duplicated most of the necessary functions for its economy; collaborations among different national financial markets were often no more than the execution of a given set of operations in each of the countries involved, as in clearing and settlement. With few exceptions, such as offshore markets and a relatively small number of large banks, the international system consisted of a string of closed domestic systems.

The global integration of markets makes many of these activities redundant and makes collaboration a far more complex matter, one that has the effect of sharpening the division of labor within the network. Beyond the necessary range of specialized services present in all these centers, we now also see a trend toward the formation of specialized capabilities that partially differentiate centers and simultaneously integrate them into a larger global network. This configuration also promotes the formation of strategic alliances. In this context London and New York with their enormous concentrations of resources and talent continue to be powerhouses in the global network for the most strategic and complex operations of the system as a whole. They are the leading exporters of financial services and typically part of any major international public offering, whether it is the privatization of British Telecom or of a large public sector utility in Latin America. Similarly, the formation of the Eurozone is strengthening the position of Frankfurt and of Paris, each of which is, in turn, becoming part of a crisscross of alliances among major European centers.

The incorporation of a growing number of financial centers is one form through which the global financial system expands: each of these centers is the nexus between that country's wealth and the global market and between foreign investors and that country's investment opportunities. The overall sources and destinations of investment therewith grow in number. The financial centers of many countries around the world are increasingly fulfilling gateway functions for the circulation in and out of national and foreign capital. Gateway functions emerge as a key mechanism for integration into the global financial market. In contrast, among key functions in leading centers are the production of innovations to package the capital flowing in and out. Further, most of the complex operations involved in gateway functions tend to be executed by many of the top investment, accounting, and legal services firms, through affiliates, branches, direct imports of those services, or some other form of transfer. Thus the development effects, even in the narrow sense of building these types of skills, may well be quite limited. These gateways for the global market are also gateways for the dynamics of financial crises: capital can flow out as easily and quickly as it flows in. And what was once thought of as "national" capital can now as easily join the exodus: for instance, during the Mexico crisis of December 1994, we now know that the first capital to flee the Mexican markets was national, not foreign.

In my reading the globally integrated financial system is not only about competition among countries as is typically assumed. The trend is toward an increase in specialized collaborative efforts among these centers. Further, insofar as markets are integrated, growth overall is maximized through growth in all centers. The crisis in Tokyo or Hong Kong does not create advantages for other centers, except perhaps in some very particular segments of the market. The sharp growth of London, New York, Paris, or Frankfurt is in part fed by the global network of financial centers. The global capital market needs a network of state-of-the-art financial centers. Hence simply to reduce the interaction among even the leading cities in the network to competition is inadequate. For instance, there is little gain for the larger financial system in Hong Kong's or Tokyo's decline. Since its inception, Hong Kong has been a strategic exchange node for firms between China and the rest of the world, as well as among all the overseas Chinese communities (Meyer, this volume). Few other centers in the world can replicate this advantage, but they can benefit from Hong Kong's specialized role.[15] Today, even after a severe crisis, Hong Kong still has one of the most sophisticated concentrations of advanced services that puts it in the group of top-ranked centers. A parallel argument can be made for Tokyo: even as its economy is in crisis, it will continue to be a crucial cog in the global financial system given its enormous concentration of financial resources and its role as the leading exporter of capital in the world.[16] The interactions among financial centers are multifaceted, and competition is just one element.

The rapid growth of electronic networks and markets raises a question about the ongoing importance of financial centers.[17] Insofar as the latter combine multiple resources and talents necessary for executing complex operations and servicing global firms and markets and insofar as this combination cannot easily be relocated to electronic space, financial centers will remain important. The question then becomes: How far can the new communications technologies go in eliminating the need for actual financial centers and the network of such centers, especially given the increasingly global and electronic nature of the capital market.[18] An important distinction in my research on the subjet is that between centers and exchanges: financial centers cannot be reduced to their exchanges. They are part of a far more complex architecture, and they encompass far more than exchanges. It is far easier to make a financial exchange electronic than a financial center. The next two sections develop these issues.

IN THE DIGITAL ERA: MORE CONCENTRATION THAN DISPERSAL?

What really stands out in the evidence for the global financial industry is the extent to which there is a sharp concentration of the shares of many financial markets in a few financial centers.[19] London, New York, Tokyo (notwithstanding a national economic recession), Paris, Frankfurt, and a few other cities regularly appear at the top *and* represent a large share of global transactions. London, followed by Tokyo, New York, Hong Kong, and Frankfurt account for a major share of all international banking. London, Frankfurt, and New York account for an enormous world share in the export of financial services. London, New York, and Tokyo account for more than one-third of global institutional equity holdings, and this as of the end of 1997 after a 32 percent decline in Tokyo's value over 1996. London, New York, and Tokyo account for 58 percent of the foreign exchange market, one of the few truly global markets; together with Singapore, Hong Kong, Zurich, Geneva, Frankfurt, and Paris, they account for 85 percent in this, the most global of markets.

This trend toward consolidation in a few centers even as the network of integrated financial centers expands globally also is evident within many countries. In the United States, for instance, New York concentrates a disproportionate share of the leading investment banks and international exchanges. Sydney and Toronto have equally gained power in their respective countries and have taken over functions and market share from what were once the major commercial centers, respectively Melbourne and Montreal. So have São Paulo and Bombay, which have gained share and functions from respectively Rio de Janeiro in Brazil and New Delhi and Calcutta in India. One might have thought that such large countries with multiple cities and powerful economies could sustain several major financial centers. In France, Paris today concentrates larger shares of most financial sectors than it did ten years ago, and once-important stock markets like Lyon have become "provincial," even though Lyon is today the hub of a thriving economic region. Milano privatized its exchange in September 1997 and electronically merged Italy's ten regional markets. Frankfurt now concentrates a larger share of the financial market in Germany than it did in the early 1980s, and so does Zurich in Switzerland, which once had Basel and Geneva as significant competitors. Further, the trend towards the consolidation of one leading financial center in each country is a function of rapid growth in the sector, not of decay in the losing cities.

There is both consolidation in fewer major centers across and within countries *and* a sharp growth in the numbers of these national centers that become part of the global network as countries deregulate their economies. São Paulo and Bombay, for instance joined the global financial network after Brazil and India (partly) deregulated their financial systems. This mode of incorporation into the global network is often at the cost of losing functions that they had when they were largely national centers. Today the leading, typically foreign, financial, accounting, and legal services firms enter their markets to handle the new cross-border operations. Though they add to the total volume in the global market, incorporation typically happens without a gain in the share of the global market that they can command even as capitalization may increase, often sharply, and enrich investors.

Why is it that at a time of rapid growth in the network of financial centers, in overall volumes, and in electronic networks, we have such high concentration of market shares in the leading global and national centers? Both globalization and electronic trading are about expansion and dispersal beyond what had been the confined realm of national economies and floor trading. Indeed, one might well ask why financial centers matter at all.

WHY THE NEED FOR CENTERS IN THE GLOBAL DIGITAL ERA?

The continuing weight of major centers is, in a way, countersensical, as is, for that matter, the existence of an expanding network of financial centers. The rapid development of electronic exchanges, the growing digitization of much financial activity, and the fact that finance produces a dematerialized and hypermobile product, all suggest that location should not matter. In fact, geographic dispersal would seem to be a good option given the high cost of operating in major financial centers. Further, the last ten years have seen an increased geographic mobility of financial experts and financial services firms.

There are, in my view, at least three reasons that explain the trend toward consolidation in a few centers rather than massive dispersal (Sassen 2001). Several of the chapters in this volume also provide us with detailed empirical specifications of some of these trends (see especially Garcia; Schiffer; Parnreciter; Meyer).

a) *The importance of social connectivity and central functions.* First, while ICTs do indeed enable geographic dispersal of economic activities without losing system integration, they have also had the effect of strengthening the importance of central coordination and control functions for firms and even for markets. Indeed for firms in any sector, operating a widely dispersed network of branches and affiliates and operating in multiple markets has made central functions far more complicated. Their execution requires access not only to top talent but also, more generally, to innovative milieux—in technology, accounting, legal services, economic forecasting, and all sorts of other, many new, specialized corporate services. Major centers have massive concentrations of state-of-the-art resources that allow them to maximize the benefits of ICTs and to govern the new conditions for operating globally. Even electronic markets such as NAS-DAQ and E*Trade rely on traders and banks that are located somewhere, with at least some in a major financial center.

One fact that has become increasingly evident is that to maximize the benefits of ICTs firms need not only the infrastructure but a complex mix of other resources. Most of the value added that these technologies can produce for advanced service firms lies in so-called externalities—material and human resources such as state-of-the-art office buildings, top talent, and the social networking infrastructure that maximizes connectivity. Any town can have fiber optic cables, but this is not sufficient (see Garcia, this volume; Graham, this volume; Meyer, this volume).

A second fact that is emerging with greater clarity concerns the meaning of "information." There are two types of information (Sassen 2001: chap. 5 and 7). One is the datum, which may be complex yet is standard knowledge: the level at which a stock market closes, a privatization of a public utility, the bankruptcy of a bank. But there is a far more difficult type of "information," akin to an interpretation/evaluation/judgment. It entails negotiating a series of data and a series of intepretations of a mix of data in the hope of producing a higher-order datum. Access to the first kind of information is now global and immediate from just about any place in the highly developed world thanks to the digital revolution. But the second type of information requires a complicated mixture of elements, which we could think of as the social infrastructure for global connectivity. It is these specialized kinds of social connectivity that give major financial centers a leading edge.

It is possible, in principle, to reproduce the technical infrastructure anywhere, but the same cannot be asserted for specialized kinds of social connectivity. While the leading financial and business centers have the highest levels of connectivity, this is a key feature of cities generally, and of spaces of centrality particularly. When the more complex forms of information needed to execute major international deals cannot be gotten from existing databases, no matter what a firm can pay, then one needs the social information loop and the associated de facto interpretations and inferences that come with bouncing off information among talented, informed people. It is the importance of this input that has given a whole new importance to credit rating agencies, for instance. Part of the rating has to do with interpretation and inference. When investors accept these as "authoritative," they become "information" available to all. The process of making inferences/interpretations into "information" takes quite a mix of talents and resources.

In brief, financial centers provide the specialized social connectivity that allows a firm or market to maximize the benefits of its technological connectivity.

b) *Cross-border mergers and alliances.* Global firms in the financial industry need enormous resources, which is leading to rapid mergers and acquisitions of firms and strategic alliances among markets in different countries. These are happening on a scale and in combinations few would have foreseen as recently as the early 1990s, with growing numbers of mergers forged among financial services firms, accounting firms, law firms, insurance brokers—in brief, firms that need to provide a global service. A similar evolution is also possible for the global telecommunications industry, which will have to consolidate in order to offer a state-of-the-art, globe-spanning service to its global clients, among which are the financial firms (see Graham, this volume).

I would argue that yet another kind of "merger" is the consolidation of electronic networks that connect a very select number of markets. In the late 1990s several financial exchanges sought to form highly integrated alliances. The most important and visible of these was the attempted alliance between the London Stock Exchange and Frankfurt's Deutsche Borse. The complexities of these mergers are such that at this time most of them have failed to sort out the difficulties. Yet the will to merge continues, and it is likely that workable formulas will be built eventually. Europe's more than thirty stock exchanges have been seeking to shape various alliances. Euronext (NEXT) is Europe's largest stock exchange merger, an alliance among the Paris, Amsterdam, and Brussels bourses. The merger created the world's fifth largest stock exchange, with more than thirteen hundred listed companies. But it is not only the largest exchanges that are merging: in March 2001 the Tallinn Stock Exchange in Estonia and its Helsinki counterpart created an alliance. A new pattern toward takeovers is also evident among these exchanges, such as the attempt by the owners of the Stockholm stock market to buy the London Stock Exchange (for a price of U.S. $3.7 billion). This was the first time that a stock exchange faced a hostile takeover. While the efforts to form strong alliances have failed, a number of looser networks connecting markets have been set up in the last few years. In 1999 NASDAQ, the second largest U.S. stock market after the New York Stock Exchange, set up Nasdaq Japan and in 2000 Nasdaq Canada. This gives investors in Japan and Canada direct access to the market in the United States.[20] The Toronto Stock Exchange has joined an alliance with the New York Stock Exchange (NYSE) to create a separate global trading platform. The NYSE is a founding member of a global trading alliance, Global Equity Market (GEM) which includes ten exchanges, among them Tokyo and NEXT. (For a fuller discussion see Sassen 2001: chap. 4, 5, and 7.)

These developments are likely to strengthen inter-city links in the worldwide network of about forty cities through which the global financial industry operates. We now also know that a major financial center needs to have a significant share of global operations to be such. Another indication of this intercity system is the fact that the worldwide distribution of equities under institutional management is spread among a large number of cities that have become integrated in the global equity market with deregulation of their economies and the formulation of "emerging markets" as an atractive investment destination in the 1990s. In 1999, institutional money managers around the world controlled approximately U.S. $14 trillion. Even as there is a growing number of cities that participate in this broad network, there is sharp concentration. Thomson Financial (1999), for instance, has estimated that at the end of 1999, twenty-five cities accounted for about 80 percent of the world's valuation of these assets. These twenty-five cities also account for roughly 48 percent of the total market capitalization of the world, which stood at U.S. $30 trillion at the end of 2000.

These various centers don't just compete with each other: there is collaboration and division of labor. In the initial stages of deregulation in the 1980s there was a strong tendency to see the relation among the major centers as one of straight competition among New York, London, and Tokyo, then as today the major centers in the system. But in my research on these three centers I found clear evidence of a division of labor already in the 1980s. What we are seeing now is an additional pattern whereby the cooperation or division of functions is somewhat institutionalized: strategic alliances not only between firms across borders but also between markets. There is competition, strategic collaboration, and hierarchy.

c) *Denationalized elites and agendas.* National attachments and identities are becoming weaker for these global firms and their customers. Deregulation and privatization have further weakened the need for *national* financial centers. The nationality question simply plays differently in these sectors than it did even a decade ago. Global financial products are accessible in national markets and national investors can operate in global markets.[21] For instance, some of the major Brazilian firms now list on the New York Stock Exchange and bypass the São Paulo exchange, a practice that has caused somewhat of an uproar in financial circles in Brazil. The major U.S. and European investment banks have set up specialized offices in London to handle various aspects of their global business. Even French banks have set up some of their global specialized operations in London, inconceivable even a few years ago and still not avowed in national rhetoric.

One way of describing this process is as an incipient denationalization of certain institutional arenas (Sassen 1996: chap. 1; 2003). It can be argued that such denationalization is a necessary condition for economic globalization as we know it today. The sophistication of this system lies in the fact that it only needs to involve strategic institutional areas—most national systems can be left basically unaltered. China is a good example. It adopted international accounting rules in 1993, necessary to engage in international transactions. To use these standards it did not have to change much of its domestic economy. Japanese firms operating overseas adopted such standards long before Japan's government considered requiring them. In this regard the "wholesale" side of globalization is quite different from the global consumer markets, in which success necessitates altering national tastes at a mass level. On the organizational side of the global economy, the changes are bounded, strategic, and confined largely to what is absolutely necessary. This process of denationalization has been strengthened by state policy enabling privatization and foreign acquisition. In some ways one might say that the Asian financial crisis has functioned as a mechanism to denationalize, at least partly, control over key sectors of economies that, although allowing the massive entry of foreign investment, had never relinquished that control.[22]

Major international business centers produce what we can think of as a new subculture, a move from the "national" version of international activities to the "global" version. Many of the countries that are becoming incorporated into the global economic system need to overcome often deeply rooted business cultures that are at odds with key aspects of the new global economic culture. For instance, the long-standing resistance in Europe to M&As, especially hostile takeovers, or to foreign ownership and control in East Asia, are elements of national business cultures that are somewhat incompatible with the new global economic culture of liberalizing capital flows and acquisitions of foreign firms. I would posit that major cities, and the variety of so-called global business meetings (such as those of the World Economic Forum in Davos and other similar occasions), contribute to denationalize corporate elites. Whether this is good or bad is a separate issue (see Sassen 2001: part 3).[23] But it is, I would argue, one of the conditions for setting in place the systems and subcultures necessary for a global economic system.

IN CONCLUSION

Economic globalization and the new information and communications technologies have contributed to produce a spatiality for the urban that pivots on cross-border networks as well as territorial locations with massive concentrations of resources. This is not a completely new feature. Over the centuries cities have been at the crossroads of major, often worldwide processes. What is different today is the intensity, complexity, and global span of these networks, the extent to which significant portions of economies are now dematerialized and digitized, hence the extent to which they can travel at great speeds through some of these networks, and the numbers of cities that are part of cross-border networks operating at vast geographic scales. What is also different today is the development of cross-border regulatory regimes necessary to accommodate the global economic system. Governments have had to produce new legislative instruments to privatize and deregulate vast sectors of their economies and to guarantee rights of contract and the private property of foreign firms and investors. While typically formulated for the global and national levels, the impacts of these regimes and instruments are made concrete in specific transactions and places: among the most important of these are global cities and their inter-city networks.

The growth of mostly specialized transactions connecting cities contributes to patterned networks. These include, among others, the global networks of firms' affiliates, the particular architecture of connectivity emerging from the interests of those actors with the powers to shape it, the formation of regional cross-border hierarchies enabled by free trade zones and international growth corridors, the integration of a growing number of financial centers into the global capital market. All of these are examined in this book.

Engaging in these highly specialized transactions has required often massive transformations in growing portions of these cities. The development of global city functions is embedded in infrastructural, structural, and policy developments that can amount to a new political, economic, and spatial order in these cities alongside the continuing dynamics of older orders. The depth of these transformations can be partly submerged under the megacity syndrome in some of these cities and the fact that large cities tend to have multiple social, economic, and spatial dynamics. The new urban spatiality produced as cities become sites for cross-border transactions is, then, partial in a double sense: it accounts for only part of what happens in cities and what cities are about, and it inhabits only part of what we might think of as the space of the city. New articulations with global circuits and disarticulations inside the city are thus produced.

Each of the chapters in this book examines a particular combination of these conditions and dynamics. Abstracting, it is possible to identify at least the following questions to which these chapters provide often detailed empirical answers.

Much has been written about the decisive difference that access to advanced ICTs makes for firms, markets, and urban economies. In their respective chapters, Garcia, Graham, and David Meyer examine how economic dynamics are embedded in complex configurations and the ways in which this sets limits on the capabilities of technology: meeting the technological requirements of our era is a necessary but not a sufficient condition for the development of the type of economic systems we have today. The ascendance of ICTs raises the importance of technical connectivity for firms, markets, and cities.

But it is becoming clear that the relationship between technical connectivity and economic growth is complicated.

A second issue concerns the scales at which these networking technologies operate. Much attention has gone to their globe-spanning capacities and hence their overriding of place and locality. Patrice Riemens and Geert Lovink dissect the creation of a local digital network aimed at strengthening relations among a city's inhabitants and thereby its civic fabric. The multiplication of such local digital cities can conceivably produce intercity collaborations leading to the emergence of community-oriented cross-border networks. Digital City Amsterdam (DCA) was the first major such local network and the best known one, and it was emulated by cities worldwide. Riemens and Lovink's analysis captures a unique moment in the hisory of these networking technologies in the 1980s and early 1990s, when they were less common than today so there was the need to develop a culture within which these technologies would make sense and acquire meaning and usefulness (see, e.g., ADILKNO 1998). This is another version of the embeddeness of technical networks examined by Garcia, Graham, and Meyer. Riemens and Lovink also examine the diruptive power of commercial interests for such civic efforts. The founding, managing, and evolution of DCA captures a broad spectrum of matters often neglected in the more general discussions about networking technologies.

A third issue concerns the capabilities of these technologies for enabling widespread connectivity and hence, one might infer, for reducing gaps and inequalities. Most of the chapters in this book document the development of ICT infrastructure from various angles and in various cities, and find that it has contributed to a growth in the spatial differentiation inside cities even as they can strengthen their cross-border transactions. Further, although a growing number of cities develop better infrastructure and some of their economic sectors experience upgrading and vigorous growth, these conditions do not reduce the inequalities in the global hierarchy, as is shown in both Graham's chapter and this introduction. This is partly so because the benefits that these technologies can provide firms, markets, and urban economies are in good part predicated on a variety of nontechnical conditions, be it the networks of capital that Meyer describes for Hong Kong or the impacts of different histories of economic advantage in the world economy.

How these older histories of advantage play into the current dynamics of globalization is one of the subjects addressed by Parnreiter for Mexico City, Sueli Ramos Schiffer for São Paulo, and Ali Parsa and Ramin Keivani for the Iran-Dubai corridor. São Paulo and Mexico City have long been dominant cities in their national economies, with massive their concentrations of resources and a disproportionate share of national wealth or its control. Does this make a difference in their current positioning on cross-border circuits connecting these cities to the global economy and in their national economies? Both Mexico City and São Paulo, emblematic of other such older cities, have lost enormous numbers of manufacturing companies and jobs, as well as share of national population, all variables of enormous significance for certain types of issues. Yet they also account for some of the most dynamic sectors in their national economies and control a disproportionate share of the cross-border transactions of their national economies. Parnreiter finds that notwithstanding many aggregate indicators showing declines for Mexico City, a more detailed examination shows its enormous and growing control over key international processes, which in turn are gaining ascendance in the national economy, and how the city has also gained more than any other region in Mexico when it comes to some of the leading, highly specialized economic sectors. Understanding the production of these current histories of advantage requires using a combination of variables that is not the one frequently used in aggregate level studies or in measuring past histories of economic advantage.

One of the key issues in much discussion about globalization concerns the weight of history and the specificities of a city. Except when the subject does not warrant it, these chapters examine the trajectories that produced the enabling environments for current forms of globalization. It is clear from these accounts that many of the so-called effects of globalization are actually the outcome of explicit and highly developed government policies in each of the countries and cities involved. These may range from the centrally planned development of global city capabilities in Shanghai to the enormous concessions that governments have made to private enterprises in the cases of São Paulo, Buenos Aires, Mexico City, and the most extreme case, Beirut.

Another major issue is the extent to which globalization brings with it growing competition among cities or a division of functions at both the global and regional scales. In the case of the global geography of a firm's overseas affiliates, examined by Taylor et al., it is crucial that there exist many cities that offer the requisite conditions for successful operation. This is a different inter-city relation from that between cities competing for a single factory. Since globalization also entails expanding into new areas, including ones that are not necessarily well provisioned, there is a push toward upgrading infrastructures and the built environment. Firms and markets with global operations require a network of well-provisioned cities to execute the operations. At a more specialized level, one can identify a variety of modalities through which this need for a network of cities functions and gets implemented. The chapters in this volume examine a broad range of particular cases in addition to the framing analysis in this introduction. They include Beirut's reconstruction aimed at reentry into various specialized global circuits and complementarity with other regional centers; the particular division of functions in the emerging Iran-Dubai corridor; the geography of the global network of firms' offices and of airline connections; and Hong Kong's deeply embedded networks of capital exchange. In none of these instances can the complex inter-city links be reduced to a relation of competition.

Finally, a key issue concerns the impacts of becoming part of global circuits on the cities themselves. Beyond the aspects discussed above, there are questions concerning the functioning of various markets, from real estate to labor, and questions concerning poverty and income inequality, all addressed by most of the chapters in this book. At the heart of these diverse subjects lies the broader question about the positive and negative consequences of economic globalization for the socioeconomic structure of cities that are global or, at the least, have global city functions. The results produced by the research of the authors in this volume show, on the one hand, a pronounced upgrading of select urban infrastructures and built environments, and on the other, a multiplication and sharpening of spatial and social inequalities.

Let me conclude by summarizing the focus of each part of the book.[24]

In part 1, the focus is on the architecture of networks. The chapters address two of the concerns in this book. One is the tension between global span and particular sites, explored here through an examination of both the global architecture of these networks and their interactions with the specific environments of different cities. The second concerns the complex interactions between technical networks and social or economic networks, explored through the cases of business networks, capital exchange networks; and transport networks. Garcia, Graham, Taylor and his colleagues and David Smith and Michael Timberlake, each examine particular instantiations of these issues. (The complex interactions between urban civic networks and ICTs are examined in chapter 12.)

Using a new and pioneering data set, Taylor, Walker, and Beaverstock map the global networks of offices of the leading firms in accounting, law, advertising, and finance. These networks of offices can be used to classify cities in terms of their participation in cross-border networks. Smith and Timberlake have been among the first to develop ways of applying network analysis to cross-border transactions. In their chapter they focus on air travel networks showing how some of the cities in this book and, more generally, in the global networks under discussion, have only indirect connections with one another. It brings to the fore one of the central concerns in this book, which is to capture the presence or absence of cross-border interactions among cities that are in the middle range of various global hierarchical networks and, more generally, in the global south. It is also an interesting juxtaposition with the evidence presented by Taylor and his associates for the geography of offices of some of the most powerful firms in the global economy. Air travel includes a far broader range of cross-border transactions than the networks of affiliates in law and finance.

Part 2 of the book moves to the urban and regional scale and examines the role of leading cities in the internal articulation of cross-border regions and in locating the region on global circuits. In several regards this is further developed in part 3, which examines cities as nodes in cross-border networks. Parnreiter's examination of Mexico City shows us its location on multiple global circuits and the complex history of economic internationalization that characterizes the country. In their chapter, Parsa and Keivani focus on the emergent Dubai-Iran corridor in the Hormuz Strait. Though little discussed in Western scholarship on these issues, it plays a crucial role in the decentered map of the global economy presented in this part of the book. Under current economic and political conditions as described in the chapter, older cross-border networks are becoming reactivated and new ones are being formed. There is an emergent division of functions between Dubai, which has positioned itself as a leading financial and trading center in the region, and southern Iran, which has the labor and land resources lacking in Dubai and the other members of the United Arab Emirates. Schiffer examines the role of São Paulo in articulating the South American region, specifically the range of transactions encompassed by the Mercosur free-trade agreement. Schiffer shows us that São Paulo is at the intersection of regional cross-border circuits and global circuits, and that it is the leading global node in the region. Eric Huybrechts examines the rebuilding of Beirut under a leadership intent on reconnecting the city to key global circuits both in finance and port-linked trade. This has become a largely physical and technical process, and has proceeded without attending to the need for internal reconciliation after a long and brutal war.

The chapters in part 3 examine the work of developing the infrastructures, urban spaces, and policies necessary for global city functions. Except for chapter 12, all chapters in part 3 focus on the restructuring of urban space to enable global city development. Each captures a particular combination of conditions that dominates this process and might also be evident in other cities in the world: a long history of economic interdependence with a major global power, either central government planning or private corporate leadership aiming at connecting a city to global circuits, and private and foreign investment-led restructuring of urban space. Meyer, long a student of Hong Kong, examines the role of this city as a strategic node for capital exchange between China and the world. What is extraordinary in this history is the extent to which it is Hong Kong's social connectivity that produced and reproduced this strategic role. The actors changed in terms of their origins and nationalities and their competitive advantages, but the machinery that secured Hong Kong its privileged role continued to grow. Meyer focuses particularly on the difference that the new communication and information technologies might make for this historic role. In contrast, Felicity Rose Gu and Zilai Tang show us how tight government control, leadership and initiative in Shanghai are producing the technical connectivity that might give this city a key role in global networks. The question that jumps out of this detailed account of the constructing of the technical base is whether Shanghai can produce the social connectivity that is the crucial factor for maximizing the benefits of technical infrastructure. Pablo Ciccolella and Iliana Mignaqui have done some of the most extensive and detailed research on the new forms of sociospatial polarization evident in Buenos Aires. Their chapter documents the actual work of developing a city's capabilities to host global city functions, and examines the urban fabric that is being configured. Riemens and Lovink examine the capacity of the new networking technologies to strengthen local interactions inside a city. Theirs is one of the first detailed accounts of the formation of Digital City Amsterdam, the most famous of the urban public digital spaces and the first freenet of its kind. Being among the founders and active participants in the project and the larger public media culture that made it possible, they dissect the trajectory of this experiment until its current transformation into a private enterprise. The efforts and setbacks they describe are a microhistory that is taking place in multiple cities around the world as people struggle to make these new technologies work for them.

NOTES

1. For illuminating examinations of the general issue of cultural complexity, see Hannerz 1992; Appadurai 1996; Maldonado 1997; Low 1999.

2. In this sense, global cities are different from the capitals of erstwhile empires, in that they are a function of cross-border networks rather than simply the most powerful city of an empire. There is, in my conceptualization, no such entity as a single global city as there could be a single capital of an empire; the category "global city" only makes sense as a component of a global network of strategic sites. The corporate subsector which contains the global control and command functions is partly embedded in this network.

3. This distinction also matters for questions of regulation, notably regulation of cross-border activities. If the strategic central functions—both those produced in corporate headquarters and those produced in the specialized corporate services sector—are located in a network of major financial and business centers, the question of regulating what amounts to a key part of the global economy will entail an effort different from that which would be the case if the strategic management and coordination functions were as dispersed geographically as the factories, service outlets, and affiliates generally.

4. There are multiple specifications to this argument. For instance, the development of financial instruments that represent fixed real estate repositions the latter in various systems of circulation, including global ones. In so doing the meaning of capital fixity is partly transformed and the fixed capital also becomes a site for circulation. For a fuller elaboration see Sassen 2001, chapter 2.

5. In contrast to the notion of globalization as signaling the transformation of the world into a single place or as denoting the "global human condition," it can be argued that globalization is also a process that produces differentiation. But the alignment of differences is of a kind very different from that associated with such differentiating notions as national character, national culture, national society. For example, the corporate world today has a global geography, but it isn't everywhere in the world: in fact it has highly defined and structured spaces; it also is increasingly sharply differentiated from noncorporate segments in the economies of global cities or countries where it operates. There is homogenization along certain lines that cross national boundaries and sharp differentiation inside these boundaries. The hierarchical nature of global networks is yet another form of differentiation even within the somewhat homogenized geography of centrality discussed earlier. Globalized forms and processes, though homogenizing, tend to have a distinct geography. (For discussions of particular aspects, see, e.g., Bonilla et al. 1998; Ong and Nonini 1997; Staeheli 1999; Cochrane, Peck, and Tickell 1996; Clark and Hoffman-Martinot 1998; Eade 1996; Olds et al. 1999).

6. We need to recognize the specific historical conditions for different conceptions of the international or the global (Arrighi and Silver 1999; Isin 2000; Ong and Nonini 1997). Today there is a tendency to see the internationalization of the economy as a process operating at the center, embedded in the power of the multinational corporations and, in the past, in colonial enterprises. One could note that the economies of many peripheral countries are thoroughly internationalized because of high levels of foreign investment in all economic sectors, and of heavy dependence on world markets for "hard" currency (see Parnreiter, this volume; Ciccolella and Mignaqui, this volume). What the highly developed countries have is strategic concentrations of firms and markets that operate globally, the capability for global control and coordination, and power. This is a very different form of the international from that which we find in the global South.

7. The fact of systemic conditions in the new geoeconomics is a significant factor for the question of regulation. The orders of magnitude and the intensity of transactions in the North Atlantic system facilitate the formation of standards even in the context of strong differences between the United States and Continental Europe in their legal, accounting, antitrust, and other rules. It is clear that even though these two regions have more in common with each other than with much of the rest of the world, these differences matter when it comes to the creation of cross-border standards. The fact of shared Western standards and norms, however, in combination with the enormous economic weight, has encouraged the circulation and imposition of U.S. and European standards and rules on transactions involving firms from other parts of the world. There is a sort of globalization of Western standards. Much has been said about the dominance of U.S. standards and rules, but European standards are also evident, for instance in the new anti-trust rules being developed in central and eastern Europe.

8. There is a fourth case, which I have addressed elsewhere (2001), that consists of electronically generated spaces of centrality.

9. In the case of a complex landscape such as Europe's we see in fact several geographies of centrality, one global, others continental and regional. A central urban hierarchy connects major cities, many of which in turn play central roles in the wider global system of cities: Paris, London, Frankfurt, Amsterdam, Zurich. These cities are also part of a wider network of European financial/cultural/service capitals which articulate the European region and are somewhat less oriented to the global economy than the top five listed above. And then there are several geographies of marginality: the East-West divide and the North-South divide across Europe as well as newer, more finely grained divisions. In eastern Europe, certain cities and regions, notably Budapest, are rather attractive for purposes of investment, both European and non-European, while others will increasingly fall behind, notably in Rumania, Yugoslavia, and Albania. We see a similar differentiation in southern Europe: Madrid, Barcelona, and Milan are gaining in the new European hierarchy; Naples, Rome, and Marseille are struggling.

10. For instance, the globalization of investment banking and fund management, two areas in which New York firms are major players, may well have been more important in strengthening London's position as a financial center than England's *national* growth *per se*. In the original 1991 edition of *The Global City* I posited that the globalization of markets reduces the importance of national economic health for major cities to thrive as international business centers—not necessarily a desirable feature of the global economic system. I found this trend again in the research for the second edition (2001). For instance, several European countries with thriving stock markets have had slow economic growth and high unemployment throughout the 1990s. Schiffer (this volume) and Parnreiter (this volume) find similar patterns in, respectively, São Paulo and Mexico City.

11. This also holds in the highly developed world. For instance, the Paris region accounts for more than 40 percent of all producer services in France, and more than 80 percent of the most advanced ones. New York City is estimated to account for between a fourth and a fifth of all U.S. producer services exports though it has only 3 percent of the U.S. population. London accounts for 40 percent of all exports of producer services in the United Kingdom. Similar trends are also evident in Zurich, Frankfurt, and Tokyo, all located in much smaller countries.

12. We can think of the producer services, and most especially finance and advanced corporate services, as industries producing the "organizational commodities" necessary for the implementation and management of global economic systems (Sassen 2001: chap. 2–5). Producer services are

intermediate services bought by firms. They cover financial, legal, and general management matters, innovation, development, design, administration, personnel, production technology, maintenance, transport, communications, wholesale distribution, advertising, cleaning services for firms, security, and storage. Central components of the producer services category are a range of industries with mixed business and consumer markets; they are insurance, banking, financial services, real estate, legal services, accounting, and professional associations (for more detailed discussions see, e.g., Noyelle and Dutka, 1988; Daniels 1991; Veltz 1996).

13. Indeed, several scholars have argued that the producer services sector could not exist without manufacturing (Cohen and Zysman 1987; Markusen and Gwiasda 1994). A key proposition for these and other authors is that producer services are dependent on a strong manufacturing sector in order to grow. Others disagree (Noyelle and Dutka 1988; Drennan 1992; Drennan, Tobier, and Lewis 1996). Drennan, Tobier, and Lewis find that a strong producer services sector is possible without manufacturing growth. In a variant on both positions, I (2001: chap. 5) argue that manufacturing indeed is one factor feeding the growth of the producer services sector, but that it does so whether located in the area in question, somewhere else in the country, or overseas.

14. For a detailed analysis of and data on the issues discussed briefly here, see Sassen (2001: chap. 4, 5, and 7).

15. Its historic advantage as a nexus between the world and China, and its concentration of state-of-the-art specialized services secure a strategic role for Hong Kong. David Meyer's impressive *Hong Kong as a Global Metropolis* is one of the best explanations of this peculiar Hong Kong advantage as an intermediary for global networks of capital. See also Wasserstein, forthcoming.

16. For instance, according to the most recent data available, in 1999 Japan had U.S. $1 trillion in assets under institutional management and U.S. $10 trillion in savings and similar accounts that are about to be deregulated.

17. Electronic trading will also contribute a radically new pattern whereby one market, for instance Frankfurt's Deutsche Eurex, can operate on screens in many other markets around the world, or whereby one brokerage firm, Cantor Fitzgerald, can (as of September 1998) have its prices of U.S. Treasury futures listed on screens used by traders all around the United States.

18. For instance, the typical emphasis in much commentary on the electronic features of the futures market in Frankfurt veils the fact that this electronic futures network is actually embedded in a network of financial centers. And the brokerage firm Cantor Fitzgerald, which has computerized the sale of U.S. Treasury futures, actually has an alliance with the Board of Trade of New York to handle these sales.

19. Among the main sources of data for the figures cited in this section are the Bank for International Settlements (Basle); International Monetary Fund national accounts data; specialized trade publications such as the *Wall Street Journal's WorldScope;* Morgan Stanley Capital International; *The Banker;* data listings in the *Financial Times* and *The Economist;* and, especially for a focus on cities, the data produced by Technimetrics, Inc. (now Thomson Financials). Additional names of standard, continuously updated sources are listed in Sassen 2001.

20. The first step in this alliance includes the installation of terminals at ten securities firms in Montreal to allow Canadian investors the ability to trade more than five thousand stocks listed on NASDAQ, including more than 140 Canadian companies traded in the U.S. markets.

21. For example, investment banks used to split up their analysts team by country to cover a national market; now they are more likely to do it by industrial sector (see, for example, Latin American Finance, various recent issues).

22. For instance, after the crisis erupted in 1997, Lehman Brothers bought Thai residential mortgages worth half a billion dollars for a 53 percent discount. This was the first auction conducted by the Thai government's Financial Restructuring Authority, which is conducting the sale of $21 billion in financial companies' assets. It also acquired the Thai operations of Peregrine, the Hong Kong investment bank that failed. The fall in prices and in the value of the yen has also made Japanese firms and real estate attractive targets for foreign investors. Merrill Lynch has bought thirty branches of Yamaichi Securities; Societe Generale Group was set to buy 80 percent of Yamaichi International Capital Management; Travellers Group became the biggest shareholder of Nikko, the third largest brokerage; and Toho Mutual Insurance Co. announced a joint venture with GE Capital. These are

but some of the best-known cases right after the 1997 crisis. Much valuable property in the Ginza—Tokyo's high-priced shopping and business district— is now being considered for acquisition by foreign investors, in a twist on Mitsubishi's acquisition of Rockefeller Center a decade earlier.

23. Denationalization has multivalence. If it produces a hollowing out of a national economy it could be seen as negative; if it strengthens the human rights regime in a country, as positive (Sassen 2002).

24. Originally the project on which this book is based was to include Johannesburg and Bombay, two key cities for global-city analysis. For various reasons this could not be organized. For treatments of these cities see Gugler 2000.

REFERENCES CITED

Abbott, Carl. 1996. "The Internationalization of Washington, D.C." *Urban Affairs Review* 31 (5): 571–594.

Abu-Lughod, Janet L. 1999. *New York, Los Angeles, Chicago: America's Global Cities.* Minneapolis: University of Minnesota Press.

ADILKNO. 1998. *The Media Archive. World Edition.* New York: Autonomedia; Amsterdam: ADILKNO.

Allen, John, Doreen Massey, and Michael Pryke. (ed). *Unsettling Cities.* London: Routledge, 1999.

Amin, Ash (eds.). 1997. *Post-Fordism.* Oxford: Blackwell.

Amin, A., and N. Thrift. 1995. *Globalization, Institutions, and Regional Development.* Oxford: Oxford University Press.

Appadurai, Arjun. 1996. *Modernity at Large.* Minneapolis: University of Minnesota Press.

Arrighi, Giovanni, and Beverley Silver. 1999. *Chaos and Governance in the Modern World System.* Minneapolis: University of Minnesota Press.

Ascher, Francois. 1995. *Metapolis ou L'Avenir des Villes.* Paris: Editions Odile Jacob.

Aspen Institute. 1998. *The Global Advance of Electronic Commerce. Reinventing Markets, Management, and National Sovereignty.* Washington, D.C.: The Aspen Institute, Communications and Society Program.

Castells, M. 1996. *The Networked Society. Oxford:* Blackwell.

Baum, Scott. 1997. "Sydney, Australia: A Global City? Testing the Social Polarisation Thesis." *Urban Studies* 34 (11): 1881–1901.

Beauregard, Robert. 1991. "Capital Restructuring and the New Built Environment of Global Cities: New York and Los Angeles." *International Journal of Urban and Regional Research* 15 (1): 90–105.

Bonilla, Frank, Edwin Melendez, Rebecca Morales, and Maria de los Angeles Torres (eds). 1998. *Borderless Borders.* Philadelphia: Temple University Press.

Boyer, Kenneth 1996. "Network Externalities," in Donald L. Alexander, Werner Sichel, *Networks, Infrastructure and the New Task for Regulation*, Ann Arbor: Michigan, pp. 13–19.

Brenner, Neil. 1998." Global Cities, Glocal States: Global City Formation and State Territorial Restructuring in Contemporary Europe." *Review of International Political Economy.* 5, 2: 1–37.

Castells, M. 1989. *The Informational City: Economic Restructuring and the Urban Regional Process.* London, UK: Blackwell.

Castells, Manuel, and Peter Hall. 1994. *Technopoles of the World: The Making of Twenty-First Century Industrial Complexes.* London: Routledge.

Clark, Terry Nichols, and Vincent Hoffman-Martinot (eds). 1998. *The New Political Culture.* Oxford: Westview.

Cochrane, Allan, Jamie Peck and Adam Tickell. 1996. "Manchester Plays Games: Exploring the Local Politics of Globalization." *Urban Studies* 33 (8): 1319–1336.

Cohen, Stephen S. and John Zysman. 1987. *Manufacturing Matters. The Myth of the Post-Industrial Economy.* New York: Basic Books.

Cohen, Michael A., Blair A. Ruble, Joseph S. Tulchin, Allison M. Garland (eds.). 1996. *Preparing for the Urban Future. Global Pressures and Local Forces.* Washington, D.C.: Woodrow Wilson Center Press. (Distributed by Johns Hopkins University Press.)

Daniels, Peter W. 1991. "Producer Services and the Development of the Space Economy." Pp.

135–150 in Daniels, Peter W. and Frank Moulaert (eds.) *The Changing Geography of Advanced Producer Services*. London and New York: Belhaven Press.

Davis, Diana E. 1994. *Urban Leviathan. Mexico City in the Twentieth Century*. Philadelphia: Temple University Press.

Drennan, Matthew P. 1992. "Gateway Cities: The Metropolitan Sources of U.S. Producer Service Exports." *Urban Studies* 29 (2): 217–235.

Drennan, Matthew P., Emanuel Tobier, and Jonathan Lewis. 1996. "The Interruption of Income Convergence and Income Growth in Large Cities in the 1980s." *Urban Studies* 33 (1): 63–82.

Eade, John (ed.). 1996. *Living the Global City: Globalization as a Local Process*. London: Routledge.

Elliott, James R. 1999. "Putting 'Global Cities' in Their Place: Urban Hierarchy and Low-Income Employment During the Post-War Era." *Urban Geography* 20 (2): 95–115.

Fincher, Ruth, and Jane M. Jacobs (eds.). 1998. *Cities of Difference*. New York: Guilford.

Graham, Daniel and Nigel Spence. 1997. "Competition for metropolitan resources: 'the crowding out' of London's manufacturing industry?" *Environment and Planning A* 29 (3): 459–484.

Gravesteijn, S. G. E., S. van Griensven, and M. C. de Smidt (eds). 1998. *Timing Global Cities, Nederlandse Geografische Studies*, 241. Utrecht.

Gugler, Joseph (ed.). Forthcoming. "Introduction." *World Cities in Poor Countries*.

Hannerz, U. 1992. *Cultural Complexity. Studies in the Social Organization of Meaning*. New York: Columbia University Press.

Harris, Nigel, and I. Fabricius (eds.). 1996. *Cities and Structural Adjustment*. London: University College London.

Isin, Engin F. (ed.) 2000. *Democracy, Citizenship, and the Global City*. London and New York: Routledge.

Jessop, Robert. 1999 "Reflections on Globalization and Its Illogics." Pp. 19–38 in *Globalization and the Asian Pacific: Contested Territories*, ed. Kris Olds. London: Routledge.

Jimenez, M., Bo-Sin Tang, Murat Yalcintan and Ertan Zibel. 2001. "The Global-City Hypothesis for the Periphery: A Comparative Case Study of Mexico City, Istanbul and Guangzhou." In A. Thornley and Y. Rudin (eds.) *Planning in a Globalised World*. London: Ashgate.

Keil, Roger. 1993. *Weltstadt- Stadt der Welt: Internationalisierung und lokale Politik in Los Angeles*. Munster: Westfaelisches Dampfboot.

King, A.D. (ed.). 1995. *Representing the City. Ethnicity, Capital, and Culture in the 21st Century*. London: Macmillan.

Kostinsky, Grigory. 1997. "Globalisation de l'economie et notions urbanistiques." Pp. 17–25 in *Metropolisation et Politique*, ed. P. Claval and A.-L. Sanguin. Paris: L'Harmattan.

Landrieu, Josee, Nicole May, Dirige Par, Therese Spector, and Pierre Veltz (eds). 1998. *La Ville Eclatee*. La Tour d'Aigues: Editiones de l'Aube.

Lo, Fu-chen, and Yue-man Yeung (eds.). 1996. *Emerging World Cities in Pacific Asia*. Tokyo: United Nations University Press.

Low, Setha M. 1999. "Theorizing the City." Pp. 1–33 in *Theorizing the City*, ed. Setha M. Low. New Brunswick, NJ: Rutgers University Press.

Machimura, Takashi. 1998. "Symbolic Use of Globalization in Urban Politics in Tokyo." *International Journal of Urban and Regional Research* 22 (2): 183–194.

Maldonado, Tomas. 1997. *Critica della ragione informatica*. Milano: Feltrinelli.

Marcuse, Peter, and Ronald van Kempen. 2000. *Globalizing Cities. A New Spatial Order*. Oxford: Blackwell.

Markusen, A., and V. Gwiasda. 1994. "Multipolarity and the Layering of Functions in the World Cities: New York City's Struggle to Stay on Top." *International Journal of Urban and Regional Research* 18: 167–93.

Meyer, David R. 2000. *Hong Kong as a Global Metropolis*. Cambridge: Cambridge University Press.

Moulaert, F., and A. J.Scott. 1997. *Cities, Enterprises, and Society on the Eve of the 21st Century*. London and New York: Pinter.

Nijman, Jan. 1996. "Breaking the Rules: Miami in the Urban Hierarchy." *Urban Geography* 17 (1): 5–22.

Noyelle, T., and A. B. Dutka, 1988. *International Trade in Business Services: Accounting, Advertising, Law, and Management Consulting.* Cambridge, MA: Ballinger.

Olds, Kris, Peter Dicken, Philip F. Kelly, Lilly Kong, and Henry Wai-Chung Yeung (eds). 1999. *Globalization and the Asian Pacific: Contested Territories.* London: Routledge.

Ong, Aihwa, and Nonini, Donald (eds). 1997. *Underground Empires.* New York: Routledge.

Orum, Anthony and Xianming Chen. 2002. *Urban Places.* Malden, Ma: Blackwell.

Peraldi, Michel, and Evelyne Perrin (eds.). 1996. *Reseaux Productifs et Territoires Urbains.* Toulouse: Presses Universitaires du Mirail.

Persky, Joseph, and Wim Wievel. 1994. "The growing Localness of the Global City." *Economic Geography* 70 (2): 129–143.

Pirez, Pedro. *Buenos Aires Metropolitana.* 1994. Buenos Aires: Centro.

Pozos Ponce, Fernando. 1996. *Metropolis en reestructuracion: Guadalajara y Monterrey 1980–1989.* Guadalajara: Universidad de Guadalajara

Santos, Milton, Maria Adelia A. De Souze, and Maria Laura Silveira (eds). 1994. *Territorio Globalizacao e Fragmentacao.* São Paulo: Editorial Hucitec.

Sassen, Saskia. 1996. *Losing Control? Sovereignty in an Age of Globalization.* New York: Columbia University Press.

———. 1989. *Cities in the World Economy.* London, UK: Blackwell.

———. 2000. *Cities in a World Economy.* Thousand Oaks, CA: Pine Forge/Sage Press (new updated edition; originally published in 1994).

———. 2001. *The Global City: New York, London, Tokyo.* Princeton, NJ: Princeton University Press (new updated edition; originally published in 1991).

———. 2003. *De-Nationalization.* Princeton, NJ: Princeton University Press.

Scott, A. J. 2000. *Global City-Regions.* Oxford: Oxford University Press.

Skeldon, R. 1997. "Hong Kong: Colonial City to Global City to Provincial City?" *Cities 14* (5): 265–271.

Souza, Maria Adelia Aparecida de. 1994. *A Identidade da Metropole. A Verticalizacao em São Paulo.* São Paulo: Hucitec.

Staehli, Lynn A. 1999. "Globalization and the Scales of Citizenship." *Geography Research Forum* 19: 60–77. (Special issue *On Geography and the Nation-State*, edited by Dennis Pringle and Oren Yiftachel.

Storper, M. 1997. *The Regional World: Territorial Development in a Global Economy.* New York: Guilford.

Stren, Richard. 1996. "The Studies of Cities: Popular Perceptions, Academic Disciplines, and Emerging Agendas." Pp. 392–420 in *Preparing for the Future,* ed. Michael A. Cohen et al., Washington, D.C.: Wilson Center Press.

Sum, Ngai-Ling. 1999. "Rethinking Globalisation: Re-articulating the Spatial Scale and Temporal Horizons of Trans-Border Spaces." Pp. 129–145 in *Globalization and the Asian Pacific,* ed. Kris Olds et al. London: Routledge.

Tardanico, Richard, and Mario Lungo. 1995. "Local Dimensions of Global Restructuring in Urban Costa Rica." *International Journal of Urban and Regional Research* 19 (2): 223–249.

Veltz, Pierre. *Mondialisation Villes Et Territories.* 1996. Paris: Presses Universitaires De France.

Wajcman, Judy. 2002. *Information Technologies and the Social Sciences.* Special Issue of *Current Sociology.* (Summer)

Warf, Barney, and Rodney Erickson. 1996. "Introduction: Globalization and the U.S. City System." *Urban Geography* 17 (1): 1–4.

Wasserstrom, Jeff. Forthcoming. *Shanghai's Past and Present as a Global City.* (On file with author, Department of History, Indiana University).

Wissenschafs Forum. 1995. Special issue: *Global City: Zitadellen der Internationalisierung* 12, No. 2 (June) 1995.

Yeung, Yue-man. 2000. *Globalization and Networked Societies.* City?: University of Hawaii Press.

PART ONE

THE URBAN ARCHITECTURE OF GLOBAL NETWORKS

Chapter 1

THE ARCHITECTURE OF GLOBAL NETWORKING TECHNOLOGIES

D. Linda García

The role that communication and information technologies can play in affecting economic outcomes is now widely recognized.[1] Less certain, however, is our understanding of how these technologies will affect the locus of economic activity. Emphasizing the enhanced ability of information and communication technologies to overcome barriers of time and space, a number of scholars contend, for example, that nonmetropolitan areas are less likely to be disadvantaged in the future, given a global economy in which they can access a greater number and variety of resources (Parker et al. 1995; Hudson 1995). Others disagree. They contend that profits and growth opportunities in an information-based global economy will be ever more closely linked to transaction costs. Under such circumstances, cities—which benefit greatly from economies of agglomeration—will have an even greater economic advantage over nonmetropolitan areas than they have today. In fact, cities will themselves be ranked depending on their size and importance, with those at the top of the hierarchy serving as central hubs and access ramps to the global economy (Gottman 1983; Sassen 2000; Castells 1989). Some go even further in characterizing the spatial impacts of communication technologies, claiming that in a networked, global economy, economic activities will become deterritorialized, with resources and power being shifted from geographically bounded nation-states to large transnational firms (O'Brian 1992).

This lack of clarity and consensus can be explained, in part, by the fact that many analysts neither differentiate among information and communication technologies in terms of their capabilities nor characterize them according to how they are each—given their differences—likely to mediate social and economic exchanges.[2] Communication and information technologies are hardly the same in these regards. One need only compare, for example, the impact of the railroads and the telegraph versus those of the telephone on rural areas. Because the railroads and telegraph were point-to-point technologies, they served to deplete rural areas of their resources. In contrast, the telephone, with its meshed, network architecture, served instead to reinforce local ties. Today's information-based networking technologies are far more varied—as well as variable—than networks in the past.[3] Defined by software, and supporting almost all forms of communication, today's advanced networking technologies are extremely flexible and versatile so they can easily be customized to the task at hand. This flexibility means that the impact of today's networking technologies will—to a considerable degree—be a matter of the social, economic, and political forces driving their evolution. Depending on these forces, networking technologies can be designed and deployed either to empower or to weaken the position of parties in an exchange.

To anticipate the architecture of global networks, this chapter first lays out a framework for analyzing and differentiating among networks and their socioeconomic impacts. Next it examines how networking technologies will likely evolve given the technological, economic, and political forces at work. Based on this analysis, the chapter argues that although advanced networking technologies have the potential to promote and sustain more decentralized and widely distributed economic activities, such an outcomes is highly unlikely under the present circumstances. Operating in a deregulated environment, and responding to the most lucrative business demands, networked industries will design and deploy networks to mirror the existing flow of trade and financial transactions between major city regions (Sassen, this volume). Moreover, while operating globally, these industries will at the same time base their organizations in major cities where they can better service their business clients as well as interconnect their networks through central international hubs. The existing first mover advantages enjoyed by these city regions in the global hierarchy will thereby be reinforced as technology networks generate even greater externalities and increasing returns. The increased role of cities and globally networked actors will diminish, but certainly not eliminate, the role of nation-states. National government will continue to play an active role in the economy—both domestically, in setting national priorities, and internationally, by advocating in support of national objectives and on behalf of national economic players.

COMMUNICATION NETWORKS

Communication processes do not occur in a vacuum; they are facilitated and sustained by an underlying network of individuals, institutions, and technologies that provide the means and mechanisms for formulating, exchanging, and interpreting information, and for creating the necessary linkages among these activities.[4] As part of the infrastructure, communications networks not only support communication processes; they also mediate them, restructuring the way in which these processes take place.

Networking technologies can affect communication processes in a variety of ways. For example, they can alter the speed and cost of communication, the distance that information can travel within any given time period, the amount of intelligence/functionality that can be transferred, the density and richness of information flows, the relationships and interdependencies among parties to an act of communication, and the perceptions of the parties communicating.

It is these changes in communication processes—*and not the actual deployment of technology*—that eventually give rise to social and economic opportunities and impacts. Thus, for example, communications technologies such as fiber optics and optical switches, which increase the speed and reduce the cost of communication, can foster economic growth by permitting a greater number of transactions to take place. Similarly, search engines and filtering devices, by restructuring economic relationships and directly linking consumers to the products and services that they desire, can eliminate the role of traditional middlemen.

The technical characteristics of communications networks also affect the way in which networking providers are structured and organized, and the rate at which networking technologies are likely to be deployed and diffused. Thus, for example, the higher the fixed costs of building network facilities, the greater the number of users and applications required to support them, and the greater the likelihood that network providers will vertically integrate themselves (Gong and Srinagesh 1997). Likewise, the more interoperable the components of a network, the lower the costs, the more rapidly it will be diffused, and the greater the prospects for competitive provisioning.

Because the impacts of communication technologies are indirect, however, socioeconomic changes are likely to take place in an evolutionary fashion.[5] Moreover, the path such change follows is not direct; it zigzags and meanders in response to the openings and obstacles encountered along the way. Technology advances, for example, are tempered by social and economic forces as well as by the historical conditions under which new technologies are brought into use. Made in the context of existing institutional structures, laws, and practices, technology choices will depend on who the key decision makers are; how they perceive their needs, interests, and objectives in the light of new technology; and the power and authority that they have to determine events. To anticipate the architecture of global networking technologies, all these variables must be taken into account.

NETWORKING TECHNOLOGIES

Although communications networks have many properties in common, they are not all alike. They differ with respect to the components that constitute them, their architectures, as well as the capabilities that they can support. Together, these three network aspects help to determine the socioeconomic impacts of networking technologies.

Network Components

Each network component performs a function essential to the communication process. Network components serve not only to determine the capabilities of networks, but also the relationship among their parts. Equally important, components have an impact on the power relationships within a network as well as on the way in which industry players organize themselves to provide services (Hakansson and Johanson 1993). Network functions can be executed via hardware, software, or human "ware."

Whatever their makeup, network components are functionally interdependent; so they must work together for communication to take place. Because of the interdependencies among components, any network changes with respect to them will have far-reaching repercussions (Antonelli 1992). For example, the interdependencies of networking components give rise to both positive and negative externalities. Thus, for example—up until a certain point—adding another participant to a network will likely enhance the value of the network for existing participants. Similarly, new network applications are likely to increase the value of existing applications as well as the value of the network to users (Boyers 1986). On the other hand, to the extent that they cause congestion, additional applications and users can give rise to negative externalities.[6]

These interdependencies and externalities explain why networks, once they gain momentum, assume path dependent trajectories (Arthur 1989: 116–131). Having become part of an established network, users tend to get locked in. Unwilling to forgo the positive externalities, they are likely to stay put. Because networks represent a large installed base, users are, moreover, unlikely to purchase incompatible components. Instead, they may postpone the adoption of new technologies—even when new components are far superior to old ones—until their entire network can be written off. On the other hand—and for the same reasons—if a number of users come to constitute a critical mass moving to a new technology, others will likely jump on the bandwagon, fearing that they will be left behind (Farrell and Saloner 1987).

Network interdependencies are also a source of constraint. Because a network's performance is limited by its weakest link, each component is a potential bottleneck. In today's computer networks, bottlenecks can occur in many places: the rate at which data can be sent from the computer's memory to the network; the time required for data to pass through the links; and the time that switches take to route data to another network node. Unblocking a bottleneck in one portion of the network, however, may serve only to exacerbate the problem by generating bottlenecks elsewhere.

Bottlenecks, it should be noted, are also a source of network power and control. Not surprisingly, network providers often seek to gain control over bottleneck facilities as part of their business strategies. Given network interdependencies, businesses can leverage control of the bottleneck to gain a competitive advantage in all component markets throughout the network. Such control can be achieved—as some claim Microsoft has done with its operating system—by owning a critical network standard (Farrell and Saloner 1987; Morris and Ferguson 1993). Or companies may try to gain control by buying up and vertically integrating the bottleneck into their business. To this end, many traditional carriers are today seeking alliances and/or buying up stakes that control set-top boxes, cable modems, and Internet portals.

Network Architecture

When network components are considered together and in relationship to one another, they have a definable structure. This structure and the rules that govern how components function within the network constitute the network's architecture. Although some communications networks are more pronounced and concrete than others, all have an architecture, which serves to structure and constrain the way in which communication takes place.

The transportation network, for example, is a complex hierarchical network of roads, rails, shipping routes, and airways. Although the network has many disparate parts, it appears seamless to the user. Despite its fixed nature, the network is somewhat flexible insofar as it can carry a wide range of cargo along a number of alternative distribution routes (Tennenhouse et al. 1995). Capacity and quality, however, are distributed unevenly. Each network consists of layers of distribution channels that are linked together into hubs arranged and spoked out in a decreasing order of size.

People-based networks also exhibit architecture, and with equally significant consequences (Scott 1998). Consider, for instance, social networks such as kinship groups or caste systems. As in any communication network, information is formulated, exchanged, and distributed by an integrated set of functionally related components—in this case individuals acting in roles—in accordance with certain rules and protocols. Over time, patterns of human communication generate a lasting structure that takes on an existence all its own.[7] Embedded in a complex set of social relationships, human-based communication networks tend to be closed, inflexible systems, both reflecting as well as reinforcing the powers that be.[8]

Virtual networks—such as the Internet—are no exception to the rule. Although they can be dynamically reconfigured, virtual networks also have an architecture that serves to mediate information flows. However, whereas the architecture in physical networks is determined by the fixed relationships between links and nodes, and in social networks by the psychological ties that bind, in virtual networks the structure is to be found in the logical relationships that are written into the software code (Mitchell 1991).

Network Capabilities

Taken together, network components and network architecture help to determine network capabilities and, hence, the range of applications that networks can support. These capabilities are described below. Although they are listed separately, network capabilities are interdependent and thus may serve to reinforce one another, or alternatively involve trade-offs—as, for example, in the cases of capacity versus cost, or flexibility versus functionality.

Network Capacity. Capacity is generally measured in terms of bandwidth over some measure of time—the number of bits per second. Bandwidth requirements will differ, depending on the application, the specific needs of users, as well as on the location and number of users. Generally speaking, however, the richer the application, the higher the capacity requirements.[9] To accommodate future educational, e-commerce, and scientific applications in a distributed computer environment, networks with gigabit capacity and even higher will be required.

Network Reach. Network media differ in terms of their reach. For example, some media—such as geosynchronous satellite systems (GEOS)—have a wide footprint and thus are inherently more capable of providing reach than others. Other technologies—if they are interoperable and interconnected on a broad enough basis—can also be used to provide global services. For example, the Internet, given its widely accepted TCP/IP standards, can provide worldwide communication irrespective of the transmission media used to provide services.

Information Density. Like network reach, the density of information flows is, in part, a function of the media employed and the applications they can support. Thus, a fiber optic network that supports multimedia applications will be far richer in information than a narrow-band network that can support voice alone. Information density is also related to network architecture and, in particular, to the mode of communication that it supports. A real-time, two-way interactive multimedia communication—such as videoconferencing—will be richer in information than a communication carried out in a one-way point-to-multipoint store and forward mode. Functionality is also a factor. The more processing capacity in a network, the more information can be targeted to the most appropriate recipients and/or tailored to a user's particular needs.

Modes of Communication. Network coverage will also be affected by the mode in which communication takes place. Communication can occur, for example, on a one-to-one basis (point to point); a one-to-many basis (point to multipoint); and on a many-to-many basis (multipoint to multipoint). Communication can also be one-way and asynchronous, as in the case of the telegraph or e-mail. Or, it can take place synchronously, in real time, on a two-way interactive basis, as in the cases of a telephone conversation or a real-time videoconference. Generally speaking, the mode of communication determines the topology of the network and, with it, the structure of communication flows.

Network Costs. Network costs comprise the resources required to build, operate, and supply network services. Because of the externalities associated with network interdependencies and the potential for joint production, the provisioning of all networking services are subject to significant economies of scale and scope. Putting facilities into place generally entails high up-front and long-lived capital investments. Once a network is built, however, the cost of adding users approaches zero. This cost structure plays a critical role in defining many networking parameters—from the size and organization of networked industries to patterns of deployment and use.

Network Versatility. Network versatility refers to the extent to which a communications system can support a wide range of applications and services. Versatility is a function of the capacity and processing capabilities of a network, the way in which information is formatted, as well as the level of interoperability among network components and network applications. Versatility helps to determine the types of services that can be provided, the costs of these services and the rate of their deployment, as well as the structure and business strategies of networking industries.

Network Flexibility. Network flexibility refers to the ease with which a network can be modified and reconfigured. Network flexibility is determined by a number of interrelated factors, including: (1) the location of intelligence in the network; (2) the technical characteristics of network components; (3) the level of interoperability; (4) the degree of network unbundling; and (5) the level of competition within the networking industry. Flexible networks reduce the costs of provisioning services, promote competition and product diversity, and enhance user control.

Network Accessibility. Network accessibility refers to the ability not only to access a network, but also to take full advantage of the myriad opportunities and functionality associated with networking technologies. Accessibility is related to five major factors: (1) patterns of deployment and diffusion; (2) cost of services; (3) levels of interoperability; (4) rules for interconnection; and (5) technological complexity and ease of use.

Network Functionality. Network functionality is a measure of the extent to which communications networks can execute processes and procedures in the course of communicating information. Functionality depends on network capacity and the extent and distribution of intelligence within the network. Functionality provides a number of benefits. At the level of systems operations, for example, it increases both the efficiency and effectiveness of networking operations. Network functionality reduces the need for network administration, and thus for large-scale, hierarchical operations; microlevel functionality greatly increases users' opportunities and choices.

NETWORKS, INFORMATION, AND ECONOMIC ORGANIZATION

Care must be taken not to generalize about the effects of networking technologies. Their impact will depend not only on their technical capabilities, but also—a factor just as important—on the social and organizational context in which these technologies are deployed. Thus, to assess the potential impact of networking technologies, one needs to consider them in relationship to their intended purposes and the specific environment in which they will be used.

To anticipate the impact of today's advanced networks on the global economy, three interrelated factors must be taken into account. First, it is necessary to understand the fundamental role that information and communication play in the economy, and the incentives to which it gives rise. Second, based on that role, one needs to determine the criteria for economic success and how, in the light of communication flows, these criteria drive economic outcomes and the organization and location of economic activities. Third, it is necessary to consider how a change in communication patterns, brought about by new technological advances, might lead to different types of outcomes.

The Role of Information and Communication in the Economy

Information and communication are inherent in coordinating and sustaining all economic activities. The exchange of information, for example, is at the heart of the market system. Capitalism depends on it both to allocate resources efficiently and to generate and disseminate knowledge essential for innovation and economic growth. Likewise, within firms, the delivery of timely and accurate information is key to decisions about whether to enter or exit markets; how to secure financing; how to organize and manage workers effectively; and how to distribute and market goods.

The time, energy, and money spent in gathering, processing, and using economic information entail considerable costs, typically referred to as transaction costs (Williamson 1985). The level of transaction costs is a function of uncertainty and the inclination and opportunity for economic actors to cheat one another.[10] Such conditions are most likely to prevail, for example, when economic activities are carried out at great distances from one another; when there are many different economic actors who—rarely interacting—are unknown to one another; when market information is unavailable or unevenly distributed; and when production processes, worker skills, and products and services are highly differentiated and not substitutable. Not surprisingly, transaction costs and the value of economic information have increased over time as markets have expanded in scope and as economic processes and products have become more complex (North and Thomas 1973).

High transaction costs not only reduce economic returns; they also inhibit economic growth. In fact, when transaction costs become too high, markets cease to exist (Ackerlof 1970). Thus, in the face of rising information costs, a wide range of social, political, economic, and technological mechanisms have been adopted to cope with them. Among these, for example, have been a reliance on social norms, the use of close-knit social networks, the establishment of geographically based trading regions, the imposition of political rules and regulations, as well as the deployment of networking technologies (Putnam 1993).

Though such mechanisms can solve the problem of transaction costs in the short term, they are unsustainable in the long run. For, while reducing information-related costs in one part of the transaction chain, these solutions serve simultaneously to generate new transaction costs elsewhere in the chain, thereby creating anew the need for organizational and technological innovations. In the economic reshuffling that follows, those who are best positioned to access information and to employ it strategically are likely to be winners, while those excluded from access will fall behind. This sequence is depicted in figure 1.

Networks and the Rise of the National Economy

As described by Sassen in chapter 1, this sequence of interactions is today leading to both the unbundling of the nation as a spatial unit of production as well as the rise of other spatial units and scales. To understand how networking technologies can engender such changes, it is useful to examine the dynamics among the model's four components over time to see how vertically integrated firms and national markets have been linked to advances in networking technologies.

Consider, first, the market before the age of transport, when economic activities were confined to the town square. As the market existed then, neither economic and social relationships nor products were highly differentiated. In this context, proximity and overlapping relations reduced transaction costs, making markets more efficient. Buyers and sellers were known to one another.

FIGURE 1

COPING WITH TRANSACTION COSTS

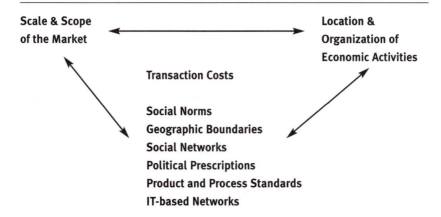

Given their common expectations and established level of trust, credit was generally available, and social sanctions served to some degree to constrain people from exploiting one another. When necessary to prevent monopoly practices, local authorities intervened, setting caps on prices and interest rates.

Improved transportation—in particular, large sailing ships—led not only to the extension of markets over much larger geographic areas; innovative practices were also required to reduce the increased uncertainties associated with markets operating on such scale. Thus, trading intermediaries emerged who specialized in accumulating, transporting, and distributing market information, as well as in brokering and financing deals and exchanges.[11] As trade grew and became more complex, trade was organized—much as Sassen describes the global hierarchy of city economies today—not only horizontally across time and space, but also vertically according to intermediaries' roles and functions in the overall scheme of economic affairs.[12] Thus, at the bottom of the rung were the small local fairs and merchants who conducted minor transactions, most often involving perishable goods. Next up the ladder were larger fairs frequented by long-distance merchants who dealt in more expensive luxury items. Just like the major financial centers of today, at the top of the pyramid were bankers and large merchant families whose revolving fund of cash and credit linked all the players.[13]

Although these networks of intermediaries were essential, they also introduced new uncertainties and bottlenecks into the economy, thereby skewing the flow of trade and financial transactions and concentrating it in a given geographic location. Just as New York, Paris, Frankfurt, Tokyo, and London play a central role today in the global economy, so Venice, Genoa, Lisbon, Antwerp and Amsterdam, were major information hubs for the Mediterranean economy. Take the case of Venice. To secure its place, the city's political leaders partnered with the private sector to build a vast commercial shipping infrastructure—the *galere da mercato*. Complementing this transportation infrastructure was an elaborate network of commercial institutions, all working together to reduce the costs of transacting. These tightly knit social, economic, and political relationships confined in one geographic locale not only reduced transaction costs; they also gave rise to significant economies of agglomeration as well as a first mover advantage.[14] More and more trade was attracted to Venice as a result.[15]

As the model above might suggest, these city-based networks were unable to support the emergence of national markets, integrated within a territorial state. The transaction costs were simply too high. To develop national markets, it was necessary not only to transcend the barriers of time and space but also to overhaul the feudal system. For such purposes, state intervention was required (Polanyi 1957). Social and economic forces, working together, also played a critical role. With the increasing density of the market, a new merchant class emerged, with a distinct culture of its own (Lux 1990). These merchants set national standards of behavior that helped to unify the disparate cultures and political jurisdictions that made up the nation, thereby reducing the transaction costs and risks associated with trade (Hirschman 1977).

To carry out these fundamental and far-reaching social, economic, and political changes, only an advanced and tightly networked communication system would suffice (Braudel 1992a). Nowhere was the impact of an advanced network infrastructure better illustrated than in the development of a mass market in the United States. Here, the telegraph and the railroads greatly increased the size and scope of the market, and—of equal importance—provided the means by which businesses could revamp their operations and reorganize their activities for mass production (Chandler 1977). With the expansion of trade came new risks and thus the need for even greater information, coordination, and control. Economic activities took on such complexity that the previous means of minimizing transaction costs no longer served. Thus, instead of relying on intermediaries to process and convey market information, businesses sought to eliminate the need for many middlemen by standardizing their processes and vertically integrating their organizations (Williamson 1951; Giedion 1954).

The Urban/Rural Divide

By changing the nature and distribution of transaction costs, networking technology expanded markets and redirected the location of economic activities. Above all, increases in the size and scope of markets, together with the vertical integration of firms, fostered the growth of urban economies at the expense of rural areas. Prior to the industrial era, for example, rural economies had been relatively self-sustaining (Swanson 1990). Although populations and resources were sparse, the agricultural economy did not require the extensive differentiation of roles. Thus, low population densities did not disadvantage rural communities. Equally important, rural communities were able to compensate for their remoteness and thin institutional structures by taking advantage of their dense social relationships and cooperative norms (Ensiminger 1978: 295). In the industrial economy, in contrast, rural communities found themselves at a distinct disadvantage. The vast network of transportation and communications technologies that fostered and sustained industrialization channeled resources away from rural communities and helped create conditions for economic success that rural communities were increasingly unable to fulfill.

To compete in the new economy, rural communities required—at a minimum—access to advanced transportation and communication networks. These communities, however, typically lagged urban areas in the diffusion process. Because of the high fixed costs entailed in constructing networks, networking providers focused on deploying technologies first to high-density urban areas where the costs of deployment were lower and could be shared across a wider and more lucrative customer base. As a result, favorably situated businesses in high-density urban corridors usually enjoyed a head start of several decades in utilizing networking technologies, thereby gaining a significant competitive advantage (DuBoff 1983).

Having access to networking technologies was no guarantee of economic success, however. In fact, many networking technologies favored urban economies over rural ones by vastly increasing the scale and scope of the national market.[16] Using the telephone and telegraph, for example, businesses were able to expand their spheres of operation and centralize decision making in distant headquarters. As firms extended their reach, transaction costs increased, forcing firms to become larger and larger. While urban communities had the resources to support business organization on such a grand scale, rural economies did not.

The advent of the mass media also reinforced the development of a national marketplace, exacerbating the growing disparity between rural and urban areas. With the emergence of inexpensive popular magazines such as the *Saturday Evening Post,* the *Ladies Home Journal,* and *Country Gentleman,* small local retailers who had once served their communities with little competition suddenly faced a succession of new challengers—department stores, mail-order companies, and chain stores.

The development of modern highways reinforced this uneven pattern of development and its socioeconomic impacts. Although road building brought rural and urban areas closer together, it forced many small communities to deal with urban values for the first time. Highways also stimulated massive rural outmigration. Concomitantly, by encouraging specialization in agriculture, highways reduced the need for farm labor, inducing many rural residents to seek urban jobs. Highways also contributed to population decentralization. Nonfarm employment expanded in the hinterlands along freeways and modern roads. Industrial belts grew up in the towns and countryside along highways, especially in the southern and border states. The nation's midsize cities linked by freeways also grew at the expense of rural communities.

ANTICIPATING CHANGES IN THE NETWORKED ECONOMY

Just as new networking technologies restructured economic relationships in the past, advanced networks are engendering significant changes in the organization and location of economic activities today. To anticipate their impact, we must first identify the distinct attributes of today's networks and the forces likely to determine their evolution.

Major Technology Advances

Technology advances are greatly enhancing the capacity of all networking technologies, allowing faster communication and denser communication flows. This improved capacity is likely to have a synergistic effect. It will reduce networking costs and increase the applications and functionality that can be supported and hence the demand for network services.

Network Reach. Technology advances are greatly extending network reach. Most notable in this regard are advances in satellite technology. Satellites are inherently more capable of providing greater reach at lower cost than other technologies. Because of their reach, geosynchronous satellite systems (GEOS) have traditionally been used to transmit broadcast signals and voice over very long distances. With the development of very small aperture terminals (VSATs), businesses can now leverage satellite's long-range broadcast capabilities to build private networks. At the same time, GEO technology continues to advance, bringing more efficient, higher capacity satellites to the fore.[17] Satellites rotating in orbits close to the earth—such as medium Earth-orbiting satellites (MEOS) and low Earth-orbiting satellites (LEOS)—offer even greater reach, allowing communication services to be relayed almost anywhere in the world.[18]

The Density of Information Flows. Not only is network coverage likely to be extended spatially. Equally important, today's advanced networking technologies also allow much richer and denser information flows (Evans and Wurster 1999). One major factor contributing to richer information flows is digitization.[19] Digital switching and data processing are the centerpieces of modern networking. Given this convergence, networks are becoming more and more versatile, so they can support a wider range of applications and services. The development of lightwave technology and advances in compression technologies also allow for greater information density. With the use of laser systems and dense wavelength division multiplexing (DWDM) on a single fiber, it is possible to transport 40+ channels of information yielding capacities up to 2 terabytes (2 trillion bits per second).[20] Today, such high-capacity, high-performance fiber optic networks are being built to expand coverage across the globe. For example, between 1996 and 1999, transatlantic cable capacity increased approximately tenfold.

Network Accessibility. Not surprisingly, given these developments, today's networks are likely to be more accessible than ever before. Advanced networking technologies will not only be more evenly deployed; new services and applications will be provisioned much more quickly. Wireless technologies will play a major role in this regard. Today's wireless technologies are not only less costly than wireline technology, they increasingly match—if not exceed—wire-line technologies in terms of performance.[21] Unlike wire-line technologies, wireless technologies are independent of distance. Moreover, they can be rapidly deployed and are easy to maintain. In addition, because wireless systems provide service on a point-to-multipoint basis, their capital costs can be shared across all users, instead of—as in the case of wire-line systems—on a customer-by-customer basis.[22] Equally important, wireless technologies can be deployed in response to demand, so costs are not fixed but variable. Also, because these costs are incurred only when customers purchase the service, the return on capital is quicker, and hence the cost of capital much lower. Likewise, wireless operators are unlikely to have stranded capital; they can easily redeploy their systems if their customers relocate or terminate their services (Arora and Nagpaul 1998). Deployment will also be fostered by greater network versatility. Offering multiple services over a common network, vendors can gain considerable economies of scale and scope. Moreover, by integrating media content and functions, they can add value and create new products and services.

Network Flexibility. Network flexibility is another new and unique aspect of networking today.[23] Continued improvements in the performance of computer technologies and their convergence with communications technologies have allowed for the dispersal of intelligence and control throughout communications systems. More and more, systems are becoming defined and driven by software, which can be easily reconfigured, giving users greater control over network access and use.[24] Equally important in this regard is the ability to unbundle components from the network, allowing users to separately purchase services or functions that were formerly made available only as a single unit. Flexibility is also enhanced, given interoperable, modular components. Most notable in this regard is the Internet.[25] With its modular design and open, interoperable communications protocols, the Internet's service interface is totally independent of the underlying networking technology as well as the applications that are in use.[26] Thus, new networks and applications can be added without fundamentally altering the basic system (Computer Science Research Board 1994).

Network Functionality. Today the software that drives the network is itself becoming more intelligent, greatly enhancing the ability of networks to carry out intelligent tasks. In contrast to traditional software, which treats data and procedures independently, today's object-oriented programs integrate data together with the procedures that operate on that data in an "object." When data and procedures are combined in this fashion, a program can instruct an object to execute a process that is already embedded in it.[27] Because of their functionality and modularity, software objects are likely to provide the building blocks for the distributed intelligent networks of the future. Object-oriented software will also be used to create "intelligent agents" that will be used to automate an ever-growing number of information-related tasks. As intelligence is distributed both horizontally and vertically, network layers are collapsing so that technology-based and socially-based networks can jointly execute functions in a virtual space.

ANTICIPATING TECHNOLOGY IMPACTS IN THE GLOBAL ECONOMY

Given today's technology advances, networks can be both locally based as well as globally extended. At the same time, they can target access to customized information as well as provide interactive forums for communication and intelligent transactions among multiple actors. Configured in a layered, networked architecture, advanced information technologies can greatly enhance the density and functionality of market transactions, thereby generating the kinds of economies of agglomeration that hitherto were available only in tight-knit urban markets. How will these technologies affect the organization and location of economic activities? To answer this question, one has to consider opportunities and economic imperatives associated with new technologies and the new transaction costs to which they might give rise.

Opportunities and Imperatives Associated with the Global Economy

Gaining competitive advantage in a knowledge-based global economy no longer depends on efficiency and cost reduction. Increasingly, it depends on businesses' ability to innovate, respond just-in-time, focus on quality, and establish more cooperative interfirm and intrafirm relationships. To enhance their effectiveness, businesses must take advantage of more timely and appropriately packaged information to help them shift from business models based on mass production to those that center on the concept of flexible, decentralized production.[28] In this new environment, information will be a primary resource, and a prerequisite for the development of all other resources.

Providing positive externalities and economies of agglomeration, networking technologies will be critical in helping businesses to maximize the value of their information resources. Using these technologies, businesses can integrate and compress the time from product innovation to marketing to drive demand and maximize customer responsiveness. Coupled together loosely, they can rearrange their activities around teams and networks to bring together everyone involved in the life cycle of a product. Working together and sharing the same information, they can carry out all business processes in parallel. This kind of networked economic structure reduces the time involved in product development and leads to higher quality products.

As networking technologies and their various functions are brought together into integrated and interactive networks, more and more economic activities will take place electronically, in a virtual environment. Already, companies are moving more and more key activities on-line (Hoff 2000). Not surprisingly, given these developments, business-to-business e-commerce is predicted to increase from $50 billion in 1998 to $300 billion in 2003; similarly, worldwide revenue from application service providers is expected to increase from $7.7 billion in 1999 to 22.87 billion in 2003 (Bruno 2000: 161).

Worldwide networking technologies are also essential for conducting business on a global scale. To fully benefit from the availability of global resources and markets, businesses must have a truly transnational perspective that harmonizes operations in service of a single corporate strategy. Transnational corporations must be able to balance their global operations with the requirements of local markets—such as the need to establish special sales channels, service contracts, and work relationships. Thus, as companies spread their corporate boundaries they will need to make far more complex decisions based on information and data that reflect cultural and political disparities.

Networked information technologies will similarly be a prerequisite for enterprise restructuring and reengineering. Networking technologies can serve not only to support such activities but also as a catalyst for organizational change. In a highly complex and rapidly changing global economy, vertical bureaucracies are being pushed to their limits. Businesses everywhere are rearranging their activities to carry them out in networks and teams. Some businesses, for example, are entering into highly integrated, long-term relationships with customers and suppliers; others are setting up short-term ad hoc alliances to address a particular problem at hand. Many of these networks, moreover, transcend national as well as organizational boundaries. The result has been the widespread vertical disintegration of business activities on a global basis.[29]

New Sources of Transaction Costs

Notwithstanding the potential benefit of networking technologies, their effect will depend not only on the technical characteristics and capabilities of advanced networking technologies but equally on whether these technologies generate new transaction costs, and whether their deployment is accompanied by new organizational innovations and institutional mechanisms that can reduce transaction costs. In the knowledge-based networked economy, transaction costs and new information bottlenecks will stem from three major sources: 1) the decline of embeddedness given a shift from hierarchical business relationships to more atomized market relationships; 2) the potential for bottlenecks in the network itself; and 3) the lack of well-defined property rights.

Loss of Embeddedness in a Networked Environment

As the above historical account makes clear, economic activities and relationships do not exist in a vacuum. They are embedded in a complex set of social and organizational relationships that serve to generate knowledge and reduce transaction costs (Granovetter 1985). Thus, one major challenge that businesses will face in an electronically networked environment is how to promote these locational externalities in the absence of continued face-to-face relationships and organizational routines.

Establishing trust in a networked environment will be particularly challenging.[30] Already, many businesses are finding it difficult to cooperate with their networked partners, with whom they have no shared history. As a result, businesses often defeat the purpose of computer-integrated manufacturing and electronic data interexchange (EDI) by their reluctance to share proprietary product data, or to let their customers or competing suppliers share their cost data (Everett 1993; Munday 1992). Failure to share information within firms also inhibits partnering, because effective interorganizational relations require cooperation across sectors of all related firms (Kleiner and Bouillon 1991).

New ways of establishing trust and loyalty between management and the workforce will also be required. Throughout the industrial era, employees worked in a bureaucracy, in what were predictable and somewhat committed relationships, exchanging loyalty of service for salary, benefits, and career mobility. Today, more and more people work in a variety of settings—home, satellite offices, rented or temporary offices, even at the offices of suppliers, partners, or competitors; they also were under a variety of arrangements with their employers—part time, contractual, temporary, or some other individually negotiated arrangement. Without new social and organizational mechanisms for assuring loyalty and compliance under these many circumstances, the transaction costs entailed in orchestrating flexible processes, assuring quality, and monitoring performance will be exceedingly high.

An equally serious problem related to embeddedness is that of organizational learning and innovation. Like trust, learning in a business takes place in the context of social interactions. It occurs not by individuals acting on their own, but rather in the course of people working together to execute tasks and carry out routines. The shared conventions that result from such interactions constitute organizational learning. Providing the basis for innovation, organizational learning is critical in a knowledge-based economy, where new product development and product differentiation are key (Lundvall 1992). Organizational learning is also a competitive resource that serves as a barrier to entry.[31] Insofar as it is tacit knowledge, which cannot be easily replicated, organizational learning provides the only sustainable basis for competitive advantage.[32] The problem for businesses in a networked environment is how to foster and maintain organizational learning in the absence of structured organizations.

The Network as Bottleneck

In the networked economy, the network may itself serve as a bottleneck and source of new transaction costs. Because exchange transactions will increasingly be carried out electronically and on-line, the network will in many cases constitute the market. Where this occurs, economic outcomes will depend not only on the relationship among economic actors, but also on the network's architecture and the type of economic incentives that network service providers face in a knowledge-based global economy.

Network architecture and the rules of access and interconnection will be critical in determining their economic impacts. The design and structure of networks, for example, will affect the overall efficiency of the economy, the size and scope of markets, the ability to conduct trade, the distribution of economic costs and benefits throughout the economy, the nature of work, and the quality of jobs. To reduce transaction costs, the network architecture must be flexible and open. Without such versatility, businesses will be unable to rapidly reconfigure their networks to respond to changing circumstances and market demand. Nor will they have the leeway needed to customize applications and networks to support changing business processes and flexible working relationships. Moreover, without the freedom to mix and match a wide variety of network components, businesses will be less able to add value and develop new products and services.

To reap the benefits of networking fully, networks will also need to be interoperable and open for interconnection. Proprietary systems with closed standards increase the cost of doing business and create significant barriers to market entry. Open, interoperable systems, in contrast, reduce transaction costs, provide greater network flexibility and improved ease of use, and reduce the costs of networks. Moreover, given standardized platforms, diffusion will be more rapid and equitable, and new products and innovations will be encouraged.

In the absence of government regulation, network providers—responding to the signals of the market—will determine the design and evolution of the global network infrastructure. Although network providers are likely to provide an integrated platform for electronic commerce, they may be much less inclined to offer their networking services on an open and ubiquitous basis. In contrast to the downsizing characteristic of many other industries, network service providers have little incentive to break up and outsource their operations. To the contrary, by integrating infrastructure services and applications, they can benefit not only from economies of scale and scope, but also from the many positive externalities associated with networked technologies. Equally important, integrated networks will command higher service prices than nonintegrated networks in the marketplace.

Not surprisingly, network providers are scurrying to take advantages of these opportunities. Mergers and acquisitions in the information technology, communications, and media industries jumped 97 percent in 1998, to $488 billion (Reinhardt 1999). Nor are Internet companies immune to these developments. In fact, given the lack of barriers to market entry, they are far more inclined to engage in mergers and acquisitions than established, lower technology companies.[33] Even in the burgeoning e-commerce area, one can see evidence of a trend toward industry concentration. In the short run, the proliferation of start-ups and fierce competition is the norm. Over the long term, however, the cost barriers associated with acquiring a critical mass of properties, strategic pricing, and advertising are likely to give rise to first mover advantages.[34]

The Lack of Well-defined Property Rights

Property rights are the building blocks of the economy. Prescribing the rights and obligations of those engaged in economic activities, they help to determine the structure of prices, the allocation of resources, as well as the level and distribution of consumer welfare (Libecap 1993). Hence the way in which property rights are structured will have profound implications for economic performance (North 1990). Establishing a property rights regime to maximize economic performance is problematic, however. Property rights are not natural; they are contrived. Emerging in the context of a struggle for economic and political advantage, property rights are more likely to reflect and reinforce existing power relations than they are to conform to an ideal set of governance rules (Sened 1997). Even given agreement about the need for change, achieving consensus on a new regime will be difficult, requiring bargaining and side payments among heterogeneous groups of stakeholders.[35]

Major technological advances such as we are witnessing today will serve to challenge existing property rights regimes. As more and more economic activities are shifted on-line, the value of access and market information increases geometrically. As a result, the informal rules that have governed cyberspace until now will no longer suffice. Major disputes have already arisen, for example, with respect to privacy, security, intellectual property, access and interconnection, as well as to proprietary rights to business practices.

Resolving these competing claims is likely to go on for a very long time. Because the networked economy is global in scope and incorporates such a wide range of activities, the number and variety of stakeholder interests that need to be reconciled are unprecedented. The level of uncertainty is also high, because of our lack of experience with both the technology and the notion of information as a commodity. Compounding the problem, there is no universally accepted third party or governance structure to resolve competing claims. Until there is a clear institutional framework and set of rules for operating in the networked economy, uncertainty and transaction costs will likely abound.

REVISITING THE THREE HYPOTHESES

How do the three hypotheses posited at the outset of this chapter hold up in the light of the analysis presented here? Overall, it is clear that—given the complexity of the problem at hand—each of these three scenarios is too starkly drawn. Because today's networks are so malleable, in each case there is room for considerable leeway. Nevertheless, based on the discussion of the factors laid out in this chapter, some conclusions about place/space relationships in a networked economy can be drawn.

The Shift of Power from the Geographically Based Nation-state to the Transnational Firm

Looking at the evolution of technology alone, the notion that power will shift in the future from the geographically based nation-state to the transnational firms is quite plausible. Because of the reach and flexibility of today's networks, businesses can easily bypass national boundaries, creating their own global networks or purchasing worldwide services from the increasing number of global service providers. As described by one observer, "The Old World is quickly becoming the telecommunications new frontier."[36] What this scenario fails to take into account, however, are the new transaction costs that are likely to emerge in a global economy, and how they might serve to reinforce the need for the nation-state. As history bears witness, the more trade has expanded, and the greater its value, the more government has intervened, whether to build infrastructure or to secure property rights.

In today's global environment, instituting a private governance structure for electric markets presents a much more formidable challenge. Notwithstanding the demise of the Soviet Union and the worldwide trend toward privatization and market liberalization, economic actors from different areas of the world continue to operate in accordance with diverse cultural norms and political rules of the game. Thus, some Western firms have found it difficult to enter foreign markets because they don't understand the unwritten rules and information codes of conduct (Orru, Hamilton, and Suzuki 1989). Equally significant, to overcome these institutional trade barriers, or to negotiate a way around them, businesses are turning not to their counterparts in other countries but rather to their own national governments.

Especially problematic for the private sector are conflicting perspectives—both domestically and worldwide—about the nature of information. Some people view information as a commodity to be bought and sold in the marketplace; others perceive it as a public good to be widely shared; still others consider information to be potentially dangerous and want it secured and protected. These conflicts over information, although always present, have intensified as the value of information has risen. Moreover, these info-skirmishes have given rise to market disputes involving fundamental societal issues—among them freedom of speech, the protection of privacy, cultural integrity, and national security.

Businesses, moreover, will not go unchallenged in their efforts to redefine property rights. Governments, representing a broader citizenry, have their own, sometimes competing, interests in securing new governance regimes, especially in the area of national security and defense. As proved true in the heated debate in the United States over encryption technologies, the property rights regime proffered by government and that sought by industry don't always coincide. And though global expansion of electronic commerce will yield numerous economic benefits, it will also undermine international mores and accepted rules of behavior, creating new sources of political and economic vulnerability. Increased terrorism, drug trafficking, electronic fraud, and money laundering are all likely upshots of the growth in electronic commerce—ills that ultimately would force governments to intervene.

New Opportunities for Nonmetropolitan Areas

The claim that networking technologies will redress the urban/rural divide is plausible in a number of key respects. In the past, networking technologies enhanced the speed of communications but increased transaction costs, requiring the establishment of vertically integrated firms, situated in central urban locations. In contrast, today's networks offer much greater functionality, allowing them to reduce some transaction costs in the course of communication.[37] Equally important, today's networks, given their decentralized, flexible architecture, can, in contrast to the railroads and the telegraph, which served to deplete rural areas, reinforce local, horizontal ties.

By aggregating supply and demand horizontally, networking technologies can overcome many of the market failures associated with rural economies and generate new economic synergies based on economies of agglomeration. Equally important, such networks, when designed to strengthen local and regional ties, can provide a counterforce to the external drain on local resources that might otherwise occur in a globally networked economy. Put more concretely, just as businesses employ networking technologies to establish industry-based portals, so too might rural communities use these technologies to establish regionally based rural portals that can serve as "virtual industrial districts."[38]

When operating in a virtual environment, rural and urban areas are more likely to be on equal ground. A regional rural portal, for example, would allow remote communities from across an entire region to link up and cooperate with like communities elsewhere, thereby reinforcing local knowledge, restraining destructive competition among communities, and limiting the drain of resources to more urbanized areas. Moreover, by participating in such a regional rural portal, rural communities would benefit not only from greater economies of agglomeration but also from the external economies associated with industrial districts. These locational economies would serve not only to reduce overall costs but to allow communities to use their limited resources in the most cost-effective manner.

Succeeding in such endeavors will be extremely difficult, however. Rural communities will not only have to act strategically; they will also need to have access to, as well as control over, the design of local networks. While rural telephone cooperatives have a long history of providing communication services to their communities, they are less positioned to do so today in an increasingly competitive communication marketplace. As in the past, most of the deployment of advanced networking technologies is being focused almost exclusively in large cities and urbanized regions, where demand is highest and the customer base the most lucrative.[39] What's worse, a number of large companies in the United States are actually abandoning their rural customers. Thus, for example, since 1994, US West—which provides service in fourteen states—has sold off more than four hundred of its exchanges (Selwyn, Kratin, and Coleman 1999).

Even if rural communities were successful in carrying out the economic endeavors described here, there would be limits to what they might accomplish.

In a knowledge-based economy, keeping pace with transaction costs will be an uphill battle, notwithstanding the functionality and flexibility of advanced networking technologies. More than likely the traditional division of labor between urban and rural areas will be maintained, with the former focusing on highly complex, specialized goods, and the latter on standardized products (Storper 1991).

The Rise of Global Cities at the Expense of Nonmetropolitan Economies

In contrast to the two previous hypotheses, which discount future transaction costs, the proposition that a chain of cities will provide the hubs of the global economy is premised on the notion that transaction costs are on the rise. According to this thesis, in an information-based economy, global cities will be advantaged precisely because they are suited best to handle transaction costs, given their strong economies of agglomeration. As in the two previous cases, there is much to be said for this scenario. However, while emphasizing transaction costs, it fails to take into account the flexible architecture and functional capabilities of advanced networking technologies. Given these attributes, we can expect that the vertical impetus driving cities to link together at the global level may very well be counteracted and balanced by forces that establish horizontal ties, grounding cities and their economies in a larger regional context.

In the new economy, local places will continue to matter. However, these places will not remain untouched by the global expansion of markets; on the contrary, in order to survive, local communities will have to redefine themselves in relationship to them. Where the local and the global meet, two interrelated forces are likely to be at work. On the one hand, globalization is operating to eliminate the key economic distinctions that are associated with specific places. Thus, for example, we are witnessing the standardization of tastes, technologies, and techniques on a global scale. However, and somewhat paradoxically, this aspect of globalization is giving rise to totally new types of products and production techniques that are embedded in territorial locales.[40]

In this globally, networked economy, old industrial cities, which were designed to accommodate mass production, will continue their decline. However, urbanization will continue apace. Given the breakdown of economic and political boundaries, metropolitan areas will extend their connection by incorporating urban regions into their vastly expanded networks that stretch across the globe (Gereffi and Korezeniewic 1994). At the same time, new industrial regions are likely to emerge in places that were previously undeveloped.[41] The result is the rise of the "Galactic" city, which extends from one major metropolis to another (Lewis 1995). Nation-states will not disappear in this new environment. However, they will serve less and less as the geographic unit that bounds economic activities and provides a stimulus to economic growth. Nation-states, moreover, will devolve authority both upward and downward. More and more they will assume the role of orchestrating a loose confederation of regional economies.

NOTES

The author thanks the Institute for Advanced Study, United Nations University (Tokyo) for its support, and the Center for Advanced Study in the Behavioral Sciences (Palo Alto, CA), for hosting one of the meetings of the research network.

1. Based on statistical analysis, for example, a number of recent studies have demonstrated clear causal links between telecommunications deployment and economic growth. In explaining these relationships, researchers have pointed to the ability of telecommunications not only to reduce transaction costs within markets; they note that these benefits also spill over to make other institutions more efficient (Hardy 1980; Cronin, Parker, et al. 1991: 529–535; Cronin, Colleran, et al. 1993: 677).

2. As noted by Kellerman, "[The] hidden dimension of telecommunications, and the technical nature of network structures could be counted as major reasons for an almost lack of interest among geographers in the topology, structure, and design of telecommunications" (1993). Unfortunately, Kellerman, though noting the problem, does not systematically address it.

3. As described by Fleck, information-based networks can be characterized as "configurational technologies" insofar as they can be customized to meet specific needs (1994: 637–652).

4. A network is a group of functionally related elements that together form a complex whole. A communication network can be defined as "a set of interdependent components, each of which performs a function necessary to support, or execute, communication processes."

5. As described by Braudel with respect to the industrial revolution, "When one is talking about social phenomenon, rapid and slow changes are inseparable. For no society exists which is not constantly torn between the forces—whether perceived as such or not—working to undermine it. Revolutionary explosions are but the sudden and short-lived volcanic eruption of this latent and long term conflict" (1992b: 537–538).

6. Thus, flat-rate pricing, while encouraging usage, has led to congestion on the Internet, especially at the Network Access Points in the United States where most of the traffic between backbones is exchanged. As noted by the OECD (2000:9), the average performance of backbone networks—as measured by the speed of downloading—declined by 4.5 percent in 1997.

7. As described by Katz and Kahn, "As human inventions, social systems are imperfect. They can come apart at the seams overnight, but they can also outlast by centuries the biological organisms that originally created them. The cement that holds them together is essentially psychological rather than biological. Social systems are anchored in the attitudes, perceptions, beliefs, motivations, habits and expectations of human beings" (1978: 37).

8. Thus, for example, a single-line voice conversation in a digitized format can be accommodated at the rate of 56 Kbps. High-speed Internet access and medium-quality videoconferencing can be provided using basic rate ISDN, which operates at 144,000 bits per second. However, very good quality, full-motion teleconferencing will require 2.54 Mbps, while multimedia applications will need rates of 45 Mbps and more.

9. Williamson (1985) refers to these two factors as "bounded rationality" and "opportunism with guile."

10. Commenting on the role of intermediaries in facilitating trade, Braudel notes, for example, "Another effect of the organization of the London market was the dislocation (inevitably, in view of the scale of the enterprise) of the traditional open market, the public market where nothing could be concealed, where producer-vendor and buyer-consumer met face to face. The distance between the two was becoming too great to be traveled by ordinary people. The merchant, or middleman, had already, from at least the thirteenth century, made his appearance in England as a go-between for town and country, in particular in the corn trade. Gradually, chains of intermediaries were set

up between producer and merchant on the one hand, and between merchant and retailer on the other; along these chains passed the bulk of the trade in butter, cheese, poultry, produce, fruit, vegetables and milk. Traditional habits and customs were lost or smashed. Who would have thought that the belly of London or the belly of Paris would cause a revolution? Yet they did so simply by growing" (1992b, 42).

11. At the bottom of the rung were the small local fairs and merchants who conducted minor transactions, most often involving perishable goods. Next up the ladder were larger fairs frequented by long-distance merchants who dealt in more expensive luxury items. At the top of the pyramid were bankers and large merchant families whose revolving fund of cash and credit served to link and bring together all the players.

12. Six annual fairs alternated every two months, like clockwork, between Champagne and Brie. Connecting the trade routes from the Netherlands to northern Italy, these regional fairs provided the hub of European economic activity (Braudel 1992a).

13. Agglomeration economies include scale economies that result from spatial concentration instead of the scale of a specific, individual firm. Moreover, whenever businesses are concentrated together they also benefit from the law of large numbers, which allows them to share risks. Agglomeration economies also result from complementarity in labor supply and in production. In addition, spatial concentration can foster personal interaction, which in turn generates new ideas, products, and processes (Mills and Hamilton 1984).

14. Seeking to benefit from this expanded trade without sacrificing its own competitive advantage, Venice restricted access to trade-related information, going so far as to segregate and conduct strict surveillance over all foreign merchants. As Braudel has described this policy: "All trade to and from the Terra Firma, all exports from her islands in the Levant or cities in the Adriatic (even goods traveling to Sicily or England) were obliged to pass through the port of Venice. Thus Venice had quite deliberately ensnared all the surrounding subject economies, including the German economy, for her own profit; she drew her living from them, preventing them from acting freely and according to their own lights" (1992a: 228).

15. The development is clearly illustrated by a convergence of prices across the nation. As Richard DuBoff notes with respect to the cotton market, "Data on cotton prices in New York show diminishing fluctuations over time. The average spread between lowest and highest prices narrowed steadily, except during the Civil War and its aftermath, and the steepest declines in high-low price ranges and dispersion of prices from decade averages came in the 1850s—'the telegraph decade,' as it might be called" (1983: 257).

16. Thus, for example, Hughes Electronics has recently announced its plays for Spaceway—a $1.4 billion North American satellite network that would provide high-speed bandwidth for data, Internet access, videoconferencing, and other applications on demand. In addition, Space Station Loral now expects to launch a satellite that will carry more than 150 transponders—or the equivalent in on-board digital signaling processing equipment—allowing it to serve multiple regions with an unlimited range of applications. Estimates are that between 1996 and 2002 approximately 155 GEOS will have been launched (Janders 1999; Pfeifenberger and Houthakker 1998).

17. These systems use a number of small satellites rotating in a lower earth orbit, which act like cells in a cellular phone system, but instead of being fixed, these satellites are in motion with respect to the user. Lower earth orbiting systems are less costly to manufacture and easier to deploy than GEOS. In addition, they experience less signal delay, and have fewer power requirements, allowing for smaller terminals and more flexible types of services (Sawyer 1998).

18. One major technological advance contributing to this trend is digitization—the process of transforming analog messages (a spoken word, a picture, or letter) into a signal made up of discrete pulses that can be transmitted, processed, and stored electronically. Transmitting digital data is much more efficient than transmitting analog data; in digital systems data need not be converted into tones simulating a voice signal. Moreover, when in digital form, audio, video, and text-based messages can be combined and recombined, allowing information to be integrated in a way that was previously impossible.

19. With wave division multiplexing, each fiber optic cable can accommodate multiple channels by assigning each data stream a different wave length or color. With dense wave division multiplexing, carriers can greatly enhance the capacity of installed fiber.

20. Mobile systems were introduced in the late 1980s and early 1990s. They used analog cellular and cordless telephone technologies. Second-generation systems could digitize speech, allowing for advanced calling features and some data services. The idea of a third-generation system, which originated in the International Telecommunications Union, was referred to as the future public mobile telephone system. Today, the general term is International Mobile Telecommunications-2000, although the Europeans employ the term "universal mobile telecom systems" (UMTS) when referring to their own version of a third-generation system. As originally conceived, IMPTS-2000 would have a common radio interface and network. It would support higher data rates than do second-generation systems, but be less expensive (Computer Science and Telecommunications Board 1997).

21. For example, the average cost of a 5–kilometer local loop ranges from $1,000 to $1,800 per subscriber. A wireless local loop costs one-quarter to one-third as much as this (Swasey 1999: 44).

22. In the past, building networks was a highly complicated endeavor, entailing large sums of investments, sunk costs, and twenty-year depreciation cycles. To cope with the complexity, amass the required capital, and provide the necessary interconnection, network industries were organized hierarchically on a monopoly basis. Fixed in hardware, the network was very rigid, making it difficult to adapt to changing circumstances and needs.

23. Within the public switched network, this trend is well illustrated by the "intelligent network." With the advent of powerful microprocessors, high-speed computers, and enhanced memory devices, telephone companies have been able to locate network intelligence not just in the central office switch, but also at nodes throughout the network. Because these intelligent nodes can communicate in real time with one another, as well as with software, network providers cannot respond to network problems and to changes in user demand, optimize network capacity, and ensure greater system and service reliability. Moreover, because software databases and intelligent switches can be assessed and modified by customers as well as by service providers, the integration of intelligence into the network allows users greater control over the provisioning of their services.

24. As characterized by Anthony Rutkowski, "The only physical components of the Internet are the computers and paths that transit its data; it is the software running on the computers that creates everything else usually in modularized layers of functionality that allow different activities to invoke each other without knowing much about each other's details. It is the software that has enabled the amazing diverse deployment of the Internet as well as the applications that run on it" (1997).

25. Unlike networks in the past, the Internet has no center of control. Switching and processing functions are carried out in a nonhierarchical fashion, via routers that are located at the outer bounds of the network and that communicate with one another on a peer-to-peer basis. Equally important, the most intelligent network functions are situated not in the routers but rather at the very edge of the network, in the applications and services. As a result, it is the users who decide what content is accessed and which service providers to use (Blumenthal 1999; Gillett and Kapor 1997).

26. Object-oriented programming is not only functional, it is also efficient to deploy and flexible to use. Because software objects are entities unto themselves, they can be combined, disassembled, and recombined to create a wide variety of networking applications (Lauden and Lauden 1998).

27. Flexible, decentralized production systems allow businesses to customize production without sacrificing economies of scope. Using such an approach, businesses seek to control a particular market niche rather than maximize market size. As a result, scale economies are no longer such an important factor for success (Ayers 1992).

28. As described by Grabher, "The strategy of vertical integration was successful 'when the pace of technological change was relatively slow, production processes were well understood and stan-

dardized, and production runs turned out large numbers of similar products. Today, however, such large-scale vertical integration has serious weaknesses: inability to respond quickly to competitive changes in international markets: resistance to process innovations that alter the relation between different stages of the production process; and relative lack of willingness to introduce new products" (Grabher 1993: 16).

29. As Storper notes: 'In the American economy . . . total vertical integration declined from 30 percent to 21 percent between 1987 and 1997, and even manufacturing vertical integration decreased from 30 percent to 27 percent. In most of the specific sectors said to be increasingly flexibly specialized, these declines were even more dramatic' (1997a: 6).

30. As described by Ring and Van den Ven, "Reliance on trust by organizations can be expected to emerge between business partners only when they have successfully completed transactions in the past and they perceive one another as complying with norms and equity. The more frequently the parties have successfully transacted, the more likely they will bring higher levels of trust to subsequent transactions. As the level of trust increases, greater reliance may be placed on the actions of the trusted party" (1992: 483).

31. As described by Michael Storper, "Those firms, sectors, regions, and nations which can learn faster or better (achieving higher quality or cheaper price for a given quantity) become competitive because other knowledge is scarce and therefore cannot be immediately imitated by new entrants, via codified and formal channels, to competitor firms, regions, or nations" (1997a: 31).

32. Storper refers to these learning resources as "untradable interdependencies." As he notes, "Technology involves not just the tension between scale and variety, but that between the codifiability or noncodifiability of knowledge; its substantive domain is learning and *becoming*, not just diffusion and deployment. Organizations are knit together, their boundaries defined and changes, and their relations to each other accomplished not simply as input-output relations or linkages, but as untraded interdependencies subject to a high degree of reflexivity" (1997a, 28).

33. As noted by one consulting firm, for the top twenty-five Internet companies, the average number of years before significant merger and acquisition activity take place is six years, compared with seventy-two years for the top fifty U.S. companies (*Business Week* 1999).

34. This kind of integration will not be limited to large scale, infrastructure industries. As described by Hoff, "That could prove all the more true thanks to a rapidly emerging new class of net middlemen in a wide range of consumer and industrial markets. Online, with few limitations of time and geography, these new market makers can quickly generate a virtuous loop of buyers and sellers whose very presence attracts yet more buyers and sellers. For this reason, they're expected to dominate many industries from chemical suppliers to rolled steel (1999).

35. As described by North and Davis, "It is the possibility of profits that cannot be captured within the existing arrangemental structure that leads to the formation of new (or the mutation of old) institutional arrangements" (1971: 39).

36. Given WorldCom's global reach and British-based Vodafone's bid for the German telecommunications firm Mannesmann, a rash of global mergers can be expected. Among those will likely be big national players such as British Telecom, Deutsche Telecom, and Japan's NTT (Baker 1999).

37. One need only consider, for example, computer-integrated manufacturing. CIM improves efficiency and product quality because the data describing the engineering parameters of a product—once created and stored electronically—can be retrieved by any other member of a project team in a form appropriate for his or her needs. Redundancies and discrepancies are avoided because everyone uses the same information.

38. In an industrial district, small and medium-size firms are networked together in a geographic region. Each firm within the network specializes in some aspect of a common production system, allowing them to jointly reap many of the benefits of vertical integration, hitherto available only to large firms.

39. Thus, for example, the top seven metropolitan areas host 62 percent of the nation's Internet backbone capacity, and the top twenty-one metropolitan areas 87.5 percent.

40. Storper has emphasized that the type of globalization that we are experiencing today "opens

up markets to products based on superior forms of 'local knowledge'; it consolidates markets and leads to such fantastic product differentiation possibilities that markets refragment and, with them, new specialized and localized divisions of labor reemerge; and it in some ways heats up the competitive process (albeit among giants), creating new premia on technological learning that requires the same firms that become global supply oligopolists to root themselves in locationally specific relational assets' (1997b: 35).

41. Describing the new geography of the networked global economy, as it is presently unfolding, Scott notes: "the developed areas of the world are represented as a system of polarized regional economies each consisting of a central metropolitan area and a surrounding hinterland (of indefinite extent) occupied by ancillary communities, prosperous agricultural zones, smaller tributary centers and the like. . . . Each metropolitan nucleus is the site of intricate networks of specialized but complementary forms of economic activity, together with large, multifaceted local markets, and each is a locus of powerful agglomeration economies and increasing return effects. As such they are not only large in size but also constantly growing yet larger. These entities can be thought of as the *regional motors of the new global economy*" (1998: 8).

REFERENCES CITED

Abler, R. F. "What Makes Cities Important?" *Bell Telephone Magazine* 49 (2): 10–15.

Ackerlof, George. 1970. "The 'Market for Lemons': Qualitative Uncertainty and the Market Mechanism." *Quarterly Journal of Economics* 84: 488–500.

Antonelli, Cristiano. 1992. "The Economic Theory of Information Networks." 5–25 *The Economics of Information Networks,* edited by Cristiano Antonelli. The Netherlands: North Holland.

Arora, Suresh, and Alike Nagpaul. 1998. "Broadband Wireless Solutions for Global Business." *Telecommunications* (September): 83–84.

Arthur, Brian. 1989. "Competing Technologies, Increasing Returns, and Lock-in by Historical Events." *Economic Journal* 99: 116–131.

Ayers, R. U. 1992. "CIM: A Challenge to Technology Management." *International Journal of Technology Management* (December): pp. numbers here.

Baker, Stephen. 1999. "Running Scared: Telecoms Are Rushing to Bulk Up before a New Giant Emerges." *Business Week,* December 6, 60–64.

Bluenstein, Rebecca. 1999. "Lucent to Buy Data-Networking Firm." *Wall Street Journal,* September 11, 6.

Blumenthal, Marjorie S. 1999. "Architecture and Expectations: Networks of the World Unite!" pp. 1–52 in *The Promise of Global Networks.* Queensland, MD: Institute for Information Studies.

Boyer, Kenneth 1996. "Network Externalities," in Donald L. Alexander, Werner Sichel, *Networks, Infrastructure and the New Task for Regulation,* Ann Arbor: Michigan, pp. 13–19.

Braudel, Fernand 1992a, *The Perspective of the World: Civilization and Capitalism, 15th–18th Centuries.* Vol. 3. Berkeley: University of California Press.

———. 1992b, *The Wheels of Commerce: Civilization and Capitalism, 15th–18th Centuries.* Vol. 2. Berkeley: University of California Press.

Bruno, Leo. 2000. "The Broadband Era." *The Red Herring,* February, 161.

Business Week. 1999. "Internet Companies: Merging Young" December 6, 8.

Castells, M. 1996. *The Networked Society. Oxford:* Blackwell.

Chandler, Alfred D. 1977. *The Visible Hand: The Managerial Revolution in American Business.* Cambridge, MA: Harvard University Press.

Computer Science and Telecommunications Board. 1997. *The Evolution of Untethered Communications.* Washington, D.C.: National Academy Press.

Computer Science Research Board. 1994. *Realizing the Future.* Washington, DC: National Academy Press, 1994.

Cronin, Francis J., Elisabeth K. Colleran, Paul L. Herbert, and Steven Lewitzky, eds. 1993. "Telecommunications and Growth." *Telecommunications Policy* 17 (December): 677–691.

Cronin, Francis J., Edwin B. Parker, Elisabeth K. Colleran, and Mark A. Gold, eds. 1991.

"Telecommunications Infrastructure and Economic Growth: An Analysis of Causality." *Telecommunications Policy* 15 (6): 529–535.

Davis, L. E., and D. E. North eds. 1971. *Institutional Change and American Economic Growth.* Cambridge, England: Cambridge University Press.

Dolenga, Howard E. 1992. "Management Paradigms and Practices for the Information Age." *Advanced Management Journal* (Winter): 25–29.

DuBoff, Richard. 1983. "The Telegraph and the Structure of Markets in the United States, 1845–1890." *Research in Economic History* 8: 253–257.

Ensiminger, Douglas. 1978. "Rural Neighborhoods and Communities." In *Changes in Rural America: Causes, Consequences, and Alternatives,* ed. Richard Rodenfeld et al. St. Louis, MO: C.V. Mosby.

Evans, name, and name Wurster. 1997. "Strategy and the New Economics of Information," *Harvard Business Review* (September-October): 73–74.

Everett, Martin. 1993. "Why Partners Sometimes Part." *Sales and Marketing Management* (April): 69–74.

Farrell, Joseph. 1989. "Standardization and Intellectual Property." *Jurimerics Journal of Law, Science and Technology* 30, 1: 35–55.

Farrell, Joseph, and Garth Saloner. 1987. "Horses, Penguins, and Lemmings." In *Product Standardization and Competitive Strategy,* ed. H. Landis Gabel. The Netherlands: North Holland.

Fleck, James 1994. "Learning by Trying: The Implementation of Configurational Technology," *Research Policy,* v. pp. 637–652.

Gereffi, G., and M. Korezeniewicz, eds. 1994. *Commodity Chains and Global Capitalism.* Westport, CT: Greenwood.

Giedion, Siegfried. 1954. *Mechanization Takes Command: A Contribution to Anonymous History.* New York: Scribner.

Gillett, Sharon Eisner, and Mitchell Kapor. 1997. "The Self-Governing Internet: Coordination by Design." In *Coordinating the Internet,* ed. Brian Kahin and James H. Keller. Cambridge: MIT Press.

Gong, Jiong and Srinagesh, Padmanabhan. 1997. "The Economics of Layered Networks," in Lee McKingt and Joe Bailey, Internet Economics, Cambridge, MA: MIT Press, pp. 63–76.

Gottman, J. 1983. *The coming of the Transnational City.* College Park, MD: Institute for Urban Studies.

Grabher, Gernot. 1993. "Rediscovering the Social in the Economics of Interfirm Relations." Pp. 1–31 in *The Embedded Firm; On the Socioeconomics of Industrial Districts,* ed. Gernot Grabher. New York: Routledge.

Granovetter, Mark. 1985. "Economic Action and Social Structure: The Problem of Embeddedness." *American Journal of Sociology* 93: 481–510.

Hakansson, Hakan, and Jan Johanson. 1993. "The Network as a Governance Structure: Interfirm Cooperation beyond Markets and Hierarchies." Pp. 35–51 in *The Embedded Firm: On the Socioeconomics of Industrial Network,* ed. Gernot Grabher. London, UK: Routledge.

Hardy, Andrew P. 1980. "The Role of the Telephone in Economic Development." *Telecommunications Policy* 4 (December): 278–286.

Heywood, Peter. 1998. "Brave New York, Brave New Vendors." *Data Communications* (October): 61–74.

Hirschman, Albert O. 1977. *The Passions and the Interests: Political Arguments for Capitalism before Its Triumph.* Princeton, NJ: Princeton University Press.

Hof, Robert D. "A New Race of Giants?" *Business Week,* July 26, 1999, EB 72.

Hoff, Karla, Avishay Braverman, and Joseph E. Stiglitz 1993. "Imperfect Information and Rural Credit Markets." Pp. 33–52 in *The Economics of Rural Organization: Theory, Practice, and Policy.* Washington, DC: The World Bank.

Hudson, Heather E. 1995. *Economic and Social Benefits of Rural Telecommunications: A Report to the World Bank.* March.

Janders, Mary. 1999. "High Speed Satellite Data Network Planned." *Tech Web* (March).

Joseph, Farrell. 1989. "Standardization and Intellectual Property." *Jurimetrics: Journal of Law, Science, and Technology* 30 (1):35–55.

Kalis, Lisa. 2000. "In the Pipeline." *The Red Herring,* February, 164.

Katz, Daniel and Robert L. Kahn. 1978. *The Social Psychology of Organizations.* New York: John Wiley & Sons.

Kellerman, Aharon 1993. *Telecommunications and Geography,* New York, NY: Belhaven Press, p. xv.

Kleiner, Morris M., and Marvin L. Bouillon. 1991. "Information Sharing of Sensitive Business Data with Employees." *Industrial Relations* 30: 480–491.

Lauden, Kenneth C., and Jane P. Laudon. 1998. *Management Information Systems: New Approaches to Organization and Technology.* (5th ed.) Saddle River, NJ: Prentice Hall.

Lazonik, William. 1994. *Business Organization and the Myth of the Market Economy.* New York: Cambridge University Press.

Lewis, Pierce. 1995. "The Urban Invasion of Rural America." In *The Changing American Countryside: Rural People and Places,* ed. Emery Castle. Lawrence: University Press of Kansas.

Libecap, Gary D. 1993. *Contracting for Property Rights.* New York: Cambridge University Press.

Lundvall, B. A. 1992. *National Systems of Innovation: Toward a Theory of Innovation and Interactive Learning.* London: Pinter.

Lux, Kenneth, 1990. *Adam Smith's Mistake: How a Moral Philosopher Invented Economics and Ended Morality.* Boston: Shambhala.

Max, Munday. 1992 "Buyer-Supplier Partnerships and Cost Data Disclosures." *Management Accounting* (June): 28–36.

Meyers, Cheryl. 1999. "'The Shrinking Telecommunications Food Chain." *The Red Herring,* September.

Mills, Edwin S., and Bruce W. Hamilton. 1984. *Urban Economics.* 3rd ed. Glenview, Ill Scott, Foresman.

Mitchell, William J. 1991. *City of Bits: Space, Place, and the Infobahn.* Cambridge: MIT Press.

Morris, Charles R., and Charles H. Ferguson. 1993. "How Architecture Wins Technology Wars." *Harvard Business Review,* March/April.

North, Douglas C. 1990. *Change and Economic Performance.* Cambridge: Cambridge University Press.

North, Douglas C., and Robert P. Thomas. 1973. *The Rise of the Western World: A New Economic History.* Cambridge, England: Cambridge University Press.

North, S. N. D. 1884. *History and Present Condition of the Newspaper and Periodical Press of the United States.* Washington, DC: U.S. Government Printing Office.

O'Brien, R.O. 1992. *Global Financial Integration: The End of Geography.* London, UK: Royal Institute of International Affiars.

OECD. *Internet Traffic Exchanges: Developments and Policy.* Paris: OECD, 2000: p. 9.

Orru, M., G. G. Hamilton, and M. Suzuki. 1989. "Patterns of Inter-firm Control in Japanese Businesses." *Organizational Studies* 10 (4): 459–474.

Parker, Edwin B., Heather E. Hudson, Don A. Dillman, Sharon Strover, and Frederick Williams. 1995. *Electronic Byways: State Policies for Rural Development through Telecommunications.* 2nd ed. Washington, DC: Aspen Institute.

Peterson, Theodore. 1964. *Magazines in the Twentieth Century.* 2nd ed. Urbana: University of Illinois Press.

Pfeifenberger, J. P., and H. S. Houthakker. 1998. "Competition to International Satellite Communication Services." *Information Economics and Policy* 10.

Polanyi, Karl. 1957. *The Great Transformation: The Political and Economic Origins of Our Time.* New York: Beacon.

Putnam, Robert D. 1993. *Making Democracy Work: Civic Traditions in Modern Italy.* Princeton, NJ: Princeton University Press.

Reinhardt, Andy. 1999. "The Main Event: Bernie vs. Mike." *Business Week,* October 18, 44.

Ring, Peter Smith, and Andrew H. Van den Ven. 1992. "Structuring Cooperative Relationships between Organizations." *Strategic Management Journal* 13: 483–498.

Rutkowski, Anthony. 1997. "The Internet: An Abstraction in Chaos." In *Internet as Paradigm*. Queensland, MC: Institute for Information Studies.

Sassen, Saskia. 2000. *Cities in a World Economy*. 2nd ed. Thousand Oaks, CA: Pine Forge/Sage.

Sawyer, Douglas. 1998. "Net Satellite Services to Bridge the Gap." *Telecommunications* (September): 24.

Scott, Allen J. 1998. *Regions of the World Economy: The Coming Shape of Global Production, Competition, and Political Order*. New York: Oxford University Press.

Selwyn, Lee, Patricia D. Kratin, and Scott A. Coleman. 1999. *Building a Broadband America: The Competitive Key to the Future of the Internet*. Boston: Economics and Technology.

Sened, Itai. 1997. *The Political Institutions of Private Property*. New York: Cambridge University Press.

Shironzu, Norihiko, and Robert L. Siminson. 2000. "Toyota Weighs Joining Web Supply System" *Wall Street Journal*, January 14: B10.

Storper, Michael 1991. *Industrial Economic Development and the Regional Question in the Third World: From Import Substitution to Flexible Production*. London: Pion Limited.

———. 1997a. *Territorial Development in a Global Economy: The Regional World*. New York: Guilford.

———. 1997b. "Territorial Flows and Hierarchies in the Global Economy." In Spaces of Globalization: Reasserting the Power of the Local, ed. Kevin R. Cox. New York: Guilford.

Swanson, Louis. 1990. "Rethinking Assumptions about Farm and Community." in *American Rural Communities*, ed. A. E. Luloff and Louis E. Swanson. Boulder, CO: Westview Special Studies in Contemporary Social Issues.

Swasey, Laurence. 1999. "Waiting for a Wireless Local Loop." *The Red Herring*, March.

Williamson, Harold, ed. 1951. *The Growth of the American Economy*. New York: Prentice Hall.

Williamson, Oliver. 1985. *The Economic Institutions of Capitalism*. New York: Free Press.

Wingfield, Nick. 1999. "Inside the Tangles of AT&T's Web Strategy." *Wall Street Journal*, October 13, B1.

Chapter 2

COMMUNICATION GRIDS:
CITIES AND INFRASTRUCTURE

Stephen Graham

"Telecommunications," writes Barney Warf, "is one of the few topics in geography that richly illustrates the plasticity of space, the ways it can be stretched, deformed, or compressed according to changing economic and political imperatives" (Warf 1998: 255). The growing centrality of key large urban regions, or "global cities," to the economic, social, political, and cultural dynamics of the world presents a particularly potent example of the reconfiguration of space through telecommunications.[1] In such cities, the most sophisticated, diverse, and capable electronic infrastructures ever seen are being mobilized to compress space and time barriers in a veritable frenzy of network construction.

Such processes seem likely to maintain the electronic competitive advantages of the largest global cities for some time to come. But the "wiring" of cities with the latest fiber optic networks is also extremely uneven. It is characterized by a dynamic of dualization. On the one hand, seamless and powerful global-local (or "glocal") connections are being constructed within and among highly valued spaces, based on the physical construction of tailored fiber networks to the doorsteps of institutions. On the other, intervening spaces—even those that may geographically be cheek-by-jowl with the favored zones within the same city—seem to be largely ignored by telecommunications investment plans. Such spaces threaten to emerge as "network ghettos," places of low telecommunications access and social disadvantage (Thrift 1995). As with many contemporary urban trends, then, uneven global interconnection via advanced telecommunications becomes subtly combined with local disconnection in the production of urban space.[2]

The contexts for such transformations are now clearly established. Global cities research, in particular, has detailed at length how an interconnected network of such cities has recently grown to attain extraordinary status. Such research has demonstrated how such cities are necessary to "hold down" the globalizing economic, societal, and cultural system. Such cities bring together and interweave (in various combinations) the greatest multidimensional concentrations of control—financial, service, cultural, institutional, social, informational, and infrastructural assets—worldwide, in various configurations (Sassen 2000, 2001).

All aspects of the development and functioning of global cities are increasingly reliant on advanced telecommunications networks and services; such cities concentrate the most communications-intensive elements of all economic sectors and transnational activities within small portions of geographic space (Leyshon and Thrift 1997; Corbridge, Martin, and Thrift 1994). It is no surprise, therefore, that there is growing evidence that such city-regions heavily dominate investment in, and use of, such technologies (Graham and Marvin 1996).

Rather than simply eroding the territorial governance of modern nation-states, however, globalization and the strengthened roles of global cities seem to be supporting the rescaling of institutional, regulatory and territorial governance (Brenner 1998a). By the mid-1980s, all Western national states had "substantially re-scaled their internal institutional hierarchies in order to play increasingly entrepreneurial roles in producing geographic infrastructures for a new round of capitalist accumulation." In the infrastructural arena, this meant a widespread shift to privatizing, liberalization, opening up public infrastructure to private investment, and allowing increasing freedom for private capital to develop limited, customized infrastructures in specific spaces, without worrying about the need to cross-subsidize networks in less favored zones.

Thus, public, national telecommunications regimes that were ostensibly about throwing electronic networks universally across national space economies are being materially and institutionally "splintered" (Graham and Marvin 2001). In their place, national, regional, and local states are developing glocal strategies aimed at ensuring that global cities are equipped with the assets and electronic infrastructures that will further support the development of global centrality. Efforts here center on developing connective, customized infrastructures linking the hearts of global cities with planetary networks through other global cities. Brenner (1998b) calls these new approaches to infrastructural development glocal scalar fixes. To him, they differ totally from the styles of infrastructure development that characterized the latter stages of the modern ideal. In stark contrast to the Fordist-Keynesian project of "homogenizing spatial practices on a national scale," he writes, "a key result of these processes of state re-scaling has been to intensify capital's uneven geographical development" (p. 476).

As authors like Kellerman (1993) and Warf (1989; 1995) have shown, not only do the diversifying electronic infrastructures that girdle the planet have specific geographies and spatialities, it is global city-regions that dominate these geographies and spatialities. The current global shift toward liberalized, privatized, and internationalized telecommunications regimes seems to be accentuating the centrality of global cities to telecommunications investment patterns. The national planning of monopolistic telecommunications grids, characteristic of Keynesian and developmental states, was geared, at least to some extent, toward discursively and relationally binding national space economies. In the developed world, for example, policies were aimed at the universal geographical rollout of national telephone grids, supported by cross-subsidies between profitable and nonprofitable routes. This national-territorial model is now giving way to a global process of market-driven competition. In global cities, complex, superimposed telecommunications networks of many private firms now jostle for the attention of the spaces of maximum communications demand. They connect directly with transoceanic optic fibers and satellite connections, to offer seamless local-global connections in ways that seem to mirror the hub-and-spoke patterns of global interurban airline networks (Smith and Timberlake 1995).

But many research challenges remain to be faced before we can satisfactorily understand the complex interlinkages between telecommunications grids, global cities, and planetary urban networks. One, in particular, is the focus of the current chapter. Here, my aim is to explore the linkages between the growth of a planetary network of global financial, corporate, and media capitals and the emerging global and urban information infrastructures that interlink and underpin such centers.

As Peter Taylor (1997) suggests, relational connections among world cities remain poorly understood. Certainly, very little is known about how the global wiring of the planet with a new generation of optic fiber grids interconnects with the development of intense concentrations of new communications infrastructures within global cities. Through a relational and multiscalar perspective (see Amin and Graham 1997; 1998), my aim in this chapter is to develop such an understanding by attempting to address intraurban, interurban, and transplanetary optic fiber connections (and disconnections) in parallel. I would argue that such an approach is necessary given the logics inherent within the Network Society, which force us to collapse conventional hierarchical notions of scale—"building," "district," "city," "nation," "continent," or "planet." As a result, it is difficult to be a specialist on urban landscapes, intraurban shifts, or urban systems in separation. For discussions of restructuring *within* cities increasingly must address the changing relations *among* them, while also being cognizant of the importance of these changing relations within broader dynamics of geopolitics and geoeconomics.

For example, through the logics of the network society, global relational connections can, in certain circumstances, become much more intense than local ones. They can, in fact, be combined with very powerful local *disconnections*. People, machines, institutions, buildings, and urban districts can become intensively woven together across international space through the mediating power of local-global infrastructure networks. But such spaces can, at the same time, cease to be articulated in any meaningful way with their local hinterlands or districts, backed up by processes of urban restructuring, the widespread "fortress" impulse, architectural and urban design strategies, police practices, and so on (see Boyer 1996). As a result, traditional notions that cities, regions, and nations have any necessary coherence as territorial "containers" become extremely problematic.

This chapter has four parts. First, I set the context by briefly exploring the complex relations among urban centrality, global cities, and telecommunications investment and use. Second, I look in detail at how global financial, media, and corporate capitals are assuming dominant positions within global trends toward telecommunications liberalization and explore how such investment might be understood to relate to the "competitiveness" of global cities. The third section focuses on the urban scale, addressing the case of London. Here I explore in particular how telecommunications liberalization in the United Kingdom has bolstered the competitive position of London as a global city. Finally, I look at the global, interurban scale, looking at some examples of new global optic fiber grids, which are tying intraurban optic fiber networks together into networks that directly parallel the emerging system of global cities across the planet.

GLOBAL CITIES: THE SOCIAL PRODUCTION OF LANDSCAPES OF MULTIPLE RELATIONAL CENTRALITY

It is now clear that global cities grow by cumulatively concentrating the key assets relied on by corporate headquarters, high-level service industries, global financial service industries, national and supranational governance institutions, and international cultural industries operating within a volatile, globalizing environment (Markusen and Gwiasda 1994). The growing extent of globally "stretched" corporate, financial, and media webs, mediated by telecommunications, computer, and transport networks, seems to support a parallel need for the social production and management of places of intense centrality. This is especially so when one adds the volatilities thrown up by global shifts toward financial globalization, economic liberalization, and the opening up of regional blocks to "free" trade. As Mitchelson and Wheeler suggest, "in times of great uncertainty, select cities acquire strategic importance as command centers and as centralized producers of the highest order economic information" (1994: 88). To use Boden and Molotch's terminology, the complex mediation of economic activity in extremely volatile contexts necessitates high levels of "face-to-face co-present interaction" within the high-level managerial and control functions that concentrate in global cities (1994). Particular, grounded, and place-based social relations become central to the economic survival of high-level corporate, media, and financial organizations.

Such arguments have important implications for the way we view global cities and their development within the context of globalization. To Michael Storper, for example, "the nature of the contemporary city is as a local or regional 'socio-economy,' whose very usefulness to the forces of global capitalism is precisely as an assembly of specific, differentiated, and localized relations" (1997: 222). Such relations are mediated by complex and subtle combinations of place-based, face-to-face meetings, and telemediated exchange, both at the intra- and interurban scales. Most important, there is not a simple substitution of the latter for the former, as so often suggested in "information age" business rhetoric (Graham 1997). Nigel Thrift, for example, has recently argued (1996) that, in London at least, telecommunications technologies may actually *increase* the demand for on-going, face-to-face interaction in global financial service firms, as the information glut that is associated with them requires ever-more continuous, reflexive effort at interpretation, merely to make sense of it all. Jean Gottmann, one of the pioneers of studying the links between cities, communications, and centrality, powerfully captures the subtle interrelations among them:

> In the modern world, with its expanding and multiplying networks of relations and a snowballing mass of bits of information produced and exchanged along these networks, the information services are fast becoming an essential component, indeed a cornerstone, of transactional decision making and of urban centrality. (1990: 197)

The Dominance by Global Cities of National and International Telecommunications Flows

As mediators of all aspects of the reflexive functioning and development of global cities, convergent media, telecommunications, and computing grids (known collectively as "telematics") are thus basic integrating infrastructures underpinning the shift toward intensely interconnected planetary urban networks. Interurban telecommunications networks (both transoceanic optic fibers and satellites) comprise a vital set of "hubs," "spokes" and "tunnel effects" linking urban economies together into "real" or "near real time" systems of interaction that substantially reconfigure the production of both space and time barriers within and between them (De Roo 1994). Such technologies help integrate distant financial markets, service industries, corporate locations, and media industries with virtual instantaneity and rapidly increasing sophistication. But they underpin the enormously complex communications demands *within* global cities, generated by the intense clustering of reflexive practices in space.

In short, the most sophisticated and innovative developments of telecommunications effectively grow *out of* the larger and more internationally oriented cities. Such dynamics mean that the very small geographical areas of the main global finance, corporate, and media capitals dominate the emerging global political economy of telecommunications to a degree that is rarely appreciated because of the dominance of national figures in available data.

Two sources of data can help give an indication of this dominance. First, we can see how the economic sectors that are overwhelmingly located in global cities tend to dominate international telecommunications flows as a whole. For example, more than 80 percent of international data flows are taken up by the communications, information flows, and transactions in the financial services sector (Sussman 1997: 38). More than 50 percent of all long-distance telephone calls in the United States are made or received by 5 percent of phone customers, largely transnational corporations whose control functions still cluster in the global metropolitan areas of the nation.

Second, there is a small amount of available data on the dominance of national telecommunications patterns by particular global cities. A recent survey by the Yankee Group and *Communications Week International,* for example, found that around 55 percent of all international private telecommunications circuits that terminate in the United Kingdom do so within London (Finnie 1998). And about three-quarters of all advanced data traffic generated in France comes from within the Paris region (see Finnie 1998).

Telecommunications and the Geographies of Intraurban Restructuring

Beyond this general picture, however, we still know little about the fine-grained relationships between telecommunications and the growth, dynamics, and development of the many sectors that combine to drive the development of global cities. Equally, we know little about the ways in which new telecommunications technologies are enrolled into processes of restructuring within the geographical landscapes of global cities. How, for example, are telecommunications infrastructures and applications increasingly bound up in the production and restructuring of built environments, with the proliferation of "intelligent buildings," "smart" office complexes, "tele-villages," and "smart" highways and infrastructure networks (what William Mitchell (1995) calls "recombinant architecture")?

Noticeable trends have been identified toward the decentralization and "back officing" of routine services (see OTA 1995; Graham 1997; Richardson 1994) at urban suburbs, peripheral smaller cities, sometimes even peripheral global locations (such as Bangalore, the Caribbean, Jamaica, the northern Philippines, etc.; see Sussman and Lent 1998; Graham and Marvin 2001). But their intrinsic reflexivity means that there are limits on how far the decentralization of higher-level services can currently go. Instead, in the cores of global cities, a physical restructuring process has recently been observed, caused by the needs for new corporate financial architectures with large dealer floors that can accommodate modern electronic dealing systems and technologies. These do not simply decentralize to the periphery of cities or further afield, to rely purely on electronic interaction; rather, such processes seem to fashion complex new intraurban geographies of service location. Longcore and Rees recently showed that the larger floorplate demanded by financial service firms in New York may "offset the perceived need for face-to-face contact" and lead them to shift out from Wall Street to a doughnut ring around the edge of Manhattan (1996: 354).

The Metropolitan Dominance of Noncorporate Telecommunications

It is important to stress that global cities dominate much broader realms of telecommunications activity than those usually addressed in global cities literature: financial services, corporate finance, and trading. Such is their concentration of demands for information, communications, and transaction, and such is their propensity for broad-scale technological innovation and application, that global cities also dominate phone, mobile phone, media communications, and Internet use outside the corporate and financial sectors.

Manhattan, for example, has more telephones than all forty nations in sub-Saharan Africa put together (Sussman 1997: 231). It also provides the highest concentration of Internet activity anywhere on Earth, as the Internet and its spiraling mass of information, communication, transactions, and specialized media flows flows in to support every aspect of the functioning of the City.

Manhattan is also home to a booming set of industrial sectors as New York's Silicon Alley emerges as a dominant global provider of Internet and multimedia skills, design and high value-added content of all sorts. As in San Francisco's so-called Multimedia Gulch district, several downtown urban neighborhoods have been refurbished and gentrified to sustain the clustering demands of interlocking micro, small, and medium-sized firms in digital design, advertising, publishing, fashion, music, multimedia, computing and communications. More than twenty-two hundred firms provided fifty-six thousands jobs in these sectors in 1998, an increase of 10,500 over 1996. (Rothstein 1998). Here, as with global financial services sectors, the need for ongoing face-to-face contact, to sustain continuous innovation and reflexivity, is combined with exceptionally high use of advanced telecommunications to link relationally and continuously with the rest of the planet.

As a result, in 1997 Manhattan had twice the domain density (i.e., concentration of Internet hosts) of the next most Internet-rich U.S. city—San Francisco—and six times the U.S. average (Moss and Townsend 1997). In fact, in the late 1990s the metropolitan dominance of the Internet in the United States was actually growing rather than declining, despite its association with rural "electronic cottages." The top fifteen metropolitan core regions in the United States in Internet domains accounted for just 4.3 percent of national population in 1996. But they contained 12.6 percent of the U.S. total of domains in April 1994, and by 1996 had almost 20 percent, as the Internet became a diffused and corporately rich system. As Moss and Townsend suggest, "the highly disproportionate share of Internet growth in these cities demonstrates that internet growth is not weakening the role of information-intensive cities. In fact, the activities of information-producing cities have been *driving the growth of the Internet* in the last three years" (1997: page 8, emphasis added).

TELECOMMUNICATIONS LIBERALIZATION, GLOBAL CITIES, AND URBAN COMPETITIVENESS

It is altogether unsurprising, given the above discussion, that global cities exert a critical influence in shaping emerging global geographies and geopolitics of telecommunications infrastructure development. Central business districts (CBDs) within global cities, in particular, play a predominant role within extremely fast-moving communications landscapes. They provide leading foci of rapid technological change, liberalized service provision, and highly concentrated patterns of investment in new telecommunications infrastructures, from multiple competing providers (Graham and Marvin 1996; 2001). Global financial service industries, in particular, are especially important in driving telecommunications liberalization. With telecom costs taking up around 8 percent of expenditure on goods and services in global financial firms, world-class telecommunications infrastructure and a business-friendly, fully liberalized regulatory environment, are key assets in the race between global cities to lure financial and corporate operations and their telecommunications hubs (Moss 1987).

For transnational companies (TNCs) of all kinds, liberalized telecommunications markets allow the benefits of competition to be maximized. The spread of liberalization also minimizes the transaction, negotiation, and interconnection costs that stem from constructing global networks within the diverse regulatory and cultural contexts of multiple postal, telegraph, and telephone companies (PTTs) across the globe. Global telecoms liberalization is thus critical given the strategic centrality of private telecommunications networks to the functioning of all transnational, financial, and media firms. The emerging global, private regime allows lucrative corporate and financial market segments to benefit from intense, customized, and often very localized competition in high-level telecommunications infrastructure and services, when this was impossible through old-style PTTs.

In short, for financial, transnational, and media firms, sophisticated telecommunications are essential to business success. Such firms demand an increasingly complex and seamless package of broadband connections and services, within and between the global cities where they operate. Such demands include leased lines, so-called virtual private networks connecting their sites in a seamless manner, private optic fiber connections, dedicated satellite circuits, video conferencing, and, increasingly, highly capable mobile and wireless services.

In addition, such powerful corporate, financial, and media users are pressing hard to enjoy the fruits of competition between multiple network providers in global cities. Such competition tends to increase discounts, improve efficiency and innovation, and, above all, reduce risks of network failure by increasing network "resilience." Meanwhile, however, peripheral regions and marginalized social groups often actually lose out and fail to reap the benefits of competition, as they are left with the rump of old PTT infrastructures, relatively high prices, and poor levels of reliability and innovation. Highly uneven microgeographies of splintered telecommunications development thus replace the relatively integrated and homogeneous networks developed by national telephone monopolies (Graham and Marvin 2001).

Global Cities and International Telecommunications Liberalization

As a result of such liberalizing pressures, a global wave of liberalization and/or privatization is transforming national telecommunications regimes. The key lobbying pressures driving this shift derive from transnational companies, the World Trade Organization, and G7, telecommunications industries and, especially, the corporate, financial, and media service industries that concentrate in global cities (Graham and Marvin 2001). In the context of the recent World Trade Organization (WTO) agreement to move toward a global liberalized telecommunications market, and with most regions of the globe now instigating regional trading bloc agreements (EU, NAFTA, ASEAN, Mercosur, etc.) based on removing national barriers to telecoms competition, a profound reorganization of the global telecommunications industry is taking place.

The initial example of metropolitan network competition (or "bypass" as it was then called) was set by New York in the 1980s. Then, a whole new competitive urban telecommunications infrastructure was developed in the city by the teleport company and Port Authority (Warf 1989). As the pressures of the global neoliberal orthodoxy in telecommunications have grown, even the most resistant nation-states (such as France, Germany, Singapore, and Malaysia) are now succumbing to calls for national PTT monopolies to be withdrawn, to be replaced by uneven, multiple, telecoms infrastructures which inevitably center in large metropolitan markets.

In the shift to a seamlessly interconnected global telecoms industry, national PTT monopolies are thus being rapidly privatized and/or liberalized across the globe. Private telecom firms are aggressively "uprooting" to make acquisitions, strategic alliances, and mergers with other firms, in a global struggle to build truly planetary telecommunications service firms, geared toward meeting the precise needs of transnational corporations and financial firms within the whole planetary network of global cities, on a "one stop, one contract" basis (Finnie 1998).

For example, in an effort to position themselves for this one-stop corporate market, BT and AT&T, both trying to reposition themselves from national to global players, formed a global alliance called Concert. AT&T has also merged with the huge U.S. cable firm Tele-Communications company to improve its position within home U.S. markets. The Swedish, Swiss, Spanish and Dutch PTTs, meanwhile, have their Global One umbrella. France Telecom and Deutsche Telekom have an alliance with the U.S. international operator Sprint. As we shall see later in the chapter, new, small, specialized telecom firms like WorldCom/MCI and City of London Telecommunications (COLT) are growing, using their flexibility and responsiveness to target only the most profitable business centers for network construction. A myriad of other firms are offering services based on reselling network capacity leased in bulk from other firms' telecommunications networks. Finally, there is a process of alliance formation between telecoms, media, and cable firms. All are jostling to position themselves favorably for corporate and domestic markets, especially in the information-rich global city-regions, for a future for which many envisage a globally liberalized telecommunications environment with perhaps four or five giant, truly global, multimedia conglomerates.

The position of global cities is therefore being substantially reinforced by the shift from national telecommunications monopolies (PTTs) to a globalized, liberalized communications marketplace. As cross-subsidies between rich and poor, and core and periphery spaces within nations are removed (with the associated notion of universal tariffs), infrastructure development, innovation and service provision now reflect unevenness in communications demand in a much more potent way than has been witnessed for the last half-century, taking on an increasingly integrated global appearance in the process. Prices and tariffs are being unbundled at the national level, revealing stark new geographies that compound the advantages of valued spaces within global cities as attractive and highly profitable telecommunications markets, dominating telecommunications investment patterns within nation-states.

The Microgeographical Imperatives of "Local Loop" Connection

It is paradoxical, however, that an industry which endlessly proclaims the "death of distance" actually remains driven by the old-fashioned geographic imperative of using networks to drive physical market access. The greatest challenge of these multiplying telecommunications firms in global cities is what is termed the problem of the "last mile": getting satellite installations, optic fiber "drops" and whole networks through the expensive "local loop," under the roads and pavements of the urban fabric, to the buildings and sites of target users. Without the expensive laying of hardware it is not possible to enter the market and gain lucrative contracts. Fully 80 percent of the costs of a network are associated with this traditional, messy business of getting it into the ground in highly congested, and contested, urban areas.

This is why precise infrastructure planning (through the use of sophisticated Geographic Information Systems) is increasingly being used to ensure that the minimum investment brings the highest market potential. It also explains why any opportunity is explored to string optic fibers through the older networks of ducts and leeways that are literally sunk deep within the archaeological root systems of old urban cores. Mercury's fiber grid in London's financial district, for example, uses the ducts of a long-forgotten nineteenth century hydraulic power network. Other operators thread optic fibers along rail, road, canal, and other leeways and conduits. While satellite infrastructures are obviously more flexible, they are nowhere near as capable or secure as physical optic fiber drops to a building. And they, too, ultimately rely on having the hardware in place to deliver services to the right "footprint."

Mapping and Measuring the "Competitiveness" of Global Cities' Telecommunications Infrastructure

How, then, are all these dynamics coming together to shape the wiring of global cities currently? How can we understand the position of different global cities within this apparent maelstrom of technical and regulatory change, changing firm strategies, and physical network development? Above all, what does "competitiveness" mean in world city electronic infrastructure today?

A survey by the Yankee Group, a U.S. telecommunications consultancy, and *Communications Week International,* attempted to rank the competitiveness of telecommunications provision in early 1998 in twenty-five global cities encompassing 5 percent of the world's population (see Finnie 1998). Their resulting scored rankings (see table 1) were based on technical definitions of the pricing of services, the choice of physical infrastructure connections available, and the availability of the most advanced and sophisticated connections (for example, "dark fiber," which is unconnected to other user and very broadband services).

TABLE 1

RANKED SCORES OF GLOBAL CITIES BY THE 'COMPETITIVENESS' OF THEIR TELECOMMUNICATIONS INFRASTRUCTURES, MARCH 1998

Rank	City	Total Score	Tariffs	Choice	Availability
1	New York	438	148	182	108
2	Chicago	428	154	166	108
3	Los Angeles	428	152	168	108
4	San Francisco/San Jose	425	149	168	108
5	Atlanta	409	141	160	108
6	London	391	131	161	99
7	Stockholm	386	129	149	108
8	Toronto	361	123	148	90
9	Paris	337	118	129	90
10	Sydney	331	123	118	90
11	Hong Kong	328	107	149	72
12	Frankfurt	321	78	135	108
13	Amsterdam	308	100	118	90
14	Tokyo	300	77	133	90
15	Brussels	294	97	107	90
16	Mexico City	283	93	118	72
17	Zurich	276	100	86	90
18	Milan	267	101	94	72
19	Kuala Lumpur	256	90	94	72
20	Tel Aviv	230	110	66	54
21	Singapore	206	108	44	54
22	Johannesburg	161	76	50	36
23	São Paulo	135	44	55	36
24	Moscow	134	26	72	36
25	Beijing	105	48	39	18
Maximum possible scores		**500**	**171**	**221**	**108**

Note: Scores are based on a technical assessment of tarifss, choice of networks and availability of services.

Source: adapted from Finnie (1998, p. 21).

Their results give a revealing portrait of the degree to which intense competition is focusing on the small number of global cities that concentrate particularly high demand, are located within the core geoeconomic regions of the world, and are placed within nations that have enthusiastically embraced telecommunications liberalization. The researchers concluded that "cities large and small around the globe are integral to the fortunes of the world's economy, yet the [telecommunication] infrastructure in each can vary greatly. . . . Although the gap between the best and worst of infrastructure is narrowing, particularly in the middle ground, it is still very wide" (Finnie 1998: 20).

The five U.S. cities included in the sample ranked highest and most competitive. New York led the way with nine separate optic fiber infrastructures. London was the most competitive city outside the United States, with six separate optic fiber grids. Cities that are currently experiencing a proliferation of urban fiber infrastructures, following recent liberalization, came next: Stockholm, Paris, Sydney, Hong Kong, Frankfurt, and Amsterdam. The rest trailed further behind because of insufficient network competition, relatively high tariffs, and a lack of access to the most sophisticated services. Eleven out of the twenty-five cities only had one optic fiber network, tying firms into sole, monopoly suppliers. Interestingly, though, the researchers believed that such was the rate of current shifts toward global archipelagos of competitive global city optic fiber grids that all global cities will have at least five optic fiber grids (Finnie 1998: 22).

Global cities in the developing world tended to be at the bottom of the table because of their nation-states' general reluctance to privatize and/or liberalize their telecommunications regimes. Here, the authors portrayed foreign-owned telecom infrastructures as the "silver bullet" to such cities' lack of competitiveness.

> The "poorer" cities in our survey—defined as such in terms of GDP per capita—trail far behind, victims by and large of local reluctance to allow competition. Of these four "poorer" cities—Mexico City, Johannesburg, Beijing and Kuala Lumpur—only Mexico City makes a reasonable showing, mainly because it has been efficiently colonized by foreign owned telecoms operators taking advantage of Mexico's liberal regulatory structure. The others still have a long way to go before they can join the global elite. (Finnie 1998: 22)

TELECOMMUNICATIONS LIBERALIZATION AND GLOBAL CITY COMPETITION: THE CASE OF LONDON

Continuing our focus on the metropolitan scale for the moment, London provides a particularly illuminating case study of the detailed processes through which global cities develop multiple, competing telecommunications infrastructures. As the above survey suggests, London's position as the preeminent European global finance capital has been significantly bolstered by the very early, and very radical, liberalization of U.K. telecommunications. The Corporation of London argues that the United Kingdom's liberalization of telecommunications since 1981 has contributed directly to London's continued competitiveness as a global information capital. "Product innovation and service provision in telecommunications . . . have been directed towards the financial services. Competition between telecom providers appears to have had a considerable effect on customers. Services have been redefined and costs reduced" (Simmons 1994).

In the mid-1990s, London's City Research Project analyzed London's telecommunications infrastructure in considerable detail. Like the Yankee Group/*Communications Week International* survey, it found it to be superior to any other equivalent global city outside the United States (New York, for example, was found to have both lower costs and better service quality than London) (Ireland 1995). Since the United Kingdom liberalized its telecommunications in 1981, more than a thousand new telecommunications licenses have been awarded, many offering specialized, tailored services to financial and corporate industries in the City, either over new infrastructures or by resale and leased lines over the existing telecom grids of other telecom companies. The fact that the financial services sector accounts for 15 percent of the U.K. telecommunications market has meant that the City of London has been the prime beneficiary of this shift to competition, attracting intense infrastructure investment and localized competition from all the main global telecommunications players. The overall telecommunications market for London was recently estimated at more than £1.3 billion, around the same as that for Paris and more than four times that for Frankfurt (£253 million) (COLT Telecommunications website).

The Proliferation of Dedicated Optic Fiber Grids

The City of London now has six overlaid fiber optic grids superimposed beneath the Square Mile—the heart of the district—and the rest of the main business areas of the City (BT, Mercury, City of London Telecommunications [COLT], WorldCom-MCI, Energis and Sohonet). Roads, canal pathways, old hydraulic power ducts, underground railway tubes, sewers, and other utility pipes provide the conduits for this massive concentration of electronic infrastructure. Increasingly, these urban networks link directly into transatlantic and transglobal optic fiber grids, maximizing the quality and reliability of transglobal connectivity. The direct, digital, broadband connections that are essential for extremely fast and increasingly multimedia financial service telematics applications are now available at very competitive rates. The City has also par-

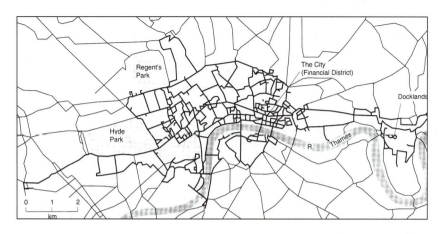

Source: http://www.colt-telecom.com/english/countries/uk/mn_technology.html.

ticularly benefited from the rebalancing of tariffs with radical reductions in the costs of international calls and leased lines (which are usually discounted substantially for bulk users).

Gaining detailed information on the urban geographies of these competing infrastructures is not easy (Kellerman 1993). But details are available of one of these six networks that operated COLT (fig. 1). The geographies of the other five are unlikely to vary considerably. Figure 1 thus shows how dedicated fiber networks tend to be tightly focused, at least at first, on the central areas with the most intensive concentration of communications-intensive activities. In the COLT network fiber is laid especially thickly in the City of London financial district. A broader grain of network coverage exists in the West End. And an extension runs out to the new international business spaces in the Docklands.

London's Advantages in Other Services

In addition to dedicated fiber networks, London has many satellite data and voice facilities, a comprehensive suite of microwave communications grids, and dozens of reselling service operators from all over the world (which lease infrastructure capacity from telecom operators for resale, offering discounts and customized service portfolios to corporate and financial firms in the City). A host of value-added and consultancy firms are also concentrated in the City, supporting state-of-the-art innovation in financial telecoms service and corporate telematics applications (Ireland 1995).

While this remarkable concentration of localized investment and infrastructure can be confusing for customers, it generally leads to improved service quality, lower costs, faster innovation, much improved reliability, radically reduced risks and improved "resilience" (a term meaning that the network services are much less likely to go down because multiple routes are built into them—a critical consideration when even a small connection problem can cost millions, even billions, of dollars in lost revenue and exchange).

Such advantages have allowed the City of London to emerge as the main telecommunications and computer networking hub in Europe, with many German firms connecting to the City directly for their global networks to access the better networks, tailored services and, most important, lower-priced services (Germany has long resisted telecoms liberalization and is only now offering limited competition in business services and infrastructure).

Dedicated Digital Media Connections to Hollywood: The "Sohonet" Initiative

But London's advantages in telecommunications infrastructure extend into cultural and media industries sectors, too. For example, a specialized telecommunications network was constructed in 1997 by a consortium of London film companies called Sohonet. This system links the tight concentration of film and media companies, TV broadcasters, publishers, Internet providers, graphic designers, and recording studios headquarters in London's Soho and West End district directly to Hollywood film studios via seamless transatlantic fiber connections. Sohonet allows online film transmission, virtual studios, and editing over intercontinental scales via highly capable, digital, broadband connections. The network is seen as a critical boost to the broader global ambitions of the U.K. film and cultural industries. Other connections are planned to other global cities, leading to a dedicated, global, interurban system in the near future. Thus, once again, it is clear that patterns of tight geographical clustering, relying on intense, ongoing, face-to-face innovation and contact, linked globally and locally through sophisticated telemediated networks, is a feature of many of the industries that concentrate in global cities (not just financial services and corporate services).

GLOBAL GRIDS OF GLASS: INTERCONNECTING URBAN FIBER NETWORKS

This brings us to our final scale of analysis: that of planetary interconnection and the geopolitics of infrastructure construction across oceans and continents. Of course, dedicated optic fiber grids *within* the business cores of global cities are of little use without interconnections that allow seamless corporate and financial networks to piece together to directly match the hub-and-spoke geographies of international urban systems themselves. To this end, WorldCom-MCI and many other internationalizing telecommunications companies are currently expending huge resources within massive consortia, laying the satellite and optic fiber infrastructures necessary to string the planet's urban regions into a single, highly interconnected communications landscape. Such efforts are especially focusing on the high-demand corridors linking the geostrategic, metropolitan zones of the three dominant global economic blocs: North America, Europe, and East and Southeastern Asia. Wiring North America and the North Atlantic is proceeding at a particularly rapid pace, with AT&T, Sprint, WorldCom-MCI, and the regional "Baby Bells" fighting it out with newcomers like Qwest to provide the pipes that will keep up with demand, especially from the Internet. Other lesser infrastructures are also being laid, designed to link southern metropolitan regions in Australia, South Africa and Brazil into the global constellation of interurban information infrastructures.

Currently, transoceanic and transterrestrial optic fiber and satellite capacities concentrate overwhelmingly on linking North America across the North Atlantic to Europe and across the North Pacific to Japan, reflecting the geopolitical hegemony of these three regions in the late twentieth century (Warf 1995). The first transoceanic fiber networks, developed since 1988 across the Atlantic, Pacific, and Indian oceans, with AT&T playing a leading role, tended to stop at the shorelines, leaving terrestrial networks to connect to each nation's markets (see Warf 1998). Increasingly, however, transoceanic fiber networks are being built explicitly to link metropolitan cores, in response to their centrality as generators of traffic and centers of investment.

WorldCom-MCI, in its efforts to connect together its many metropolitan fiber infrastructures, is one of the leaders of this process. As well as constructing a transatlantic fiber network known as Gemini between the centers of New York and London, WorldCom-MCI is building its own pan-European network, called Ulysses, to link its city grids in Paris, London, Amsterdam, Brussels, and major U.K. business cities beyond London. Elsewhere in the world, too, WorldCom-MCI is exploring the construction of transnational and transoceanic fiber networks to connect its globalizing archipelago of dedicated city networks. The strengthened importance of direct city-to-city connection is not lost on telecommunications commentators. As Finnie argues:

> It should be no surprise . . . that when London-based Cable and Wireless PLC and WorldCom laid the Gemini transatlantic cable—which came into service in March 1998—they ran the cable directly into London and New York, implicitly taking into account the fact that a high proportion of international traffic originates in cities. All previous cables terminated at the shoreline. (1998: 20)

At the strategic global scale, globalization, and the rapid growth of newly industrial countries, means that much effort is being spent filling in gaps in the global patterns of optic fiber interconnection, particularly between Europe and Asia. One project, for example, known as FLAG (or Fiber Optic Link Around the Globe) provides a new ultra-high-capacity (120,000 simultaneous phone calls) telecoms grid over 28,000 km from London to Japan, via many previously poorly connected metropolitan regions and nation-states. The route first goes by sea from England via the Bay of Biscay and Mediterranean to Alexandria and Cairo. Then it crosses Suez and Saudi Arabia overland to Dubai, crosses the Indian Ocean to Bombay and Penang and Kuala Lumpur, traverses the Malay peninsula to Bangkok, finally going by sea again to Hong Kong Shanghai and Japan. Nynex, the New York phone company, organized the construction of the project with support from a huge range of private investors in the 1990s. FLAG also connects with the 12,000-km Pacific Cable Network linking Japan, South Korea, Taiwan, Honk Kong, the Philippines, Thailand, Vietnam, and Indonesia (Warf 1998: 260).

Other similar projects are proliferating across the globe. A 30,000-km China-U.S. cable network, the first direct linkage between the two nations, was constructed by a fourteen-firm consortium between December 1997 and 1999. Other transoceanic cables are also being constructed in the Caribbean (the Eastern Caribbean Fiber System); between Florida and the Mediterranean urban system; by AT&T around the African continent (offering a high level of security while providing fiber drops to all the main cities on the African coast); and by Telefónica of Spain from the United States and Europe to the main metropolitan regions of Latin America (Fortaleza, Rio, São Paulo, Buenos Aires), again with the involvement of WorldCom.

CONCLUSIONS

This chapter has sought to extend our empirical and conceptual understanding of the ways in which global cities, and global city networks, are related to both intraurban and interurban information infrastructures. It has emerged that current advances in telecommunications are a set of phenomena that are overwhelmingly driven by large, internationally oriented, global metropolitan regions. The activities, functions, and urban dynamics that become concentrated in global city-regions rely intensely on the facilitating attributes of advanced telecommunications for supporting relational complexity, distantiated links, and snowballing interactions, both within and between cities. Such "telereliance" is particularly high in internationally oriented industries with products and services that are little more than telemediated flows of exchange, information, communication, and transaction, backed up also by intense face-to-face contact and supporting electronic coordination.

It should then be no surprise that in an increasingly demand-driven media and communications landscape, global cities should dominate investment in and use of advanced telecommunications infrastructures and services to the extent that they do. Global cities are the main focus of the highly uneven emerging geographies of network competition. They dominate all aspects of telecommunications innovation, from dedicated, proprietary, corporate networks to electronic commerce and transactions, to advanced phone services and consumption and dedicated digital media networks, to the production of Internet services.

As we have seen, such cities are now developing their own superimposed and customized fiber networks, linked together seamlessly across the planet into a global cities communications fabric, while often (at least in the initial stages of development) separating them from traditional notions of hinterland, urban and regional interdependence, and national infrastructural sovereignty. City fiber networks, for example, demonstrate that the emerging urban communications landscape is rapidly becoming dominated by tailored, customized infrastructures. Through these, dominant corporate, media, and financial players can maintain and extend their powers over space, time, and people. Such infrastructures are carefully localized physically to include only the users and territory necessary to drive profits and connect global corporate, financial, and media clusters.

But, in so doing, such networks seem likely to further urban sociospatial polarization by carefully bypassing nonlucrative spaces within the city. They are, in other words, physical, infrastructural embodiments of the splintering and fracturing of urban space described within Castells's recent "network society" thesis in which 'space organizes time' (1996: 366). The combination of intra- and interurban fiber networks thus materially supports the dynamic and highly uneven production of space-times of intense global connectivity, made up of linked assemblies of high-level corporate, financial, and media clusters, and their associated socioeconomic elites, within the spaces of global cities.

Finally, it seems inevitable that the customized combinations of intra- and interurban fiber networks analyzed in this chapter will also drive uneven development at the national level. They will exclude nondominant parts of national urban systems from the competitive advantages that stem from tailored, customized urban information infrastructures. Such infrastructures lay to rest any prevailing assumptions that there necessarily remains any meaningful connection between the sovereignty of nation-states as territorial "containers" (Taylor 1994), and patterns of infrastructural development, especially for telecommunications infrastructures. The traditional modern notion that nationhood is partly defined by the ability to roll out universally accessible infrastructural grids to bind the national space is completely destroyed by the new infrastructural logic (Elkins 1995).

NOTES

The author thanks the Institute for Advanced Study, United Nations University (Tokyo) for its support, and the Center for Advanced Study in the Behavioral Sciences (Palo Alto, CA), for hosting one of the meetings of the research network. Thanks also to *Urban Studies* for permission to reprint here some material from the article "Global Grids of Glass: On Global Cities, Telecommunications, and Planetary Urban Networks," Vol. 36, 929–949.

1. For a review of the global cities argument, see Knox and Taylor 1995.

2. For a detailed explanation of this relation, see Amin and Graham 1998.

REFERENCES

Amin, A., and S. Graham. 1997. "The Ordinary City." *Transactions of the Institute of British Geographers* 22: 411–429.

———. 1998. "Cities of Connection and Disconnection." In *Understanding Cities: Movement and Settlement*, ed. J. Allen, D. Massey, and M. Pryke. London: Open University Press.

Boden, D., and H. Molotch. 1994. "The Compulsion of Proximity." P. 257–286 in *Now/Here: Space, Time, and Modernity*, ed. R. Friedland and D. Boden. Berkeley: University of California Press.

Boyer, C. 1996. *Cybercities*. NJ: Princeton Architectural Press.

Brenner, N. 1998a "Between Fixity and Motion: Accumulation, Territorial Organization and the Historical Geography of Spatial Scales." *Environment and Planning D: Society and Space* 16: 459–481.

———. 1998b "Global Cities, Glocal States: Global City Formation and State Territorial Restructuring in Contemporary Europe." *Review of International Political Economy* 5 (2): 1–37.

Castells, M. 1996. *The Rise of the Network Society*. Oxford: Blackwell.

Colt Communications website, http://www.colttelecom.com/english/corporate.

Corbridge, S., R. Martin, and N. Thrift, (eds.) 1994. *Money, Power, and Space*. Oxford: Blackwell.

De Roo, P. 1994. "La metropolité." Pp. 9–17 in *Les Villes, Lieux Europe*, ed. A Sallex. Mouchy, Datar.

Elkins, D. 1995. *Beyond Sovereignty: Territory and Political Economy in the Twenty-First Century*. Toronto: University of Toronto Press.

Finnie, G. 1998. "Wired Cities." *Communications Week International*, May 18: 19–22.

Gottmann, J. 1990. *Since Megalopolis: The Urban Writings of Jean Gottmann*. Baltimore: John Hopkins University Press.

Graham, S. 1997. "Telecommunications and the Future of Cities: Debunking the Myths." *Cities* 14 (1): 21–29.

Graham S., and S. Marvin 1996. *Telecommunications and the City: Electronic Spaces, Urban Places*. London: Routledge.

———. 2001. *Splintering Urbanism: Networked Infrastructures, Technological Mobilities and the Urban Condition*. London: Routledge.

Ireland, J. 1995. *The Importance of Telecommunications to London as an International Financial Center*. London: Corporation of London and London Business School.

Kellerman, A. 1993. *Telecommunications and Geography*. London: Belhaven.

Knox, P., and P. Taylor (eds.). 1995. *World Cities in a World System*. Cambridge: Cambridge University Press.

Leyshon, A., and N. Thrift. 1997. *Money/Space*. London: Routledge.

Longcore, T., and P. Rees. 1996. "Information Technology and Downtown Restructuring: The Case of New York City's Financial District." *Urban Geography* 17 (4): 354–372.

Markusen, A., and V. Gwiasda. 1994. "Multipolarity and the Layering of Functions in World Cities: New York City's Struggle to Stay on Top." *International Journal of Urban and Regional Research* 18: 167–93.

Mitchell, W. 1995. *City of Bits: Space, Place, and the Infobahn*. Cambridge, MA: MIT Press.

Mitchelson, R., and J. Wheeler. 1994. "The Flow of Information in a Global Economy: The Role of the American Urban System in 1990." *Annals of the Association of American Geographers* 84 (1): 87–107.

STEPHEN GRAHAM

Moss, M. 1987. "Telecommunications, World Cities, and Urban Policy." *Urban Studies* 24: 534–546.

Moss, M., and A. Townsend. 1997. *Manhattan Leads the Net Nation.* Available at http://www.nyu.edu/urban/ny_affairs/telecom.html.

Office Of Technology Assessment. 1995. *The Technological Reshaping of Metropolitan America.* Washington D.C.: Congress of United States. U.S. Government Printing Office.

Richardson, R, 1994. "Back Officing Front Office Functions—Organizational and Locational Implications of New Telemediated Services." Pp. 309–335 in *Management of Information and Communication Technologies,* ed. R. Mansell. London: ASLIB.

Rothstein, M. 1998. "Offices Plugged In and Ready to Go." *New York Times,* February 4.

Sassen, S. 2000. *Cities in a World Economy.* 2nd ed. Thousand Oaks, CA: Pine Forge/Sage.

———. 2001. *The Global City: New York, London, Tokyo.* 2nd ed. Princeton, NJ: Princeton University Press.

Simmons, T. 1994. "Telecoms Contribute to Cities World Status." *Municipal Review* (January/February): 210.

Smith, D., and M. Timberlake. 1995. "Cities in Global Matrices: Toward Mapping the World Systems City-system." In *World Cities in a World System.* Cambridge: Cambridge University Press.

Storper, M. 1997. *The Regional World: Territorial Development in a Global Economy.* New York: Guilford.

Sussman, G. 1997. *Communication, Technology, and Politics in the Information Age.* London: Sage.

Sussman, G., and L. Lent. 1998. *Global Productions: Labour in the Making of the Information Society.* Creskill, NJ: Hampton.

Taylor, P. 1994. "The State as Container: Territoriality in the Modern World System." *Progress in Human Geography* 18: 151–162.

———. 1997. "Hierarchical Tendencies Amongst World Cities: A Global Research Proposal." *Cities* 14 (6): 323–332.

Thrift, N. 1995. "A Hyperactive World." Pp. 18–35 in *Geographies of Global Change,* ed. R Johnston, P. Taylor, and M. Watts. Oxford: Blackwell.

———. 1996. "New Urban Eras and Old Technological Fears: Reconfiguring the Goodwill of Electronic Things." *Urban Studies* 33 (8): 1463–1493.

Warf, B. 1989. "Telecommunications and the Globalization of Financial Services." *Professional Geographer* 41 (3): 257–271.

———. 1995. "Telecommunications and the Changing Geographies of Knowledge-transmission in the Late 20th Century." *Urban Studies* 32: 361–378.

———. 1998. "Reach Out and Touch Someone: AT&Ts Global Operations in the 1990s." *Professional Geographer* 50 (2): 255–267.

Chapter 3

FIRMS AND THEIR GLOBAL SERVICE NETWORKS

Peter J. Taylor, D. R. F. Walker, and J. V. Beaverstock

Although the lineage of world city studies can be traced back to well before 1980, it is only in the last two decades that a concerted research effort has emerged. This development has been intimately related to new ways in which social scientists have conceptualized the world economy, first as "the new international division of labor" and subsequently as "globalization." Specifically, the emergence of advanced computer-communications technologies has been emphasized for creating powerful control capabilities in a new global space of flows. The most explicit example of these developments has been in financial markets. This has led to important work on cities as "international financial centers" (Cohen 1981; Thrift 1987). A second strand has taken a broader view of what is happening in the world's major cities. John Friedmann (1986; Friedmann and Wolff 1982) has identified a process of "world city formation" of which financial markets are only one, albeit important, aspect. We follow Friedmann's lead in adopting a more holistic approach to the study of today's major cities.

A key question to be answered in contemporary urban studies is why under conditions of instantaneous communication, which would seem to favor decentralization or even homogenization, there is still a functional need for large world cities. Answering this question has produced two distinctive schools of thought, one specifically "urban," the other keeping the "network" to the fore. The first is best represented by the work of Michael Storper (1997), and the second by Saskia Sassen (2000; 2001). For Storper the new enabling technologies—he calls them new "metacapacities"—have not resulted in dispersion; rather, particular concentrations of economic activities have developed. He argues that the contemporary world economy is characterized by a reflexive economics in which entrepreneurs, if they are to be successful, have to be engaged in a knowledge-rich, continual learning process. Such processes can only be collective and very specific to the places in which they occur: they result in local assets that are difficult to duplicate elsewhere. He uses Hollywood as an obvious example of such processes. Cities enter his argument as privileged sites of such reflexivity, dense networks of learning practices, which steer the contemporary world economy. This urban theory provides a very good explanation of why cities are prospering as places, but has little or nothing to say about networks of cities. For this we have to turn to Sassen's identification of global cities. In an argument similar to that of economic reflexivity she identifies the production of advanced producer services as the distinguishing characteristic of contemporary world cities. Narrower in conception than Storper's definition reflexivity is to be found in industrial production as well as services—Sassen's global cities are, nevertheless, much more than places where large numbers of financial transactions take place. Advanced producer services provide worldwide assistance to global capital but they are much more than that; they are creative in making new products in finance, law, accountancy, and so on, which require the rich knowledge base in cities that Storper describes. The key difference is that for Sassen these cities are part of a network of strategic locations—hence the learning has to transcend particular places. The network of world cities, and not just single cities, is intrinsic to the process. We follow Sassen's lead here by focusing upon world city *network* formation.

The Globalization and World Cities (GaWC) Research Group and Network is a real and virtual organization[1] dedicated to the study of intercity relations under conditions of contemporary globalization. We introduce GaWC in this paper in two stages. In the first section we describe the need, origin, rationale, and operation of GaWC. In the second section we present a selection of results from GaWC research projects culminating in a preliminary quantitative presentation of a world city network.

OVERCOMING EMBEDDED STATISM

The most familiar of all world maps is that which depicts the sovereign states of the world. This mosaic of territories defines a world of boundaries, emphasizing national differences while totally ignoring spatial connections. This omission of the space of flows from a basic popular cartography is much more than a geographer's problem. It reflects a taken-for-granted world image that prioritizes nation-states as the basic units of humanity. As such its influence far transcends the map that hangs on all geography classroom walls. We describe this as embedded statism, a geopolitical feature of the modern world, which entails viewing social relations through the distorting lens of state centrism. GaWC is part of a research program dedicated to overcoming embedded statism.

PETER J. TAYLOR, D. R. F. WALKER, AND J. V. BEAVERSTOCK

This section is divided into three parts, which develop an argument from quite abstract considerations through to specific measurement questions. Embedded statism can be described as the dominant metageography of contemporary society: in the first part we set this in the context of alternative metageographies. State centrism is so pervasive, however, that even the information we have to understand our world is indelibly linked to a metageography of states. Part 2 introduces a research initiative that attempts to go beyond "stateistics." Loughborough University's *Globalization and World Cities (GaWC) Study Group* was set up to develop a web site that provides data alternatives to counter the inherent bias in the usual data sources. In the final part we focus on the data problems to be found in world city research as a prelude to the second empirical section of the paper.

Alternative Metageographies

Metageographies are the basic large-scale spatial frames by which people order their world (Lewis and Wigen 1997). These exist at different scales and may be vague in conception but are no less important for that. Hence broad dualities such as North-South and East-West have been crucial to recent geopolitical positions but have not fully replaced the traditional division into continents—the geographical entity "Africa," for example, currently exists as a social construct with largely negative images. However, underpinning all such representations is the map of sovereign states, the multicolored wall map that, despite recent political upheavals, seems to exude an almost "natural" aura (Jackson 1990). This is the metageography behind embedded statism. This is because territorial sovereignty is the basic building block of the politics of the modern era (Taylor 1999a). It is a metageography rooted in bounded spaces. Globalization is a direct challenge to the dominance of such territorial thinking.

Geographical boundaries are never completely sealed. There are links and connections between areas, which will vary by circumstance. These define a space of flows to exist alongside the space of territories. Such a space of transnational transactions has always been crucial to the development of the modern world system (Arrighi 1994), but it has not figured prominently in modern people's geographical imaginations. Globalization is changing this as it provides an alternative metageography. This is best represented by Manuel Castells (1996) with his work on the "network society." He describes a space of flows existing at several levels starting with the basic electronic infrastructure; the world city network represents one of the higher levels of spatial organization. It is the latter that has the potential to create an alternative metageography and that is our concern here.[2]

We juxtapose our alternative metageography of a network of world cities— a space of flows—against the dominant, conventional metageography of nation-states—a space of territories (Taylor 2002).

Beyond State-istics: GaWC

Despite its critical credentials, social science has not escaped embedded statism (Taylor 1996). In fact it can be argued that the reason for the success of the three core social sciences—economics, political science, and sociology—in the twentieth century is that they have each met the policy reform agendas of states. The social sciences are thus both the creations and the creatures of states. This has become particularly evident when their state-centric theories have been confronted by trans-state processes of globalization (Taylor 1996, 1997). Quite simply, theory begets data; data beget theory. This elementary synergy makes breaking out of state-centric thinking a difficult undertaking. We have chosen world cities with their associated flows as the route "beyond state-istics," hence the creation of GaWC.

When Riccardo Petrella (1995), the official futurist of the European Union, was asked not long ago to speculate about the near future he chose to contrast "two mental maps of the world system" in which major city regions (our world cities) would have either a positive or negative impact by the year 2025. The details of his predictions need not concern us here, but what is of interest is the fact that neither prediction is state-centric: both are city-centric. It is entirely appropriate that this metageography should be coming to the fore in this continent where states first subsumed cities in the construction of modern capitalism (Tilly 1990; Taylor 1995). The irony is that the European Union of states is likely to result in a new Europe of cities. Hence although the launch of the euro was seen as a pooling of state financial sovereignties, perhaps its most important long-term effect will be the setting up of the new European Bank in Frankfurt, not London. London versus Frankfurt as Europe's leader within global finance and banking is just the sort of issue, the type of world, that GaWC has been set up to study.[3]

GaWC is organized around three major related activities. First, we are a research group based around a collection of projects about world cities. So far, projects have been based at Loughborough, but we are actively working on new projects that will involve research partners from other universities. Ultimately this type of global research will require multiple-site studies so as to create the necessary broad knowledge base. Currently our projects are focused on London (to meet British ESRC [Economic and Social Research Council-UK] national efficiency concerns) with comparisons reaching New York and Singapore. Plans are in development for further work on Amsterdam, Caracas, Chicago, Frankfurt, Hong Kong, Istanbul, Miami, and Shanghai. Second, beyond our research partners, we aspire to be the world clearinghouse for world city research. In this we take advantage of the speed and flexibility inherent in GaWC's electronic existence. In the slow world of conventional article publication, with two years between initial writing and publication not uncommon, we offer an electronic outlet of immediate issuing as "GaWC Research Bulletins." In this electronic publication series, papers are made available in early form (as submitted to journals, for instance) and then as regularly revised through to the final version, which may still have to wait more than six months for hard-copy publication. The latter now represents only the final solid record of the paper, as it were.

The third major GaWC activity is also its initial raison d'être: the production and development of intercity data. This derives from our previous arguments; for instance we have much information on relations between France and the United Kingdom but relatively little on relations between Paris and London. Data come from three sources. First, the data from all our projects are automatically posted in our data bank. Second, we invite researchers with intercity data to post them on our site or else allow us to point to them from GaWC. Third, we are proactive in trying to stimulate the generation of intercity data. This has involved creating standardized data-collection procedures for use in graduate research projects so that generated data are comparable across case studies (Beaverstock, Lorimer et al. 2000). The end result is a data bank accessible to anyone across the world with Internet technology. It is therefore public data but not state-centric data. As with all other information of this type, we promote its use in research and teaching and ask only that appropriate acknowledgment be made.

The Paradox of World City Research

Before we look at some of the early results of GaWC projects, it is useful to say a little more about the research niche we have occupied. Our starting point is the identification of a curious paradox in the literature on world cities. This can be stated simply: whereas the essence of world cities is their relations to each other, researchers have generally not focused on this aspect of their being (see Taylor 1999b for direct evidence of this). Studies of world cities belong largely to two types: case studies and comparative studies. Whether looking at the one or the few, such studies leave relations between cities as either assumed or asserted. This is a specific case of the data problem described above: researchers can use urban data from national census returns to describe and analyze patterns within cities but there is little information on trans-state intercity relations. Ipso facto, intercity relations are neglected; hence the paradox we began with.

Smith and Timberlake (1995) have constructed a typology of intercity linkages based upon the form (human, material, information) and function (economic, political, cultural, and social) of flows. Twelve types are thus identified, which the authors admit constitute little more than a wish list for world city research. Some intercity flow data are available, for instance on airline traffic and telephone calls, but these tend to be very general in nature, so their relevance to world city formation is compromised. For instance, scheduled flights into Miami include the holiday and the seasonal retirement market as well as the economic growth associated with the city's role as an important center in the world city network.[4] For the most part, until GaWC is fully developed, researching intercity relations means collecting and creating new and original sets of data.

The research we have been funded for thus far has been within an area of study known as the new economic geography of services. This attempts to understand the growth of services in the contemporary economy through studies of service firms. We combine this with Sassen's insight that it is advanced producer services that particularly distinguish world cities to turn the focus from firm to city: firms are our subjects, cities are our objects of study. In practice this means collecting information on the office network of producer service firms. Although this does not directly measure flows between cities, a firm's global strategy—in whatever cities it chooses to set up branch offices—must imply both control and information connections. Aggregating large numbers of such strategies across several services will, therefore, indicate intercity relations. This is what we report upon in the next section.

In summary, world city research is a classic example of state-centric data distorting research output: the dearth of intercity data causes a neglect of intercity analysis.

GLOBAL STRATEGIES, WORLD CITIES

This section is a review of early findings of some GaWC research. It is intended to show the empirical potential of GaWC; given the neglect of inter-city studies, some relatively elementary measurement exercises can provide new and original insights into world city network formation. Hence the emphasis below is upon empirical results to the detriment of both details of production of the data (see Taylor and Walker 2001) and full reflection on the theoretical implications of the research (see Taylor 2001; 2002).

The data we employ consist of the distribution of offices of producer service firms across cities. Hence we are looking at the location strategies of firms under conditions of globalization. By tracking the global geography of firms' foreign affiliates we obtain information about corresponding intercity networks. We report on six separate analyses, with a core data set of sixty-nine firms (five accountancy, fourteen advertising, eleven banking/finance, and thirty-nine law) across 263 cities for 1997–98. The choice of firms is that they are global producer service firms, otherwise the choice is in terms of data availability (i.e., we have been able to find information on their complete global network of offices). The numbers in each sector reflect degrees of corporate concentration from the

PETER J. TAYLOR, D. R. F. WALKER, AND J. V. BEAVERSTOCK

"Big Six" in accountancy to law as the least globalized service. Data collected varied by firms, from simple presence/absence in a city to information on the relative importance of offices, notably in terms of how many practitioners in a firm are based there. Not all analyses use the same information from the data, which will become clear as we proceed.

The GaWC Inventory of World Cities

There is no agreement as to the roster of world cities. There is obvious agreement for the leading cities (London, New York, etc.) but no clear cutoff point as to when a city should not be considered a world city. The most commonly referenced rosters are those of Friedmann (1986; 1995), but these are not based upon any substantial or systematic analysis of the evidence. Is Lisbon a world city? Is Kuala Lumpur or Mumbai? It depends who you read (Beaverstock, Smith, and Taylor 1999, table 2). Hence the first task of GaWC has been to create a preliminary roster of world cities based on our initial data collection. This is carried out in two stages. First, we estimate the *global capacity* of cities separately for each of the four services we have data on. We use information on the presence, size, and roles of offices in cities across the world. Second, we aggregate these sector results to define levels of "world city-ness." We designate fifty-five cities to be world cities and find another sixty-seven cities as showing evidence of world city formation (see Beaverstock, Smith, and Taylor 1999).

The first stage consisted of finding global service centers at various levels for the four sectors. In order to avoid any idiosyncratic feature of a single firm (e.g., one having additional offices in their home country), for each sector only cities in which at least two firms are represented were considered to be global service centers. This resulted in 78 cities for accountancy, 67 for advertising, 68 for banking/finance, and 72 for law. With much overlap between sectors this produced 122 cities as candidates for world city status. For each service sector three levels of presence were identified—prime, major, and minor—on the basis of size and importance of offices. Thus each of the 122 cities can be scored 0 (not qualified) to 3 (prime center) for each sector. Sums of these scores produce a figure that indicates a city's world city-ness up to a maximum of 12. For instance, London is a prime center for all four sectors and thus scores 12; Wellington, New Zealand scores just 1, featuring only as a minor center in the advertising data. Table 1 shows all 122 cities from London to Wellington allocated to the 12 levels of world city-ness.

The division of these cities into different classes of world city formation has been carried out using simple logical criteria. Any city scoring 10 or above must feature as a service center in all four sectors. Furthermore, if it is a minor center in one sector, this would have to be compensated for by it being a prime center in the other three sectors. In addition it must be prime in at least two

PETER J. TAYLOR, D. R. F. WALKER, AND J. V. BEAVERSTOCK

TABLE 1

THE GAWC INVENTORY OF WORLD CITIES*

A. ALPHA WORLD CITIES

12: London, Paris, New York, Tokyo
10: Chicago, Frankfurt, Hong Kong, Los Angeles, Milan, Singapore

B. BETA WORLD CITIES

9: San Francisco, Sydney, Toronto, Zurich
8: Brussels, Madrid, Mexico City, São Paulo
7: Moscow, Seoul

C. GAMMA WORLD CITIES

6: Amsterdam, Boston, Caracas, Dallas, Dusseldorf, Geneva, Houston, Jakarta, Johannesburg, Melbourne, Osaka, Prague, Santiago, Taipei, Washington
5: Bangkok, Beijing, Rome, Stockholm, Warsaw
4: Atlanta, Barcelona, Berlin, Buenos Aires, Budapest, Copenhagen, Hamburg, Istanbul, Kuala Lumpur, Manila, Miami, Minneapolis, Montreal, Munich, Shanghai

D. EVIDENCE OF WORLD CITY FORMATION

Di Relatively strong evidence
3: Auckland, Dublin, Helsinki, Luxembourg, Lyon, Mumbai, New Delhi, Philadelphia, Rio de Janeiro, Tel Aviv, Vienna

Dii Some evidence
2: Abu Dhabi, Almaty, Athens, Birmingham, Bogota, Bratislava, Brisbane, Bucharest, Cairo, Cleveland, Cologne, Detroit, Dubai, Ho Chi Minh City, Kiev, Lima, Lisbon, Manchester, Montevideo, Oslo, Rotterdam, Riyadh, Seattle, Stuttgart, The Hague, Vancouver

Diii Minimal evidence
1: Adelaide, Antwerp, Arhus, Baltimore, Bangalore, Bologna, Brazilia, Calgary, Cape Town, Colombo, Columbus, Dresden, Edinburgh, Genoa, Glasgow, Gothenburg, Guangzhou, Hanoi, Kansas City, Leeds, Lille, Marseille, Richmond, St. Petersburg, Tashkent, Teheran, Tijuana, Turin, Utrecht, Wellington

* Cities are ordered in terms of world city-ness with values ranging from 1 to 12.

TABLE 1 (CONTINUED)

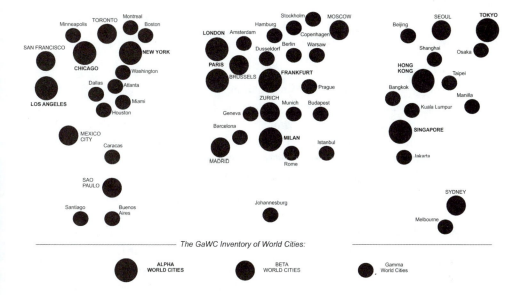

The GaWC Inventory of World Cities:

ALPHA WORLD CITIES

BETA WORLD CITIES

Gamma World Cities

sectors, and the other two would have to be major designations. Ten cities qualify in this top class and are designated *alpha world cities*. As we might expect, there are no surprises at this end of the distribution with four cities from western Europe, three from the United States, and three from Pacific Asia.

For the second class of world cities, we identify any city scoring 7 to 9. Such a city must be a global service center for at least three of the four service sectors and must be a prime or major center in at least two sectors. Ten cities qualify as *beta world cities*. The same three world regions are represented as for prime world cities but with "outer" cities appearing such as Sydney, Toronto, Mexico City, and Moscow. In addition, a Third World region appears: São Paulo of South America.

As mentioned previously, it is at the bottom end of the scale where uncertainty reigns for designating world cities. We have decided to define cities scoring 4 to 6 as *gamma world cities*. With these scores, all cities must be a global service center for at least two service sectors. This definition catches thirty-five further cities again distributed largely across the three main regions but with another three representatives of South America. Africa has its first city in our list, Johannesburg, but there are still no world cities found in South Asia or the Middle East (if we count Istanbul as European). The remaining sixty-eight cities are designated as having evidence of world city formation processes but the evidence is not strong enough to really call them world cities. The interesting cities are those twelve scoring 3, and here we find one Middle East city, Tel

Aviv, and two South Asian cities, Mumbai and New Delhi, which perhaps, signify the early stages of filling in the voids on the global world city map.

This is the first time a roster of world cities has been identified and classified on the basis of a systematic analysis of empirical data.

The Question of Regions and Hierarchies

As originally suggested by Friedmann (1986), many world cities seem to operate by articulating their national economy into the world economy. But there are others which have a wider regional role. Perhaps the most obvious example of this is Singapore, which is a city-state and the most important world city in Southeast Asia. Hence between the global headquarters of producer service firms and the national economy articulators there are regional world cities. Data for eleven of our firms (two in accountancy, two in advertising, five in banking/finance, and two in law) provide some preliminary evidence for this aspect of world city network formation (for further discussion, see Taylor 2000). As before, we avoid idiosyncratic results by including only cities that feature in at least two firms' regional organization. Despite being based upon relatively little data, the results are quite stark: we find only nine cities with regional responsibilities in our data. Of these are five that dominate: London has a total of nine regional responsibilities; Hong Kong, Miami, and Singapore have six each; and New York has five. Discussion will be based around them.

London. At the regional level London operates as the main center for both Europe (with only Brussels as minor rival), sometimes including the Middle East, and as extramural center for Africa, with Paris (for francophone Africa) and Johannesburg as minor rivals.

New York/Miami. There seems to be a simple division of labor here: where there is a single center for the Americas it is New York, where there is a division, New York is the North America center and Miami appears as the center for Latin America. Hence Miami operates as an extramural center with respect to Latin America in the way London does for Africa.

Hong Kong/Singapore. This is the example with explicit rivalry. Although these two cities are centers for their own regions, Northeast and Southeast Asia respectively, when no such division is made (for instance as in Asia or Asia-Pacific office designations) Hong Kong edges out Singapore only by 3 to 2 for the larger regional responsibility. It should be noted that where Tokyo appears as a regional headquarters, its region is limited to Japan; this city seems not to have developed responsibilities beyond its own state.

Our preliminary results are clear here: the world city network is regional-

PETER J. TAYLOR, D. R. F. WALKER, AND J. V. BEAVERSTOCK

FIGURE 1
GAWC PAN-REGIONS IN GLOBAL SERVICE PROVISION

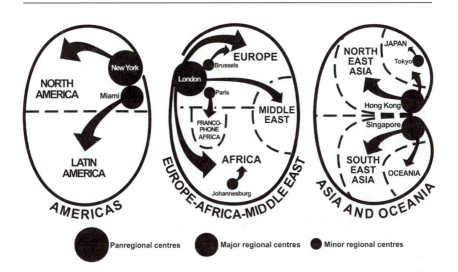

ized into three pan-regions with few smaller world cities emerging as regional centers (see fig. 1). The great exception is Miami. This is the first time the world hierarchy of world cities has been as defined and described by world regional organization (rather than the simple ranking of cities to be found in the literature).

Detecting Concentration Processes: The "Enhanced Tail" Feature

Our full data set records 2,925 presences of firms across the 263 cities. Such large sets of data lend themselves to elementary distribution analyses. This involves creating a frequency distribution showing the numbers of cities housing different totals of firms. Such distributions can be modeled as probability functions to provide insights into the empirical pattern. The frequency distribution for this data set is shown in fig. 2. One very noticeable feature is the long right-hand tail indicating many cities housing relatively large numbers of firms. This can be compared to a random allocation of firms to cities that would generate a Poisson probability distribution. In such a theoretical distribution no cities would be expected to have more than fifteen firms, which means our empirical distribution has a very enhanced tail: sixty-five cities have more than fifteen firms. This indicates that there are exceptional nonrandom concentration processes operating to produce such distribution. This is not surprising, of course, in an urban analysis where some form of hierarchy is the norm, but the length and size of the tail in this case will reflect the particular concentration

FIGURE 2

OVERALL FREQUENCY DISTRIBUTION OF FIRMS IN CITIES

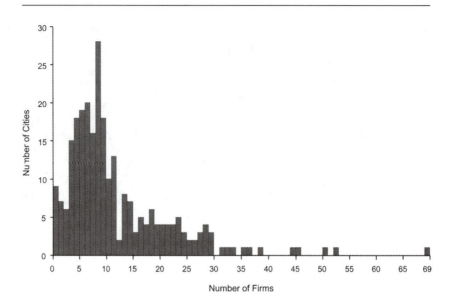

processes that Sassen (2000) argues are operating under contemporary conditions of globalization.

All the global firms we are dealing with are London-located global firms (LLGFs). Looking at the data from the perspective of London does produce interesting results. For instance, if the particular numbers of firms are converted into percentages of the maximum (69), then we can interpret the results as the chances of a firm in a given city having a direct (intrafirm) office link to London. For instance, Hong Kong has the highest total of LLGFs (fifty-two) in our data, which translates into a 75 percent probability that if a client enters an advanced producer service office in Hong Kong, there will be a direct organizational link to London. The top ten cities in terms of these probabilities are shown in table 2. No surprises here: all the alpha world cities appear except Chicago, and they are joined by Brussels and Moscow, two cities with obvious but different appeals to London-based firms (EU headquarters, and center for post-Soviet transition respectively). This points to further London-centric analysis, but before we present this, it is instructive to look at the service-specific distributions of offices (see Taylor 2000).

The frequency distributions of 262 cities (not including London) in terms of how many LLGFs they house for each sector show that accountancy differs from the other three services in having its mode at its maximum frequency: all five accountancy firms are to be found in 136 of our cities. This distribution

TABLE 2

TOP TEN CITIES SHARING FIRMS WITH LONDON: PERCENTAGE PROBABILITIES

RANK	%	CITY
1	75	Hong Kong
2	72	New York
3	65	Paris
3	65	Singapore
5	64	Tokyo
6	55	Brussels
7	52	Frankfurt
8	51	Moscow
9	48	Los Angeles
10	46	Milan

reflects the fact that accountancy is the most globalized of producer services. Although this is not a surprising result, the stark contrast with the other services is instructive. The three other services have their mode at zero presence although the dominance of this mode decreases in the order law-banking/finance-advertising, which suggests an ordering in their respective levels of globalization with law the least developed. This is not a surprise, but this has never before been illustrated so directly.

Most of our data contain much more information than merely presence as analyzed above. In order to retain as much information as possible we have created an ordinal-level set of measures by combining all the different types of information we have (see Beaverstock, Smith, and Taylor 2001). Since the data combined to ordinal level maintain more information, analysis of the data will be more instructive. We begin the analysis, as before, with frequency distributions for all 262 cities for each service sector. Again the accountancy distribution is distinctive but, compared to simple presences, it is much more suggestive with its central mode and two tails. The other three distributions continue with their zero modes and enhanced tails, but the cities are more widely dispersed compared to simple presences.

The tails of all four distributions have been abstracted from the distributions in this analysis. For advertising, banking/finance, and law, turning points for the enhanced tail are used; for accountancy the abrupt change in declining levels is used as break point. All scores are converted to percentage of the maximum possible to facilitate comparison. The lists of cities with high levels of

TABLE 3

ACCOUNTANCY

CITIES WITH MAJOR LEVELS OF LINKAGE TO LONDON

(Numbers are percentages of maximum possible (= 15) from sum of ordinal/ized scores)

Percent	City
93	Dusseldorf, New York, Paris, Tokyo, Toronto
87	Chicago, Milan, Sydney, Washington, DC
80	Atlanta, Brussels, Frankfurt, San Francisco
73	Amsterdam, Dallas, Hamburg, Hong Kong,
67	Berlin, Boston, Copenhagen, Madrid, Melbourne, Mexico City, Rotterdam, Seoul, Stockholm, Zurich
60	Birmingham, Jakarta, Lyon, Manchester, Philadelphia, Rome, São Paulo, Santiago, Stuttgart, Vancouver

TABLE 4

ADVERTISING

CITIES WITH MAJOR LEVELS OF LINKAGE TO LONDON

(NUMBERS ARE PERCENTAGES OF MAXIMUM POSSIBLE (= 21) FROM SUM OF ORDINAL/IZED SCORES)

Percent	City
90	New York
76	Brussels, Madrid, Sydney, Toronto
71	Milan, Paris
67	Los Angeles, Singapore, Stockholm
62	Amsterdam, Auckland, Copenhagen, Istanbul, Lisbon
57	Athens, Dusseldorf, Melbourne, Prague, San Francisco, Vienna, Zurich
52	Barcelona, Helsinki, Hong Kong
48	Bangkok, Frankfurt, Mexico City, Montreal
4	Beijing, Caracas, Jakarta, Manila, San Francisco, Santiago, Seoul, Taipei, Tokyo, Warsaw
38	Budapest, Buenos Aires, Hamburg, Johannesburg, Kuala Lumpur, Miami, Moscow, Mumbai, Oslo

TABLE 5

BANKING/FINANCE

CITIES WITH MAJOR LEVELS OF LINKAGE TO LONDON

(Numbers are percentages of maximum possible (= 38) from sum of ordinal/ized scores)

Percent	City
95	New York
79	Singapore
76	Hong Kong, Tokyo
66	Frankfurt
61	Paris, Zurich
55	Madrid
50	Milan, Taipei
47	Mexico City, Seoul
45	São Paulo
42	Jakarta, Los Angeles
39	Buenos Aires, Dublin, Kuala Lumpur, Moscow, San Francisco, Toronto
37	Bangkok, Dubai, Geneva
34	Luxembourg, Manama, Manila, Mumbai
32	Abu Dubai, Athens, Chicago, Johannesburg, Labuan, Melbourne, Prague, Santiago, Shanghai
29	Barcelona, Rio de Janeiro
26	Amsterdam, Beijing, Brussels, Cairo, Caracas, Houston, Miami, Warsaw

connectivity to London are shown in table 3 for accountancy, table 4 for advertising, 5 for banking/finance, and 6 for law. This analysis shows New York as London's main partner in all sectors, as might be expected, but there are noteworthy contrasts in degree of dominance and in which cities are at the top of the rankings. For instance, accountancy produces the only table in which New York shares top spot with other cities. In banking/finance New York is dominant and is followed by three Pacific Asian cities (Singapore, Hong Kong, and Tokyo). In advertising and law, New York's dominance is similarly clear; in law, the important political capitals of Washington, D.C., and Brussels feature prominently.

This is the first time a comprehensive analysis of cities has detected concentration processes and the cities in which they are manifest.

The GaWC Index of London's External Relations

Focusing on just the other fifty-four world cities, the levels of linkage to London are brought together in figure 3 where average scores across the four

TABLE 6
LAW
CITIES WITH MAJOR LEVELS OF LINKAGE TO LONDON
(Numbers are percentages of maximum possible (= 65) from sum of ordinal/ized scores)

Percent	City
68	New York
60	Washington, DC
54	Brussels, Hong Kong
48	Paris
34	Los Angeles
32	Tokyo
31	Singapore
28	Moscow
23	Frankfurt
20	Chicago
18	San Francisco, Warsaw
17	Budapest
15	Beijing
14	Dallas, Houston, Prague

FIGURE 3
THE GAWC INDEX OF LONDON'S RELATIONS

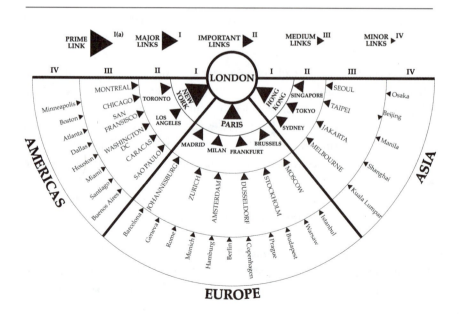

TABLE 7

AVERAGE PERCENTAGE LINKAGE TO LONDON BY REGIONS

Region	No. of Cities	Average Linkage
Western Europe	16	41
Pacific Asia	12	40
USA	11	39
Eastern Europe	5	33
Latin America	5	37
Old Commonwealth	5	45

producer services are computed to define the GaWC Index of London's External Relations (Beaverstock, Smith, and Taylor 2000). The fifty-four world cities (other than London) are arrayed in five groups. The overall dominance of the London-New York link, with score out on its own at 87, is designated as London's 'prime link'. The next two highest links (Paris-London at 68 and Hong Kong-London at 64) each connect London to the other two major world regions and are designated 'major links'. Other connections scoring over 50 then become 'important links' with two lower levels of links also identified. The clear message of this diagram is the worldwide scope of London's linkages and this is neatly confirmed by a regional analysis.

The fifty-four world cities fall neatly into five world regions plus an additional British Commonwealth noncontiguous class of cities: sixteen are in Western Europe, twelve in Pacific Asia, eleven in the United States, five each in Eastern Europe, Latin America, and the old Commonwealth (Australia, Canada, South Africa). Average levels of connection for these groups of cities are shown in table 7. Perhaps the lack of major variation in average scores is the main feature of this table, which confirms London's worldwide reach. The highest score for the old Commonwealth indicates longer-term linkages than contemporary globalization, but the three main "globalization arenas" (Western Europe, Pacific Asia, and the United States) have very similar scores. This shows that London is much more than just Europe's representative, articulating Europe with the world economy, in a twenty-four-hour globalizing financial market. The geographical reach of London confirms its location in the contemporary space of flows as truly, using Sassen's (2001) terminology, a global city (Beaverstock, Smith, and Taylor 2001). This is not only the first time London as a major world city has been analyzed comprehensively in terms of its linkages with other world cities; it is the first time this type of analysis has been done for any world city.

Local Mixes of Firms across World Cities

In the final two sections we report on ongoing work that uses a slightly different data set, one that focuses upon the larger firms. We have identified forty-six firms which have offices in fifteen or more different cities. The main difference from the previous list of firms is the removal of many small London-based law firms and the addition of three U.S. law firms without London offices. In addition this data set is limited to the fifty-five world cities previously identified. The result is a 55 x 46 data matrix with each cell scoring a firm's position in a city from 0 (no presence) to 3 (major presence).

The simplest analysis of such data is to correlate the cities in terms of how similar they are as per the mix of firms they house. The higher the correlation between two cities, the more firms they share and with similar levels of presence. To illustrate this form of analysis, table 8 shows correlations between the alpha world cities; the higher correlations are displayed in figure 4. The two highest correlations are between London and New York and between Hong Kong and Singapore, which is what we might expect although there is no previous analysis of this. However, when we look at the overall pattern of the higher correlations, some interesting features appear (fig. 4). Certainly the former pairing seems more isolated than the latter. This implies the global cities of London and New York have between them quite distinctive mixes of firms.

A full analysis of the data matrix involving all fifty-five cities has been carried out using a principal components analysis. This uses the correlations to define the main dimensions in the data, in this case grouping cities in terms of their mixes of firms. This work is in progress (Taylor and Walker 2001) but preliminary results show a complex pattern of interregional, regional, and city dimensions. For instance, London and New York appear as a separate 'global city component' replicating figure 4, and two other cities define their own individual components: Moscow, a gateway to post-Soviet economies, and Miami, a gateway to Latin America (see fig. 1). Other components highlight major regions such as Latin America, Pacific Asia, western Europe, eastern Europe, and the United States. In fact the locational clusters in these results show that even among large firms, location strategies under conditions of globalization seem to be more regional than worldwide in nature.

This analysis is the first to group world cities into types in terms of the firms they house. Classification is a necessary beginning to understand world cities beyond hierarchies.

A Preliminary Description of a Network of World Cities

Assuming that intrafirm knowledge and information flow in servicing clients is greater than interfirm flows, the previous analysis can be used to infer a network pattern. This is no doubt the reason for the regional findings and also some ele-

PETER J. TAYLOR, D. R. F. WALKER, AND J. V. BEAVERSTOCK

FIGURE 4

CORRELATIONS AMONG ALPHA WORLD CITIES

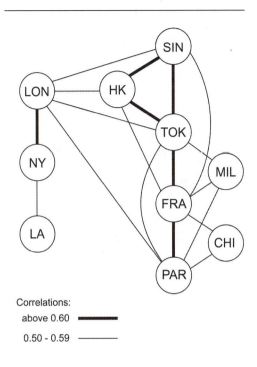

Correlations:
above 0.60 ━━━━
0.50 - 0.59 ────

TABLE 8

CORRELATIONS BETWEEN ALPHA WORLD CITIES IN TERMS OF MIXES OF FIRMS HOUSED

	CH	FF	HK	LN	LA	ML	NY	PA	SG	TK
Chicago										
Frankfurt	0.52									
Hong Kong	0.46	0.57								
London		0.43	0.37	0.5						
Los Angeles	0.42	0.35	0.24	0.34						
Milan		0.35	0.58	0.37	0.42	0.06				
New York	0.43	0.21	0.46	0.7	0.52	0.26				
Paris		0.55	0.64	0.48	0.58	0.2	0.53	0.25		
Singapore	0.24	0.5	0.79	0.58	0.2	0.42	0.33	0.46		
Tokyo		0.51	0.63	0.67	0.57	0.1	0.59	0.47	0.57	0.64

note: negative coefficients are underlined

TABLE 9

MATRIX OF OFFICE PERCENTAGE PROBABILITIES FOR OFFICE CONNECTIONS BETWEEN ALPHA WORLD CITIES

LINKAGE FROM:					LINKAGE TO:					
	CH	FR	HK	LN	LA	ML	NY	PA	SG	TK
Chicago	—	89	89	100	91	79	100	89	83	100
Frankfurt	67	—	93	100	72	87	100	95	94	95
Hong Kong	60	82	—	100	80	80	100	85	92	90
London	59	77	87	—	78	78	98	83	83	86
Los Angeles	67	73	89	100	—	70	97	84	81	89
Milan	59	88	93	100	67	—	100	88	91	93
New York	59	77	87	98	77	77	—	79	83	85
Paris	64	85	90	100	80	81	97	—	90	90
Singapore	60	87	98	100	78	83	100	92	—	95
Tokyo	64	84	93	100	83	81	100	87	88	—

FIGURE 5

VECTORS SHOWING RELATIONS AMONG ALPHA WORLD CITIES

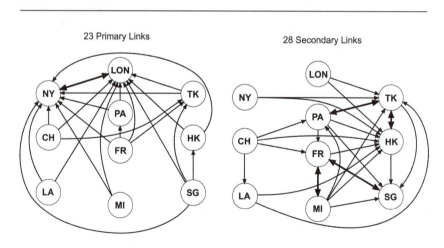

23 Primary Links   28 Secondary Links

PETER J. TAYLOR, D. R. F. WALKER, AND J. V. BEAVERSTOCK

ments of hierarchy that are found in the structures (Taylor and Walker 2001). But there is a way of going beyond such inferences to a more direct measure of intercity relations. This relates to some of our previous London analysis, which we extend to all cities.

From each city, we can compute the total level of intra-firm service to each other city. Currently this has been carried out for just alpha cities and using only presences (Beaverstock, Lorimer et al. 2000). Table 9 is an asymmetric matrix showing probabilities of connections between cities. Each cell contains the percentage probability that a firm in city X will have an office in city Y. Thus, table 9 shows that if you do business with a Chicago-based firm, then there is a 89 percent probability that that firm will also have an office in Frankfurt. On the other hand, a Frankfurt-based firm has only a 67 percent probability of having an office in Chicago. These probabilities of connection define vectors that are shown for two different levels: prime vectors highlighting the dominance of London and New York, and secondary vectors in which the Pacific Asian cities feature prominently (fig. 5). Notice the marginal positions of Los Angeles and especially Chicago. We describe this as the New York shadow effect: it seems that many firms that do business in the United States focus upon having just one single office in New York (Beaverstock, Lorimer et al 2000). This is unlike other globalization arenas which are more politically fragmented, necessitating firms to locate in cities in different countries. This may have profound effects on U.S. cities in world city competition.[5]

This is a preliminary glimpse at a world city network defined by office relations between cities. Until work such as this is completed we do not even have the basis for understanding world city network formation.

CONCLUSION: FIRST STEPS ONLY

The fact that every summary in the empirical second section of the paper has been able to claim "firsts" in what are very basic and ultimately elementary empirical analyses provides very strong support for the arguments in the first section of the paper on the dearth of trans-state data and analysis. All that is being reported is the barest skeleton of a global structure, but one not previously revealed despite two decades of world city research. It is an indicator of the difficulty of doing global research in the social sciences that these first steps have been so delayed.

NOTES

The authors thank the Institute for Advanced Study, United Nations University (Tokyo) for its support.

1. The GaWC web address is: http://www.lboro.ac.uk/departments/gy/research/gawc.html

2. During one of the early Apollo flights one of the astronauts experienced a fundamental revelation: looking back to Earth he noticed there were no political boundaries. In fact it is often said that the Great Wall of China is the only human feature on the Earth's surface that can be seen from

space. This is not strictly correct; once day turns to night the archipelago of modern human settlements is visible from the artificial light created. And this shows a pattern dominated by the great cities of the world. The apocryphal visitor from another planet would certainly get the impression of a city-dominated civilization on Earth. For the people living on Earth, however, it is the political boundaries that loom large in their geographical imaginations.

3. For a local example of where the space of cities is confronting the space of territories, as Barcelona versus Catalonia, see Morata 1997.

4. In their chapter in this volume, Smith and Timberlake develop this methodology further.

5. The end result of this research will be structural analyses of directed graphs for all fifty-five cities; this work is in progress.

REFERENCES

Arrighi, G. 1994. *The Long Twentieth Century.* London: Verso.

Beaverstock, J. V., H. Lorimer, R. G. Smith, P. J. Taylor and D. R. F. Walker. 2000. "Globalization and World Cities: Some Measurement Methodologies." *Applied Geography* 19: 43–3.

Beaverstock, J. V., R. G. Smith, and P. J. Taylor. 1999. "A Roster of World Cities." *Cities* 16: 445–458.

———. 2000. "World City Network: A New Metageography." *Annals, Association of American Geographers* 90: 123–134.

———. 2001. "The Global Capacity of a World City: A Relational Study of London." In *Globalization: Theory and Practice,* ed. E Kofman and G. Youngs. 2nd ed. London: Routledge.

Castells, M. 1996. *The Rise of the Network Society.* Oxford: Blackwell.

Cohen, R. J. 1981. "The New International Division of Labor, Multinational Corporations and Urban Hierarchy." In *Urbanisation and Urban Planning in Capitalist Society,* ed. M. Dear and A. J. Scott. London: Methuen.

Friedmann, J. 1986. "The World City Hypothesis." *Development and Change* 17: 69–83.

———. 1995. "Where We Stand: A Decade of World City Research." Pp. 21–47 in *World Cities in a World System.* ed. P. L. Knox and P. J. Taylor Cambridge: Cambridge University Press.

Friedmann, J., and G. Wolff. 1982. "World City Formation: An Agenda for Research and Action." *International Journal of Urban and Regional Research* 3: 309–344.

Jackson, R. H. 1990. *Quasi-States.* Cambridge: Cambridge University Press.

Lewis, M. W., and K. E. Wigen. 1997. *The Myth of Continents.* Berkeley: University of California Press.

Morata, F. 1997. "The Euro-Region and the C-6 Network: The New Politics of Sub-National Co-Operation in the Western Mediterranean Area." In *The Political Economy of Regionalism,* ed. M Keating and J. Loughlin. London: Frank Cass.

Petrella, R. 1995. "A Global Agora vs. Gated City-Regions." *New Perspectives Quarterly* Winter, 21 (2).

Sassen, S. 2000. *Cities in a World Economy.* 2nd ed. Thousand Oaks, CA: Pine Forge Press.

———. 2001. *The Global City: New York, London, Tokyo.* 2nd ed. Princeton, NJ: Princeton University Press.

Smith, D. A., and M. Timberlake. 1995. "Cities in Global Matrices: Toward Mapping the World-System's City System." In *World Cities in a World System,* ed. P. L. Knox, and P. J. Taylor. Cambridge: Cambridge University Press.

Storper, M. 1997. *The Regional World.* New York: Guilford.

Taylor, P. J. 1995. "States and World Cities: The Rise and Demise of their Mutuality." In *World Cities in a World-Economy,* ed. P. L. Knox, and P. J. Taylor. Cambridge: Cambridge University Press.

———. 1996. "Embedded Statism and the Social Sciences: Opening Up to New Spaces." *Environment and Planning A* 28: 1917–1928.

———. 1997. "Hierarchical Tendencies Amongst World Cities: A Global Research Proposal." *Cities,* 14: 323–332.

———. 1999a. *Modernities: a Geohistorical Interpretation.* Cambridge, UK: Polity, and Minneapolis: University of Minnesota Press.

———. 1999b. "'The So-Called World Cities: An Evidential Structure of a Literature." *Environment and Planning A* 31: 1901–1904.

———. 2000. "World Cities and Territorial States Under Conditions of Contemporary Globalization." *Political Geography* 18: 5–32.

———. 2001. "Specification of the World City Network." *Geographical Analysis* 33.

———. 2002. "Metageographical Moments: A Geohistorical Interpretation of Embedded Statism and Globalization." In *Odysses*, ed. B. Denemark and M. A. Tetreault. London: Routledge.

Taylor, P. J., and D. R. F. Walker. 2001. "World Cities: a First Multivariate Analysis of their Service Complexes." *Urban Studies* 38: 23–47.

Thrift, N. 1987. "The Fixers? The Urban Geography of International Commercial Capital." pp. 203–233 in *Global Restructuring and Territorial Development*, ed. J. Henderson and M. Castells. Beverly Hills, CA: Sage.

Tilly, C. 1990. *Coercion, Capital, and European States, AD 990–1990,* Oxford: Blackwell.

Chapter 4

HIERARCHIES OF DOMINANCE AMONG WORLD CITIES: A NETWORK APPROACH

David Smith and Michael Timberlake

The world's centers of gravity are always in process of change. Old centers lose their relative importance as new factors enter to disturb the equilibrium. Some of these factors are temporary and accidental; others are associated with permanent trends. . . . New centers of dominance are arising.

Roderick McKenzie, 1927

The world's great cities are crucial nodes in the global political economy. They are the geographic basing points in terms of not only production and consumption, but also of political-economic control and social reproduction. Though they are often conceptually recognized as the spatial loci of global processes, how relations among cities are structured is not commonly understood. Usually studies of the "world system" theorize about and describe interrelations among broad regions of the world, usually by nations. Here we depart from this usual strategy by improving upon our earlier efforts (e.g., Smith and Timberlake, 1995a and b) to identify one important aspect of global structure in the relations among a score of "world cities," many of which Friedmann so identified (1986, 1995). Thus, cities are seen as fundamental territorial nodes in the global political economy. Systematic exchanges among them are an important dimension of the world system's structure. Moreover the way in which any particular city is embedded, through these exchanges, in the global structure influences its own peculiar character. We are concerned, then, with the network relations of world cities, as defined by the exchanges that link them. Our work is indebted to that of much earlier scholars of urbanization who were concerned with "systems of cities" and the relative dominance of cities within a system, including, for example, Gras (1922), McKenzie (1968), and Duncan et al.

(1960). We are also heirs to the more recent globally contextualized case-oriented research on some of the world's most populous and important cities (for example, King 1990; Ross and Trachte 1990; Sassen 2001; Abu-Lughod 1999; Meyer 1991b). This work has largely substantiated John Friedmann's notion that there is a distinct category of "global" or "world cities" housing activities and organizations that exert international coordination and control. We are also heir to historical comparative case studies of cities which indicate that we should not assume that situating cities in the global political economy is useful only in the contemporary era (for example, Rodriguez and Feagin 1986; Feagin and Smith 1987; Hill and Feagin 1987; Feagin 1988).

CONCEPTUAL BACKGROUND

We conceive of world cities as nodes in multiple networks of economic, social, demographic, and information flows. This allows us to begin to conceptualize them in relational terms. In turn, this relational view allows us to begin to think about mapping cities in terms of their structural relationships to one another. As we have discussed this at length elsewhere (Smith and Timberlake, 1995a and b, 1998, and 2000) we will only sketch our perspective. A key point of departure for our work is the commitment to examining relationships among cities, not merely attributes of cities (see also Meyer 1986, 1991a, 1991b). What kinds of interrelations are important? Earlier (1995a, b) we posited a typology of important intercity flows based on function and form. Cities are linked through economic, political, cultural, and social reproductive exchanges, and these take many forms. Broadly, "the stuff" that flows among cities must be human, other material, or communication. Everything we can think of that moves from city to city can be classified in the matrix defined by these two typologies. A person migrates (human, social reproduction) from one city to another to join a spouse who has moved there for work (human, economic). An order of Nike athletic shoes is shipped from a distribution center to a retail outlet in another city (material, economic—like most commodities). A corporate CEO telephones a manager of a plant located in another city with orders to lay-off 15 percent of the plant's workers (economic, communication). Thus shoes, tomatoes, FAXes, e-mail, vacationers, businesspeople, circuses usually originate (or germinate) in particular locales and end up in another—usually a city. Cities can thus be conceived within a network of places, including other cities.

Once conceived as constituting a network, the next logical step is to conceptualize relative dominance as an attribute of cities in this network context. As in McKenzie and other early urban ecologists and geographers, cities in a system of cities are related to one another along a dimension of power. Certainly this was an important component of Friedmann's (1986, 1995) and Friedmann's and Wolff's (1982) theorizing about world cities:

World cities can be arranged hierarchically, roughly in accord with the economic power they command. They are cities through which regional, national, and international economies are articulated with the global capitalist system of accumulation. A city's ability to attract global investments ultimately determines its rank in the order of world cities. However, its fortunes in this regard, as well as its ability to absorb external shocks from technological innovations and political change, are variable. Cities may rise into the rank of world cities, they may drop from the order, and they may rise or fall in rank. (Friedmann 1995: 25–26)

Friedmann proposes a list of these world cities, according to their supposed role in the new global order, and he urges us to consider "the existence of differences in rank and investigate the articulations of particular world cities with each other" (1995: 23). However, his work contains little direct evidence on such linkages provided. Instead, his 1995 list of hierarchically arranged "world cities" is based, mainly, on indirect indicators of how each are situated in the global order. Thus there is a methodological disjuncture between Friedmann's network conceptualization and his empirical identification of world cities.

NETWORK ANALYSIS

Quantitative network analysis is particularly well suited to the network-theoretical imagery on which both world-system analysis and the literature on global cities rely. In principle, network methodology allows us to simultaneously analyze multiple patterns of flows, exchanges or linkages between cities (or other nodes) for the purpose of illuminating the patterning of connections between them as well as the structure of the entire network. It is a powerful tool uncovering the structure of the global flows of people, commodities, capital, information, and more. It is a rigorous way to operationalize theoretical conceptions about the world economy and the global city system. Indeed, a number of researchers use network analysis to examine the structure of the world system (e.g., Snyder and Kick 1979). But we alone have used this methodology to map the world city system.

Formal network analysis provides a method for empirically revealing social structures based on relational data. Social network analysis has evolved from the effort to operationalize the concept "social structure." Social structures as regularities in patterns of social interaction and the persistent relationships arise "from aggregated effects of individual interactions" (Smelser 1988: 1181). Here we use network analysis to measure the relations among the world's large cities. With a set of world cities analyzed as a network, we can assess the centrality (or dominance) of each city in this system, as well as changing patterns of dominance over time. Network analysis generates measurements of a variety of formal properties of structures and relationships. Here, we will focus on the measure of POWER from the network analysis STRUCTURE (Burt and Schott 1991). This variable measures a node's prominence or centrality in a social network hierarchy.

Our earlier empirical efforts included using formal network analysis of airline passenger travel between twenty-three world cities (Smith and Timberlake 1995b) for one specific time (1985) in an effort to evaluate some of the claims of Friedmann and of Sassen about the relative importance of particular cities. More recently, using data on 1991 airline passengers between all pairs of 110 cities, we measured the flows between cities to create "images of the world urban hierarchy" (1998: 214). We corroborated the early claims about the relative importance of leading world cities (Friedmann 1995; Sassen 2001; Smith and Timberlake 1995b). In equivalence analysis, we identified London, New York, Frankfurt, and Tokyo, joined by Amsterdam and Zurich, as the structurally dominant global cities, and we identified "gateway" cities, such as Miami, Los Angeles, Hong Kong, and Singapore, which seemed to link different economic zones. Here, we will follow most closely the twenty-three-city study (1995b). However, because we now have data for more time points, we will examine changes in the structure of dominance relations among these cities over time. This will allow us to focus on most of the "world cities" identified by Friedmann, assessing their relative dominance over time in terms of the network of air passenger travel.

TOWARD OPERATIONALIZING INTERCITY LINKAGES FOR NETWORK ANALYSIS OF THE GLOBAL CITY SYSTEM

The primary reason why few others have used network analysis to analyze city systems is undoubtedly because of the strict and unusual data requirements of the technique. First, network analysis is all about *relations*. Thus the data must consist of measures of *relations*. Most other quantitative analysis relies on measures of actors' *attributes*: their size, their wealth, their number of Fortune 500 headquarters, and so on. But in order to directly assess the structure of networks, we must have measures of one or more ways in which the actors are related to every other actor in the stipulated network. There are obviously many important ways that cities are interconnected through the flows of people, materials, and communications, and many of these are in principle measurable. For example, labor migration frequently accounts for the movement of people from one city (or village) to another. In fact one oft-cited characteristic of global cities is that they are destinations for a diverse array of international migrants. However, population surveys, such as censuses, rarely inquire into the exact locale from which migrants originate. At best, we can determine the country of origin, but not the city. Thus, the kind of network analysis we hope to produce is not possible, so far as we know, with existing migration data even though in terms of our theoretical/conceptual framework such data would provide an extremely useful depiction of the world city network.

The literature on commodity chains underscores the theoretical importance of the flows of commodities from the point of production to sites where value is added to the final points of consumption. But, as is the case with international migration, the systematically available information on international commodity flows is available only at the level of nations. The intercity network described by FAXes, telephone calls, and Internet communications would also provide an extremely relevant map of the network of world cities. But we are not aware of any publicly available systematic accounting of the flows of such communications across the web of international cities.

The second serious methodological restriction is that network analysis is severely constrained by missing values. The data requirements can best be understood as an in-flow/out-flow matrix. There must be a measure of the relationship between each city pair in the network; that is, every cell must have a value (including zero). Every single actor (city, for us) must be described in terms of a known relationship with every other actor in the network. Thus, formal network analysis on the international city system must be based on a thorough compilation of relational data among all possible pairs of cities to be included in the analysis.

Despite long-standing scholarly interest in migration, commodity chains, and (more recently) information technology, there is presently no way to obtain direct measures of how they relate to locales as specific as cities across national borders for even three or four cities. However, there is one source of relational data for a large number of international cities, and that is the International Civil Aviation Organization, which has compiled estimates of the volume of civil airline traffic (e.g., in terms of passengers) between pairs of international cities since about 1977. We hope this paper will help stimulate a wider search for other indicators of intercity flows that would be suitable for network analysis, but for now, it is these airline data that allow us to depict the network of some of the top world cities for several points in time. What we will provide will be analogous to a series of time-lapsed photographs of the structure of relations of these world cities in 1980, 1985, 1991, 1994, and 1997.

We cannot justify identifying world city networks on the basis of airline passenger travel unless the air travel to and from cities is more than trivial in terms of the global political economy. Though perhaps not as fundamental as labor migration, commodity flows, and telecommunications, there is good reason to regard air passenger travel as significant. In addition to the important feature that air travel data are collected for particular cities, Keeling (1995) presents a strong argument for both generic claims about transport's key role in the world city system (116), as well as specific ones that the air passenger links that we will examine are an excellent source of data:

> Airline linkages offer the best illustration of transport's role in the world city system for five reasons: (i) global airline flows are one of the few indices available of transactional flows of inter-urban connectivity; (ii) air networks and their associated infrastructure are the most visible manifestations of world city interactions; (iii) great demand still exists for face-to-face relationships, despite the global telecommunications revolution . . . (iv) air transport is the preferred mode of inter-city movement for the transnational capitalist class, migrants, tourists, and high-value, low-bulk goods; and (v) airline links are important components of a city's aspirations to world city status. (p. 118)

Keeling also points out that airports and air connections often become important political issues in various cities. For symbolic reasons as well as for economic self-interest, members of growth coalitions and of the capitalist class seek to gain public support to develop "their" city's airline capacity.

Only a few scholars have used air travel in empirical studies comparing cities. In her study of the degree to which European cities are "internationalized," Nadine Cattan argues that "because of its relatively rapid capacity to reply in terms of supply and demand, air traffic provides a pertinent indicator in the quest to evaluate the international character of western European cities" (1995: 303). She condenses airline travel data to attributional data to show that variation among European cities' international "attractivity" (in terms of air traffic) is explained by a variety of factors, including each city's relative standing in its national territorial system. David Simon, too, employs air traffic as an indicator of a city's standing in the world system. "The progressive expansion of civil aviation reflects continued growth in business and international tourism" (1995: 139). We have used air traffic relation data in several other studies (Smith and Timberlake 1995b, 2000; see also Shin and Timberlake 2000). However, this chapter marks the first time we have looked at the air traffic–defined network of cities over time. Thus, for the first time we will be able to discern change or stability in the hierarchy of world cities, as defined by air travel.

ANALYSES OF AIR PASSENGER LINKAGES AMONG GLOBAL CITIES

The Data. Our primary data source is On-Flight Origin and Destination from the International Civil Aviation Organization (ICAO) in Montreal for 1980, 1985, 1991, 1994, and 1997. Based on reports from states on airline activity to and from each city within their boundaries to or from any city outside of their boundaries, ICAO compiles quarterly and annual figures on numbers of airline passengers traveling between cities in different countries. Following our earlier

(1995b) approximate test of Friedmann's "world city hypothesis" (Friedmann 1986), we examine the hypothesized network of key world cities. There we included twenty-three cities for 1985. Here we identify the hierarchy for as many of these same twenty-three cities as data allow for the four time points.

There are two important limitations to these data. First, in order to preserve the confidentiality of states and airlines, the ICAO provides data on travel between international city-pairs only when "at least two airlines representing at least two different States have reported" (ICAO 1993: II). Thus (a) in the absence of another data source, at most only one city from a given nation can be used in the network analysis, and (b) cities served by only one airline are not available for analysis. The second limitation should not present a problem for our research, because the select group of cities on which we focus are all served by more than one airline. According to Friedmann, however, several world cities share that status with at least one city in the same nation. The ICAO data do not allow us to include cities from the same country. So far we have been able to overcome this limitation only for U.S. cities, for which we can fill in their mutual air traffic flows with data from the Air Transport Association in Washington, D.C. We also estimated the volume of air passenger traffic between one pair of cities, London and Hong Kong, which the ICAO apparently does not consider to be an international pair—at least not until 1997. We did this by assigning passenger totals between this pair at levels comparable to other similar pairs and based on patterns of air traffic between each of London's and Hong Kong's other partners. Our resulting matrix of network data, thus, includes twenty-two cities for 1985, 1991, 1994, and 1997.

Findings. We will focus our analysis on the estimate of "POWER" available in the STRUCTURE network software program. According to Ronald Burt and Thomas Schott, "power concerns (an actor's) ability to dominate the whole system across spheres" (1991: 188). This measure of network prominence takes into account the number of mutual relations with other actors in the network and their strength. Moreover, this measure takes into account the relative prominence of the positions of the nodes with which each other node relates. Thus, in our data, other things being equal, the most dominant city in our network of world cities will have air passengers traveling to and from a larger number of other cities in the network and in greater volume than less dominant cities; moreover, the cities with which it exchanges air passengers will themselves be relatively more dominant. Other cities will be scored lower in the measure of prominence to the extent they have fewer passenger exchanges with fewer and less prominent other network cities. The most dominant city in a network receives a score set at "1," and the other cities' POWER scores are set as the ratio of their power to the power of the most dominant city (Burt and Schott 1991: 188–193).

	1980 Power	1980 Rank	1985 Power	1985 Rank	1991 Power	1991 Rank	1994 Power	1994 Rank	1997 Power	1997 Rank
London	1.00	1	1.00	1	1.00	1	1.00	1	1.00	1
Tokyo	0.323	6	0.64	3	0.68	2	0.82	2	0.81	2
Frankfurt	0.405	4	0.36	7	0.54	6	0.63	4	0.70	3
Paris	0.799	2	0.57	4	0.56	5	0.61	5	0.67	4
New York	0.729	3	0.69	2	0.58	4	0.60	6	0.65	5
Seoul	0.136	14	0.24	12	0.21	17	0.32	14	0.58	6
LA			0.37	6	0.44	8	0.54	8	0.58	7
Hong Kong	0.274	9	0.48	5	0.61	3	0.66	3	0.53	8
Singapore	0.196	12	0.30	11	0.39	9	0.47	9	0.51	9
San Francisco			0.22	13	0.27	12	0.33	10	0.38	10
Milan	0.259	10	0.16	15	0.26	14	0.32	13	0.37	11
Madrid	0.304	7	0.16	17	0.27	11	0.32	15	0.37	12
Chicago			0.17	14	0.25	15	0.33	11	0.37	13
Amsterdam	0.291	8	0.31	10	0.48	7	0.55	7	0.36	14
Zurich	0.23	11	0.34	8	0.31	10	0.32	12	0.35	15
Mexico City	0.349	5	0.16	16	0.26	13	0.29	16	0.29	16
Miami			0.13	18	0.23	16	0.24	17	0.27	17
Sydney	0.097	15	0.33	9	0.15	19	0.20	19	0.21	18
Boston			0.13	19	0.17	18	0.20	18	0.20	19
Montreal	0.182	13	0.12	20	0.15	20	0.17	20	0.16	20
Houston			0.08	22	0.12	21	0.13	16	0.16	21
Seattle			0.08	21	0.071222		0.06	22	0.06	22

The five time points allow us to use STRUCTURE to estimate five hierarchical networks. Aside from the fact that a few of the cities are not included in the 1980 time period, we have the same core of cities for each network. Thus we are able to observe change or stability in the degree to which each city is powerful, or dominant, in the whole network of world cities. Table 1 shows the POWER scores for each city for each of the five measurement years along with the rank order of each, ordered according to their rank in the most recent time period (1997).

Figure 1 provides a graphic representation of the rank-power score distribution of the fifteen cities available in 1980. London is dominant in the 1980 network, and maintains this position in the subsequent years as well. Following

London in 1980 are Paris and New York, each with power scores above .7 (which indicates their ratio of power relative to London). Though Friedmann includes Paris as a "core-primary" city in his 1986 article, its extremely high standing in the air passenger network is not otherwise predicted by the literature on world cities. However, it replicates our earlier analysis (1995a). No doubt Paris is preeminent among the major world cities as a tourist destination, and it is possible that tourism rather than its economic role in the world system accounts for its level of dominance here. But France is also economically powerful in the world economy, and Paris is by far the country's leading city. After New York in rank (4th), but far lower in terms of its POWER score (.40) is Frankfurt. Frankfurt's dominance is no doubt partly an artifact of its role as hub for travelers to central and eastern Europe, but it also reflects its role as the leading urban center, in economic terms, in Germany, the strongest economy in Europe. Following Frankfurt with POWER scores between .35 and .29 are, respectively, Mexico City, Tokyo, and Madrid. Mexico City's standing seems surprisingly high, but in 1980 the Mexican economy was in relatively good shape, and there was significant optimism over the capital city's role in the world economy. Holding the ranks of 8 through 11, with POWER scores between .29 and .23, are Amsterdam, Hong Kong, Milan, and Zurich. The 12th and 13th positions are held by Singapore and Montreal, with similar POWER scores (.20 and .18), followed by Seoul (.14). Taking up the last position in 1980, with a very low score indeed is Sydney (.10). Figure 1 nicely reveals the spread of cities in term of their relative dominance (the POWER scores), with London clearly in a class by itself, followed by Paris and New York, with fairly similar (and high) POWER scores. The remaining cities are far less dominant, and the first nine of them have a rather small range in score (from .40 to .20), indicating very gradually declining dominance, such that, except for Sydney, consecutive cities in the rank-power score distribution have relatively similar levels of dominance to one another. That is, except for London, Paris, and New York, the distribution of world cities in 1980 is fairly "flat" below the top three, indicating small differences in the relative dominance of cities.

With the addition of cities in 1985 and with changes in the relative centrality of other cities, the entire distribution becomes more hierarchical in comparison to 1980 (see fig. 2). Once again London is the leading city in terms of airline passenger flows, and now New York is the second-ranked city, despite a slight drop in its power score from 1980. Its higher ranking is a result of Paris's declining prominence (from .80 in 1980 to .57 in 1985). At the same time, Tokyo moves from the relatively equal heap of cities below the middle of the 1980 graph up into the top five of the distribution, into the number 3 spot. Hong Kong increases its POWER rating equally dramatically, moving from

FIGURE 1

RANK: POWER 1980

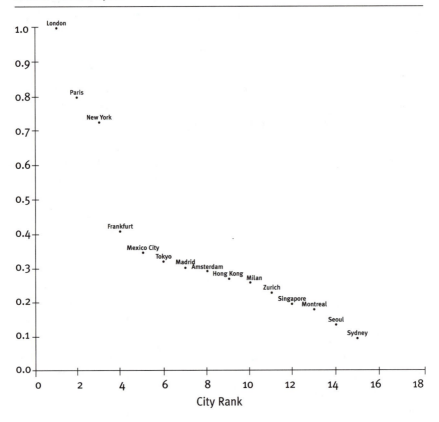

9th in 1980 to 5th in 1985, with a large increase in its estimate of power. Compared to 1980, the bottom three-fourths of the distribution is more hierarchical. Between 1980 and 1985 the cities in this group became more distinct from one another, with increasing POWER scores for many indicating their increasing importance as points of origin and destination for air travelers among all these cities. Los Angeles, Frankfurt, Zurich, Sydney, Amsterdam, and Singapore, in that order, constitute a clearly distinguishable group of cities lying between the top five and those lower in the hierarchy. Except for Frankfurt, which had a slightly higher power estimate in 1980, and Los Angeles, which was not included in 1980, these cities all have higher estimated POWER scores in 1985. Between this group and a relatively homogeneous bottom tier are Seoul and San Francisco. San Francisco was missing in 1980, and Seoul was near the bottom. The bottom of the distribution is occupied by the "new" U.S. cities and Montreal, Madrid, and Mexico City.

The 1991 network of top world cities, described in the rank-POWER

FIGURE 2
RANK: POWER 1985

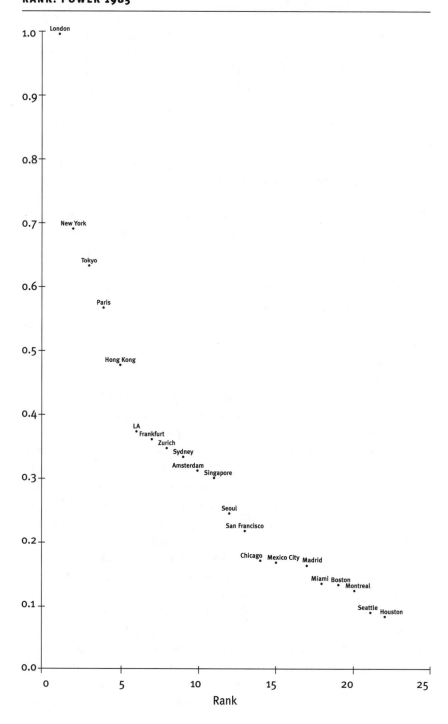

scatterplot in figure 3, indicates that London remains secure in its position as the most dominant city, once again leading the second-ranked city about .3. Following London are Tokyo (POWER=.68), Hong Kong (.61), New York (.58), Paris (.56), and Frankfurt (.54), Amsterdam (.48), and Los Angeles (.44), ranked 8th. Thus compared to 1980, when there were only two cities with POWER scores between 1.00 and .4 and 1985 when there were four cities in this range, there are now six cities in this tier, and once again, there are marked differences between most of them, as indicated by the steepness of the slope. Hong Kong replaces New York as the 3rd city in the distribution. New York is 4th, and Frankfurt and Paris are virtually tied for 6th. Amsterdam, then Los Angeles, round out this tier. These last two cities appear to have clearly become more dominant in the 1991 network than in 1985. Singapore also has a significantly higher prominence score in 1991 than in 1985, with a score of nearly .40. Following Singapore is Zurich, also with a relatively unique score in this distribution. After Zurich, there is relative equality among the next eight cities, with Madrid, San Francisco, Mexico City, Milan, Chicago, Miami, and Seoul, with Madrid and Seoul separated by only .06 in terms of their POWER scores, indicating that these cities are virtually equal in terms of their dominance in the air passenger network. (The difference between the scores of Tokyo and Zurich is .37). The tail of the distribution includes three secondary cities in the United States, and Montreal and Sydney.

Figure 4 depicts the network hierarchy for 1994. London remains the preeminent city in the network; Tokyo remains in the number 2 position but gains considerably in power over its 1991 score. In 1994 its POWER score is .82 (compared to .68 in 1991). After London and Tokyo, the distribution is less steep for the next seven cities, which are Hong Kong, Frankfurt, Paris, New York, Amsterdam, Los Angeles, and Singapore. These are the cities with POWER scores between 1.00 and .40. Overall, the composition of this group of cities is the same as in 1991, although Frankfurt and New York have switched places, with Frankfurt in 4th position and New York in 6th. However, this was not the result of New York's becoming less dominant vis-à-vis London; its POWER score actually increased slightly. Rather Frankfurt gained even more relative to London (.54 in 1991, .63 in 1994). In fact, the overall level of dominance for the cities in this group increased somewhat over the three years, indicating that these cities, as a whole, became more dominant as centers of airline passenger exchanges among cities in the entire world city network. In addition to Tokyo and Frankfurt, note the change in the POWER scores for Singapore in 1991 and 1994. Although remaining in 9th place, its score increased from .39 to .47. Also note that two consecutive pairs of cities in this group, Paris–New York and Amsterdam–Los Angeles are indistinguishable in terms of their POWER scores, but overall there is marked hierarchy through

FIGURE 3
RANK: POWER 1991

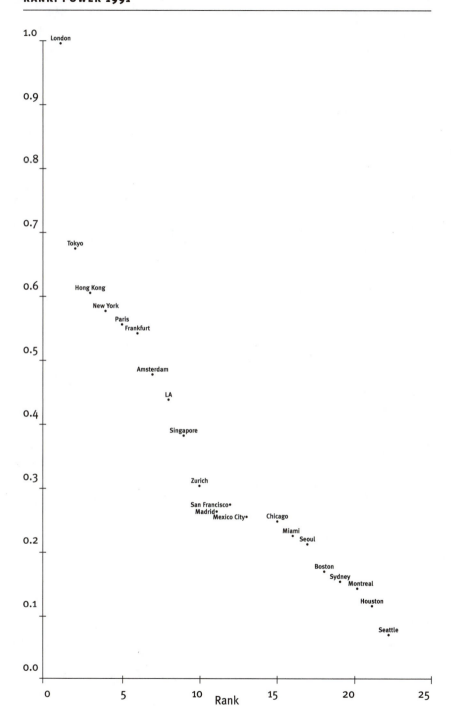

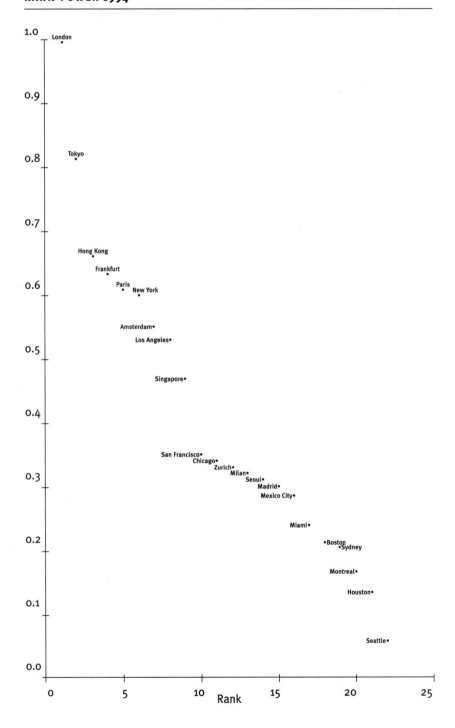

FIGURE 4
RANK-POWER 1994

this top group of nine cities. However beginning with the 10th city, the distribution becomes flat, with San Francisco, Chicago, Zurich, Milan, Seoul, Madrid, Houston, and Mexico City (10th through 17th) having nearly identical power scores. Over the bottom six cities there is once again a clear hierarchical ordering, with 18th-ranked Miami (.24) clearly more central to the network than 22nd-ranked Seattle (.06), and the three other cities (Boston, Sydney, and Montreal) occupying clear steps between the two. As in 1991, the 1994 network indicates that there is a relatively clearly marked top hierarchy of eight or nine top world cities. Beginning with London at the top of the hierarchy, each subsequent city (or two) in this top group is clearly less dominant than the immediate higher-ranking city. Following this group, the distribution is flat for the next five to eight cities of relatively equal relative dominance, suggesting that the cities in this group occupy similar roles as nodes of air passenger exchanges.

The 1997 air passenger network (fig. 5) is a little more competitive among the top five cities than in 1994. London once again dominates the whole network of world cities, followed by Tokyo, Frankfurt, Paris, and New York. The difference between the top of the distribution in 1994 and 1997 is that these next four cities are somewhat closer to London in terms of their POWER scores. The remaining distribution of cities is quite similar in shape to that of 1994. There is a clear hierarchical distribution through the 10th city (San Francisco), with the caveat that, along the way, Los Angeles and Seoul are nearly identical in terms of relative dominance. Once again, the distribution is very flat in the lower middle, with San Francisco, Milan, Madrid, Chicago, Amsterdam, and Zurich occupying the 10th through 15th ranks but separated in terms of their POWER scores by only .03. Again, the bottom of the distribution is more hierarchical. Mexico City, ranked 16th (POWER = .29) follows Zurich, and Seattle is once again the least dominant, with a score of only .06. Actually, the descent from Mexico City to Seattle is in paired steps, with Miami achieving the same level of dominance as the Mexican capital, Sydney and Boston following at roughly the same level, and Montreal and Houston closely matching. Seattle stands—or sits—alone at the bottom in terms of dominance.

Overall, the four snapshots of the network of world cities presented above indicate that, though there are small differences in the distribution of POWER, or dominance, there are certain similarities. There is one preeminently dominant city, and that is London. London's dominance relative to the next most dominant three to five cities varies somewhat. In 1985 New York was the 2nd-ranked city with .69. Tokyo replaced New York in 2nd place in 1991 with a score of .68, and remained in 2nd for the last two time periods but with relatively more power in the network (.82 and .81, indicating its ratio of dominance relative to London). Also note that the scores of the top cities become greater

FIGURE 5
RANK-POWER 1997

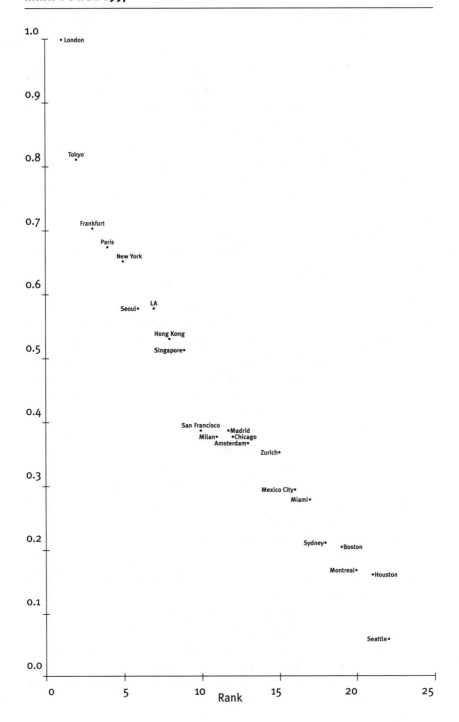

over the time period covered. In 1985 only three cities had POWER scores between .5 and 1.00, but by 1997 eight cities had scores in this range.

Also consistent over the time period studied is the distribution of relative dominance among the top ten or so cities. They are hierarchically ordered, overall, with clear differences in the relative prominence of higher-ranked cities to subsequent cities in the order (except that some adjacent pairs of cities might be very similar in power). More striking is the flatness of the curve across the seven or eight cities beginning near the middle of the distribution, indicating that after approximately the top ten cities, there is relative equality in the dominance of these world cities, at least in terms of their role in the air passenger travel among world cities. These cities cannot be distinguished from each other–they are equally dominant (or subdominant). Following this group is a third tier of cities that are, once again, hierarchically arranged. This group usually consists of four or five cities. In summary, there are consistently three tiers of cities in these air passenger networks, including a top tier of more prominent cities that are themselves hierarchically ordered, indicating that even among the top world cities, there are important differences among them. Below a top ten or so of such cities, there are typically about seven cities that are very similar in terms of their scope of dominance. These are important world cities, subordinate to the top tier but still influential with respect to the remaining four to six cities in the networks. These last cities are subordinate in the network, but like the cities at the top of the distribution, they are hierarchically arranged, indicating that substantively important differences exist among them in terms of the power each has in the whole system.

We can also venture a few generalizations about the specific composition of the three tiers of the hierarchy. In 1985, New York, Tokyo, Paris, and possibly Hong Kong constitute, with London, a top tier above a closely clustered group of cities in the middle. Included are all three of Sassen's global cities, and eight of Friedmann's nine "core-primary" cities[1] (Friedmann 1986). Hong Kong is the only city that appears out of place relative to Friedmann's early placement. It is at the top of our network of world cities for 1985, but in his 1986 article, he considered it a peripheral "secondary" city. Chicago, which Friedman considered a core-primary city, is ranked 14th, with a POWER score of only .17.

Six years later, in 1991, our network analysis results in more change at the top of the distribution. London remains in the top position, far ahead of the next most dominant city in terms of the POWER score. Moreover, Tokyo takes the second position and Hong Kong the third. These are followed by the more familiar list of New York, Paris, Frankfurt, Amsterdam, Los Angeles, Singapore, and Zurich. By 1991 the Asian economy was certainly the focus of a much larger share of the world's economic activity than had been the case in 1985, and this is reflected in the ascendance of Tokyo, Hong Kong, and

Singapore in the hierarchy of world cities (see also Shin and Timberlake 2000). Again, the top ten overlap considerably with Friedmann's (1986) list of primary world cities. The exceptions, again are that Chicago is 15th in the network and Hong Kong is 3rd. Our results suggest that Friedmann underestimated Hong Kong's importance to the world economy through the mid-1980s to the mid-1990s. He recognizes this in his later work. "The capitalist foothold in China is being widened and, without political disaster, the Hong Kong economy is likely to remain an important and increasingly strategic outpost of global capitalism, articulating much of the south China economy with the rest of the world" (Friedmann 1995: 36). Three years later, in 1994, the picture had not changed much. The top nine cities are the same ones. Frankfurt, Paris, and New York all become more prominent in absolute terms (i.e., the POWER scores) but Frankfurt's increases were sufficiently great to put it ahead of New York and the French capital in 1994. In the 10th position in 1994 there is a virtual deadlock between six cities with nearly identical POWER scores. Zurich, which was alone in this position in 1994 is joined by Chicago, San Francisco, Milan, Seoul, and Madrid, all of which have significantly higher POWER scores in 1994 than 1991.

The last data point is 1997. Again there is a distinct tier of top nine cities, and the tier's composition is similar to 1994 and 1991, but identical to neither. The most dramatic difference is that Seoul joins the elite nine for the first time, moving to 6th position from 14th in 1994. Figures 6–9 graph the POWER scores for each city over the five time periods covered, using their grouping in the 1997 network as a basis for inclusion in their respective figures. Figure 6 shows that Seoul's scores increased steadily and dramatically over the five time points, indicating that it became more and more prominent as a center for airline passenger traffic among these world cities. The top tier of nine cities includes four Asian cities, one West Coast U.S. city, New York, and three European cities, with London once again occupying the dominant position. Following 9th-ranked Singapore, once again, is a tier of six cities with nearly identical POWER scores. These cities are San Francisco, Milan, Madrid, Chicago, Amsterdam, and Zurich.

Throughout the periods when multiple U.S. cities are included, Seattle occupies a lowly position at the bottom of each time period except 1985. In fact, its POWER scores are so low (.08 or less for all four time periods in which it is included) that its inclusion as a "world city" is questionable. Friedmann (1995) includes it as a "subnational/regional articulation," but goes on to suggest that it and Vancouver should be considered part of a single economic region. But treating Vancouver-Seattle as a single region is conceptually problematic. They are in different nations, and they are about as near to one another as a few other pairs of large cities, such as New York and Philadelphia and Rio

FIGURE 6

POWER SCORE CHANGES, 1980–1997, FOR CITIES 2–7

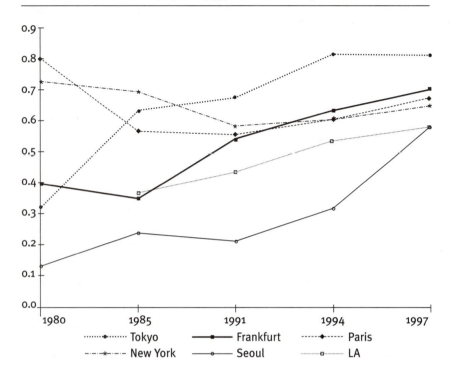

de Janeiro and São Paulo (neither of which we could include in this analysis). Seattle may be an important regional hub in the U.S. Northwest, but it certainly does not qualify as a top twenty world city in terms of air passenger traffic.

On the other hand, including Houston, second from the bottom in two out of three 1990s time points, in this group does seem to be justified on the basis of our analysis. Its POWER scores, though low in most instances, are similar to those of Montreal. In terms of airline passenger exchanges, Houston is more than the hub of a local region. It seems to be fairly well connected internationally, and this is consistent with what is known about its role as financial and producer service center in relation to oil production in the world economy (e.g., see Feagin 1988).

Figure 6 shows changes in the POWER scores for the six cities that were at the top in the 1997 network, after London. Remember, the computation for POWER assigns "1" to the most prominent actor in the network, and the other scores can be thought of as their ratio of prominence in the network relative to number 1. Since London is at the top for all five time points with a score of "1.00," it is omitted from the graph. The scores for the next six cities are more interesting. These cities are Tokyo, Frankfurt, Paris, New York, Seoul, and Los Angeles. Relative to 1985, five of the six cities became more dominant in the network of world cities. Seoul made the biggest gains: beginning with a POWER score of .24, it steadily became more dominant with the rise of the Asian economy throughout the time period covered. By 1997 its score was greater than .5 (and it moved from being ranked 12th to 6th. Seoul's dominance in our analysis is somewhat at odds with how some scholars of world cities see it. Friedmann, for example, says, "The South Korean capital appears to be losing some of its appeal to outside . . . capital. . . . it remains cut off from North Korea and so provides no access to markets other than its own. Korean capital is outward-bound . . . Seoul is not so much a world city, rather it is the capital city of South Korea" (1995: 37). Why, then, would Seoul have become so important as a destination and point of origin for travelers among world cities? Some evidence suggests that South Korean firms are increasingly playing a "brokerage" role as intermediaries between U.S.-based buyers and manufacturers elsewhere in the Pacific Rim (especially China and Southeast Asia) (Smith 1996b). So it is possible that Seoul's role in the world economy is underestimated (or undervalued) by other scholars, but it is also possible that the airline data exaggerate the South Korean capital's economic importance.

Tokyo also gained somewhat in its relative dominance. Beginning with a POWER score a little more than .6 in 1985, by 1997 its score was greater than .8. Frankfurt also became significantly more prominent over this time period, and Los Angeles's dominance increased over the four time periods. Its scores steadily increased through the 1990s time points, moving from about .45 to .58. Of course Los Angeles is the crucial U.S. link to Asia, and it is therefore not surprising that its rise parallels that of the four leading Asian cities in the 1990s. Paris, Tokyo, and Frankfurt were all more dominant in the air passenger network by the late 1990s than New York. But this is not because New York became less dominant relative to London in the network. Rather it is because these other cities became more competitive with London as centers for receiving and dispensing world-city airline passengers. New York's POWER score declined slightly, while the scores of Tokyo, Paris, and Frankfurt all increased substantially.

Figure 7 is a graph of the POWER scores, over time, for the cities ranked 8–12 in 1997. The most interesting changes here are for Hong Kong and Singapore. Although Hong Kong's dominance declined significantly between 1994 and 1997 (with the approach of reunification with China?), its score increased dramatically throughout the earlier time points, from less than .3 to greater than .6 before dropping to .53 in 1997. Singapore's rise was steadier. It became increasingly dominant throughout the time period covered (.2 to .52), joining Hong Kong as nearly equally dominant nodes in 1997, integrating Asia and interlinking it to the rest of the world. These two cities were nearly tied for

FIGURE 7

POWER SCORE CHANGES IN CITIES 8–12

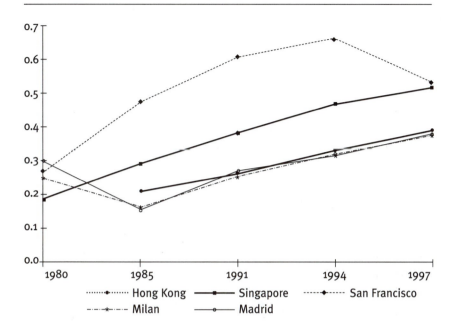

the 8th-ranked position in 1997 and were set apart from the next-ranked city by a substantial margin.

Space does not permit a detailed description of the changing levels of dominance of other world cities. The reader is referred to figures 6 through 9. In general, cities in the rest of the distribution increased their share in the global airline traffic somewhat, which indicate increasing integration in the global system over the twelve years covered. Exceptions are rare. Amsterdam increased in power through the first four time periods before declining in dominance to a level similar to its initial starting point. Zurich, at about the same level in 1997 as Amsterdam, remained atypically stable over these twelve years. Boston and Montreal also had only minute increases in dominance, and Seattle declined in dominance throughout the four time periods. Houston and Sydney have dramatically unstable POWER estimates. In the case of Houston, this could be linked to its role as a producer service center for the global oil economy. On the other hand, measurement error could also be involved for these cases.

CONCLUSIONS

The literature on the role of cities in globalization has centered on "global cities" and "world cities," defining them as crucial nodes where capital, human

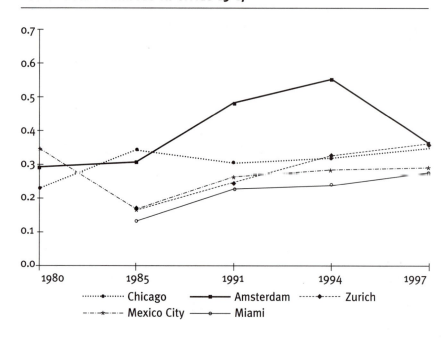

FIGURE 8
POWER SCORE CHANGES IN CITIES 13–17

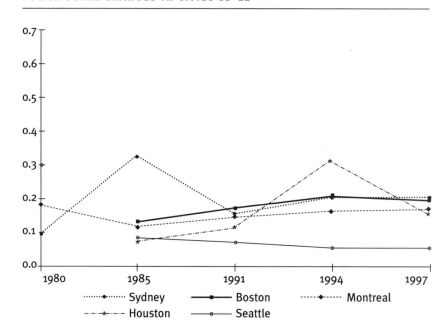

FIGURE 9
POWER SCORE CHANGES IN CITIES 18–22

resources, information, and commodities are produced, exchanged, and consumed. World cities are seen as spatial articulations of the global flows that constitute the world economy. Here we have tried to develop a network operationalization of dominance of cities within the world city network. We have done this on the basis of information on airline passenger flows among pairs of cities in a network of twenty-two world cities from 1985 to 1997. Our results indicate that there is a sharply defined hierarchy of dominance within a tier of the most important world cities, and this top tier has grown to include more cities over the last twelve years. It comprises the familiar cities identified by Sassen and Friedmann: New York, Tokyo, London, Paris, Frankfurt, and Los Angeles. But by 1997, upstarts were there as well—namely, the rising Asian cities of Seoul, Hong Kong, and Singapore. We also identified a second tier of relatively equally important secondary world cities. These include the secondary cities of the United States and Europe, each of which can be seen as serving a narrower, more specialized role in the network. Following this second layer of world cities is a bottom tier of hierarchically organized world cities that are rather marginal to the top tier. Included are Mexico City, Sydney, and Montreal in addition to several less important U.S. cities.

This research intends to contribute in three ways to the literature on cities and globalization. First, it is meant to demonstrate the utility of a network methodological approach to this substantive area of inquiry. Network language runs thick through the world city literature, but aside from our own work, there have been few, if any, attempts to match this with a network methodological approach–one that relies on information on direct relations among cities rather than information about the attributes of cities. (See also Taylor et al., this volume.) Second, we sought to describe patterns of dominance among world cities over recent time as indicated by their interrelations in the air passenger networks for several recent time points. Third, we tried to relate these patterns of dominance to other research and theory on world cities, using our analysis as a partial test of some of the claims made by others about the relative importance of particular cities at different times.

Clearly, making too much of our analysis of airline passenger exchanges would be a mistake. Our hope is that we and others will identify detailed information on the other ways in which the world's great cities are interlinked. Data on communications flows among cities would be very exciting to have, for example. With different types of intercity relational data over longer periods of time, we would be able to produce more accurate descriptions of the network of world cities. We think this will also lead to more complete knowledge about how global processes articulate with local communities, and how community groups can resist, ameliorate, or harness globalization in efforts to create more humane places to live.

NOTES

The authors thank the Institute for Advanced Study, United Nations University (Tokyo) for its support, and the Center for Advanced Study in the Behavioral Sciences (Palo Alto, CA), for hosting one of the meetings of the research network.

1. This is true if we substitute Amsterdam for Rotterdam in his list of nine core-primary cities. Friedmann suggests that this should be the case in his 1995 reassessment of the world-city hypothesis (p. 40).

REFERENCES CITED

Abu-Lughod, Janet. 1999. *New York, Chicago, Los Angeles: America's Global Cities.* Minneapolis: University of Minnesota Press.

Burt, Ronald. 1982. *Toward a Structural Theory of Action: Network Models of Social Structure, Perception, and Action.* New York: Academic Press.

Burt, Ronald, and Thomas Schott. 1991. Structure: A General Purpose Network Analysis Program Providing Sociometric Indices, Cliques, Structural and Role Equivalence, Density Tables, Contagion, Autonomy, Power and Equilibria in Multiple Network Systems. Version 4.2; Reference Manual. Center for the Social Sciences, Columbia University, New York.

Cattan, Nadine. 1995. "Attractivity and Internationalisation of Major European Cities: The Example of Air Traffic." *Urban Studies* 32: 303–312.

Duncan, Otis Dudley, W. Richard Scott, Stanley Lieberson, Beverly Duncan and Hal Winsborough. 1960. *Metropolis and Region.* Baltimore: Johns Hopkins University Press.

Feagin, J. R. 1988. *The Free Enterprise City.* New Brunswick, NJ: Rutgers University Press.

Feagin, J. R., and Michael P. Smith. 1987. *The Capitalist City.* New York: Basil Blackwell.

Friedmann, John. 1986. "The World City Hypothesis." *Development and Change* 17: 69–83.

———. 1995. "Where We Stand: A Decade of World City Research," Pp. 21–47 in *World Cities in a World-System,* ed. Paul Knox and Peter Taylor. Cambridge: Cambridge University Press.

Friedmann, John, and G. Wolff. 1982. "World City Formation: An Agenda for Research and Action." *International Journal of Urban and Regional Research* 6: 309–344.

Gras, N. S. B. 1922. *Introduction to Economic History.* New York: Harper.

Hill, Richard C., and Joe R. Feagin. 1987. "Detroit and Houston: Two Cities in Global Perspective." Pp. 155–177 in *The Capitalist City.* ed. M. P. Smith and J. R. Feagin. New York: Basil Blackwell.

International Civil Aviation Organization. 1993. "On-Flight Origin and Destination: Year and Quarter Ending 31 December 1991." Montreal.

Keeling, David J. 1995. "Transport and the World City Paradigm." Pp. 115–131 in *World Cities in a World-System,* ed. Paul Knox and Peter Taylor. New York: Cambridge University Press.

King, A. 1990. *Global Cities: Post-Imperialism and the Internationalization of London.* London: Routledge.

McKenzie, Roderick. 1927. "The Concept of Dominance and World-Organization." *American Journal of Sociology* 33: 28–42.

———. 1968. *Roderick D. McKenzie on Human Ecology.* Edited by Amos H. Hawley. Chicago: University of Chicago Press.

Meyer, D. 1986. "World System of Cities: Relations Between International Financial Metropolises and South American Cities." *Social Forces* 64 (3):553–581.

———. 1991a. "Change in the World System of Metropolises: The Role of Business Intermediaries." *Urban Geography* 12 (5): 393–416.

———. 1991b. The Formation of a Global Financial Center: London and Its Intermediaries. Pp. 97–106 in *Cities in the World-System, Studies in the Political Economy of the World-System.* ed. K. Resat. New York: Greenwood.

Rodriguez, N., and J. R. Feagin. 1986. Urban Specialization in the World System: An Investigation of Historical Cases. *Urban Affairs Quarterly* 22: 187–220.

Ross, R. and K. Trachte. 1990. *Global Capitalism: The New Leviathan.* Albany: State University of New York Press.

Sassen Saskia. 2000. *Cities in a World Economy,* 2nd ed. Thousand Oaks, CA: Pine Forge Press.

————. 2001. *The Global City: New York, London, Tokyo.* 2nd ed. Princeton, NJ: Princeton University Press.

Shin, Kyoung-Ho, and Michael Timberlake. 2000. "World Cities in Asia: Cliques, Centrality, and Connectedness." *Urban Studies* 37 (12): 2257–2285.

Simon, David. 1995. "The World City Hypothesis: Reflections from the Periphery," pp. 132–155 in *World Cities in a World-System,* ed. Paul Knox and Peter Taylor. New York: Cambridge University Press.

Smelser, Neil, ed. 1988. *Handbook of Sociology.* Newbury Park, CA: Sage.

Smith, David A. 1996a. "Going South: Global Restructuring and Garment Production in Three East Asian Cases." *Asian Perspective* 20 (2): 211–241.

————. 1996b. *Third World Cities in Global Perspective: The Political Economy of Urbanization.* Boulder, CO: Westview.

Smith, David A., and Michael Timberlake. 1995a. "Cities in Global Matrices: Toward Mapping the World-System's City-System." Pp. 79–97 in *World Cities in a World-System,* ed. Paul Knox and Peter Taylor. New York: Cambridge University Press.

————. 1995b. "Conceptualising and Mapping the Structure of the World System's City System." *Urban Studies* 32: 287–302.

Snyder, David, and Edward Kick. 1979. "Structural Position in the World System and Economic Growth, 1955–1970: A Multiple Network Analysis of Transnational Interaction." *American Journal of Sociology* 84: 1097–1126.

PART TWO

CROSS-BORDER REGIONS

Chapter 5

MEXICO: THE MAKING OF A GLOBAL CITY

Christof Parnreiter

With a population of 17.9 million people in the year 2000, Mexico City[1] is the third-largest urban agglomeration in the world, behind Tokyo and Bombay. This leads into thinking of it merely as a Third World megacity, which is a simplified picture, because beyond the large size, new dynamics of urbanization—related to economic globalization—may be at work. Though these new dynamics are far more easily seen in First World metropolises—in part because First World countries do not have the megacity syndrome—they are also present in Third World cities. In the case of Third World cities the new elements in urban processes tend to be submerged under the size of the population, which impedes one from grasping the structural transformation that cities like Mexico City are undergoing.

To overcome this deficit I focus on the global integration of Mexico City. My main argument is that it is not quantity—in terms of population size—which shaped Mexico City's destiny in the last two decades, but the changing quality of relations with the national economy on the one hand, and with the world economy on the other hand. I maintain that the city's development was strongly biased by the radical shift in the country's economic strategy toward foreign markets, because this shift implied a revalorization and reordering of economic activities, of space, and of capital–labor relations. Thus, the emphasis of this chapter is on: (a) transformations of Mexico City that occurred with the deeper integration of Mexico into the international division of labor; and (b) the specific role of Mexico City in this process of globalization. By concentrating on global embeddedness, this chapter aims to contribute to our knowledge of Mexico City, which derives from rich studies on the city's economic, spatial, and social development (see, for example, Garza 1985; Schteingart 1991; Ward 1998).

My approach is based on the global or world cities research, which reemerged in the 1980s and has created a theoretically and—to a lesser extent—empirically compelling body of literature (see, for example, Friedmann 1986; Sassen 1991; Knox and Taylor 1995; Lo and Yeung 1998).[2] In short, the argument is that globalization processes give rise to a new form of centrality, in which a certain number of cities emerge as key places. These global cities link larger regional, national, and international economies with the global economy, and by doing so serve as nodal points where the flows of capital, information, commodities, and migrants intersect and from which they are directed. Concentrating command and control functions, global cities are both production sites and trade places for specific goods, namely financial and other advanced producer services, which are essential for global integration (Sassen 2001). Finally, global cities are linked to each other by flows of capital, information, commodities, and migrants, thus creating a cross-border network of cities. The emergence of a global urban system alters the geography of the world system (perceived traditionally as a collection or hierarchy of nation-states), because it operates both through nation-states and by bypassing their boundaries.

Until recently, global city research gave priority to metropolises in the centers of the world system. Most (though not all) studies on Third World urbanization used to place cities in a nation-state framework.[3] In addition, they showed a strong bias toward demographic questions, "urban primacy," and urban problems. In recent years, however, the call has become louder to prioritize on the research agenda the conceptual and theoretical relationship between core world cities and the megacities of the peripheries (Friedmann 1995: 43; Knox 1995: 16; Sassen 1996: 14–16; Gugler 1999: 1f; Taylor 1999b: 2). There are, in fact, good reasons to expand global city research to Third World cities. First, there are serious limitations in the conceptual framework and database for adequate assessments of megacities. The deficiencies can be illustrated by the fact that the main cities in Latin America, Africa and Asia are still called simply "megacities," which is of course a quantitative definition, compared to the qualitative approach of "world city" or "global city." Second, a country's position in the international division of labor influences its economic and social development. Accordingly, urbanization in the Third World is linked to broader dynamics such as colonialism, merchant capitalism, dependent industrialization, or the crisis of the world economy (Chase-Dunn 1985; Gilbert 1992; Feldbauer et al. 1993). Third, if the postulate is taken seriously that today's world economy is shaped as a network, and if cities are, as argued, nodal points in this network, then the major cities of the Third World should be expected to be key places for globalization, too. From this perspective, a city like Mexico City presumably is the place where the integration into the global system of economic activities, territories, and societies of a Third World country such as Mexico is organized, controlled, and managed. Thus, one can conclude that the megacities of the periphery are an essential element of the cross-border urban system.

In the following sections I will analyze major developments in Mexico City in light of global embeddedness. Though results are still tentative, they show that the deep crisis of the early 1980s, the subsequent recovery and restructuring of the urban economy, the turn toward an era of net emigration, and impoverishment and social polarization are closely linked to the particular way in which Mexico and its capital have been integrated into processes of globalization. However, it is not only that forces operating on a global scale have affected Mexico City. Certain parts of the city assume more economic activities that are of global—or at least of regional—reach. Thus, because of globalization, and as part of it, Mexico City turns from a national metropolis into a pivot between the Mexican and the global economy. By doing so, Mexico City contributes to the "production" of globalization.

MEXICO IN THE GLOBAL ECONOMY

The integration of Mexico into the world system is by no means a recent phenomenon. From the Spanish conquest to the externally stimulated and pushed modernization during the rule of Porfirio Díaz (1876–1911), to massive indebtedness at the end of import substitution, Mexican destiny has been shaped to a great extent by factors beyond its territory. However, in the two decades following the debt crisis in 1982, Mexico's integration into the international division of labor has become ever deeper and has changed its form. By joining the General Agreement on Tariffs and Trade (today the World Trade Oganization) in 1986 and the North American Free Trade Agreement (NAFTA) in 1994, the country's government institutionalized its course toward globalizing Mexico.

The collapse of import substitution, marked by the debt crisis, forced Mexico to a radical change of its economic strategy. In order to guarantee the payment of interest (and, to a smaller extent, the repayment of debt), to restore public finance and to create opportunities for highly profitable investment for both foreign capital owners and national business elites, governments implemented neoliberal policies. A good part of the country's economy and labor market was deregulated, the financial sector liberalized, land reform halted, tariff protections dismantled and import restrictions eliminated, state-owned enterprises privatized, manufacturing and agriculture reorientated toward foreign markets, and wages and social transfers reduced. All these changes show that globalization thus did not simply "happen" to Mexico. Rather, the state—or the elite controlling it—was a crucial agent. Globalization resulted from a deliberate reshaping of relations of capital, state, labor, and space, carried out to assert the interests of a specific set of private firms, namely those operating on a global scale.

As a result, the character of the Mexican economy has changed profoundly in the last two decades.[4] Inward development was replaced by outward development, as demonstrated by the drastic growth of foreign trade and foreign investment. Annual exports grew more than sixfold between 1983 and 2000, up to $166 billion. Imports grew fifteenfold, amounting to $174 billion in 2000. The share of foreign trade in the national gross domestic product increased from less than 20 percent of GDP in the late 1970s to 59 percent in 2000.[5] Increase in exports was caused to a large extent by the fast expansion of the so-called maquiladora industry.[6] While exports originating outside these export processing zones grew fourfold, exports of the maquiladora industry increased by a factor of more than twenty (from $3.6 billion in 1983 to $79.4 billion in 2000). As a result, the maquiladora industry's share of total Mexican exports grew from 14 percent in 1983 to 48 percent in 2000.[7] Another result of the greater opening of Mexico to the world market is that foreign capital flew into the country at unprecedented levels. Annual foreign direct investment (FDI) increased eightfold between 1980 and 2000, amounting to $13.1 billion in 2000. Between 1980 and 2000, $124.1 billion was invested in Mexico as FDI, and an additional $91.5 billion came into the country as portfolio investment. As a consequence of this increase, FDI reached 13.9 percent of all investment and 2.5 percent of the GDP in 1998, compared to 3.3 percent of all investment and 0.8 percent of GDP in 1980 (Dussel Peters 2000b: 68, 85; Dussel Peters 2000a: 73; INEGI 2001b; Banco de México 2001).

Data unmistakably indicate a shift from inward development, as was pursued in the era of import substitution, to an economy that is strongly oriented and tied to the world market. This shift implies a profound transformation of the Mexican economy, increasing the importance of export production (in particular the maquiladora industry) and of the financial sector. Thus, in the last two decades both the mode of Mexico's insertion into the world economy and the nature of the Mexican economy itself have changed radically.

ECONOMIC, SOCIAL, AND DEMOGRAPHIC TRANSFORMATIONS IN MEXICO CITY

For the purpose of this chapter it is crucial to ask what this transformation meant for Mexico City (the Zona Metropolitana de la Ciudad de México, or ZMCM). At first glance, transformation reduced the economic weight of Mexico City. The combined share of the Federal District and the state of Mexico in the national GDP went down by nearly 10 percent, reducing the share of Mexico City to 33.1 percent (see table 1).[8] This decline was mainly due

TABLE 1

SHARES OF REGIONS IN THE NATIONAL GDP, 1980–1999 (PERCENT)

	1980	1985	1994	1999
Mexico City	36.2	32.1	34.2	33.1
Central region	43.5	40.0	42.4	41.6
Extended North/Central region: all those above plus Guanajato, Jalisco, Xacatecas, Aguascalientes, San Luis Potosi.	56.6	53.2	56.5	55.6
Northern border region	19.3	19.4	21.9	23.3
Gulf region	10.3	11.9	7.1	6.6
South	4.1	4.1	3.4	3.2
Southeast	1.1	1.6	2.6	3.0

Source: Author's calculations based on INEGI 2001b.
Central region: Federal District, State of Mexico, Hidalgo, Morelos, Puebla, Querétaro, Tlaxcala
Northern border region: Baja California, Chihuahua, Coahuila, Nuevo León, Sonora, Tamaulipas
Gulf region: Campeche, Tabasco, Veracruz
South: Chiapas, Oaxaca
Southeast: Yucatán, Quintana Roo

to the breakdown of the manufacturing sector in Mexico City in the early 1980s. Industrial output shrank in absolute terms (down 5.8 percent annually between 1980 and 1985), and its share in Mexican manufacturing fell from 48.6 to 32.1 percent (Pradilla Cobos 1997: fig. 2; Garza and Rivera 1994: 13f). Additionally, the Federal District lost importance as a national center of economic decision making. Though 287 of the Mexican "Top 500" companies were there in 1982, this number had declined to 145 by 1989 (*Expansión*, various dates).

Due to the losses of the ZMCM, the share of the country's central region in the national GDP also declined. At the same time some states in the country's center or north of it (Aguascalientes, Querétaro, Guanajuato) increased their share. States in the northern border region (particularly Baja California, Chihuahua, Coahuila and Nuevo León), where most of the maquiladora industry is located, increased their share of the national GDP considerably. Finally, the Southeastern state of Quintana Roo (the destination of a good part of international tourism) also augmented its share of national GDP (see table 1).

As regards the labor market, it is even more obvious that transformation weakened economic concentration in Mexico City. Though in 1980 nearly 41 percent of the workforce employed in the formal sector was counted in the ZMCM, this share had dropped to less than 30 percent in 1994. The reduction was strongest in Mexico City's manufacturing sector, where even the absolute number of workers declined (Aguilar 1996: fig. 8.1, 8.2). For the second half of the 1990s, complete data on the whole urban agglomeration of the ZMCM are not accessible. However, available data suggest that the downward trend continued. According to the most recent economic census (INEGI 2001a), both federal states on whose territory Mexico City is located employed fewer people in 1998 than in 1993. While in the case of the state of Mexico the reduction was small (9.7 percent compared to 9.8 percent), it was significant in the case of the Federal District (17.5 percent compared to 20.5 percent). In a similar vein, both states employed fewer workers in manufacturing in 1999 than in 1993 (Katz 2000: 162f). Finally, the reduction of the absolute number of workers in manufacturing in the Federal District continued, falling by more than 7 percent to 513,118 in 1999 (Fideicomiso 2000: 57). On the other hand, maquiladora employment had risen to 1.3 million workers by 2000 (INEGI 2001b). Thus, while in 1980 the relation of employment in manufacturing between Mexico City and the maquiladora industry was 7.9:1, by the end of the 1990s it had reversed to 1:2.3. As a consequence of the northward move of manufacturing, the northern border states increased their share in national employment by more than 6 percent between 1993 and 1998 (Aguilar 1996: fig. 8.2; INEGI 2001b; Fideicomiso 2000: 57; INEGI 2001a).

With the beginning of neoliberal restructuring in the second half of the 1980s Mexico City's share in the national GDP rose again, although without reaching 1980 levels (see table 1). The recovery was driven mainly by an upswing of the Federal District where growth rates of GDP amounted to 3.5 percent annually (1988–1996), which was markedly higher than the national average (2.5 percent). The extent to which the city's economy recovered is shown also by the fact that the Federal District is one of the few regions in Mexico where GDP per capita was higher in 1995 than in 1980. Though it stagnated nationwide and grew only slightly (0.2 percent annually) in the dynamic northeastern border region, it increased by 1.4 percent in the capital. Consequently, GDP per capita in the Federal District was 3.3 times the national average in 1995, while in 1980 it was only 2.6 times higher. This increase points to the concentration of highly productive economic activities (Fideicomiso 2000: 31, 34).

Economic recovery in Mexico City stems mainly from two trends. First, manufacturing in the Federal District overcame the crisis, regaining annual growth rates of nearly 4 percent from 1993 to 1999. Consequently, the share of the Federal District's industrial GDP in the total Mexican manufacturing GDP remained constant in the 1990s, at a level slightly over 20 percent. Although this is, of course, much lower than in the 1970s, it is important to note that the downward trend in terms of production was stopped (INEGI 2001b). Thus, speaking of a "deindustralization" of Mexico City would be misleading for various reasons. First, due to its historical weight and the stabilization of the manufacturing sector, the ZMCM still is by far the most important single city for manufacturing in Mexico, although states like Tamaulipas, Aguascalientes, Chihuahua, or Baja California have far higher growth rates in manufacturing. Second, employment that was formerly counted as manufacturing might appear as part of the service sector because of the internal reorganization of firms, even though the employment may still be attached to manufacturing. Third, part of the city's manufacturing might have become informalized, which would mean a reduction in statistical employment but not in output.

For the economic recovery of Mexico City the growth of the service sector was even more important than manufacturing. Services became the city's most important sector both in terms of the GDP and employment. Yet, the growth of the service sector does not simply reflect a shift toward services in general, since the subsectors "trade, restaurants, and hotels" and "municipal, social, and personal services" barely grew. Rather, growth was concentrated on "transportation and communication" and "finance, insurance, and real estate." Both subsectors had annual growth rates of about 5 and 4 percent, respectively (1993–1999). Consequently, the weight of "finance, insurance, and real estate" within the Federal District's GDP nearly doubled over the last 15 years (from 10.7 percent in 1985 to 19.0 percent in 1999). Within advanced producer services, financial services in particular expanded rapidly. With an annual growth rate of more than 8 percent, banking outperformed any other subsector of the urban economy (INEGI 2001b; Fideicomiso 2000: 51).

A strong expansion of employment in producer services also indicates that the economic upswing of Mexico City in the 1990s was very much linked to advanced services. Employment in "real estate, financial, and professional services" grew by 75 percent between 1987 and 1997. In addition, advanced services accounted for nearly a third of all new employment in the Federal District in the second half of the 1990s. Amounting to 8.6 percent of the city's total formal employment in 1997, advanced services employed about half as many people as did manufacturing (INEGI, various years [a]; Fideicomiso 2000: 51–57, 60). Finally, headquarters returned to the capital in the 1990s. In 1998, 213 of the Mexican Top 500 were located in the Federal District (up from 145 in 1989), while the state of Nuevo León, where Monterrey is situated, had 59 (up from 51 in 1989), and Jalisco, housing Guadalajara, had 40 (the same as it had in 1989) (*Expansión*, 21 July 1999).

During the process of recovery, the city underwent two major socioeconomic transformations. First, its economic profile was changed. Until the 1970s trade and manufacturing were the most important sectors. By 1999, "municipal, social, and personal services" dominated (30.4 percent of the capital's GDP), followed by "trade, restaurants, and hotels" (21.4 percent), "manufacturing" (19.6 percent), and "finance, insurance, and real estate" (19.0 percent). Already in 1993 the Federal District had become, according to the Coefficient of Local Specialization, highly specialized in services related to finance and insurance, and, to a lesser degree, in professional services (INEGI 2001b; Garza and Rivera 1994: 67, 73f, 90f, 106–110; Iracheta Carroll 1999: 118f). Second, economic recovery was reached at the expense of employment and social standards. Though employment grew throughout the 1990s, it grew slower than the Mexican average, resulting in a further decrease of Mexico City's share in national employment. In particular, manufacturing did not recover its capacity to generate employment. Industry, which provided more than 50 percent of formal employment in the ZMCM in 1980, employed only 20 percent of all (formally) occupied people in 1999 (Aguilar 1996: figs. 8.1, 8.2; Cárdenas Solórzano 1999: 239).

Economic recovery was also obtained at the expense of income. In general, real wages in Mexico have declined severely in the last two decades, losing 43 percent of their purchasing power from 1980 to 1998. Real minimum wages shrank even more by 60.5 percent (Dussel Peters 2000b: 72). Yet, the decrease was even more pronounced in the Federal District. Though in 1980 real minimum wages paid in the capital were about 20 percent higher than the national average, this difference had almost disappeared by the second half of the 1990s (Boltvinik 1995: 37; Cárdenas Solórzano 1999: 246). Furthermore, ever greater numbers of people worked in the unregulated informal economy, where work tends to be poorly paid. Although by the very nature of the informal economy it is difficult to assess exactly how many people work there, some studies (of the International Labour Organization [ILO], for example) estimate that the number might reach up to 50 or 60 percent of the economically active population— a sharp increase since the 1980s. Even the National Institute for Statistics, Geography, and Computer Sciences (INEGI) points out that the number *and* the share of people who work under precarious conditions increased notably in the 1990s. For example, 50 percent of the workers in the ZMCM have no welfare benefits. It is interesting to note that various indicators suggest that informality is higher in Mexico City than the national average (*El Universal,* 31 March 1997; Delgado Selley 2000; OECD 1999; INEGI 1999: 56; INEGI, various years [a]; Cárdenas Solórzano 1999: 243–245).

As to social polarization, data on the income structure of the employed population in the ZMCM (INEGI, various years [a]) have to be analyzed carefully because the INEGI does not reflect on the loss of the real value of wages.

Yet this loss is a decisive factor, since a person earning five times the minimum wage in 1999 in reality obtained only slightly more real purchasing power than did a person earning twice the minimum wage in 1987. If this sharp contraction of real wages is taken into account, the notable decrease of people earning less than double the minimum wage between 1987 and 1999 (from 83.6 to 56.1 percent) does not mean that the actual share of people earning incomes below the poverty line really declined. On the contrary: taking five times the minimum wage as the income necessary to purchase the basic basket of goods at the end of the 1990s, compared to twice the minimum wage in the mid 1980s (*La Jornada*, 27 December 1996; *El Financiero*, 21 January 2000), the share of the employed population that obtained incomes below or up to the poverty line increased slightly (from 83.6 in 1987 to 85 percent in 1999). On the other extreme of the income scale the group with the highest earnings grew, although it remained very small (amounting to 2.8 percent in 1993). Thus, in terms of earnings, a trend toward polarization can be identified, though this trend is not very strong. However, data on the income distribution among households of Mexico City point to a somewhat declining inequality during the first half of the 1990s. The richest tenth obtained 34.6 percent of all income in 1996, compared to 39.5 percent in 1989. Conversely, the poorest 30 percent of the urban population expanded their share from 8.9 to 10.1 percent (INEGI, various years [b]). However, this result has to be taken carefully since some distortion might result from the fact that city-related data for the 1980s are missing. This decade was, at least on the national level, one of pronounced growth of inequality (CONAPO 1999: 154). Thus, it is likely that despite a decrease in inequality in the first half of the 1990s, the level was still higher than in 1980.

The labor market, too, shows rising inequalities. Aguilar (1996: fig. 10) identified a growing polarization between jobs at the top and at the bottom of the hierarchy for the period between 1970 and 1990. This tendency seems to have continued through the 1990s, although in an altered and less pronounced way. Between 1992 and 1998, petty traders and street vendors, a group that certainly corresponds to the bottom of the labor market hierarchy, expanded their share of total urban employment by 5 percent. By doing so, this segment of the labor market grew faster than any other sector (INEGI, various years [a]).[9]

A final transformation happening in Mexico City that is worth mentioning is the turnaround regarding migration patterns. Mexico City, which has been the most important destination of migrants for decades, turned—in only one decade—into the country's main sending area. The migration balance of the ZMCM became negative in the second half of the 1980s, amounting to a net loss of 223,700 people (Parnreiter 1998: 118–130).[10] In other words, Mexico City grew not because of immigration, but despite emigration. Population growth was driven only by birthrates being higher than mortality. Most researchers (Porras Macías 1997: 43, 62–65; Gómez de León Cruces and Partida Bush 1996: 17) expect the trend toward emigration to have continued in the 1990s, although maybe to a lesser extent than in the 1980s. As a consequence, between 1980 and 2000, the combined share of the state of Mexico and the Federal District (that is, in essence, the share of Mexico City) of all internal migrants shrank from 47 percent to 40.2 percent. Federal states attracting a growing number of migrants are Baja California and Chihuahua in the North, Morelos and Puebla in the country's center, and Quintana Roo in the Southeast. The emergence of new patterns of migration becomes even more evident if one excludes intraurban mobility from data and focuses on migration balances instead of gross immigration, in which case the most important destination for internal migrants between 1985 and 1990 was Baja California, followed by Chihuahua and Quintana Roo. The state of Mexico came in fourth, and the Federal District had, as already mentioned, a negative migration balance (Parnreiter 1998: table A-11, A-14).

DEBT CRISIS AND THE END OF IMPORT SUBSTITUTION

The loss of Mexico City's share of national GDP and employment and the emergence of new migration patterns may, to a certain extent, be seen as decentralization of the country's economy and population. In fact, since the 1970s, Mexican governments had elaborated various plans to promote more balanced development. However, in the opinion of many researchers the defacto decentralization that happened in the 1980s cannot primarily be attributed to these plans (Pradilla Cobos 1993: 39; Hiernaux Nicolás 1995: 158; for a different position see Ward 1998: 45). Some authors maintain that diseconomies of scale (e.g., high land prices, traffic jams, or pollution) affected industries with high consumption of land, water, and infrastructure, which might have forced them to relocate in nearby states in central Mexico or in the northern border region (Bataillon 1992: 79; Davis 1993: 79f).

The most important changes contributing to the decrease of Mexico City's share of the national GDP in the early 1980s are the definite end of import substitution and the crisis that accompanied the transformation to an outward-oriented development. Data previously mentioned suggest that the first half of the 1980s was particularly critical to the ZMCM. In addition, evidence shows that Mexico City was harder hit by the crisis than other cities. This may be surprising, given that Mexico City was the unchallenged "epicenter" of the Mexican economy, with a rather developed and diversified economic base, above national average levels of productivity, and considerable foreign investment (Garza 1985).

The immediate cause of the crisis was that indebtedness had grown so high by 1982 that Mexico could no longer pay interest. However, this bankruptcy did not arise from simple insolvency. Rather, 1982 marked the definitive end of import substitution and thus can be seen as a watershed in Mexican history. Problems with import substitution had become apparent by the 1970s. Thanks to the oil boom in the second half of that decade and the fact that foreign credit was easily available and rather cheap at that time,[11] the Mexican government disregarded the first signs of serious economic problems. When terms of trade for oil worsened to the disadvantage of Mexico and when interest rates in the United States increased drastically in the early 1980s, Mexico could not meet its obligations (Arrighi 1994: 322–324; Dussel Peters 2000b: 45–48).

Though import substitution was relatively successful through the decades, it never developed a base for intensive growth. Rather, it had to rely on extensive growth, meaning a steady increase of inputs. In the 1970s, agriculture slid into a profound crisis, making it unable to generate enough export revenue to pay for manufacturing imports. Industry itself lost its capacity to achieve productivity gains; plants and technology became obsolete. Consequently, the Mexican economy could not generate the amount of exports and therefore foreign currency necessary to finance imports. Thus, inflation increased, problems in the balance of payments became notorious, and indebtedness rose drastically (Pradilla Cobos 1993: 15–25; Dussel Peters 2000b: 45–48).

Why was Mexico City hardest hit by the collapse of import substitution? Economic crises, like growth, entail and produce a phenomenon of social and spatial unevenness. In general, branches hardest hit by crisis are construction, durable consumer goods, and capital goods, whereas nondurable consumer goods fare better in times of recession. Uneven impacts of the crisis on different economic sectors have their spatial expression because they affect different cities to a different extent. Since nearly two-thirds of industries producing durable consumer goods and capital goods were located in the ZMCM, Mexico City was hit harder than other Mexican cities (Garza 1985: 408–420; Garza and Rivera 1994: 11–14).

The reorientation of the economy toward foreign markets further deteriorated Mexico City's position. With production gearing to exports, domestic markets lost importance, devaluing the large urban agglomerations first as markets and then as production sites. In the neoliberal model, the masses aren't needed as consumers as much as they were during the era of import substitution. As workers, the population came under pressure because economic success depends on rationalization of economic activity and gains in productivity. Moreover, wage reductions that were crucial for becoming competitive in the world market reduced domestic purchasing power, additionally contributing to the devaluation of domestic markets. By far the biggest market, Mexico City was hardest hit by these developments (Connolly 1993: 66). Moreover, the strong impact of the crisis on Mexico City is explained by the fact that precisely because it has been the epicenter of the Mexican economy, restructuring started there. New technologies and innovation in organizing production were introduced first in the ZMCM (Aguilar, Graizbond, and Crispin 1996: 187), which resulted, at least in the first years, in high social and economic costs.

The severe crisis that Mexico (City) suffered as a consequence of the collapse of import substitution was more than a "national" phenomenon. Its "global" character is seen, first, by the fact that many countries had similar problems. Import substitution collapsed practically everywhere within only a few years.[12] Second, import substitution never was separated from the world market. It was only the severe crisis of world capitalism between the late 1920s and the end of World War II that opened the way for peripheral states to implement import substitution strategies. Though these were quite successful in some respects (e.g. the production of consumer goods), when it came to capital goods it became evident that dependency on imports of technology and of capital could not be overthrown (Thorp 1998). Indebtedness grew, with well-known consequences. First World bankers also created indebtedness of Third World countries. Because of a structural crisis of the world system, investment in industries in core countries became less profitable in the 1970s. One consequence was that overabundant capital was channeled as credit to Third World countries, which turned out to be a boomerang only a few years later. In sum, the argument can be launched that the breakdown of import substitution was a worldwide phenomenon, closely linked to the structural crisis of the capitalist world system. This crisis caused the end of the specific Fordist arrangements from the 1950s to the 1970s in the centers of the world economy, and it caused the end of "incomplete Fordism" or import substitution in the peripheries (Amin et al. 1982; Frank 1990: 26; Arrighi 1994: 322–324; Altvater and Mahnkopf 1996: 405–409).

ECONOMIC RECONCENTRATION AND THE MAKING OF A GLOBAL CITY

The 1980s were, as shown in table 1, a period of economic decentralization that occured in the northern border region and the so-called "crown cities" of Mexico City in the central region (Parnreiter 2000). Yet, the obvious weakening of economic and demographic primacy of Mexico City does not point to decentralization. The notion of a "polarization reversal" (Richardson 1980) can be doubted for several reasons.

First, decentralization occurs in the form of concentrated deconcentration (Aguilar 1999: 392) or polycentric metropolitan concentration (Garza 1999: 166). The weakening of Mexico City's primacy is offset—totally, in demographic terms and partly, in economic terms—by the growth of cities in the wider metropolitan area. A dense and complex regional division of labor is emerging in the center of Mexico that consists of seven federal states (Federal District, state of Mexico, Hidalgo, Morelos, Puebla, Querétaro, Tlaxcala), of which the most important cities are (besides Mexico City) Toluca, Pachuca, Cuernavaca, Puebla, Querétaro, and Tlaxcala. Mexico City is functionally tied to these other cities through the flows of people, goods, capital, information, and so on (Delgado, Anzalso, and Laralde 1997; Pradilla Cobos 1997; Aguilar 1999; Garza 1999).

Second, the strong economic growth of cities in the northern border states suggest that instead of becoming more decentralized, the Mexican urban system is partially disintegrating. Economic and demographic growth in border cities such as Tijuana, Ciudad Juárez, or Reynosa was strongly pushed by export manufacturing. Yet the maquiladora industry represents, at least to some extent, the case of a denationalized industry, because more than three-fourths of its production value corresponds to imports of intermediate products. In fact, low-skilled labor is the only important Mexican contribution to the maquiladora industry. In addition, production of the maquiladora industry is designated nearly exclusively for exportation. It seems therefore reasonable to assume that cities whose economic growth is driven by the maquiladora industry are more closely related to the U.S. city-system than to its Mexican counterpart. Investment, machinery, managers and supervisors, advanced producer services, and so forth come from United States cities, and a majority of exports go there. That means that some of the most prosperous cities of Mexico became—at least partially—detached from the national urban system (Parnreiter 2000).

The most important argument against the notion of a 'polarization reversal' is the fact that a new form of centrality is emerging that has Mexico City as its nodal point.[13] However, this new form of centrality cannot be identified by traditional indicators for urban primacy such as population size, gross data on GDP, employment or output of manufacturing. Spatial decentralization of GDP (and in particular of manufacturing) and of population might well be accompanied by the recentralization of specific activities, namely economic command and control functions, which is suggested by the above-mentioned growth of advanced producer services in Mexico City. From that perspective one could argue that the Federal District is taking on global city functions.

Location Patterns of Headquarters

A first step to study the relationship between the new dynamic of Mexico City's economy and global functions is a closer analysis of the location patterns of the most important firms registered in Mexico. The results can be summarized as follows: the greater a firm's sales volume and the stronger its links to the global economy in terms of exports, imports and foreign capitalization, the higher the probability that its headquarters are in the Federal District (see table 2).

Regarding sales, 70 percent of the top ten Mexican companies had headquarters in the Federal District in 1998, compared to 42.6 percent of the top 500. Mexico City's dominance emerges even more clearly by including the communities of the state of México that belong to the ZMCM, in which case half of the biggest 500 companies have their main offices in Mexico City. The only other Mexican state with a significant number of main offices is Nuevo León, with its capital, Monterrey.

Since the primary concern of this article is Mexico City's global links, export orientation and foreign capital participation are among the most meaningful facts about the location of company headquarters. Companies dominated by international capital are much more likely to locate in Mexico City than are Mexican-owned private firms. Breaking the top 500 Mexican firms down according to whether they are Mexican-owned private companies or have mostly foreign capital, different location strategies emerge. Whereas 39.4 percent of companies with primarily private Mexican capital have their main offices in the Federal District, 58.3 of the foreign-controlled corporations have their headquarters there. This trend increases with the size of the firm and if one considers the whole metropolitan area (ZMCM). For example, 78.9 percent of internationally controlled companies among the top 100 firms are based in Mexico City. Regarding foreign trade (except for the maquiladora industry)[14], the results show the same tendency: Mexico City is strongly preferred for headquarters, and the preference increases the more a company exports or imports. Nine of the ten biggest export firms are located in the Federal District, and 73.4 percent of the exports of the 100 biggest export companies (again excepting the maquiladora industry) originate in the Federal District, a huge lead over Nuevo León (11.5 percent).

To sum up, the Federal District is where the biggest Mexican companies prefer to set up their headquarters. This preference increases with: 1) sales volume; 2) foreign capital participation; and 3) export production. The location of main offices in the Federal District points to a close link between the city's economy and the global economy. The data suggest that transnational companies situated in Mexico and Mexican companies capable of adapting to the world market and becoming "global players" prefer to locate their headquarters in the Federal District. Consequently, the Federal District has global city functions insofar as it is where the Mexican economy (or at least parts of it) become globalized. In that sense, Mexico City's loss of manufacturing employment suggests that deindustralization fits into a new division of labor, in which the ZMCM specializes in functions commonly attributed to global cities, while other cities in central Mexico and the U.S. border region expand manufacturing.

In this context it is important to note that the high concentration of headquarters in the Federal District does not translate into concentrated production

TABLE 2

LOCATION PATTERNS OF MAJOR FIRMS REGISTERED IN MEXICO, 1998 (PERCENT)

	Federal District	State of México	ZMCM[a)]	State of México Minus ZMCM	Nuevo León	Jalisco	Other States
Top 500 in sales	42.6	9.4	50.0	2.0	11.8	8.0	28.2
Top 100 in sales	59.0	2.0	61.0	-	23.0	4.0	12.0
Top 10 in sales	70.0	-	70.0	-	20.0	-	10.0
Top 300 in exports	43.0	11.6	51.3	3.3	12.3	6.6	26.3
Top 100 in exports	54.0	2.0	56.0	-	24.0	3.0	17.0
Top 10 in exports	90.0	-	0.0	-	-	-	10.0
Top 300 in imports	44.3	10.6	51.6	3.3	14.6	5.6	24.6
Top 100 in imports	52.0	1.0	53.0	-	24.0	4.0	19.0
Top 10 in imports	80.0	-	80.0	-	10.0	-	10.0
Firms with > 50% private national capital in the top 500 (sales) (n=413)	39.4	8.2	46.7	0.9	13.5	8.4	30.0
Firms with > 50% private national capital in the top 100 (sales) (n=80)	53.7	2.5	56.2	-	27.5	2.5	13.7
Firms with > 50% private national capital in the top 10 (sales) (n=4)	50.0	-	50.0	-	50.0	-	-
Firms with > 50% foreign capital in the top 500 (sales) (n=84)	58.3	14.2	66.6	5.9	3.5	5.9	17.8
Firms with > 50% foreign capital in the top 100 (sales) (n=19)	78.9	-	78.9	-	5.2	10.5	5.2
Firms with > 50% foreign capital in the top 10 (sales) (n=5)	80.0	-	80.0	-	-	-	20.0

Source: Author's calculations, based on *Expansión* 1999: Las empresas más importantes de México.
Note: Along with maquiladoras, the three state-owned enterprises listed among the 500 most important Mexican firms are not included in table 2. Petróleos Mexicanos (Pemex), the biggest firm registered in Mexico, has its headquarters in the Federal District, while the other two state-owned enterprises, which are of minor importance, are located in Baja California Sur.

and employment. Instead, the big firms have spread their production across various cities in the country, maintaining only specific segments in Mexico City. This points to the city's role as a central node in the international and regional division of labor.

The Mexican branches of General Motors, Daimler-Chrysler, Volkswagen, Ford and Nissan are, for example, leading enterprises in terms of sales, exports, and foreign investment. All but Volkswagen have their headquarters in the Federal District, yet production plants are spread all over the country. Although Mexico City is not totally negligible as a manufacturing site, most automobile production takes place either in central states (state of Mexico, Guanajuato, Aguascalientes, and Morelos), or in northern border states (Coahuila and Chihuahua). The same applies to the computer industry, a fast growing sector with massive exportations to the United States. IBM, which came to Mexico City in 1957, shifted its plants to the state of Jalisco in 1975, leaving only its main office in the Federal District. Future research should analyze the links between production sites, the regional headquarters in Mexico City, and foreign cities, where the capital, specific services or semi-finished products might come from. That would indicate the world economic network or commodity chain into which headquarters articulate Mexican production.

Regional Distribution of Foreign Investment

As previously stated, both FDI and portfolio investment grew significantly as a consequence of the opening of Mexico's economy. In fact, global capital flows represent one of the most important links between the Mexican and the world economy. In 1998–99 Mexico was, behind China, Hong Kong, Brazil, and Argentina, the fifth-largest recipient of FDI among Third World countries (UNCTAD 2000). Both FDI and portfolio investment are highly concentrated in the Federal District. Between 1994 and 1999, $29.4 billion or 60.3 percent of all FDI went to the Federal District (see table 3). Though the minor increase compared to the period from 1989 to 1993 (59 percent) might result from privatizations of state-owned companies (and might therefore not be sustainable), it is remarkable that the share of the Federal District remained at a very high level despite the significant growth of FDI directed to maquiladora industry. It is striking that *together* the six northern border states, which contain 86 percent of all maquiladora production (Bendesky 2000), attracted only 29.2 percent of FDI—less than half the share of FDI invested in the Federal District. Mexico City's dominance is even greater if one considers that most of the FDI in the State of Mexico may have been directed to firms located in the ZMCM. In that regard, Mexico City's share was nearly two-thirds of all FDI. Portfolio investment data on regional distribution are lacking, but it is likely that here the concentration in the Federal District is even higher than for FDI since the stock

TABLE 3

DISTRIBUTION OF FOREIGN DIRECT INVESTMENT IN MEXICO, 1989–1999 (PERCENT)

	1989	1990	1991	1992	1993	1989–1993	1994	1995	1996	1997	1998	1999	1994–1999
Federal District	51.7	58.7	67.0	56.4	61.1	59.0	74.0	58.4	67.5	55.0	48.1	51.3	60.3
Nuevo León	3.8	13.7	0.6	0.9	7.2	5.2	8.7	8.3	4.3	20.4	5.0	3.9	9.8
Baja California	3.4	1.0	1.8	2.7	3.9	2.6	2.2	6.6	5.6	5.7	9.7	16.4	6.5
Chihuahua	3.1	0.6	0.5	2.6	0.6	1.5	2.9	6.5	7.1	4.2	7.9	10.5	5.8
State of Mexico	7.4	5.7	8.8	8.7	6.0	7.3	3.1	7.5	5.6	2.3	9.7	1.5	4.7
Tamaulipas	4.5	1.2	1.7	1.0	1.0	1.9	3.3	4.8	4.5	2.5	4.7	8.2	4.1
Jalisco	2.9	2.9	6.1	4.6	2.4	3.8	0.6	1.4	2.4	1.5	3.2	6.0	2.3
Others	23.2	16.2	13.5	23.1	17.8	18.7	5.8	6.5	3.0	8.4	11.7	2.2	6.5

Source: Author's calculations based on SECOFI for the period 1989-1993 and on Dussel Peters (2000a: 91-94) for the period 1994–1999. Data for 1999 are provisional. FDI includes new investment plus investment in maquiladoras. Because of the change in methodology for measuring FDI, the absolute numbers before and after 1994 are not comparable. However, since the purpose of this article is to show the regional distribution of FDI, a comparison can still be made.

market and the headquarters of all major banks—and hence their accounting departments—are located in the capital.

However, not all capital that enters the Federal District is necessarily invested there. For example, a transnational corporation that makes a "greenfield investment" may set up a new plant anywhere in Mexico, whereas that company's regional headquarters, which controls and services "local" production, is located in Mexico City. This applies to the biggest single investments of 1998–99. Daimler-Chrysler and Ford invested $1.5 billion each, but Daimler-Chrysler's resources went toward expanding an existing plant in Coahuila, whereas Ford spent its on building a new one in Chihuahua. The same principle applies to mergers and acquisitions. The U.S. brewing company Anheuser-Busch invested $556 million to buy 13 percent of Mexico's Grupo Modelo, which brews Corona. Grupo Modelo has its main office in the Federal District and has breweries in eight cities throughout the country (Dussel Peters 1999: table 11; CEPAL 2000: 77). In these cases foreign investment is entered in the Federal District (because accountancy is carried out there) and then redistributed to production sites throughout Mexico. As in the case of the headquarters, however, it is necessary to trace capital flows from the global investor to the local use. This would reveal an urban network in which different cities occupy different positions, tasks, and degrees of power. Key issues for future research include: 1) identifying the command-and-control linkages between headquarters in the Federal District and production facilities elsewhere in the country; 2) the spatial and sectoral distributions of investment; and 3) the role played in that division of labor by banks, financial institutions, and other services located in Mexico City.

Advanced Producer Service Sector

Both headquarters and FDI are not abstract economic "things." The Mexican branch of a transnational automobile company, a foreign investor buying assets from a formerly state-owned enterprise, a Mexican beer company catering to the U.S. market or a broker speculating on currencies—they all need to be serviced by accountants, tax and financial advisers, lawyers, advertising agencies, political consultants, and so on. In other words: The work of integrating (parts of) the Mexican economy into the global economy requires specific services. Yet, global city researchers emphasize not only that advanced producer services are crucial because they provide the means by which globalization is done, but also that many of these services (particularly the ones that are not routinized) concentrate necessarily in major cities because it is there that the creative milieu needed to develop them and the markets to trade them are to be found (Sassen 2001: ch. 5). Accordingly, in Mexico the advanced service sector should have both grown and strengthened Mexico City's position, and indeed, both have happened.

Between 1980 and 2000 the proportion of "finance, insurance, and real estate" in the Mexican GDP increased from 11 to 15 percent, and national employment in "real estate, financial, and professional services" grew by 45 percent between 1992 and 1997 (INEGI 2001b; INEGI, various years [a]). This growth was strongly concentrated in Mexico City. In 1999, 27.1 percent of the national GDP in the category of "financial services, insurance, and real estate" came from the Federal District, compared to 22.5 percent of the total GDP and 20.6 percent of GDP in manufacturing. The combined share of the Federal District and the state of Mexico (that is, in essence, Mexico City) amounted to 36.8 percent. It is remarkable that Mexico City's share in the national GDP in advanced producer services increased through the 1990s, while the share of the northern border region, which takes on increasingly more manufacturing, declined slightly (see table 4).

Similarly, employment in advanced producer services is concentrated to a high degree in Mexico City. In 1997 the ZMCM had 47.8 percent of all national employment in "real estate, financial, and professional services." Additionally, with 8.6 percent of formal employment, advanced services make

TABLE 4

REGIONAL SHARES OF NATIONAL GDP IN "FINANCIAL SERVICES, INSURANCE, AND REAL ESTATE," 1993–1999 (PERCENT)

	1993	1994	1995	1996	1997	1998	1999
Federal District	26.6	27.4	26.9	26.6	27.4	27.0	27.1
State of Mexico	9.0	8.9	9.1	9.4	9.4	9.7	9.8
Mexico City	35.6	36.3	36.0	36.0	36.8	36.7	36.9
Central region	43.4	44.0	43.7	43.7	44.4	44.3	44.5
Northern border region	20.3	20.1	20.3	20.0	19.5	20.0	20.2

Source: Author's calculations based on INEGI, Banco de Información Económica.

up a higher share of urban employment in the ZMCM than in any other major Mexican city (Guadalajara: 6.8 percent, Monterrey: 7.8 percent); thus they have a greater impact on the city's economic and social development. Also, Mexico City is the only Mexican city where productivity in advanced services is above the national average in all subbranches, while rival cities such as Monterrey and Guadalajara exceed the national average in no more than half the categories (Garza and Rivera 1994: 67, 73f, 90f, 106–110).

To sum up, the evidence clearly suggests that a new form of centrality is emerging. Mexico City concentrates most activities related to economic globalization even though its share of the national GDP and employment has decreased since the 1970s. The location patterns of headquarters, regional distribution of foreign direct investment, and distribution of advanced producer services indicate that the opening of the Mexican economy and the growing orientation toward global markets has intensified the concentration of activities essential to the globalization of the Mexican economy in the Federal District. Thus, as part of the production of globalization, Mexico City has changed from a national metropolis into a pivot between the Mexican and the global economies. In other words: Mexico City increasingly takes on global city functions. The articulation of export production (aside from the maquiladora industry) with the world economy, for example, is mainly organized and controlled from Mexico City. In a similar vein, capital flows to Mexico are channeled through the Federal District and in particular its service sector.

IMPOVERISHMENT, SOCIAL POLARIZATION, AND NEW PATTERNS OF MIGRATION

The traditional factory worker or public employee, who lost his or her job during the crisis of the 1980s, is very likely to be unable to find employment in the advanced service sector. Rather, he or she might be forced to emigrate to the United States or to work in Mexico City's growing informal economy to make a living. Thus, the new role assumed by Mexico City affects social arrangements as well as economic structure. A critical issue is the fact that economic recovery happened at the expense of most of the city's inhabitants. As stated previously, the last two decades were a time of impoverishment, and they were also a time of growing polarization of the labor market structure and of earnings.

Are impoverishment and polarization linked to the deeper integration of Mexico into the world economy and to the growing importance of global city functions within the economy of Mexico City? Evidence presented so far suggests that this is the case. First, it is obvious—and admitted by high representatives of the government—that substantial wage reductions were a crucial element in the country's course of neoliberal modernization and globalization, because cheapening production allowed Mexico to become more competitive in both the world and the domestic markets. Furthermore, wage reductions were an important cornerstone in the efforts to reduce inflation. Second, the recovery of the manufacturing sector was succeeded, at least partly, by reducing employment and/or by downgrading production to the informal sector. As pointed out, industrial employment stagnated although output grew in the 1990s, and work in the informal economy expanded at the expense of formal capital-labor relations. Third, the growing importance of services contributed both to impoverishment and polarization. In the service sector, more people than in the national average earned wages under the poverty line[15] (72 percent compared to 70 percent), and slightly more people were really well-off, earning more than ten times the minimum wage (3 percent compared to 2.8 percent). In contrast, manufacturing, which also had an above-average number of poorly paid workers, was underrepresented among the high-income groups, too. The majority of the well-off people in services worked in the subsector of the advanced producer services, making this branch the one with the highest number of people earning more than ten times the minimum wage. The increase in the numbers of petty traders and street vendors also indicates a polarizing structure of the labor market (INEGI, various years [a]). Thus, as a provisional conclusion one can assume that by strengthening links to the world economy, Mexico City experiences the worsening of social problems it already had before. This is concurrent with the findings of world city researchers, who argue that a growing informalization of the relations between capital and labor and a deepening of social polarization are characteristic processes of world city formation.

While social polarization and in particular its relationship to globalization needs to be studied further, the evidence on the impacts of globalization on the reorientation of migration flows is solid (Parnreiter, forthcoming). The emergence of new patterns of internal migration in Mexico, in which Mexico City is an area of net emigration and in which the northern states of Baja California and Chihuahua and the southern state of Quintana Roo became main destinations for migrants, is closely linked to the altered position of Mexico in the national and global economy. First, since the economic crisis reduced possibilities for employment and earning in Mexico City, people may have been motivated to leave the city for other places. The Federal District[16] recently has had a negative migration balance with most of the traditional sending areas, such as the federal states of Puebla, the state of Mexico,[17] Veracruz, and Hidalgo. Another option for people who wanted to leave the capital was the removal to nearby states such as Morelos, although in such cases people normally continued to work in the Federal District. Finally, emigration from Mexico City to economically more promising cities and to the United States became of increasing importance. The northern state of Baja California has rapidly gained importance as a destination for emigrants from Mexico City.

The second consequence resulting from the economic crisis is that Mexico City lost its attractiveness for internal migrants. Between 1980 and 1985, the ZMCM attracted 76,589 fewer migrants than ten years before, which means a reduction of more than 15 percent. Taking into account the growth of immigration in the new industrial cities in the North and in the centers of tourism in the South, this reduction very likely is attributable to the greatly reduced capacity of Mexico City to create employment. The demand for labor, which drew millions of migrants to Mexico City since the 1930s, did not serve as an engine of immigration anymore. Since the 1980s, new industrial workers were needed mainly in the North, and the workforce serving international tourism was wanted primarily in the South.

MEXICO CITY IN THE CROSS-BORDER NETWORK OF CITIES
Location Patterns of Global Firms in Advanced Producer Services
Although still tentative, evidence presented so far suggests that a specific set of structural transformations going on in Mexico City is linked to globalization and to the particular role of Mexico City in this process. Parts of the city engage increasingly in global activities, so that Mexico City, and in particular the Federal District, became a pivot between Mexico and the world market. In that sense we can speak of the making of a global city.

Support for this argument comes from various studies of the Globalization and World Cities Study Group and Network (Beaverstock, Smith, and Taylor. 1999a, 1999b, 1999c, Taylor and Walker 1999; Taylor 2000; Taylor et al. in this volume). Their review of fifteen of the most relevant publications on world cities shows that Mexico City is listed by six studies as a world city, ranking 21st among all cities cited. In order to achieve a refined hierarchy, the Globalization and World Cities Study Group and Network (GaWC) analyzed the location patterns of sixty-nine firms in four key service sectors (accountancy, advertising, banking/finance, and law) among 263 cities in 1997–98. Taylor and his colleagues identified 55 world cities. Mexico City[18] ranks 15th in this hierarchy, identified as a beta world city. It shares this position with Brussels, Madrid, and São Paulo, only narrowly behind San Francisco, Sydney, Toronto, and Zurich, but ahead of Washington, Miami, Berlin, or Shanghai. In an improved measurement, Mexico City is listed in 20th place—as the highest-ranked Latin American city. With a score of 12 percent in terms of world city functions (measured as the level of service provision of the mentioned sectors relative to the top scoring city), ahead of São Paulo (with 11 percent), Buenos Aires (6 percent), Caracas (6 percent), and Santiago (5 percent). Mexico City can be compared to cities like Zurich (11 percent), Johannesburg and Milan (13 percent each), and even Los Angeles (14 percent), which is a surprisingly high classification, given skeptical judgments such as "Mexico City's future as a world city is far from clear" (Friedmann 1995, 38).

The high ranking of Mexico City is based on the strong presence of global players among service firms. Mexico City qualifies as a major global service center for all four sectors (accountancy, advertising, banking and legal services), while São Paulo is a major global service center in three (advertising, banking, and legal services), and Buenos Aires only in one (banking). The fact that Mexico City houses many of the global service firms suggests that the Mexican capital is well embedded into the cross-border network of cities. Indeed, further evidence obtained by the research of the GaWC confirms this assumption. Firms in the advanced producer service sector that are located in London but operate on a global scale tend to have a high presence in Mexico City. In finance and banking, for example, there is a 93 percent probability that a global firm located in London has branch in Mexico City. Considering that only two cities show a higher probability of direct organizational links to London (New York and Tokyo) and that Mexico City, probality compares with only three cities (Buenos Aires, Hong Kong, and Singapore), Mexico City can in fact be considered as a strategic location for globalization processes. In advertising, the organizational links to London are slightly weaker—the likelihood that a London-located advertising firm has a branch in Mexico City amounts to 82 percent. In law the ties are still very weak—the probability for a London-located law firm to have a direct link to Mexico City is only 5 percent.

Addressing not only the presence of London-based firms, but the broader question of connections of cities to London by averaging across the four producer services (accountancy, advertising, banking/finance, and law), Mexico City comes in 15th place among fifty-four cities. Of course, the alpha world cities New York, Paris, and Tokyo (in that order) have stronger links to London, as do major European cities (such as Brussels, Frankfurt, Milan, and Madrid) and the Asian world cities Hong Kong and Singapore. Mexico City's connectivity to London is the same as São Paulo's and notably stronger than that of Buenos Aires. It compares to the linkages of Chicago, San Francisco, Washington, D.C., Dusseldorf, and Amsterdam. This is, again, a surprising result, underlining Mexico City's importance as a strategic site in globalization. The significance of having strong linkages to London gains weight when one considers that Mexico City has no historical ties to London (as Hong Kong and Sydney do) and forms part of a different regional bloc in the world economy (and hence is supposed to be more closely connected to U.S. cities).

In a similar vein, by analyzing geographical strategies of U.S. law firms in 1997, the GaWC identifies Mexico City as a strategic place in the cross-border network of cities. Eight of the 368 foreign offices of U.S. law firms, or 2.2 percent, are located there. This seems to be a rather negligible number. However, a closer look reveals that though the number is small, Mexico City still classifies high in location strategies of U.S. law firms. First, one has to take into account that the number of U.S. law firms in Latin America is unexpectedly low—twenty-three altogether, suggesting that this region cannot be considered as a major globalization arena. Second, out of these twenty-three offices, Mexico City houses eight. Thus, it is the only Latin American city with a significant presence of U.S. law firms. Third, Mexico City is the most important location worldwide for U.S. law firms outside the three areas identified by Beaverstock, Smith, and Taylor (1999a) as globalization arenas (western Europe, Pacific Asia, eastern Europe). Consequently, despite having only 2.2 percent of all foreign offices of U.S. law firms, Mexico City still ranks 11th in their location strategies.

The studies of geographical strategies of firms do not provide data on the actual transactions of companies. Additionally, the analysis of the relations of London-based service firms to other cities includes firms that might have their main office elsewhere in the world. For example, the three U.S. law firms with the most pronounced global strategies (Baker & McKenzie, White & Case, and Coudert Brothers) appear in the list of London-based global firms, although they are from Chicago and New York. This means that although we can conclude from the data cited that Mexico City is a rather prominent place in the geographical strategies of global service firms, we cannot guess where an international investor buys the services to conduct transactions. It might be in London, but it seems more probable that the investor would turn to the New York or Chicago headquarters or branch. Thus, the actual *space of flows* created by services remains a subject for further investigation as well, along with the place of Mexico City within it.

Interurban Telecommunications Networks

Connections among cities need to be built up. Interurban telecommunications networks are crucial to linking distant financial markets, firms offering advanced services, and offshore sites for manufacturing. The availability of ever more sophisticated, diverse, capable, and cheap telecommunications technologies has therefore become a key asset in the competition among cities to attract financial and corporate operations. Concurrent with the findings of the GaWC summarized here, a survey that classified the competitiveness of telecommunications provision in July 1998 in twenty-five major cities reveals that Mexico City is well integrated into the interurban telecommunications networks. Mexico City ranks 16th—better than any other Third World city and better even than Zurich or Singapore. While the pricing of services is still one of the biggest disadvantages of Mexico City, the availability of sophisticated connections and infrastructure were appraised in particular (Finnie 1998, cited in Graham this volume: T1).

The high ranking of Mexico City results from efforts undertaken in the last decade to build up an adequate infrastructure to compete in the world market. Privatization of the state-owned telephone company, Teléfonos de México (Telmex), in 1990 was a key step in this direction. The Mexican Grupo Carso and two major global players among telecommunications companies—Southwestern Bell and France Telecom—took control over Telmex. The latter two groups, despite having only 10 percent of the capital of Telmex, control 49 percent of the stocks. They were crucial to the expansion and modernization of telecommunications in Mexico because they provided the latest technologies.

In fact, in the time since the Mexican telephone company was "efficiently colonized by foreign owned telecoms operators" (Finnie 1998: 22), the infrastructure needed for secure, fast, and voluminous data transmission and hence for cross-border communication has expanded and improved rapidly. The number of telephone lines doubled to more than ten million between 1990 and 1999, and the quality of lines—an equal or even more important factor for efficient data transmission—improved substantially. In 1999, more than 97 percent of all lines were digitalized—up from 29 percent in 1990. In 1994, an electronic backbone consisting of two 2-megabit fiber-optic lines and several 64–kilobit lines was set up (and expanded since then), connecting the main Mexican cities to the United States. This infrastructure helped to expand conventional telecommunications (international calls, for example, grew by 436 percent between 1990 and 1998, reaching 737 million), and allowed Mexico to join the Internet. Since the first Internet connection in Mexico was put into place in 1989, infrastructure for and usage of Internet communication have expanded rapidly. In July 1999, the number of Mexican hosts totaled 224,239—up from 13,787 in January 1996. Mexico ranks second among Latin American countries in terms of both growth rates and the absolute number of hosts—surpassed only by Brazil—and it ranks 20th worldwide. Similarly, the number of Internet users increased from 94,000 in 1995 to more than 1.3 million in 1998. The development of the infrastructure was driven mainly by business interests; though the first internet users were universities, by now business-related users represent the majority—and their dominance is growing (56 percent in 1998, up from 51 percent in 1995) (COFETEL 1998a; 1998b; 1999a; 1999b; 1999c; Fernández 1995; Gutiérrez and Daltabuit 1999: 23; ISC 1999).

These data suggest a fast-growing integration of Mexico into the cross-border information flows. However, it is not the entire country that is part of the global telecommunications network. The upgrading of the Mexican telephone system and the new telecommunications infrastrucure reinforced an uneven geography of information flows. For example, more than 38 percent of all Mexican telephone lines are concentrated in Mexico City, which is twice as much as the city's share of the country's total population, and nearly a third of all international telephone calls are made in or received from Mexico City. More significant, however, is the fact that the Federal District is the central node of the national electronic backbone. Five 2-megabit fiber-optic lines meet in the Federal District, making Mexico City the best-connected city in Mexico. To transfer information between Guadalajara and Monterrey, for example, the Federal District must be involved, since there are no direct lines between those cities (COFETEL 1998a, 1999d; Iracheta Carroll 1999: 134; Red Tecnólogica Nacional 2000).

Centralizing infrastructure, Mexico City dominates the use of telecommunications. Though available data from the Matrix Information and Directory Services (MIDS 1999) on the distribution of hosts within Mexico are not very detailed—only orders of magnitude are reported—they do show huge differences in scale among Mexican cities. In January 1999, Mexico City was the only Mexican city qualifying for the category "100,000 to 1,000,000 hosts," making it one of the three telecommunications hubs in Latin America (the other two are São Paulo and Buenos Aires). Thus, Mexico City accounted for at least 50 percent of all hosts in Mexico, given that by that time there were slightly more than 200,000 hosts in the whole country. The centrality of Mexico City in the country's telecommunications network is shown as well by the fact that only one other city—Reynosa, surprisingly—counts between 10,000 and 100,000 hosts, while other major cities such as Monterrey, Puebla, Chihuahua, and Guadalajara have even fewer. In addition, the geographical unevenness of the telecommunications system is revealed by the fact that 60 percent of all Mexican municipalities did not even have *one* computer in 1995. In federal states like Oaxaca, Yucatán, San Luis Potosí, Chiapas, and Guerrero, between 93 percent and 71 percent of the municipalities lacked the very basic infrastructure to participate in electronic cross-border flows of information (Gutiérrez and Daltabuit 1999: 22).

Telecommunications are unevenly distributed within the city, too. Basically, both the 2-megabit fiber-optic lines and the 128- and 64-kilobit lines are centralized in five of the sixteen *delegaciones* (districts) of the Federal District—Álvaro Obregón, Miguel Hidalgo, Benito Juárez, Cuauhtémoc, and Coyoacán (Red Tecnológica Nacional 2000). That comes as no surprise given that the main banks and companies, the research centers and universities, and many governmental institutions are located in these districts. As a result, 72 percent of the Federal District's GDP in services originated in those five *delegaciones*, 49 percent of the GDP in trade, and 21 percent in manufacturing in 1993 (Iracheta Carroll 1999: fig. 3). That shows that the integration in global data flows is highly concentrated both spatially and in terms of economic sectors. Thus, integration of Mexico into global data flows basically means that a few areas of the Federal District that house the service sector are becoming part of the cross-border telecommunications system.

Air Travel

Connections between cities are also established by air travel, which reflects the ways in which cities are linked by the movement of people. Analyzing air travel between twenty-two world cities between 1985 and 1997, David Smith and Michael Timberlake (in this volume; also Smith and Timberlake 1995) found that Mexico City belongs to the third of four tiers of world cities. Both in 1985 and 1997, it ranked 16th in the number of mutual relations with other cities in the network and in the strength of the connections. Mexico City is more central than Miami, Montreal, or Houston, but behind San Francisco, Chicago, Madrid, or Zurich. However, the margin to the second-tier cities is narrow.[19] Though its position in the network formed by air travel remained unchanged, Mexico City's power score (a term that Smith and Timberlake use in chap. 4 of this volume to measure intercity relations by air travel) increased notably. While in 1985 it amounted to 0.16, by 1997 the power score of Mexico City had grown to 0.29. This means that Mexico City significantly increased its share in global airline traffic, which points to growing integration in the global economy. The increase occured mainly in the second half of the 1980s—after Mexico joined GATT (WTO). NAFTA seems to have had no impact either in terms of ranking or in terms of the power score of Mexico City. Nevertheless, in very recent years international air travel to the airport of Mexico City increased by nearly 10 percent annually (Secretaría de Turismo 1998).

Regarding the spatial patterns of Mexico City's integration in the international air travel network, the extent to which U.S. cities dominate is remarkable. In 1997, slightly more than two-thirds of all international passengers came from or flew to U.S. cities (67.8 and 67.2 percent, respectively). About 12 percent of the passengers came from or flew to Europe, and about 11 percent connected to

Latin American cities. The unevenness of the integration of Mexico City into the international air travel network can be illustrated by the fact that there was more air passenger travel between Mexico City and Los Angeles (amounting to 13 percent of all passengers) than between Mexico City and all European or between Mexico City and all Latin American cities. After Los Angeles came Houston, Dallas, Miami, New York, and Chicago. Madrid ranks 7th, while San José, the top-ranked Latin American city, does not figure among the top 10. In terms of air cargo, the dominance of U.S. cities is not as impressive, although still strong. Fifty-five percent of all freight originating in Mexico City went to U.S. cities, with Los Angeles (17 percent) again being the most important destination, followed by Miami and New York. European cities together amounted to a share of 22 percent (Paris is the most important one, followed by Frankfurt), while Latin American cities remain relatively unimportant as destinations of cargo from Mexico City (13 percent)—an amount that corresponds to only 75 percent of the cargo flown to Los Angeles. In terms of cargo flights to Mexico City, U.S. cities are less outstanding—42 percent of all freight came from there, compared to 36 percent of European and 16 percent of Latin American cities. Miami is the most important city of origin (13 percent), followed by Paris, Amsterdam, and Los Angeles (Iracheta Carroll 1999: fig. 4–7).

The finding that Mexico City is a rather central place in the network of cities formed by air travel corresponds to the cited studies on advanced producer services and on telecommunications connections. However, though airline data provide good estimates of connections between cities established by the movement of people, they fail to grasp the qualitative difference of links established by different kinds of passengers, such as businesspeople, tourists, and migrants. In the Mexican case a good part of the huge volume of flights to and from U.S. cities may in fact arise from migrants moving between the two countries and not from representatives of corporations or of national Chambers of Industry and Commerce. Indeed, the new airline Taesa basically came into existence to serve the migrant market, and the airlines Mexicana and AeroMexico have added flights in response. In this context it is interesting to note that Los Angeles is not only by far the most important city in terms of air passenger travel, but also houses more than a fourth of recent Mexican immigrants to the United States. Nearly half of all recent immigrants headed to five cities—Los Angeles, Chicago, New York, Houston, and Phoenix (Durand, Massey, and Kao 2000: table 4), representing more than a third of passenger air travel. Although most of the migrant flights do not originate in the Federal District but in cities to the west, such as León, Guadalajara, Zacatecas, and San Luis Potosí (Douglas Massey, pers. com.), Mexico City became more important as a sending area for migrants to the United States in recent years (Durand, Massey, and Zenteno forthcoming). Thus, both the amount and the spatial pattern of passenger air travel between U.S. cities and Mexico City might be influenced by migration.

If that were true, one would have to deal with a different quality of connections than in the case of, for example, air travel between London and New York. Yet, this does not mean that data on air travel of migrants are irrelevant to the question of connections between cities. On the contrary, the export of labor is one of the most important mechanisms of the integration of Mexico into the global economy, and Mexican emigrants have created firm links between Mexico and the United States. These connections might even surpass trade or foreign investment in economic significance (Hinojosa Ojeda, McCleery and de Paolis 1998: 3). Thus, the air travel data on Mexico may not refer to people who are 'greasing the wheels of production, finance or commerce through face-to-face contact' (Smith and Timberlake 1995: 296), but instead to Mexican men and women who grease those wheels by *really* greasing machines, digging ditches for advanced telecommunications cables, or cleaning bathrooms. Nevertheless, this data supports the argument that Mexico City is highly connected to U.S. cities.

WHICH PLACE IN THE GLOBAL URBAN NETWORK?

Given the evidence that clearly shows that Mexico City is indeed assuming world city functions and that the city is well integrated into the cross-border urban network, two questions arise. First, do the functions that Mexico City carries out in and for the world economy exceed the national territory and economy? Differently put, is Mexico City a regional center for Central America? Second, to which other world cities is Mexico City linked, and what is, in terms of power relations, the nature of these connections?

In Latin America, there are five cities identified by the GaWC as world cities: Mexico City, São Paulo, Buenos Aires, Caracas, and Santiago. Since a majority of Latin American countries do not possess world cities, their access to the specialized knowledge of advanced producer services has to be cross-border. Could it be, that in the case of Central American and Spanish-speaking Caribbean countries, that Mexico City is the place where these services are bought? Evidence available suggests that that may not be the case. According to Taylor (2000), "where the region is the Americas, New York is the centre but where Latin America is a designated region then Miami is the centre." This argument is based on the fact that six out of eleven London-based major producer service firms have their regional office in Miami, which makes that city the clear regional center even though it is not a particularly important world city in its own right. Nijman (1996) reaches the same conclusion. Although Miami does not play an important role either on the national scene in the United States or in trade relations with most of the world's regions, it is the dominant city for U.S.–Latin American connections. In the early 1990s, the city handled more than a third of all U.S. trade with Latin America, and the tendency was growing. For Central America and the Caribbean the share was even higher (47 and 43 percent, respectively). Yet, it is crucial to note that these data *exclude* Mexico. Regarding U.S.–Mexican trade, Miami virtually plays no role—it handles less than 1 percent. Thus, one can assume that the reach of Mexico City as a global city does not exceed the national economy and territory, given that Miami seems to be the central node for the rest of Latin America. On the other hand, regarding the articulation of Mexico into the world economy, Miami is not involved. Consequently, in that case the main node is Mexico City.

From this conclusion, some questions for future research can be derived: Which cities have the most important links to the Federal District, and what is the nature of the links? Future investigations should focus mainly on financial flows and on commodity chains. Financial flows are, without any doubt, one of the most important mechanisms to tie Mexico and Mexico City to the global economy. In this regard, the Federal District is intimately linked to—and dependent on—the New York stock exchanges. Any "adjustment" of the Dow Jones would have serious effects on the Mexican financial system and on the government's current account, on investments and on monetary policy, on interest rates, and on the budget. Yet, the link to New York might not be the only one. What other stock markets, for example, list Mexican companies?

Second: Although the Federal District specializes in organizing, controlling, and servicing foreign trade (except the maquiladora industry), we know little about other cities involved in commodity chains that connect Mexico to the world market. It is highly probable that the majority of these links are with U.S. cities, since 80 percent of Mexico's foreign trade is with the United States (CEPAL 2000: 105). The same applies for oil exports, which still matter for Mexico, despite their shrinking share of the export market (about 8 percent by the end of 2000 [Banco de México 2001]). The headquarters of the national oil company Pemex is located in the Federal District, with connections to the oil-producing states (like Campeche in the southeastern part of the country). Again, it is a subject for further research to identify other cities involved in the commodity chain—from trade partners to places where the oil prices are fixed.

Regarding the nature of the integration of Mexico City into the cross-border urban system, links that connect cities can be distinguished by form and function, and also by power-related characteristics such as frequency, strength, importance, or dominance/subdominance (Smith and Timberlake this volume). Because links between cities are not even, power relations among cities—and nation-states—are crucial. Indeed, global city research investigates not only the connections among cities, but also the question of influence and hegemony among these cities. For Sassen, global cities are "highly concentrated command points in the organization of the world economy" (2001: 3), and Knox states that they are "powerful centres of economic and cultural authority within the contemporary world-system" (1995: 7). While global functions and power may be rather similar in cities like New York, London, or Tokyo, in Third World cities there is a marked inconsistency between function and power. Although Mexico City carries out important tasks in globalization processes, it is obvious that it can by no means compare to the power exercised in New York.

Although a study of power-related characteristics of cross-border links between Mexico City and other world cities is lacking, some general indications can be given. For example, in the mid-1990s the Mexican stock market attracted only 0.005 percent of the capital invested worldwide in stocks and bonds, and its turnover was only 1.6 percent of that realized on the New York Stock Exchange—a stock market to which the Mexican financial market is pegged (*La Jornada*, 15 April 1997, 24 August 1997; *El Financiero*, 14 April 1997). This quantitative dimension reflects, to a certain extent, a qualitative order—namely one of subordination. The Federal District as a financial center, and Mexico as an economy and as a state, are highly dependent on and vulnerable vis-à-vis the floating global capital. Both dependency and vulnerability are present in everyday life as shown by the financial crash in 1994–95, various devaluations, the contraction of wages, the sustained economic instability, and so on.

The uneven distribution of power in intercity relations can be illustrated further by the fact that half of the biggest firms (in terms of sales and of exports) located in the Federal District are actually local headquarters of transnational corporations. In order to refine our knowledge of power-related characteristics of the cross-border links between Mexico City and other world cities, we should know to what extent decisions concerning the Mexican branch of these companies are met (or at least influenced) by the local offices. Likewise, we should know the kind of services these corporations bring with them (and hence obtain in other cities) and the ones that are acquired locally. Of the global players (companies among the world's Top 500 listed by *Fortune* magazine), only one has its "real" headquarters in Mexico City—the (still) state-owned oil company Pemex. Among firms with headquarters in the Federal District and dominated by private national capital, only a limited number operate on the world market. Among them are, for example, Telmex, Carso, Bimbo, Cintra, Desc, Modelo (*Expansión*, 21 July 1999; Chudnovsky, Kosacoff, and López 1999: 174–179).

Uneven power relations indicate that Mexico City is not just another world city. The fact that the terms "First World" and "Third World" are not appropriate anymore to describe the geography and social hierarchy of the world—if they ever were—does not imply that "center" and "periphery" have become pointless terminologies. On the contrary, as socioeconomic categories that shape the world system's hierarchy, center and periphery still exist. They have undergone significant changes, however. In the era of globalization, center and periphery are produced and reproduced increasingly on a global and a local scale. That makes it more complicated to indicate a place for Mexico City in the global hierarchy. On the one hand, evidence presented clearly suggests that the Federal District is no center in global terms. On the other hand, Mexico City does have core areas (and people and activities) that form part of the cross-border network of cities. Thus, one might call Mexico City a "relay" global city—oriented to and dominated by one, probably two, powerful pole(s) and linked to other "relay cities" (compare Braudel 1986: 22–33). 'Relay cities' like Mexico City (or São Paulo or Buenos Aires, etc.) are, as a group and as a category, indispensable for the whole system to exist. As shown for Mexico City, they not only transmit global flows but rather generate globalization on their own. However, as single, individual cities, relay cities may be nonessential—unlike the alpha world cities identified by the GaWC.

GLOBAL PLACES IN MEXICO CITY

Though evidence clearly suggests that Mexico City is becoming a world city, it is not the whole urban agglomeration that is inserted into cross-border flows. What one observes is the making of a global city *in some parts of the city*—which does not enclose the historical center that is dominated by public services and informal street vendors. Thus, the transformation of Mexico City into a global city implies not only the emergence of new forms of centrality, but also the creation of new spaces of centrality within the city (Terrazas 2000)—the five *delegaciones* of the Federal District that were noted earlier in this chapter for their communications infrastructure. It is in these districts that nearly two-thirds of the capital's GDP and three-fourths of its GDP in services are produced, where the vast majority of companies with headquarters in the Federal District can be found, where the conversion of the use of urban space toward services is most pronounced, where infrastructure for global telecommunication is centralized, where most private investment is directed to, where many of the urban megaprojects (like shopping malls or modern office complexes) are (going to be) realized, and where prices for land and real estate are the highest (Fideicomiso 2000; Terrazas 2000).

However, the "new center" needs the urban peripheries (in economic, social, and spatial terms) because they are functionally linked to the core. An indigenous woman living in a poor neighborhood like Valle de Chalco and working as a *muchacha* (domestic servant) in a banker's household in Las Lomas is attached to the global, as is a street vendor who sells branded articles. Both contribute in a specific niche to the reproduction of global capitalism. Though rich studies on the links between the informal and the formal economy exist (see, for example, Benería and Roldán 1992), we need more research to establish whether the transformations that Mexico City is undergoing create a section of society which is functionally irrelevant to the system—as Castells (1991: 213) contended was true for whole states.

CONCLUSION

Five main conclusions can be drawn from this article. First, the specific way in which the city—and the country—are integrated into the international division of labor matters. For example, the character of the severe crisis that hit Mexico City in the 1980s can be understood only by taking into account the impacts resulting from the crisis of global capitalism. Thus, a purely urban or national approach is inadequate to grasp the recent economic, social, and spatial transformations in Mexico City. Second, Mexico City is a crucial part of the cross-border network of cities. The Federal District is well integrated into global flows of capital, services, information, and people, fulfilling global city functions and working more and more as a pivot between the national and the global economies. Consequently, one indeed observes the making of a global city. Third, this specific role of Mexico City in the global economy affects the urban economy, society, and space. Though not all changes can be attributed to the making of a global city, recent transformations such as the boom in producer services are closely linked to globalization processes. Fourth, although evidence presented here supports the argument that Mexico City is (becoming) a global city, the challenge is still to prove it. Most, if not all, of the issues touched upon here need to be investigated further to verify, modify, or falsify the main hypothesis. Consequently, this article includes not only the evidence available but sketches out an agenda for future research. Fifth, and concluding, since there is much more to Mexico City than a huge urban agglomeration, one should reconsider the concept of megacities. On the one hand, this term is highly problematic because it alludes so strongly to large population size, which leads, vice versa, to a neglect of qualitative new urban dynamics. On the other hand, global city research provides, as shown in this article, very useful tools which could help us to deepen our knowledge of the major cities of the Third World.

NOTES

The author thanks the Institute for Advanced Study, United Nations University (Tokyo) for its support, and the Center for Advanced Study in the Behavioral Sciences (Palo Alto, CA), for hosting one of the meetings of the research network. The author also thanks the Fonds zur Förderung der Wissenschaftlichen Forschung (Vienna) for granting him an Erwin Schrödinger Auslandsstipendium to the University of Chicago; the Globalization Project and the Transnationalism Project of the University of Chicago for their support; and Enrique Dussel

CHRISTOF PARNREITER

Peters, Peter Feldbauer, Gustavo Garza, Adolfo Gilly, Emilio Pradilla Cobos, and Saskia Sassen for their comments on a previous version.

1. Mexico City refers to the whole Metropolitan Area (Zona Metropolitana de la Ciudad de México [ZMCM]). The ZMCM is formed by the Federal District, which is the country's capital, and forty-one communities (*municipios*) of the surrounding state of Mexico, which have grown together with the Federal District. Nearly half of the city's overall population of 17.9 million live in the Federal District (Garza 2000: fig. 4.2.1).

2. For very rich empirical studies consult the webpage of the Globalization and World Cities Study Group and Network: http://www.lboro.ac.uk/departments/gy/research/gawc.html

3. As early as 1976 Walton called for a change in the perspective of research on Third World urbanization, arguing that it is largely shaped by economic forces operating cross-nationally. For early studies applying a global approach, see Timberlake 1985, Armstrong and McGee 1985, and Drakakis-Smith 1986.

4. For more detailed accounts, see, for example, Dussel Peters 2000b.

5. The numbers are the author's calculations based on Banco de México 2001; INEGI 2001b; and Cárdenas 1999: 90. It is interesting to note that the balance of trade, which was positive in the 1980s, became strongly negative in the 1990s, and that the current account, which was already negative in the 1980s, deteriorated markedly in the 1990s (INEGI 2001b; Dussel Peters 2000b: 73). Dussel Peters therefore speaks, contrary to the official rhetoric that calls the present model "export oriented," of an "import-oriented industrialization" (2000b: 110). In addition, the increase of exports should not lead to the assumption that the Mexican economy prospered in the last two decades. The GDP growth rate is much lower than during the era of import substitution, and GDP per capita increased only very slightly.

6. Maquiladoras are in-bond industries geared to foreign markets (mainly the United States), which are generally located in the northern border region and which process imported semifinished products to reexport them.

7. Author's calculations based on Banco de México 2001.

8. Given the lack of data on Mexico City, we have to get along by adding together the GDP of the Federal District and the state of Mexico for a reasonable approximation of Mexico City's GDP (see note 1).

9. It is important to add that in a time of growing social inequality, Mexico City is experiencing political opening. After decades of direct control by the president of the Republic, the nation's capital got an Assembly of Representatives of the Federal District in 1988, which was later transformed into the Legislative Assembly of the Federal District. Citizens of the Federal District were given possibilities for formal participation by law (*Ley participación ciudadana* [1998]), and governance is becoming somewhat decentralized. In July 1997, for the first time since 1928, the capital's citizens were able to directly elect their chief executive officer (formerly an appointee or "regent" of the president). Yet, it still remains to be seen whether the fading away of patronage, corporativism, and clientelism (which, although far away from being democratic, provided some sort of social reconciliation and political control) is followed by a system allowing for real participation and democratic control.

10. Migration data presented by the INEGI include movements between the Federal District and those communities belonging to the state of Mexico that are physically tied to the Federal District. Thus, intraurban mobility within Mexico City is counted as migration. Once these statistical distortions are corrected, the net emigration from the ZMCM is considerably lower than that quoted by INEGI (for a recalculation, see Parnreiter 1998: 118–130).

11. This was mainly due to an oversupply of the dollar. In the words of Arrighi: "First World bankers (were) begging Third World States to borrow their overabundant capital" (1994: 323).

12. São Paulo, for example, experienced a crisis very similar to that of Mexico City (Tolosa 1998: 214–216).

13. In a similar vein, studies on South Africa and Brazil point to a reinforcement of both Johannesburg's and São Paulo's position due to globalization (Beavon 1998: 363f; Tolosa 1998: 217–219).

14. There seem to be no direct links between Mexico City and the maquiladora industry. Between 1993 and 1999, 77 percent of this industry's production value corresponded to imports, and only 23 percent was value added in Mexico. Of this rather small segment, 51 percent corresponded to wages (overwhelmingly to blue-collar workers), 13 percent to profits, 8 percent to packing and raw materials, and 27 percent to other factors such as property, energy, transportation, and so on (Bendesky 2000). The low value added in Mexico and its structure show that low-skilled labor is the only important Mexican contribution to the industry. That suggests that the necessary specialized services (e.g., financial or legal) are imported, presumably from the United States.

15. Data are for 1993; the poverty line is defined by earnings of three times the minimum wage.

16. Data on the whole ZMCM are not available.

17. The migration balance with the most important sending state, the state of Mexico, is negative at a very high level (-468,069). However, due to the complexity of the spatial situation (the state of Mexico forms part of the ZMCM) this figure is misleading. Yet, excluding intra-urban mobility, the migration balance of the Federal District with the state of Mexico is still negative (-9,695)

18. The Globalization and World Cities Study Group and Network does not distinguish between Mexico City and the Federal District. It is likely that the data cited refer to the Federal District rather than to the whole urban agglomeration.

19. Unfortunately, São Paulo is not included in the data on air travel between 1985 and 1997. In an earlier article Smith and Timberlake (1995) ranked it 22nd—markedly behind Mexico City.

REFERENCES

Aguilar, Adrián Guillermo. 1996. "Reestructuración económica y costo social en la Ciudad de México. Una metrópoli periférica en la escena global." Ponencia presentada en el Seminario Economía y Urbanización: Problemas y Retos del Nuevo Siglo, organizado por el Instituto de Investigaciones Económicas, UNAM, en la Unidad de Seminarios 'Dr. Ignacio Chávez', May 22.

———. 1999. "Mexico City Growth and Regional Dispersal: The Expansion of Large Cities and New Spatial Forms." *Habitat International* 23 (3): 391–412.

Aguilar, Adrián Guillermo, Boris Graizbord, and Álvaro Sánchez Crispín. 1996. *Las ciudades* intermedias y el desarollo regional en México. Mexico City: Consejo Nacional para la Cultura y las Artes.

Altvater, Elmar and Birgit Mahnkopf. 1996. *Grenzen der Globalisierung. Ökonomie, Ökologie und Politik in der Weltgesellschaft.* Munster, Germany: Westfälisches Dampfboot.

Amin, Samir, Giovanni Arrighi, André Gunder Frank, and Immanuel Wallerstein. 1982. *Dynamics of Global Crisis.* New York: Monthly Review Press.

Armstrong, Warwick and T. G. McGee. 1985. *Theatres of Accumulation: Studies in Asian and Latin American Urbansization.* London: Methuen.

Arrighi, Giovanni. 1994. *The Long Twentieth Century: Money, Power, and the Origins of Our Times.* London: Verso.

Banco de México. 2001. "Indicadores Económicos y Financieros." http://www.banxico.org.mx/eInfoFinanciera/FSinfoFinanciera.html (March).

Bataillon, Claude. 1992. "Servicios y empleo en la economía de la ZMCM." Pp. 79–83 in *Consejo Nacional de Población: La Zona Metropolitana de la Ciudad de México. Problemática actual y perspectivas demográficas y urbanas.* Mexico City: CONAPO.

Beaverstock, J. V., R. G. Smith, and P. J. Taylor. 1999a. "Geographies of Globalization: US Law Firms in World Cities." *GaWC Research Bulletin* 4, http://www.lboro/ac.uk/departments/gy/research/gawc.html4.

———. 1999b. "The Global Capacity of a World City: A Relational Study of London." *GaWC Research Bulletin* 7, http://www.lboro/ac.uk/departments/gy/research/gawc.html7, edited and posted on the Web on July 28, 1999.

———. 1999c. "A Roster of World Cities." *Cities* 16 (6), 445–458.

Beavon, Keith. 1998. "Johannesburg: Coming to Grips with Globalization from an Abnormal Base." Pp. 352–387 in *Globalization and the World of Large Cities*, ed. Fu-Chen Lo and Yue-Man Yeung. Tokyo: UNU Press.

Bendesky, León. 2000. "La industria maquiladora." *La Jornada*, January 25, p. 17.

Benería, Lourdes and Martha I. Roldán. 1992. "Las encrucijadas de clase y género. Trabajo a domicilio, subcontratación y dinámica de la unidad doméstica en la ciudad de México." México City: El Colegio de México, Fondo de Cultura Económica.

Boltvinik, Julio. 1995. "La Satisfacción de las Necesidades Esenciales en México en los Setenta y Ochenta." Pp. 17–77 in *Distribución del Ingreso y Políticas Sociales*, ed. Luis Alberto Ganza and Enrique Nieto. Tomo I. Semenario Nacional Sobre Alternativas Para la Economía Mexicana. Mexico City: Juan Pablos Editor.

Braudel, Fernand. 1986. *Sozialgeschichte des 15.-18. Jahrhunderts. Aufbruch zur Weltwirtschaft.* Munich: Kindler.

Cárdenas, Enrique. 1999. "Lecciones recientes sobre el desarrollo de la economía mexicana y retos para el futuro." Pp. 59–105 in *Banco Nacional de Comercio Exterior: México: Transición económica y comercio exterior.* Mexico City: Bancomext / Fondo de Cultura Económica.

Cárdenas Solórzano, Cuauhtémoc. 1999. *Segundo informe de gobierno. Anexo Estadístico.* Mexico City: Gobierno del Distrito Federal.

Castells, Manuel. 1991. "Die zweigeteilte Stadt—Arm und Reich in den Städten Lateinamerikas, der USA und Europas." Pp. 199–216 in *Die Welt der Stadt.* München.

Chase-Dunn, Christopher K. 1985. "The System of World Cities, 800 A.D.–1975." Pp. 269–292 in *Urbanization in the World-Economy*, ed. Michael Timberlake. Orlando, FL: Academic Press.

Chudnovsky, Daniel, Bernardo Kosacoff, and Andrés López. 1999. *Las multinacionales latinoamericanas: sus estrategias en un mundo globalizado.* Mexico City: Fondo de Cultura Económica.

Comisión Económica para América Latina y el Caribe (CEPAL). 2000. "La inversión extranjera en América Latina y el Caribe." Santiago, Chile: CEPAL.

Comisión Federal de Telecomunicaciones (COFETEL). 1998a. "Estadísticas de Interés sobre Telecomunicaciones: RTN: Backbone + Nodos regionales." http://www.cft.gob.mx/html/5_est/graficas/img038.gif

———. 1998b. "Estadísticas de Interés sobre Telecomunicaciones: Conferencias de larga distancia." http://www.cft.gob.mx/html/5_est/ graficas/Graf4_pag6.html

———. 1999a. "Estadísticas de Interés sobre Telecomunicaciones: Líneas Telefonía en Servicio y Densidad Telefónica." http://www.cft.gob. mx/html/5_est/celulares/usumincel.html

———. 1999b. "Estadísticas de Interés sobre Telecomunicaciones: Porcentaje de Digitalización de la Planta Telefónica." http://www.cft.gob.mx/html/5_est/graficas/Graf3_pag5.html

———. 1999c. "Estadísticas de Interés sobre Telecomunicaciones: Usuarios estimados de Internet en México" http://www.cft.gob.mx/html/5_est/Graf_internet/estiminternet_01.html

———. 1999d. "Estadísticas de Interés sobre Telecomunicaciones: Lineas Residenciales, Comerciales y Totales." http://www.cft.gob.mx/html/5_est/graficas/lcomres.html

Connolly, Priscilla. 1993. "La reestructuración económica y la ciudad de México." Pp. 45–70 in *Dinámica urbana y procesos socio-políticos. Lecturas de actualización sobre la Ciudad de México*, ed. René Coulomb and Emilio Duhau. Mexico City: UAM-Azcapotzalco.

Consejo Nacional de Población (CONAPO). 1999. "La situación demográfica de México." Mexico City: CONAPO.

Davis, Diane E. 1993. "Crisis fiscal urbana y los cambios políticos en la ciudad de México: desde los orígenes globales a los efectos locales." *Estudios Demográficos y Urbanos* vol 22, no. 8 (1): 67–102.

Delgado, Javier, Carlos Anzaldo, and Adriana Larralde. 1997. "Mexico City: Towards a City-Region Formation." Paper presented to the International Geographical Union Conference: Urban Development and Urban Life, Mexico City, August 8–11.

Delgado Selley, Orlando. 2000. "Resultados macroeconómicos y nivel de vida." *La Jornada*, January 28.

Drakakis-Smith, David, ed. 1986. *Urbanisation in the Developing World.* London: Routledge.

Durand, Jorge, Douglas S. Massey, and Grace Kao. 2000. "The Changing Geography of Mexican Immigration to the United States, 1910–1996." *Social Science Quarterly* 81 (1): 1–15.

Durand, Jorge, Douglas S. Massey, and René M. Zenteno. Forthcoming. "Mexican Immigration to the United States: Continuities and Changes." *Latin American Research Review.*

Dussel Peters, Enrique. 1999. "La inversión extranjera en México. Informe 1999." Documento elaborado para la Comisión Económica para América Latina y el Caribe (CEPAL). Mimeo.

———. 2000a. "La inversión extranjera en México." Serie Desarrollo Productivo 80. Santiago, Chile: CEPAL.

———. 2000b. *Polarizing Mexico. The Impact of Liberalization Strategy.* Boulder/London: Lynne Rienner .

Feldbauer, Peter, Erich Pilz, Dieter Rünzler, and Irene Stacher. 1993. *Megastädte. Zur Rolle von Metropolen in der Weltgesellschaft.* Vienna: Böhlau.

Fernández, Jeffry S. 1995. "Development of WWW Services in Mexico, toward a National Information Infrastructure." http//www.iooe.org/HMP/PAPER/035/html/paper.html

Fideicomiso de Estudios Estratégicos sobre la Ciudad de México. 2000. *La ciudad de México en el siglo XXI, 2010–2020.* Parte I. Mexico City: Fideicomiso de Estudios Estratégicos sobre la Ciudad de México.

Frank, André Gunder. 1990. "Politische Ironien der Weltwirtschaft." In André Gunder Frank and Marta Fuentes-Frank, *Widerstand im Weltsystem. Kapitalistische Akkumulation, Staatliche Politik, Soziale Bewegung,* pp. 13–45. Vienna: Promedia.

Friedmann, John. 1986. "The World City Hypothesis." *Development and Change* 17: 69–83.

———. 1995. "Where We Stand: A Decade of World City Research." Pp. 21–47 in *World Cities in a World System,* ed. Paul L Knox and Peter J. Taylor. Cambridge: Cambridge University Press.

Garza, Gustavo. 1985. *El Proceso de Industrialización en la Ciudad de México (1821–1970).* Mexico City: El Colegio de México.

———. 1999. "Global Economy, Metropolitan Dynamics and Urban Policies in Mexico." *Cities* 16 (3): 149–170.

———. 2000. "Ámbitos de expansión territorial." In *La Ciudad de México en el fin del segundo milenio.* ed. Gustavo Garza. Mexico City: El Colegio de México.

Garza, Gustavo and Salvador Rivera. 1994. *Dinámica Macroeconómica de las Ciudades en México.* Aguascalientes: Instituto Nacional de Estadísticas, Geografía y Informática.

Gilbert, Alan. 1992. "Urban Development in a World System." Pp 14–32 in *Cities, Poverty and Development: Urbanization in the Third World,* ed. Alan Gilbert and Josef Gugler. Oxford: Oxford University Press.

Gómez de León Cruces, José, and Virgilio Partida Bush. 1996. "La Ciudad de México: tendencia demográfica y escenarios para el siglo XXI." *Federalismo y Desarrollo* 9 (56): 12–17.

Graham, Stephen. 1999. "Global Grids of Glass: On Global Cities, Telecommunications, and Planetary Urban Networks." *Urban Studies* 36 (5–6): 929–949.

Gugler, Josef. 1999. "Introduction." Paper prepared for a National Academies Workshop on World Cities in Poor Countries. Washington D.C., October 27–28th.

Gutierrez, Fernando, and Enrique Daltabuit. 1999. "Mexican Cities in Cyberspace." *Cities,* 16 (1): 19–31.

Hiernaux, Nicolás Daniel. 1995. "Reestructuración económica y cambios territoriales en México. Un balance 1982–1995". *Estudios Regionales* 43: 151–176.

Hinojosa Ojeda, Raul, Robert McCleery, and Fernando de Paolis. 1998. "Economic effects of NAFTA: Employment and Migration Modelling Results." Paper prepared for the Seminar on Migration, Free Trade, and Regional Integration in North America, organized by the OECD and the Mexican authorities with the support of Canada and the United States. Mexico City, January 15–16.

Instituto Nacional de Estadísticas, Geografía y Informática (INEGI). 1999. "Estadisticas Económicas. Indicadores de empleo y desempleo." Aguascalientes: INEGI.

————. 2001a. "Censos Económicos 1999. Enumeración integral. Resultados definitivos." Aguascalientes: INEGI. http://www.inegi.gob.mx/ (February).

————. 2001b. "Banco de Información Económica." Aguascalientes: INEGI. http://www.inegi.gob.mx/ (March).

————. Various years (a). "Encuesta Nacional de Empleo Urbano." Aguascalientes: INEGI.

————. Various years (b). "Encuesta de Ingresos y Gastos de los Hogares del Area Metropolitana de la Ciudad de México." Aguascalientes: INEGI.

Internet Software Consortium (ISC). 1999. "Domain Survey. Distribution by Top-Level Domain Name by Host Count." http://www.isc.org/ds/WWW-9907/dist-bynum.html

Iracheta Carroll, Jimena del Carmen. 1999. "Las grandes ciudades en el contexto de la globalización: El caso de la Zona Metropolitana del Valle de México." Tesis para sustentar el título de Licenciado en planeación territorial. Toluca: Universidad Autónoma del Estado de México.

Katz, Isaac. 2000. "El impacto regional del tratado de Libre Comercio de América del Norte. Un análisis de la industria manufacturera." Pp. 133–176 in *TLCAN: ¿Socios Naturales? Cinco años del Tratado de Libre Comercio de América del Norte,* ed. Betaris Leycegui and Rafael Fernández de Castro. Mexico City.: Instituto Tecnológico Autónomo de México Miguel Ángel Porrúa.

Knox, Paul L. 1995. "World Cities in a World System." Pp. 3–20 in *World Cities in a World System.* ed. Paul L. Knox and Peter J. Taylor. Cambridge: Cambridge University Press.

Knox, Paul L., and Peter J. Taylor, eds. 1995. *World Cities in a World System.* Cambridge: Cambridge University Press.

Lo, Fu-Chen, and Yue-Man Yeung, eds. 1998. *Globalization and the World of Large Cities.* Tokyo: UNU Press.

Matrix Information and Directory Services (MIDS). 1999. "The Internet in Mexico." http://www.mids.org/mmq/602/mid/intbmx.html (January).

Nijman, Jan. 1996. "Breaking the Rules. Miami in the Urban Hierarchy." *Urban Geography* 17 (1): 5–22.

OECD. 1999. "Economic Surveys. Mexico." Paris: OECD.

Parnreiter, Christof. 1998. "Migration in Megastädte der Dritten Welt. Von der importsubstituierenden Industrialisierung zur Globalisierung. Erfahrungen aus Mexiko." Dissertation zur Erlangung des Doktorgrades an der Geisteswissenschaftlichen Fakultät der Universität Wien. Vienna.

————. 2000. "Globalization, Transformation, and Urban Primacy: Towards More Balanced Systems of Cities? Lessons from Latin America with Particular Emphasis on Mexico." Paper prepared for the conference of the International Geographical Union—the Commission on Urban Development and Urban Life, August 9–13, Seoul, Korea.

————. Forthcoming. "Free Trade and Changing Patterns of Cityward Migration: The Case of Mexico." In *Global Sustainable Development. Encyclopedia of Life Support Systems,* ed. Saskia Sassen and Peter Marcotullio. City: UNESCO.

Porras Macías, Agustín. 1997. "El Distrito Federal en la dinámica demográfica megalopolitana en el cambio de siglo." Pp. 37–73 in *Bases para la planeación del desarollo urbano en la Ciudad de México, Tomo I: Economía y sociedad en la metropoli,* ed. Roberto Eibenschuts Hartman Universidad Autónoma Metropolitana-Xochimilco, Mexico D.F:

Pradilla Cobos, Emilio. 1993. *Territorios en crisis. México 1970–1992.* Mexico: Red Nacional de Investigación Urbana y Universidad Autónoma Metropolitana.

————. 1997. "La Megalópolis Neoliberal: Gigantismo, Fragmentación y Exclusión." Ponencia presentada en el Congreso Internacional Ciudad de México, Sobre Política y Estudios Metropolitanos, organizado por el Consejo Mexicano de Ciencia Sociales, A.C., 10 al 14 Marzo.

Red Tecnólogica Nacional. 2000. http://www.infocentro.com.mx/ (February).

Richardson, Harry W. 1980. "Polarization Reversal in Developing Countries. Pp. 67–85 in *Differential urbanization. Integrating Spatial Models,* ed. H. S. Geyer and T. M. Kontuly. London: Arnold.

Sassen, Saskia. 2001. *The Global City. New York, London, Tokyo.* Princeton, NJ: Princeton University Press. (Second Edition. Originally published in 1991)

———. 1996. "Cities in the Global Economy." Paper presented at the UNU-Panel on Globalization and the Urban Future, June 7, Habitat II.

Schteingart, Martha, ed. 1991. *Espacio y Vivienda en la Ciudad de México.* México City: El Colegio de México.

Secretaría de Comercio y Fomento Industrial (SECOFI). N.d. "Dirección General de Inversión Extranjera." México D.F.

Secretaría de Turismo. 1998. "Estadísticas básicas de la actividad turística." México City.

Short, J. R., Y. Kim, M. Kuus, and H. Wells. 1996. "The Dirty Little Secret of World Cities Research: Data Problems in Comparative Analysis." *International Journal of Urban and Regional Research* 20 (20): 697–717.

Smith, David A., and Michael Timberlake. 1995. "Conceptualising and Mapping the Structure of the World System's City System." *Urban Studies* 32 (2): 287–302.

Taylor, Peter J. 1997. "Hierarchical Tendencies amongst World Cities: A Global Research Proposal." *Cities* 14 (6): 323–332.

———. 1999a. "So-called 'World Cities': The Evidential Structure within a Literature." *Environment and Planning A* 31 (11): 1901–1904.

———. 1999b. "Worlds of Large Cities: Pondering Castells' Space of Flows." *GaWC Research Bulletin* 14, http://www.lboro.ac.uk/departments/gy/research/gawc/rb/rb14.html

Taylor, Peter J. 2000. "World Cities and Territorial States under Conditions of Contemporary Globalization" *Political Geography,* 19, 1, 5–32.

Taylor, P. J., and D. R. F. Walker. 1999. "World Cities: A First Multivariate Analysis of their Service Complexes." *GaWC Research Bulletin* 13, http://www.lboro.ac.uk/departments/gy/research/gawc.html13

Terrazas, Oscar. 2000. *La red de la centralidad metropolitana en la globalización.* Mexico City.: Borrador de trabajo.

Thorp, Rosemary. 1998. *Progress, Poverty and Exclusion. An Economic History of Latin America in the 20th Century.* Baltimore: Johns Hopkins University Press.

Timberlake, Michael, ed. 1985. *Urbanization in the World-Economy.* Orlando, FL: Academic Press.

Tolosa, Hamilton C. 1998. "Rio de Janeiro as a World City." Pp. 203–227 in *Globalization and the World of Large Cities.* Tokyo: UNU Press.

United Nations Conference on Trade and Development (UNCTAD). 2000. "World Investment Report 2000. Cross-Border Mergers and Acquisitions and Development." Geneva: UNCTAD.

Walton, John. 1976. "Political Economy of World Urban Systems, Directions for Comparative Research." In *The City in Comparative Perspective, Cross-National Research and New Directions in Theory.* ed. J. Walton and L Masotti. New York: John Wiley and Sons.

Ward, Peter M. 1998. *Mexico City.* Rev. 2nd ed. Chichester, England: Wiley.

Chapter 6

THE HORMUZ CORRIDOR: BUILDING A
CROSS-BORDER REGION BETWEEN IRAN AND THE UAE

Ali Parsa and Ramin Keivani

There is now general cross-disciplinary consensus among urban researchers that national and regional economies are being integrated into a global network of production, distribution, and exchange at a pace that is unparalleled in history (Sassen 2001, 2000; Sykora 1994; Goodwin 1996; Knox 1996; Dicken 1994; Persky and Wiewel 1994; Badcock 1997; Lo and Marcotullio 2000; Godfrey and Zhou 1999; Short and Kim 1999). Indeed, while some writers have warned against overexaggeration of the shift to, and domination of, globalization at this particular historic juncture, the fact that such a process is occurring at unprecedented speed is itself not under question (Budd 1995). The internationalization of capital and its rapid movements across frontiers is now so extensive that it has become the main driving engine of the world economy, overshadowing the real economy of trade in goods and services (Hoogvelt 1997; Yeung and Lo 1996). This process, moreover, is supported by the technological information revolution, which greatly reduces spatial restrictions on both the "mobility of capital and information and importantly the centralized control of decentralized production" (Sykora 1994: 115).

Globalization processes and national responses to them have important consequences for urban form and development. Many national, regional, and local governments have responded by forming specialized organizations, such as development corporations and promotion and marketing agencies, and offering special incentives, such as tax holidays, in order to promote the development and regeneration of rundown areas and attract international investment.

While such actions have undoubtedly strengthened the relative position of individual regions and cities in the global market, it is becoming increasingly clear that the complexity of requirements of international capital is such that no individual region or city can compete in an optimal manner in the world economy. The post-Fordist world of flexible accumulation has eroded the past certainties of the Fordist production/location nexus based on heavy investment in fixed capital, mass production, scale economies, and flow line technology. In their efforts to secure international investment, countries and cities are today increasingly operating in conditions of changing comparative advantage. As a result, rather than relying solely on traditional concepts of comparative advantage in terms of lowest production costs or highest investment incentives, economies must gain and sustain their competitive advantage in a manner which complements the global strategies and networks of operations of modern transnational corporations (Yeung 1998). This implies creating urban alliances and economic synergies within and across national boundaries in order to channel different urban and regional strengths into accomplishing common economic advantages. The world of modern capitalism, in the words of Yeung and Lo, is "both a world wide net of corporations and a global network of cities" (1996: 20). As such, networking and complementary activity have become the key to economic success not only at the corporate but also at the city and regional levels (Yeung and Lo 1996; Gugler 1992; Gottmann 1991; Cooke and Morgan 1993).

This chapter expands on the literature by examining regional cross-border growth triangles/corridors and complementary function between cities. After a brief discussion of these alliances in those parts of Pacific Asia where they are most developed, we evaluate the development of such a corridor in the Persian Gulf region.

GROWTH CORRIDORS: LESSONS FROM THE EXPERIENCE IN PACIFIC ASIA

With the gradual disintegration of the old political and economic alignments, a defining feature of the emerging global economic order has been the formation of supranational economic organizations to promote regional economies in the face of stiff international competition and economic uncertainties (Parsonage 1992). The emergence of growth corridors in Pacific Asia reflects this trend.

A growth corridor may be defined as an area combining different factor endowments between the constituent parts in order to enable the optimum utilization of resources for developmental objectives. This would offer "a denser, multi-layered, and synergistic network based on world-wide air and telecommunication connections, thus allowing ever-expanding multinational enterprises (MNEs) to arrange production and distribution in smaller units to take advantage of the larger number of coastal and continental locations offered by the host states with good profit potentials" (Rimmer 1994: 1731).

ALI PARSA AND RAMIN KEIVANI

A major feature of this development in Pacific Asia has been the concentration of actual or proposed growth corridors along border areas of neighboring states. For this reason some observers have referred to a new form of borderland economic integration in the region leading not only to an intensification of traditional flows of people and trade across borders, but also to the diversification of economic activities to include a range of manufacturing and service functions (Ho and So 1997).

In comparison to the more formal regional trading blocs such as the European Union (EU) and the North American Free Trade Agreement (NAFTA), the borderland growth corridors of Pacific Asia are much more informal and modest. Moreover, these initiatives have mainly originated in and involve semiperiphery and periphery nations in the region without the direct involvement of core industrial countries. Furthermore, with the exception of city-states, they span only border provinces of the involved states and not entire nations. Unlike the EU and NAFTA they are not based on the exclusion of the rest of the world and formation of "fortress" internal markets. The respective states thus have much more political and economic autonomy. The essential ingredients here are proximity, complementarity, and a shared history. As such, the formation of these zones does not preclude other types of bilateral or multilateral ventures by the member states (Ho and So 1997). Chen writes:

> Instead of being co-ordinated through formal government treaties and agreements among member nations, the cross-national growth zones are new spatial-economic complexes that envelop contiguous border areas of national economies and are shaped by linked activities of private firms, with limited government involvement. They pertain to natural economic territories or natural strategic alliances and are defined by much less formality and autonomy of the member states than the other more conventional forms. (1995: 606)

There are at present many different areas in the Pacific Asia regions that have been designated as cross-border development corridors. The best-known and most active and successful examples are undoubtedly the Singapore-Johor-Riau Triangle, better known as the SIJORI Growth Triangle, and the Hong Kong–Guangdong Axis. In both cases the main impetus for the creation of the growth corridor or triangle arose from structural shifts toward higher-order export service, command, and control, and research and development functions within the dominant industrial nations, Singapore and Hong Kong respectively (Macleod and McGee 1996; Rimmer 1994; Parsonage 1992; Ho and So 1997). These shifts resulted in the necessary relocation of much of the older, traditional, low-value-adding industrial activities to other regions that had the requisite hinterland that Singapore and Hong Kong lacked. These relocations provided the incentive for the formation of cross-border growth areas. Moreover, these cross-border hinterlands provided cheaper and more plentiful materials and labor for expansion of industrial activity while at the same time benefiting from management and technical expertise as well as capital investment from Singapore and Hong Kong.

The cross-border investment areas have attracted not only large-scale relocation and investment from the participating countries, particularly the two city-states, but significant international investment. Between 1987 and 1989 there was a threefold increase in the amount of FDI in Johor state, to about U.S.$1 billion per annum; by the middle of 1990, that figure had risen even higher, to U.S.$2.5 billion (Macleod and McGee 1996). By the mid-1990s, not only had Johor become the second most important Malaysian industrial region after Klang Valley, but it had also become one of the most popular investment destinations in Asia. In 1990 the total amount of foreign investment in the two largest cities of Guangdong—Guangzhou and Shenzhen—amounted to about U.S.$666 million, of which an estimated 60 percent came from Hong Kong (Chu 1996).

One should note, however, that with the development of the infrastructure capacities in Johor and Riau as well as Guangdong, and increasing international investment straddling national boundaries, the bargaining position of Singapore and Hong Kong is likely to decrease. There is, therefore, the potential for Johor, Riau, and Guangdong to upgrade their current low-end functions to higher levels depending on future developments. The important point to note is that such cross-border economic activities can create competitors as well as partners.

There are also several other active or proposed variations modeled on the success of these two areas, involving other combinations of border areas from practically all other countries in the region. Included are Japan, Taiwan, Thailand, Vietnam, South and North Korea, Myanmar, Laos, Cambodia, the Philippines, the Russian Far East, and Mongolia.

It is generally accepted that a major reason for the widespread acceptance of the cross-border growth corridors in the region during the past decade has been a general decline in the perception of threats and political tensions (Rimmer 1994; Chen 1995; Parsonage 1992; Ho and So 1997). This is largely a result of the ending of the cold war, the Chinese open-door policy, and the formation of pan-Asian institutional frameworks for promoting economic and political cooperation. Coupled with the changed international economic situation—that is, the crucial importance of international investment for economic growth and development and stiff competition for attracting FDI—the changed political climate has created the space for economic considerations to become paramount in national and regional political thinking. There is therefore the possibility of overcoming historical rivalries, ethnic, religious, and ideological differences and territorial disputes in order to create the necessary conditions for attracting FDI-boosting endogenous economic activities.

THE BASIC ELEMENTS OF THE PACIFIC ASIAN CROSS-BORDER GROWTH CORRIDORS

The success of the studied cases in Pacific Asia is part of a result of very specific historical, social, and economic developments. For example, the role of ethnic Chinese capital and business networks in the region is unique and impossible to replicate elsewhere. Similarly, the existence of highly industrialized and transport-hub city-states such as Singapore and Hong Kong is also an occurrence unique to the Asia Pacific region. These city-states have been the driving force behind the formation of two of the most successful corridors, albeit largely as a result of their own need for restructuring their economies and upgrading their position in the network of global cities. To this must be added the role of regional capital and well-established global multinational corporations from Japan, South Korea, and Taiwan in the planning and formation of the cross-border growth corridors, particularly those at the higher regional and continental geographical scales. Last but not least is the role of Chinese labor, resources, and markets, which underpin much of the economic activity in the region.

Given these unique characteristics, such corridors clearly cannot be replicated in other regions wholesale. Nevertheless, we are of the opinion that crucial seeds are in place in the eastern Persian Gulf that could act as a basis for the development of a corridor, albeit one with more modest aims and objectives. This point can be illustrated by considering the most common characteristics of cross-national growth corridors in the Asia Pacific region. These are:

a) the existence of a large metropolitan base and a functionally complementary urban system that can anchor supporting economic activity within the global economic system. In this respect Yeung and Lo (1996) have proposed the idea of the development of a functional city system in Pacific Asia leading to the formation of urban corridors at the local and regional levels. These corridors connect the main urban regions at different geographical scales on the basis of their accumulated functions in the regional and global economies. The crucial element determining the importance of any city within the system is the range of key functions it can attract and provide in the global division of labor.

b) complementary factor endowments, comparative advantages. These might include:
   • industrial and high-technology base and capital by at least one partner in need of expansion and cheaper land and labor;

- a relatively high degree of existing economic cooperation, links, and trading, preferably historical;
- transnational, common, ethnic businesses, as in the case of ethnic Chinese capital in the growth triangles of East and Southeast Asia;
- close geographical proximity and cultural and linguistic contiguity;
- a relatively sophisticated infrastructural capacity to provide basic services, telecommunications, and transportation. Of particular importance are telecommunications, air, shipping, road, and rail links, potential hubs that facilitate global market activity.
- the establishment of an effective supranational governance structure capable of providing political and legislative support. An example of this is appropriate regulatory frameworks in support of international investment and economic activity.
- moves toward economic harmonization within the corridor, such as:
  1. elimination or reduction of tariffs;
  2. the streamlining and reduction of bureaucratic hurdles;
  3. trade liberalization;
  4. tax elimination or reduction;
  5. easy cross-border movement of people, capital, and information.

A major question that confronts us is to what degree the experience of Pacific Asia can be applicable to the Persian Gulf region. A definitive answer to this question requires detailed research on the economic, social, and political conditions of the region. Nevertheless, we are able to shed some light on the potential for a cross-border growth area by considering the basic elements of the Pacific Asian corridors in the new context of the eastern Persian Gulf region, specifically between southern Iran and the United Arab Emirates (UAE).

TOWARD THE FORMATION OF A CROSS-BORDER GROWTH CORRIDOR IN THE PERSIAN GULF REGION

The potential democratization of Iran in the late 1990s coincided with the reduction in regional tensions and rivalry and improvement in relations between Iran and the Arab states in the Persian Gulf. This furthered economic growth and enhanced interregional mobility and cross-border trade activities.

The Iranian economy has long been dominated by the oil sector, which produced about 76 percent of the country's total exports in 1998. Accordingly, the fortunes of the Iranian economy coincided with fluctuations in world oil markets (EIA 2000a). The GDP dropped from U.S.$120,404 million in 1990 to U.S.$113,140 million in 1998 because of sharp reductions in the price of oil (ICCIN 2000). Sharp increases in oil prices during 2000 will undoubtedly increase both the share of oil in the value of the total export and overall GDP. As part of

the efforts to encourage non-oil exports, particularly for attracting foreign investment and transit trade, a number of free trade and industrial zones as well as special economic zones (specially set up to promote transit and reexport trade) have
appeared mainly along the southern and northern border areas of the country.
Three of the largest and longest established areas are the Qesham and Kish Islands
free trade and industrial zones and the special economic zone of the Shaheed
Rajaee port close to the city of Bandar Abbas in the eastern Persian Gulf.

The United Arab Emirates

The Arab state in the Persian Gulf region that has experienced the most rapid
urban development is the United Arab Emirates (UAE), a confederation of seven
emirates established in 1971. The establishment of the UAE was a direct result
of diminishing British colonial power in the region and the increasing influence
of Iran in the 1960s and 1970s. Following the British announcement, in early
1968, terminating their agreements with the Trucial States by the end of 1971,[1]
the rulers of the seven emirates—Abu Dhabi, Dubai, Sharjah, Ras al-Khaimah,
Fujirah, Umm al-Qawayn, and Ajman—met to discuss their future. The establishment of the federal state (Taryam 1987) was more a reflection of their pragmatic desire for survival than for the creation of a unified structure within the
country—a point that becomes obvious when considering the competing interests of different rulers in preserving their own territorial and geographical sphere
of political and financial power within the context of a feudal structure
(Mojtahed-Zadeh 1996). The rapid growth of the UAE since its establishment
has been phenomenal. With increased accumulation of wealth the government
launched a massive program of urban expansion and infrastructural development.

With such massive development has come the need to import workers.[2]
Although indigenous population growth has been notable, large numbers of
semiskilled and unskilled migrant workers were imported from the Indian subcontinent of Asia, and skilled technical and managerial personnel from Europe
and North America. This set in place rapid urban expansion mainly in Abu
Dhabi, Dubai, and Sharjah, the larger of the seven emirates. Between 1975 and
1980 the population of the UAE almost doubled, increasing from 557,887 to
1,042,099. By 1995 the population had reached 2.4 million, and the 1999 population estimate was put at 2.8 million (World Bank 2000b). UAE growth in
population has been characterized by a high degree of urbanization; in 1999,
about 86 percent of the population lived in cities. The indigenous population
now accounts for only 20 percent of the total population. Table 1 provides a
breakdown of the population according to ethnic origin.

In 1995, out of a total workforce of 1.2 million in the UAE, 90 percent
were foreign (Government of Sharjah 1998a). The breakdown of population
according to specific nationalities is impossible because of the UAE's national

TABLE 1

COMPOSITION OF ETHNIC GROUPS IN THE UAE, 1982 AND 2000.

Ethnic Origin	1982[a] Estimates %	2000[b] Estimates %
UAE national	19	20
Other Arabs	23*	22
South Asian	50	50
Western and East Asian	8	8
Total	**100**	**100**

Sources: a. CIA World FactBook 2000; b. EIA United Arab Emirates 2000 (www.eia.doe.gov)

* Includes Persians

security considerations. The official statistics do not provide specific data, and the only sources of information are foreign. However, it can safely be assumed that the majority of the foreign population are from the Indian subcontinent (estimated at 1.5 million) (Hirst 2001). Of these, a very large share are workers, largely in manual jobs or engaged in trade and other commercial activities. Workers from the Philippines, Thailand, Indonesia, and China are mainly engaged in semiskilled and service sectors, while the more skilled and managerial workforce generally has an expatriate European or North American background. Many Arabic-speaking nationals from Egypt, Iraq, Syria, Palestine, Lebanon, and Africa are engaged in education, trade, and other business activities. Iranian workers, who, according to estimated figures number one hundred thousand (Hirst 2001), are largely involved in trade, commerce, and skilled crafts activities.

Economically, the UAE has undergone a profound transformation. It has an open economy with a high per capita income and a healthy annual trade surplus. The gross domestic product for 2000 was estimated at $63.2 billion and the trade balance at $9.5 billion (EIA 2000b). The GDP in 1998 was $47.2 billion, and in 1997, $42.8 billion (World Bank 2000b). GDP has historically been highly dependent on oil revenues, which provide 70 to 80 percent of fiscal revenue and account for roughly 30 percent of export earnings (U.S. Department of State 1999). Estimated oil revenues for the year 2000 were $20.7 billion (26 percent of the GDP) compared with $10.1 billion in 1998, an increase that reflects the impact of changing oil prices on the overall economy. At current levels of production, oil and gas reserves should last for more than one hundred years (CIA 2000). Despite this, the UAE government has embarked on economic diversification, shifting from dominance of oil toward reexports, services, and tourism. Among the three largest emirates, Abu Dhabi and Sharjah have the biggest oil and gas reserves. Dubai's oil reserves have

TABLE 2

POPULATION AND KEY ECONOMIC INDICATORS IN THE UNITED ARAB EMIRATES, 1995–1999.

	1995	1998	1999
Total population	2.3 m	2.7 m	2.8 m
Population density (people per sq km)	28.0	..	..
Population growth	2.4%	5.4%	3.3%
Urban population (% of total)	83.8%	85.1%	85.5%
GDP at market prices (current US$)	42.8bn	47.2 bn	41.5 bn*
GDP growth (annual %)	6.1 -5.7	2.5*	
GNP, Atlas Method (current US$)	45.3 bn	48.7 bn	
GNP per capita, Atlas method (Current US$)	19,340.0	17,870.0	..
Present value of debt (current US$)	..	15.5 bn*	

Sources: The World Bank Group 2000b, United Arab Emirates, Data Profile; Central Intelligence Agency—The World Fact Book 2000a. United Arab Emirates.

* Estimated

almost been exhausted, and the emirate has been particularly successful in diversifying its economy.

The Proposed Bandar Abbas–UAE Development Corridor

The proposed area comprises the port city of Bandar Abbas and islands of Qeshm and Kish in Iran and the main cities of the UAE situated on the Persian Gulf, particularly the three major cities of Sharjah, Dubai, and Abu Dhabi. The region however provides a direct gateway to a much larger market: the rest of the Middle East, north and northeast Africa, the Indian subcontinent, central Asia, the Caucasus, and Russia. Using the basic elements of growth corridors in Pacific Asia as a guiding framework, we shall examine the potential for development of such a corridor in this Middle Eastern subregion.

Existence of a large metropolitan area. The three main cities of Dubai, Abu Dhabi, and Sharjah provide an estimated combined population of 1.7 million, and the urban population is further increased by 271,000 people from the three smaller cities of Ajman, Ras al-Khaimah, and Umm al-Quwain, which also lie on the Persian Gulf shores of the UAE. Together with Bandar Abbas and the two Iranian islands of Qeshm and Kish, these provide a large metropolitan base with a combined population of about 2.3 million. In the UAE, the three main

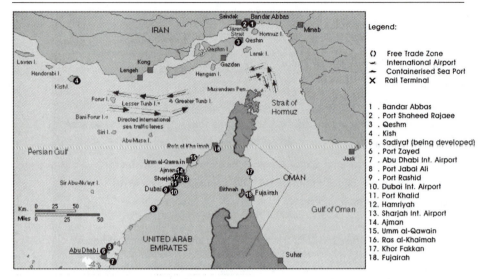

Legend:

()   Free Trade Zone
   International Airport
   Containerised Sea Port
X   Rail Terminal

1 . Bandar Abbas
2 . Port Shaheed Rajaee
3 . Qeshm
4 . Kish
5 . Sadiyat (being developed)
6 . Port Zayed
7 . Abu Dhabi Int. Airport
8 . Port Jabal Ali
9 . Port Rashid
10. Dubai Int. Airport
11. Port Khalid
12. Hamriyah
13. Sharjah Int. Airport
14. Ajman
15. Umm al-Qawain
16. Ras al-Khaimah
17. Khor Fakkan
18. Fujairah

Source: Adapted from map by M. R. Izady (The Gulf/2000 Project, SIPA, Columbia University)

cities contain around 74 percent of the urban population of that country while Bandar Abbas and Qeshm and Kish Islands have a small share of the urban population of Iran (about 0.8% of a total urban population of 38 million). However, Bandar Abbas and its port and rail facilities play an important strategic, administrative, and communication role in southern Iran. In the UAE, on the other hand, Abu Dhabi is the political capital with the strongest economy, based on vast oil resources. Dubai is the center of tourism, trade, and financial services, while Sharjah is the center for education and culture with a well-established economy based on oil and gas and regional trade and tourism.

Close geographical proximity and cultural and linguistic contiguity. All cities within the proposed growth corridor are located in very close geographical proximity. Bandar Abbas, the capital city for the Hormozgan province, on the northern coast of the Persian Gulf, is about 300 kilometers from the UAE on the southern coast of the Gulf. The flying time between Bandar Abbas and Dubai or Sharjah is approximately thirty minutes, and relatively well-developed ferry links between these urban centers cut transport by water to only a few hours. Moreover, there are frequent flights on well-established air routes between cities in the UAE and Iran.

The history of this region is mixed with the history and geography of the Persian Gulf. The Persian Gulf region was part of the Omavi (661–750) and then Abbasid (750–1285) Arab-Islamic Khalifate territory. From the very beginning of the formation of the Islamic Khalifates, the region has played a central role in facilitating trade and communication within the Khalifates and with other countries in North Africa and the Indian subcontinenet. As noted by Ibrahimi (2001), early Islamic geographers and historians such as Istakhri (951 AD) regarded the Persian Gulf and the Straits of Hormuz as the "centre of the world" emphasizing inter-connections among its cities and settlements as the main conduit for trade and communication in the entire Islamic world and beyond. From the 15th century onwards, various European colonial powers, including the Portuguese, Dutch, and British, competed with one another for dominance of the Persian Gulf region. In fact, the Portuguese directly colonized Hormuz and Qeshm Islands and built the modern port city of Bandar Abbas. The Portuguese presence in the region ranged from 1506 to 1635, when Shah Abbas I expelled them with English assistance (Amirahmadi 1996).[3]

Despite the close historical ties between the two regions, there is a lack of official linguistic congruity, with Arabic and Farsi as the official and dominant languages of the southern and northern parts of the Gulf, respectively. However, the years of close contact, particularly during the rapid development of the UAE, have led to large-scale migration from southern Iran. In some cases specific parts of a city in the UAE have been dominated by ethnic Iranians and historically known as such. An example of this is the Bastaki neighborhood in Dubai, which was named after its original inhabitants from the Bastak region of southern Iran (Boussa 2000). As a result, large numbers of the local population in the UAE, particularly Dubai, Sharjah, and Ras al-Khaimah, speak or understand variants of southern Iranian dialects such as Bandari or Bastaki. Moreover, many among the large Farsi-speaking Iranian immigrant community in the UAE, particularly Dubai, are now fluent in Arabic.

Infrastructural capacity and complementary endowments. There are six international airports in the UAE and two in Bandar Abbas and Kish Island. Qeshm Island also has a rapidly expanding international airport although at present its international flights are limited to the UAE.

There are frequent flights between the three main cities of the UAE (particularly Dubai and Sharjah) and Bandar Abbas, Qeshm, and Kish Islands in Iran (government of Dubai 2000). In addition, there are daily flights between Sharjah and Dubai and other Iranian cities, including Tehran, Shiraz, Mashad, and Bandar Lengeh. The available data on the number of passengers who flew between Iran and UAE show only those between Dubai and Tehran. In 1997, 130,857 passengers arrived in Dubai from Tehran—an increase of 50.9 percent since 1996. The number of passenger departures from Dubai to Tehran was calculated at 124,833 in 1997, which would be an increase of 48.2 percent over 1996 and would make Tehran eighth among the top ten destinations from Dubai. This compares with 137,998 passengers arriving in Dubai from Bahrain, and 82,407 from Jeddah (Saudi Arabia) both members of the Gulf Co-operation Council (GCC), showing an annual increase of only 3.7 percent and 32.6 percent respectively (Government of Dubai 2000). As noted earlier, however, this reflects only a part, albeit the majority, of air passenger traffic between the two countries. There are frequent scheduled daily flights between the UAE's three largest cities and Iran's Bandar Abbas, Kish Island and Qeshm Island by five different airlines. To this must be added flights between Tehran and Sharjah and Abu Dhabi as well as a few other Iranian cities and the UAE.

This should be viewed in the broader context of the region as a major gateway to the Middle East, Africa, Asia, and Europe. Before the Islamic revolution in Iran, Tehran was the major headquarters location for international companies operating in the region and was the only regional transport hub. Since the beginning of the 1980s however, Dubai has replaced Tehran as the major regional transport hub. This has been achieved as a result of continuous expansion, development, and modernization of Dubai International Airport. In 1997, the total number of passengers arriving, departing, and in transit at the Dubai airport exceeded 9 million, an increase of 13.7 percent over 1996 (Government of Dubai 2000). With the completion of the second terminal in April 2000, the airport's capacity was enhanced to 22 million passengers a year. A third terminal is planned that would increase capacity to between 40 million and 45 million by 2018.

In addition to Dubai, the Abu Dhabi and Sharjah international airports also play a major role in both passenger and cargo movement. Sharjah airport is the premier cargo handling and transit airport in the whole of the UAE, while at the same time gaining in importance in passenger traffic. The total number of passengers handled at Sharjah airport in 1998 was about 1 million, with 360,000 arrivals, 384,000 departures and 214,000 transit passengers (SAIF Zone 1999). Abu Dhabi airport, on the other hand, is a major regional transport hub in its own right, with forty-one international carriers having daily flights in and out of this airport. The other international airports in the region play a minor role representing only some regional passenger and cargo movements.

The available statistics for air travel do not reflect the full extent of passenger movement between Iran and the UAE. While there is accurate data for passengers arriving and departing from different cities in the UAE and Tehran, there are no specific data measuring the true extent of population movement between the different destinations. There are numerous charter flights from different locations in Iran to UAE cities and even more by traditional seagoing boats known as *Lenje* and through well-established shipping routes.

Internal communication and transport facilities in Iran are relatively well developed with an integrated rail network that links the strategic north-south from Tehran to Bandar Abbas and all major areas of the country. The rail network provides good links between the Persian Gulf and the newly independent states in central Asia, allowing reexport and transit of goods. This has been of immense benefit to the UAE for its main economic activity (i.e., reexporting to Iran, central Asia, and the Caucasus). To capture this trade traffic between UAE and the Southern CIS countries, Iran extended the rail line to Bandar Abbas and completed a line connecting Mashad and the Republic of Turkmenistan.

On the other hand, the UAE's interest in domestic travel shows primarily in its well-developed road system, with little attention given to domestic air transport routes, despite the fact that all emirates have modern airports (U.S. Department of State 1999). The limited number of flights that do occur between Abu Dhabi and Dubai are by one or two international carriers, which is the case by default rather than by design. A private commuter seaplane that started operating between the central business districts of Abu Dhabi and Dubai in 1996 was suspended in early 1997. Nor is there any rail system in the UAE.

There are ten international containerized ports within the proposed development corridor; seven are located in the UAE, and three in Bandar Abbas and Kish and Qeshm Islands. All the emirates have modern seaports. The port of Jebel Ali in Dubai is the largest man-made port in the world. As part of its drive to diversify its economy away from oil to regional trade, Dubai has developed free zones at the two main seaports and its international airports.

Based on their individual infrastructure capacities, a high degree of functional compatibility exists among the various urban centers and islands in the region, both internally within their respective national boundaries and from a cross-boundary regional perspective.

Dubai and Sharjah both have complementary urban functions. While Dubai is a major tourist, shopping, and service center, Sharjah plays a more traditional role as a cultural and tourist resource and offers less expensive housing. As a result a large population lives in Sharjah but works in Dubai. Dubai, Sharjah, and Abu Dhabi have further complementary functions, including alternative arrival and departure points and diversified and competing port facilities. To a much lesser degree the smaller cities of Ajman, Umm al-Quwaine and Ras al-Khaimah play supporting roles particularly through their port facilities. To these must be added the port cities of Khor Fakkan and Fujairah on the Gulf of Oman. However, the geographical location of these places puts them outside our immediate concern (U.S. Department of State 2000).

In Iran, on the other hand, Bandar Abbas is the country's largest port; it has grown rapidly since the 1960s, first with the establishment of a naval base, later with an expansion of port facilities to provide safe entry for Iran's imports and exports in the 1980s. Much of the reexporting of goods from the UAE cities to Iran and beyond are handled at the Shaheed Rajaee Port of Bandar Abbas. With the linking of Bandar Abbas to the national rail network in Iran and along the ancient Asia silk route, the port city has played an important transit route for the UAE's reexports to Russia and central Asia. Both Kish and Qeshm Islands act as points of entry into Iran for tourism and as locations for major export processing. Kish Island is currently undergoing major growth because of the expansion of its tourist facilities (hotels, resorts, beaches), and events such as festivals, attracting internal and foreign tourists.

From a regional perspective there is much scope for expanding cross-border functional communications. Dubai and Abu Dhabi already act as major regional transport hubs with well established air routes to most destinations and markets in the world. In addition they have well-developed infrastructural capacities for supporting regional headquarters and command and control functions as well as offering a high quality of life to foreign personnel and technical staff of national and international firms. On the other hand, Bandar Abbas and Qeshm and Kish Islands can provide plentiful cheap land and other material resources, particularly water, which is a very scarce resource in the UAE. In addition, there is a supply of cheap labor, which is augmented from Iran as a whole, with supporting infrastructural development for the physical location of production units. Table 4 indicates that unskilled, skilled, and foreman labor rates in the Qeshm and Kish Islands free zones, for example, are one-half to two-thirds the rates in the Jebel Ali and Sharjah free zones. However, the position of Bandar Abbas is more advantageous with direct road, rail, and air links to the markets of central Asia, the Caucasus, and Russia providing an added incentive for attracting international investment to the region as a whole. In addition both Kish and Qeshm Islands and designated areas in the UAE have enjoyed the status of free trade zones for several years, which could promote closer economic cooperation.

Free trade zones and special economic zones. Globalization of trade and the changing geopolitical map of the Middle East and central Asia has led to strategic policy shifts concerning Iran's interaction with the international economic and trade community. The Iranian Parliament approved the free trade zones (FTZ) Act in September 1993. According to this act, Kish Island, Qeshm Island, and the Port of Chaharbahar were declared the free trading zones of Iran. The formation of these zones has tremendously liberalized trade in Iran and has attracted new foreign investment. In addition to the three FTZs, a number of special economic zones (SEZ) have been established with the sole purpose of promoting the transit and reexport of goods without being subjected to normal customs and taxation duties and regulations. Shaheed Rajaee port in Bandar Abbas is included in this category. It is important to note that the Qeshm FTZ has been primarily designed as a location for attracting heavy and light industry as well as trade (Qeshm FZO 2001). The island also offers good opportunities for ecotourism because it has large concentrations of mangrove forests along its northern shores and is a breeding and spawning ground for giant sea turtles. These natural habitats are protected areas 60 to 100 kilometers from the free trade zone situated around Qeshm city itself. One should note that of a total area of 1,445 square kilometers, only 300 square kilometers have been devoted to the FTZ. Infrastructural development on the island includes a recently opened containerized port with a capacity to host 40,000–ton ships in its first phase of development. This will be extended to 100,000 capacity in its third phase (Qeshm FTZ 2001). In addition, future plans envisage connecting Qeshm to the Iranian railway system in Bandar Abbas through construction of a bridge between the Island and the Iranian mainland. Kish, on the other hand, is already an established trade and commercial center, which has developed its tourist facilities as a large coral island, becoming a major sight-seeing and shopping destination for internal tourism in Iran. Kish is hoping to expand its tourist appeal as it is one of only two destinations in Iran—the other is the Qeshm FTZ—that do not have any visa requirements for international visitors.

As part of its drive to diversify its economy away from oil to regional trade, Dubai has developed free zones at the two main seaports and its international airport to reexport cargo to a well-developed niche market. As mentioned above, Jebel Ali in Dubai is one of the largest free trade zones in the world. Dubai aggressively seeks out new reexport markets, and, though it still depends on its traditional reexport markets of Iran and the Gulf Co-operation Council, it has developed trade ties with the newly independent central Asian states of the former Soviet Union. Cargo unloaded at Dubai and ferried across the Gulf to Iranian ports is then taken to markets in central Asia via Iranian roads and rail routes (U.S. Department of State 2000). In its latest effort to further develop its international trade and to benefit from the "new economy" Dubai has recently designated what it says is the world's first purpose-designed Internet city that is also a Free Zone, Dubai Internet City (DIC). It boasts becoming the best location for new economic activites that want to serve a region of more than 2 billion people from Egypt to the Indian subcontinent and from South Africa to the Commonwealth of Independent Stats. The DIC is designed to host IT companies, multimedia businesses, telecommunication companies, Internet startups, service companies, incubators, venture capitalists, and so forth (Dubai Internet City 2000).

Dubai's success in reexport has been imitated by other emirates within the UAE seeking to compete for a share of this activity. Khor Fakhan Port in Sharjah and Fujairah's ports, although not as efficient as Dubai's, provide closer locations outside the entrance to the Persian Gulf, in the Gulf of Oman. Using these ports can cut up to twenty-four hours off the sailing time of international cargo ships traveling between Asia and the Far East. A number of new free zones are either in the planning stage or are currently under construction. The proposed Saadiyat Island Free Zone in Abu Dhabi would be a $3 billion project that would concentrate on bulk commodity trading rather than manufacturing. Saadiyat would provide delivery and storage centers for sixty-seven basic commodities and is planned to have a stock exchange, a futures exchange, and an offshore banking unit (Emirate of Abu Dhabi 1998). Sharjah also boasts a number of FTZs including Sharjah Airport International Free Zone (SAIF Zone) and the Hamariyah Free Zone (HFZ), established in 1995 and marketed as the UAE's Next Generation Free Zone (Government of Sharjah 2000).

The establishment and development of free trade zones by both countries demonstrate their attempt to diversify their economies away from the dominance of oil. These designated zones are designed to provide international investors with open access to the country where they can enjoy preferential tax incentives and few bureaucratic constraints. Both governments have invested heavily to develop the necessary infrastructure, including ports, airports, state-of-the-art telecommunications, and utilities. In addition, both governments have introduced special legislation in support of international investments in these zones. Common elements of such legislation are long-term tax exemptions (fifteen years in Qeshm), lifting of restrictions on repatriation of capital and profits, freedom of foreign exchange movement, offshore banking, exemptions from customs and duties, and government guarantees for foreign investment.

Within the free trade zones in the UAE, foreign labor plays a dominant role in providing the necessary skills. In Iran however, there is an abundant local workforce, both skilled and unskilled, with very competitive wages compared with those in the UAE. Workers' remittances back to their country of origin places serious constraints on the balance of payments in the UAE. Furthermore, the UAE faces serious water shortages, limiting its ability to continuously expand into new development areas. Table 3 provides a comparison of labor costs in the Iranian and main UAE free trade zones.

The figures in table 3 demonstrate the substantial cost differences between the various categories of workers in the free trade areas in the proposed development corridor. The cost difference is particularly significant for skilled and management personnel. Other costs, including office, hotel, factory, and warehousing buildings are also much cheaper on the Iranian side. In terms of quality of life, although Kish Island has well-developed leisure attractions, none of the Iranian cities in the region offers the level of leisure and entertainment offerings available in Dubai, Abu Dhabi, or Sharjah. Dubai has established itself as the most cosmopolitan city in the region and draws regional headquarters for many international firms operating in the region. Already a number of

ALI PARSA AND RAMIN KEIVANI

198

TABLE 3

COMPARISON OF LABOR COST IN THE FREE TRADE ZONES IN IRAN AND THE UAE, 1998.

	Iran		UAE	
Job Category	Kish Island*ᵃ US$ Month	Qeshm Island* US$ Month	SAIF/Sharjah*ᵇ US$ Month	Dubai (Jebel Ali Free Zone)*ᶜ US$ Month
Unskilled Construction	150	116	150-245	140-220
Unskilled	120	90-100	150-245	140-220
Semiskilled	170	90-100	165-270	160-270
Skilled	200	150-250	270-525	270-540
Technician/Engineer	300	370-525	350-550	350-490
Foreman	240	180-400	490-820	490-820
Senior Supervisor	600	590	1,090-1,900	1,090-2000
Manager	600+	1000	+ 1,500-2,700	1,600-2,700

Source: a. Kish Free Zone Organization 2000, Qeshm Free Zone Organization 2000.

b. Salamiram 2000, Sharjah Airport International Free Zone 1999.

c. Jebel Ali Free Zone Authority 1998.

* Includes cost of food and accommodation.

international firms present in southern Iran operate out of their headquarters in Dubai. This compatibility in function provides added incentive and a platform for the transfer of manufacturing and service functions to the free trade areas in Iran in order to alleviate real shortages of resources including fresh water, electricity, and development land in the UAE.

Population mobility and cross-border economic activities. As noted earlier, many people move between UAE and Iran as a result of trade links between southern cities in Iran and the coastal Arab settlements in the UAE. Such cross-border mobility has resulted in Iranian settlements in the coastal areas of the UAE, and large numbers of migrants from the emirates to the southern cities of Iran. Large-scale movement of population between these cities has been going on for generations, and though there are differences in local languages, Persian and Arabic are frequently spoken by both UAE and Iranian nationals. Consequently, there has been much intermarriage and settlement of population on both sides of the Gulf. A large Iranian expatriate community makes its home in the UAE and is mainly active in business and commerce, and a large proportion of UAE nationals are of Iranian origin. It is impossible to determine the exact number of UAE citizens of Iranian origin and difficult to ascertain the number of Iranian expatriates as they are usually grouped with other communities in the official statistics. One estimate in 1982 set the combined number of other Arab and Iranian expatriate communities at 23 percent of the total population (CIA 2000b). A more recent estimate placed the number of Iranians and other groups in the UAE at one hundred thousand, or about 4 percent of the population, in 1999 (Hirst 2001).

As we said earlier, the Islamic revolution in 1979 and Iran's isolation globally and regionally shifted economic activity and transport hubs from Tehran to Dubai, Sharjah, and Abu Dhabi. The UAE was the only alternative route for the importation of spare parts, luxury goods, and other commodities, which were subject to sanctions for export to Iran. Analysis of economic and trade statistics reveals the extent of cross-border activities between Iran and the UAE since 1980.

Within the proposed development corridor, the cross-border economic activity between Iran and the UAE exceeds that betweeen other Arab countries and the members of the GCC. Iran was the top destination for the reexport of goods from the UAE in the last quarter of 1996, amounting to AED1.014 billion (U.S.$276 million). This compares with AED849.55 million (U.S.$231 million) worth of reexports to other GCC countries and AED719.65 (U.S.$196 million) to Europe in the same period (Central Bank of UAE 1997b). As indicated in table 4, total UAE exports, including reexports, to Iran amounted to AED4.45 billion (U.S.$1.2 billion) in 1994, AED3.68 billion (U.S.$ 1 billion) in 1995 and AED3.861billion (U.S.$1.1 billion) in 1996, making Iran the top export destination and trading partner. Iran's share of total UAE exports was 36 percent in 1994, 24 percent in 1995 and 18.6 percent in 1996. This indicates a sharp fall and reduction of exports in the period that is commensurate with falls in oil revenue. Iranian customs data indicate that UAE formed the largest export destination in 1999 with a total value of U.S.$599 million, an increase of 17.81 percent over the previous year (Customs of Islamic Republic of Iran 2001). At the same time, imports from the UAE reached U.S.$769 million in 1999, an increase of 6.06 percent over the previous year. Though we are missing data for 1997 and 1998 from both UAE and Iranian sources, yearly comparison of trade for the period 1994 to 1999 would indicate a continuing reduction in trade until 1999. This pattern of trade is commensurate with a steep drop in oil prices during the period and mounting external debts and economic problems in Iran, which led to a sharp reduction in imports in general. Partly as a result of import restriction and other austerity measures, the Iranian government succeeded in reducing its external debts from a total value of about U.S.$30 billion in the early 1990s to about U.S.$13.8 billion in 1998 (World Bank 2000a).

TABLE 4

VALUE OF THE UAE NON-OIL EXPORTS AND REEXPORTS TO SELECTED COUNTRIES, 1994-1996

Destination	1994	1995	1996
Iran (US$)	1.2bn	1bn	1.1bn
India (US$)	305m	280m	381m
Saudi Arabia (US$)	242m	230m	282m
Germany (US$)	33m	55m	58.7m

Source: UAE Central Bank Annual Report 1997.

The level of cross-border trade activities between Iran and the individual emirates of Sharjah, Dubai, and Abu Dhabi is quite different. For example, in 1997, Iran was the top reexport destination from Sharjah, amounting to AED1.017 billion (U.S.$277 million) with another AED99.8 million (U.S.$27 million) worth of transit trade through Iran in the same year (Government of Sharjah 2000).

Dubai's total reexport to Iran was AED4.185 billion (U.S.$1.1 billion) in 1994, ranking first among the top 20 destinations. This was far greater than the total value of reexports of AED893 million (U.S.$243 million) to India, the second top destination (Government of Dubai 2000). During the same year the value of Dubai's imports from Iran reached AED872 million (U.S.$238 million), ranking the country 15th among the top 20 exporters to Dubai (Dubai Internet Pages 2000). Total reexports from Dubai to Iran in 1997 topped AED3.237 billion (U.S.$882 million) showing an increase of 12.71 percent over 1996 (Government of Dubai 2000).

In addition to the official trade there has long been an active and large-scale smuggling trade between the two countries, particularly through the use of high-speed boats, which can cross the straits between Bandar Abbas and Ras al-Khaimeh in about two hours.

Political environment and cross-border direct capital investment. Experience from Asia indicates that a decline in the perception of threats and reduction of political tensions have been major reasons for the widespread acceptance of cross-border growth corridors in the region (Rimmer 1994; Chen 1995; Parsonage 1992; Ho and So 1997).

The relationship between Iran and the UAE is both complex and historical. Despite a period of Omani control on both sides of the straits of Hormuz in the nineteenth century, historically Iran's dominance in the Persian Gulf, both before and after British colonial rule, has been military and economic. Since its independence from Britain, the UAE has experienced unprecedented economic growth based on its oil economy and, increasingly, reexports of goods to Iran and other countries in the region. As the only two regional powers in the Gulf, Britain and Iran had control over many small islands in the Gulf (Amirahmadi 1996). With increased economic power and accumulated wealth, the UAE roused nationalistic sentiment in a territorial dispute with Iran over its 1971 occupation of the three islands of Abu Musa and the Greater and Lesser Tunbs in the Persian Gulf (Mojtahed-Zadeh 1996). However, this territorial dispute gave way to economic realism and pragmatism and profitable mutual trade relations.

Such economic interdependence have been brought about by a number of important factors. Forces of globalization such as movement of capital and goods from Asia, western Europe, and North America has made the UAE a regional hub for import and reexport of goods to Iran and many other countries. Other international factors such as the Iran-Iraq War, the deterioration of Iran-U.S. relations, and imposition of economic and trade embargoes on Iran by the United States and its allies since the early 1980s have had the effect of expanding legal and illegal cross-border economic activities between the UAE and Iran.

Both Iran and the UAE want to develop international trade. Within the proposed development corridor, both countries have introduced far-reaching reform to attract foreign investment and to nurture international trade, commerce, and tourism. Recent political development has helped improve Iran's relations with countries in the region. Although the territorial dispute with the UAE has been a barrier to fully normal relations between the two countries, they jointly manage oil fields in the disputed area. Since 1999, there has been growing investment by UAE nationals in various joint industrial and tourism projects in Iran. For example, the Airport Services Management Group at Dubai "Marhaba" recently bid for the provision of management services at the Imam Khomeini International Airport in Tehran. In addition, UAE capital has started to invest in Qeshm Island. By the year 2000, UAE capital accounted for six out of the twenty-nine foreign and joint ventures on the island. With the easing of tensions between the two countries, a growing number of Iranian construction contracting firms have entered the UAE market competing with Western companies. These include roads, dam projects, and electrical power lines in the different emirates. Because of the economic climate and greater investment insecurity for the operation of private firms in Iran, however, there is much more investment by the Iranian business community in the UAE an outflow akin to capital flight. According to Ali Ghanbari (2001), recent estimates put the number of registered Iranian companies in Dubai alone at between three hundred and four hundred.

In order to ease regional tension, Iran has signed an agreement to supply potable water to Kuwait through the construction of a giant undersea pipeline between southern Iran and Kuwait (Ettelat 2001). This $2 billion project is to be jointly funded by a consortium of British, Kuwaiti, and Iranian investors. The consortium handling this project hopes that the same pipeline will be linked to Saudi Arabia and the UAE at a later stage.

In a further move to enhance intraregional mobility and attract foreign investment from countries of the Gulf Cooperation Council as well as a sign of goodwill toward the neighboring countries, the Iranian government waived visa restrictions for entry of GCC citizens in December 2000.

Finally, the establishment of an effective supranational governance structure and further economic harmonization are dependent on the political will of national and regional authorities to pursue such policies toward creating economic synergies that are crucial for finding a foothold in the international division of labor and the global economy.

CONCLUSION

This chapter has shown that official cross-border trade and migration are flourishing between the UAE and Iran. Our analysis points to a high level of complementary functions among Bandar Abbas and the three main UAE cities. The resulting corridor acts as the main conduit for export/import and business activities between the two countries. More important, however, both Iran and UAE are eager to improve their position in the world economy and attract international investment in export service, manufacturing, and leisure and tourist industries. This forms part of their efforts toward diversifying their economic base and moving out of the shadows of the oil economy, with one long-term unsustainable outlook as a finite resource and short-term disruptive influences because of price fluctuations.

The Pacific Asian experience has shown that creation of economic synergies based on complementary endowment factors within and across national boundaries offer the best opportunity for meeting the locational requirements of international capital. Our analysis indicates that the basic historical, economic, geographic, and cultural conditions exist for building on the existing complementary trade activities between the southern borderland area of Iran and UAE cities toward the creation of an active regional growth corridor.

Dubai and Abu Dhabi, and to some extent Sharjah, are already acting as major regional transport hubs with well-established air routes to most destinations and markets in the world. They also have relatively well-developed infrastructure for export service functions, information technology, and leisure activities, which are more than adequate to support the operation of regional headquarters and command and management functions of multinational firms.

However, the cities lack local labor and material resources for supporting large-scale industrial expansion. These shortages can easily be overcome by relying on Bandar Abbas and Qeshm and Kish Islands for the physical location of industrial expansion while the UAE cities themselves could be centers for the related higher value-adding functions and some light industrial development. Moreover, the unique position of the Iranian cities with direct road and rail links to the markets of central Asia and the Caucasus could provide an added incentive for attracting international investment. In addition, Kish Island has unique coral features, and Qeshm's natural attractions are suited for eco-tourism. These can be combined with the well-developed leisure and tourist facilities of the UAE for attracting international tourist trade. Indeed, the simplest move toward the creation of a growth corridor might begin with tourist excursions from UAE to Qeshm and Kish Islands as part of a bigger package for expanding the tourist industry in the region as a whole.

In the final analysis, however, as in Pacific Asia, the whole idea of cross-national economic zones can become credible only with the easing of political tensions and the priority of economic development and growth over more limited nationalistic concerns. But unresolved issues persist at the international level, particularly between Iran and the United States, and political instability at home may dampen the enthusiasm for international investment in Iran, be it from the UAE or other quarters, despite recent passage of laws guaranteeing international investment and repatriation of profits. Indeed, as Ali Ghanbari the deputy head of the Plan and Budget Commission of the Iranian Parliament recently noted, lack of political stability and the general feeling that security for investment is inadequate have led to a major flight of Iranian capital, paradoxically to the UAE, and to the deflection of international capital into Iran, albeit to a specially created growth corridor.

Yet, the Pacific Asian experience is a vivid reminder of the transitory nature of such political barriers to economic development. This is particularly the case in the current context of rapid economic globalization and the urgent need for developing countries to find a firm foothold in the international division of labor and the global economy. The proposed cross-border economic growth corridor provides an important and effective tool for regional economic development for UAE and southern Iran. As such it is worthy of much more serious consideration both by policymakers and academics in other developing regions as a focus for further research and policy development.

NOTES

1. Between 1820 and 1892 the British signed a series of truces with the ruling Shikhs in what is now UAE. The area then became known as Trucial States or Trucial Oman until Independence in 1971.

2. Iran, in contrast, had rapid population growth from the second half of the twentieth century

onwards. Between 1900 and 1956 the population rose from an estimated 9.9 million to 20.4 million (Halliday 1979), for an increase of 10.5 million in 56 years. Since then 43 million have been added for a total of more than 63 million today (World Bank 2000a). The urban population increased from around 21 percent in the 1930s to more than 61 percent in 1999.

3. The close cultural and historical links between this region and the Arabic cities on the southern coast of the Persian Gulf is demonstrated by the fact that Bandar Abbas and its appurtenances were leased to the sultan of Masquat (present-day Oman) according to a contract signed in the mid-nineteenth century. Due to political turmoil in Masquat in 1868 this treaty was canceled, and the city was brought back under Iranian administration. However, it was in the aftermath of World War I that the Persian Gulf gained a very important strategic and economic role as a center of petroleum export for world industrial development (Mojtahed-Zadeh 1996).

REFERENCES CITED

Amirahmadi, H. 1990. *Revolution and Economic Transition: The Iranian Experience.* Albany, NY: State University of New York Press.

Amirahmadi, H. and M. Razavi. 1993. "'Urban Development in the Muslim World: Encounter with Modernity and Implications for Planning." Pp. 2–11 in *Urban Development in the Moslem World,* ed. H. Amirahmadi and S. S. El-Shakhs. New Brunswick, NJ: New Jersey Center for Urban Policy Research, Rutgers University.

Amirahmadi, H. 1996. "The Colonial-Political Dimension of the Iran-UAE Dispute." Pp. 1–30 in *Small Islands, Big Politics: The Tonbs and Abu Musa in the Persian Gulf,* ed. H. Amirahmadi. New York: St. Martin's Press.

Amirahmadi, H., and El-Shakhs, S. S. eds. *Urban Development in the Moslem World.* New Brunswick, NJ: New Jersey Center for Urban Policy Research, Rutgers University.

Badcock, B. 1997. "Restructuring and Spatial Polarisation in Cities." *Environment and Planning D* 4: 447–464.

Boussa, J. 2000. "Vision Building and Planning in the YAE: Is there room for Heritage." Paper presented at *The Third Sharjah Urban Planning Symposium,* Sharjah, United Arab Emirates, 18–19 April.

Budd, L. 1995. "Globalization, Territory, and Strategic Alliances in Different Financial Centers." *Urban Studies* 32 (2): 345–360.

California Civil Aviation. 2000. "Teheran Counts on Airport to Turn Chapter in History." July. http://www.archives.californiaaviation.org

Central Bank of UAE. 1997a. *Statistical Bulletin Quarterly* 17 (1).

———. 1997b. *Statistical Bulletin Quarterly* 17 (2).

Central Intelligence Agency. 2000a. *World Factbook, S.V.* "Iran." http://www.odci.gov/cia/publications/factbook.

Central Intelligence Agency. 2000b. *World Factbook, S.V.* "United Arab Emirates." http://www.odci.gov/cia/publications/factbook.

Chen, X. 1995. "The Evolution of Free Economic Zones and the Recent Development of Cross-National Growth Zones." *International Journal of Urban and Regional Research* 19 (4): 593–621.

Chu, D. K. Y. 1996. "The Hong Kong-Zhujiang Delta and the World City System." In *Emerging World Cities in Pacific Asia,* ed. F. Lo and Y. Yeung. Tokyo: United Nations Press.

Cooke, P. and K. Morgan. 1993. "The Network Paradigm: New Departures in Corporate and Regional Development." *Environment and Planning D* 11: 543–564.

Customs of Islamic Republic of Iran. 2001. http://www.irica.org.

Dicken, P 1994. "The Roepke Lecture in Economic Geography. Global-Local Tensions: Firms and States in the Global Space-Economy." *Economic Geography* 70 (2): 101–128.

Dubai Internet City. 2000. http://www.dubaiinternetcity.com

Dubai Internet Pages. 2000. *Economic Facts and Figures.*

Energy Information Administration (EIA). 2000a. *Country Analysis Brief—Iran.* September.

Energy Information Administration (EIA), 2000b. *Country Analysis Brief—United Arab Emirates.* October.

Ettelaat International. 2001. 25th February.

Ghanbari, Ali. 2001. Deputy Head of Plan and Budget Commission, Iranian Parliament. Personal Interview in Hamshahri, March 4.

Godfrey, B. J., and Y. Zhou. 1999. "Ranking Multinational Corporations and the Global Urban Hierarchy." *Urban Geography* 20: 268–281.

Goodwin, M. 1996. "Governing the Spaces of Difference: Regulation and Globalization in London." *Urban Studies* 33 (8): 1395–1406.

Gottmann, J. 1991. "The Dynamics of City Networks in an Expanding World." *Ekistics*, 350/351: 227–281.

Government of Dubai. 2000. *Dubai Business: Facts and Figures.* Dubai: Department of Tourism and Commerce Marketing.

Government of Sharjah. 1998a. *Sharjah Trade*, 4th ed. Sharjah: United Arab Emirates.

———. 1998b. *Socio-Economic 97 Indicators*, 15th ed. Sharjah: United Arab Emirates.

———. 2000. *Hamriyah Free Zone Sharjah, The Next generation Free Zone.* Free Zone Authority. Sharjah: United Arab Emirates.

Gugler, P. 1992. "Building Transnational Alliances to Create Competitive Advantage." *Long Range Planning* 25 (1): 90–99.

Halliday, F. 1979. *Iran: Dictatorship and Development.* London: Penguin.

High Council for Free Trade-Industrial Zones. 1998. *Iran's Special Economic Zones.*

Hirst, D. 2001. *Le Monde Diplomatique.* (February 16).

Ho, K. C., and A. So. 1997. "Semi-Periphery and Borderland Integration: Singapore and Hong Kong experiences." *Political Geography* 16 (3): 241–259.

Hoogvelt, A. 1997. *Globalization and the Postcolonial World*, Basingstoke, England: Macmillan.

Ibrahimi, M. H. 2001. "Strengthening Urban Planning Coordination: Intercultural Exchanges and Cooperation in the Gulf Region." Paper presented at *The 4th Sharjah Urban Planning Symposium*, Sharjah, United Arab Emirates, 8–11 April.

Iran Air. 2000. Performance Highlights for 1997. http://www.iranair.com

Iran Export. 2000. "Trade Statistics." http://iran-export.com

ICMN (Iran Chamber of Commerce, Industries and Mines). 1999a. "Export Policies of the Third Plan." Quarterly Magazine 6 (2).

———. 1999b. "Industrial Investments Rise in Iran." *Quarterly Magazine* 6 (3).

———. 2000. "Review of Economic Events." *Quarterly Magazine* 7 (1).

Jebel Ali Free Zone Authority. 1998. http://www.jafz.org

Kish Free Zone Organization. 2000. http://www.kfzo.org

Knox, P. L. 1996. "Globalization and Urban Change." *Urban Geography* 17 (1): 115–117.

Lo, F., and P. J. Marcotullio. 2000. "Globalization and Urban Transformations in the Asia-Pacific Region: A Review." *Urban Studies* 27 (1): 77–111.

Macleod, S. and T. G. McGee. 1996. "The Singapore-Johore-Riau Growth Triangle: An Emerging Metropolitan Region." In *Emerging World Cities in Pacific Asia,* Ed. F. Lo and Y. Yeung. Tokyo: United Nations Press.

Mojtahed-Zadeh, Firooz. 1996. "Perspectives on the Territorial History of the Tonb and Abu Musa Islands." In *Small Islands, Big Politics: The Tonbs and Abu Musa in the Persian Gulf,* Ed. H. Amirahmadi. New York: St. Martin's Press.

Morgan, K. 1992. "Innovating by Networking: New Models of Corporate and Regional Development." In *Cities and Regions in the New Europe,* ed. M. Dunford and G. Kafkalas. London: Belhaven.

Parsonage, J. 1992. "Southeast Asia's 'Growth Triangle': A Sub-Regional Response to Global Transformation." *International Journal of Urban and Regional Research* 16 (2).

Persky, J., and W. Wiewel. 1994. "The Growing Localness of the Global City." *Economic Geography* 70 (2): 129–143.

Qeshm Free Zone Organization. 2001. http://www.qeshm.org

Rimmer, P. J. 1994. "Regional Economic Integration in Pacific Asia." *Environment and Planning A* 26: 1731–1759.

Sabahi, H. 1990. *British Policy in Persia 1918–1925.* London: Frank Cass.

SAIF Zone. 2000. "Sharjah Airport International Free Zone." Sharjah: UAE.

Sassen, S. 2000. *Cities in a World Economy.* 2nd Ed. Thousand Oaks, CA: Pine Forge.

———. 2001. *The Global City: New York, London, Tokyo,* 2nd ed. Princeton, NJ: Princeton University Press.

Sharjah International Airport. 2001. http://www.shj-airport.gov.ae

Short, J. R., and Y. U. Kim. 1999. *Globalization and the City.* Essex, England: Addison-Wesley Longman.

Sykora, L. 1994. "Local Urban Restructuring as a Mirror of Globalization Process: Prague in the 1990s." *Urban Studies* 13 (7): 1149–1166.

Taryam, A. 1987. *The Establishment of the United Arab Emirates 1950–85,* London: Croom Helm.

United Arab Emirates Internet Pages. 2000. *Quick Facts—UAE.*

U.S. Department of State. 2000. *FY 2000 Commercial Guide: United Arab Emirates.* Washington D.C.: U.S.

World Bank Group. 2000a. *Iran, Islamic Republic, Data Profile. World Development Indicators Database.* July.

World Bank Group. 2000b. *United Arab Emirates Data Profile. World Development Indicators Database.* July.

Yeung, H.W.C. 1998. "Transnational Economic Synergy and Business Networks: The Case of Two-Way Investment Between Malaysia and Singapore." *Regional Studies* 32, 8: 687–706.

Yeung, Yue-man and Fu-chen Lo. 1996. "Global Restructuring and Emerging Urban corridors in Pacific Asia." In *Emerging World Cities in Pacific Asia,* ed. Fu-Chen Lo and Yue-man Yeung. Tokyo: United Nations Press, 17–47.

Chapter 7

SÃO PAULO: ARTICULATING A CROSS-BORDER REGION

Sueli Ramos Schiffer

This chapter examines São Paulo's national and international role in specific processes of economic globalization. Particular attention goes to the Mercosur regional bloc and its capacity to articulate the cross-border region with the global economy. The centrality of São Paulo in the articulation of the Mercosur cross-border region required heavy national investments in regional infrastructure to overcome surface flow obstacles and to build digital networks. A key issue in this regard is the deregulation process that Brazil began undergoing in the early 1990s, insofar as it illuminates how national institutional reshaping conditions greater participation of both the country and its major cities in the global economy and how the challenges of international competitiveness have been mediated internally. In a developing country like Brazil, the government has a crucial role in quickly channeling investments throughout different markets. Furthermore, unlike developed countries, competitiveness here occurs in the context of a society where social exclusion is deeply rooted and has never been seriously questioned.

The chapter concludes with a specific study aimed at determining if the trade relations and the number of networks between Brazil and Japan have increased in the last decade in the wake of Brazil's economic restructuring. Brazil is today home to the world's greatest number of Japanese immigrants and a very large number of Japanese firms.

LATIN AMERICA AS A COMPETITOR FOR INVESTMENTS

The growth of foreign direct investments (FDIs) since the 1990s in developing countries indicates that the structure of local patterns for attracting capital has changed. The question of what criteria today's corporate decision-making processes are based on is raised when a foreign market is to be chosen for making new investments. Enhanced competition among firms imposes a rigorous search for competitive advantages, of which the most important site-related aspects are business opportunities, a country's institutional framework, infrastructure availability, existence of a consolidated or potential consumer market, and the necessary skilled labor force. These priorities underline the declining importance of former competitive advantages for developing countries, such as cheap, unskilled labor and local availability of raw materials.

Latin America recorded a strong decline in its share of FDI between 1986 and 1990 compared with 1981–1985 (Chudsnovsky 1997: 129), and a relative increase since 1991, particularly after 1997, when Latin America obtained almost two-thirds of the increase in overall FDI received by developing countries. Although it has not yet reached the shares of the early 1980s, the absolute amount has increased due to the large expansion in total worldwide FDI. On the whole, current foreign investment has raised the concentration of capital and production in the largest transnational corporations located in developed countries. UNCTAD (1996, 1998, 2000) credits the relative increase in FDI in Latin America since the late 1990s to national efforts to attract foreign investments, and especially to the success of privatization programs, mainly in Argentina and Chile up until 1994, and in Brazil after 1995. Privatization was also the leading factor attracting FDI in 1998 and 1999 in these countries. UNCTAD (TAD/INF 2856: 4) found that "A majority of the 50 largest privatizations in the world during 1997–1999 occurred in developing countries. In 1999 Argentina was at the top, with a volume of US$16 billion, whereas Brazil headed the list the previous year, with US$20 billion." Latin American outward FDI flows have also increased, from U.S.$2.3 billion in 1996 to U.S.$27.3 billion in 1999.

In fact, the increase in foreign direct investments to major Latin American countries can be attributed not only to the privatization process, particularly of public utilities, but also to the spread of foreign capital acquisitions of former domestic manufacturers and banks. This process has been stronger in Argentina,[1] where economic restructuring resulted from the widespread lifting of foreign trade restrictions, and from Argentina's industry being more vulnerable than Brazil's in the wake of a long period of stagnation. Yet, despite the strength of its industrial structure, Brazilian manufacturing capital has been shrinking and playing a lesser role in the economic scenario. A press release (Nov. 10, 1998) based on UNCTAD's World Investment Report of 1998 stated, "Brazil emerges [in 1997] as the champion in attracting foreign direct investment" within Latin America. This performance is attributed to "a combination of effective macroeconomic policies, the opening up of the economy and privatization programs, which alone accounted for 27 percent of FDI inflows in the last two years [1996–97]. Some 600 mergers and acquisitions have taken place in the last 6 years [1992–97], and 61 percent of these involved foreign buyers and 59 percent involved the manufacturing sector."

In 1998, foreign capital mergers and acquisitions in Brazil had reached the U.S.$29.4 billion mark, almost three times the amount recorded in 1997, whereas the total amount in 1999 declined to U.S.$9.4 billion. Argentina received an inflow of U.S.$19.1 billion in 1999 from foreign capital mergers and acquisitions, almost double the amount obtained in 1998 (UNCTAD: WIR2000).

Since 1995, the financial sector has been rife with mergers and acquisitions, a wave that began in the banking industry. Argentina was in the forefront of this process. In a period of less than four years, three of the four largest domestic banks were sold to foreign banks.[2] In Brazil, from March 1997 to the end of 1998, eight banks were acquired with foreign capital, and, coincidentally, the new owners belong to foreign financial corporations also active in Argentina, such as HSBC (Great Britain), Santander, and Bilbao Viscaya (both Spain). Foreign investments in the financial sector in Brazil are also yielding more wide-ranging diversified products in the stock market, in securities and in assets management. Recently, establishments of the largest world investment operators set up offices,[3] almost all in São Paulo, reinforcing the role of Brazilian economic deregulation.

The automobile industry is also particularly attractive to foreign investments, spurred by the great increase in demand for cars, mainly in Argentina and Brazili[4]. The lifting of trade restrictions helped market expansion and, in the case of Brazil, the arrival of new car manufacturers. Additional car plants have also been built by the formerly installed manufacturers, vying for heavy investments by Japanese, French, and German newcomer corporations (*Financial Times* 1997).

Although major foreign investments to Mercosur come from developed countries, regional investments have also increased, aiming at producing counterparts. Brazil, for instance, doubled its investments in Mercosur countries from 1990 to 1995. The amount channeled to Argentina was almost 60 percent of the total, going mostly to the manufacturing industry. Half of Brazilian investments in the service industry in Argentina, in that period, went to banks (GM 1996b). (I will return to this subject later.)

To attract foreign capital, South American countries have had to reshape their economies to offer competitive advantages to foreign capital investments and to develop regional infrastructure to allow cross-border integration. The reverberations from the economic adjustments that have had to be made have been felt even more strongly in Brazil, since the greater regional power of its industrial and financial sectors and the size of its population have required stronger government intervention to impose institutional and economic changes, in order to sustain its regional leadership .

THE BRAZILIAN DEREGULATION OF THE 1990s: GLOBAL INTENTIONS AND LOCAL OUTCOMES

Major institutional restructuring in Brazil throughout the 1990s to ensure its inclusion in the post-1980 expanding global economy was aimed at eventual monetary stabilization, lifting foreign trade restrictions, and introducing special measures to attract foreign capital. The measures put into effect to attain these goals were based on strong governmental intervention, mostly through the implementation of a compulsory plan called "Plano Real" in mid-1994, and can be summarized as follows:

i) Radical monetary reform was designed to stabilize the national currency (inflation rate declined from roughly 35 percent to 2 percent a month). This adjustment was achieved by enhancing the foreign reserves that underpinned the dollar parity anchor. The main attraction for enhancing foreign reserves has been the high interest rate[5] applied on foreign financial investment profit. These policies are still in effect and have obviously favored speculative investments for both national and foreign capital, at the expense of productive investment opportunities.[6]

ii) The abrupt opening of trade was effected by drastically reducing duties on multiple goods. Since the measure was not preceded by a negotiated industrial policy, it led to disastrous consequences for certain branches of domestic manufacture: the great increase in imports[7] has led to an unprecedented proliferation of mergers, acquisitions, and bankruptcies.[8]

iii) Specific financial sectors were deregulated to allow the inflow of foreign capital under privileged taxation (particularly as compared with the high annual interest rate), especially involving stock market rules and financial investment opportunities.[9]

iv) The constitutional concept of national corporations was broadened to allow the participation of major foreign investments in strategic branches still restricted to national capital, like telecommunications, mining, and domestic navigation.

v) A reorganization of the state was launched to enable these policy changes. This reorganization was set against an identification of the state with authoritarianism and inefficiency, and the creation of an ideological basis supporting the privatization of major industries, such as the largest metallurgical industries and public infrastructure.

The abrupt introduction of most of these measures, particularly the opening up of the economy, has had important effects on the overall performance of manufacturing. Brazilian firms—including some subsidiaries of foreign firms—have responded to the growing competition of imported goods by shrinking their hired skilled and unskilled labor force, with no relevant technological improvement. Additionally, they have reduced their end prices thereby cutting into their net profits, and promoting the decapitalization of Brazilian firms. Often these are the same firms that had participated in or pushed for the increase in mergers and acquisitions involving foreign capital, mentioned previously.

Privatization and deregulation in Brazil started, as in many other countries, with the more competitive industries owned by the state. This was the case in the steel, petrochemical, and fertilizer industries, whose privatization processes absorbed most of the efforts and skills of the state from 1991 to 1996.[10] Whereas this first cycle involved relatively few changes in the institutional organization of the state in terms of its operational branches, the privatization and deregulation of public utilities involved major restructuring of the entire institutional order both nationally and subnationally. The infrastructure and public utilities industry in Brazil until the early 1990s evolved according to a model of immense networks, with growing territorial scope and functional complexity. With the prospect of privatization, territorial and functional unbundling has become a major strategy, preventing deep technological and managerial restructuring. Within the telecommunications industry, the great diversification of scope has enabled some makeshift arrangements to be made since the early 1990s to bypass the strict national regulations for public utilities. Through a flexible interpretation of constitutional rule that establishes the state monopoly of public-utility communications services, the Brazilian Congress passed a number of subconstitutional laws that classified "special services of telecommunications" as different from public services *stricto sensu*. Based on this interpretation, a number of concessions, bids, and joint ventures were opened specifically for services like cable TV, mobile telephone networks, and wireless communication in general, years before the private takeover of the whole system in 1998.

The technological and territorial expansion of the telecommunications networks that followed were crucial to the broader integration of Brazil, and São Paulo in the international economic circuit. The construction of cross-border telematic networks connecting South America to North America and Europe (see map 2), with São Paulo as a central node, has reinforced the regional primacy of this city.

BRAZIL AND SÃO PAULO IN THE ECONOMIC GEOGRAPHY OF MERCOSUR

Brazil is the richest and most populous country in Latin America, although its excluded population has one of the worst standards of living in the continent.

TABLE 1

MERCOSUR: POPULATION AND ECONOMIC INDICATORS.

Country	population (1999) Millions	GDP (1990/99) (%)[a]	GDP (1999) Billions of Dollars	industry (1999) % GDP[b]	Manufacturing (1999) % GDP[b]	Services (1999) % GDP[b]	GNP/c* (1999) Dollars
Argentina	36.6	4.9	281.9	32	22	61	7,600
Brazil	168.1	2.9	760.3	29	23	62	4,420
Chile	15.0	7.2	71.1	33	16	59	4,740
Paraguay	5.4	2.4	8.1	22	16	52	1,580
Uruguay	3.3	3.7	20.2	29	19	62	5,900

[a] average annual growth rate/ [b] value added as % of GDP / * GNP per capita.
Source: World Development Report 2000/2001.

Average indicators, in general, are not a good expression of the reality of a country with such sharp internal differences and concentration of wealth; these indicators tend to mask the true dimensions of both scarcity and abundance. However, some selected data on Mercosur countries and Chile,[11] namely gross domestic product and gross national product per capita for 1999, as well as sector GDP shares (see in table 1), allow for rough comparisons among countries and express Brazil's economic leadership in the area.

The Regional Supremacy of São Paulo

Brazilian leadership in Mercosur is held by the state of São Paulo, which represents more than 35 percent of Brazil's GNP. With GNP at about U.S.$285 billion in 1998 (GM 1999: 164), the state of São Paulo accounted for more than 50 percent of Brazilian manufacturing production, including a million cars produced each year (as such it should be considered the tenth largest automobile producer in the world). The state of São Paulo accounted for 28 percent of Argentina's foreign trade in 1997, surpassing the United States as the major country of origin of Argentinian imports (GMLA 1997c).

The São Paulo Metropolitan Area, with thirty-nine municipalities and more than 17 million inhabitants, accounted for about 20 percent of the national GNP in 2000 (EXAME São Paulo, 2000: 7). The city of São Paulo (a major metropolitan municipality and state capital) is the nation's economic center, concentrating not only the most advanced financial and service activities, but also its representative manufacturing industry, holding a roughly 35% share of the total for the state in 1998.

Among the three energy companies set up in this state, one—CESP—is

TABLE 2

MERCOSUR METROPOLITAN AREAS AND URBAN AGGLOMERATIONS 2000

Metropolitan Area and/or Urban Agglomeration (Country)	Population		
	2000 (millions)	1990 to 1995 (% p.a.)*	National Population (%) 2000
Asuncion (Paraguay)	1.2	...	23.1
Buenos Aires (Argentina)	13.4	1.7	37.1
Montevideo (Uruguay)	1.3	0.6	39.4
Santiago (Chile)	5.6	2.0	37.8
São Paulo (Brazil)	17.5	2.0	10.1

... no data.

* annual growth rate from the United Nations—Department for Economic and Social Information and Policy Analysis, Population Division. Urban Agglomerations, 1994.

Sources : DEMOGRAPHIA (website, January. 2001) estimate by Wendell Cox Consulting;

the largest in Latin America, with an operating capacity of 10,800 megawatts. The state also has the largest Brazilian port—Santos—and forty-two airports, three of which handle international flights. With a population of more than 33 million in 2000, the GNP per capita was about US$6,200 in the same year, roughly 50 percent more than the Brazilian average (EXAME São Paulo 2000:7).

The role of the city of São Paulo in Mercosur basically mirrors that of Brazilian leadership in the area. Data shown in table 2 indicate the total population and their respective national share for major Mercosur agglomerations, as rough indirect indicators of their relative leadership in their national scenarios.

The São Paulo Metropolitan Area has been the main economic center of the Brazilian economy ever since coffee production was introduced in the state in the last quarter of the nineteenth century. The world coffee glut in the first decades of this century channeled coffee production profits to the manufacturing industry. São Paulo's industrialization gained further momentum between 1955 and 1960 with foreign capital injections in the automobile industry, pushing São Paulo manufacturing output to a national share of more than 42 percent in 1970. After the mid-1970s, there was a rise in the São Paulo state GDP tertiary sector associated with the manufacturing decentralization process in the São Paulo Metropolitan Area. This process is more a consequence of transferring some manufacturing plants to certain cities than it is a deindustrialization process, since the headquarters of the largest corporations—particularly those owned by foreign capital—have remained in the city of São Paulo (table 3). Even some corporations with administrative offices formerly in other cities,[12] have transferred their central offices to the city of São Paulo. In addition, manufacturing within the São Paulo Metropolitan Area has shifted from traditional manufacturing industries to the most technologically advanced industries. According to FSEADE: PAEP (1997/98) *(São Paulo Economic Activity Survey)*, 78.7% of the most advanced technology manufacturers of São Paulo State are located in the São Paulo Metropolitan Area (*EXAME* São Paulo 2000: 19).

Similar to what has occurred in several global cities, the city of São Paulo has experienced an even higher increase in tertiary activities, from 58.7 percent in 1985 to 67.4 percent in 1995, and a rise in financial and specialized services, to such an extent (table 4) that it has strengthened the city's leadership within the country.[13] The São Paulo Stock Exchange—the largest in Latin America—currently transacts about 10 percent of Brazil's GNP annually; the Futures Commodities Stock Exchange ranks third in the world in terms of money negotiated (GMLA 1997c).

Of the twenty largest foreign-owned companies in Latin America in 1999, twelve were in Brazil, and six of these are regionally based in the city of São Paulo (GMLA 2000b). A survey of the largest companies[14] with headquarters in the São Paulo Metropolitan Area, developed for this text in 1998, resulted in a sample consisting of twenty-six responses,[15] twenty-one from foreign companies. Of all the companies surveyed, 73.1 percent also have factories elsewhere in Latin America, 61.5 percent have factories elsewhere in Mercosur countries and 38.5 percent have their regional office (responsible for controlling Mercosur factories and the Mercosur market) in this metropolis.

THE MERCOSUR CROSS-BORDER INFRASTRUCTURE

None of the Mercosur countries had a very comfortable position in terms of infrastructure provisions in the mid-1990s.[16] Table 5 shows some general figures for regional availability of infrastructure, and clearly indicates that the entire region needs to expand and modernize its infrastructure supply.

It is not clear whether privatization is necessarily going to solve this problem best. Argentina has delved deeper into the privatization process, particularly in regard to telecommunications, beginning in 1990, almost half a decade earlier than Brazil. Yet Brazil's pre-privatization model of sectoral government corporations in heavy industry and public infrastructure has proved very receptive to joint ventures with the private sector both upstream and downstream from their core businesses.

This Brazilian "model" has also lent itself to integration with neighboring countries. This is the case of the Itaipú hydropower plant, constructed in the mid-1970s, according to a bilateral agreement between Brazil and Paraguay.

TABLE 3

HEADQUARTERS OF PRIVATE COMPANIES ESTABLISHED IN THE CITY OF SÃO PAULO

Of the Largest	1980 %	1985 %	1990 %	1992 %	1994 %	1996 %	1997 %	1999 %
100 Brazilian groups	45.0	45.0	42.0	36.0	36.0	40.0	47.0	39.0
40 foreign groups	...	...	72.5	62.5	75.0	70.0	...	67.5
100 foreign companies	51.0	54.0	47.0	45.0	47.5	68.0	65.0	63.0
50 Brazilian companies	42.0	34.0	40.0	30.0	32.0	26.0	38.0	34.0

... no data

Source: *Gazeta Mercantil*—Balanço Anual(Annual Balance Sheet, several years).

TABLE 4

HEADQUARTERS OF THE LARGEST COMPANIES IN THE FINANCIAL SECTOR ESTABLISHED IN THE CITY OF SÃO PAULO.

	1986 Units in SP / Largest	1990 Units in SP / Largest	1993 Units in SP / Largest	1996 Units in SP / Largest	1997 Units in SP / Largest	1999 Units in SP / Largest
Commercial private Brazilian banks	18/40	29/40	4/11	31/40	...	27/40
Commercial private foreign banks	15/19	14/16	14/15	23/24	...	36/40
Insurance companies	33/80	36/80	35/80	36/80	37/80	40/80
Brokerage houses	25/50	25/50	32/50	34/46	36/50	29/43

Note: The number of the largest companies varies according to different dates and sectors /
... no data

Source: *Gazeta Mercantil*—Balanço Anual (Annual Balance Sheet, several years).

TABLE 5

MERCOSUR COUNTRIES. INFRASTRUCTURE SUPPLY DENSITY.

	Electric power	Telecomm	Transportation		Water
Country	Consumption per Capita	Telephone Main Lines	Paved Roads (% of total)	Air Carried	Access to Passengers Safe Water
	1997[a]	1998[b]	1998	1998[c]	1996[d]
Argentina	1,634	203	29.5	8,447	71.0
Brazil	1,743	121	9.3	28,091	85.0*
Chile	2,011	205	13.8	5,150	...
Paraguay	759	55	9.5	222	70.0
Uruguay	1,710	250	90.0	557	99.0

[a] Kilowatt-hours / [b] per 1,000 people / [c] thousands / [d] % of a urban population / * refers to 1995 / ... no data

Source: World Development Report (2000/2001).

The plant has an installed capacity of 12,000 megawatts carried through thousands of kilometers of transmission lines crossing Brazil in the South, Southeast, and Midwest regions, as well as all of Paraguay. This is also the case of the Tietê-Paraná waterway, a 2,400–kilometer system (1,040 kilometers already operating) of river navigation connecting southeastern Brazil to Paraguay, Argentina, and Uruguay. This project is still under construction, but its conception and initial implementation date to the late 1960s.

Nevertheless, shared projects in South America have always targeted very specific goals and have not been concerned with regional development per se. Aside from the examples of partially integrated projects, an array of mismatches can be mentioned that attest to the lack of a deeper regional concern: railway track gauges often differ from country to country, jeopardizing broader continental integration and entailing growing costs for the intermodal transportation of goods; no meaningful surface connections link Atlantic and Pacific harbors in the region; differences in electric frequency hamper the sharing of output generated at Brazil-Paraguay's Itaipú hydropower plant with Argentina; air traffic among countries of the continent has so far been regulated as long-distance international air transport, with no special concern given to secondary cross-border regional links.

In electronic communications, too, little regional response has been made to the complex demands of international trade and finance operations for territorial and functional integration. A wide gap emerges between the needs of this

MAP 1

BRAZIL (1999): EVOLUTION OF THE INTERNET BACKBONE (RNP PROGRAM: 1991 (ABOVE) AND 1999 (BELOW).

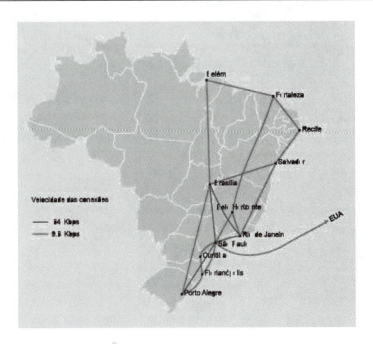

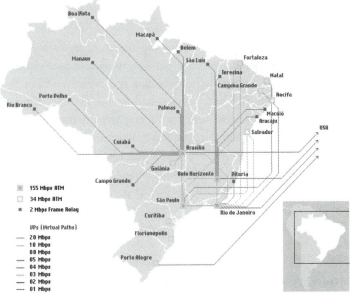

Source: Ministério da Ciência e Technologia (*Brazil's Ministry of Science and Technology*): RNP—Rede Nacional de Pesquisa (*National Research Network*) (website www.rnp.br, Feb. 2001).

MAP 2

MERCOSUR: MAIN DIGITAL NETWORKS (2000)

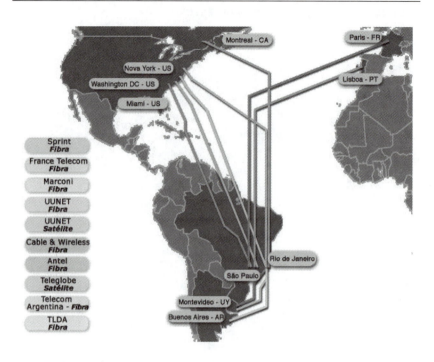

Source: Bazil: Anatal (2000: website: www.anatel.gov.br)

new geography and the dispersed existing capabilities of regulating and operating extensive and complex surface and digital networks. Those linkages tend to be centered in the cities where decision making and capital control are concentrated (see maps 1 and 2). The functional and territorial unbundling of infrastructure networks, on the one hand, is necessary to make the private operation of public utilities feasible. On the other hand, the need for extensive territorial connectivity and for cross-border links, especially in transport, energy, and communications, make wide-range regulation and standardization indispensable. In this sense, the concept of cross-border projects should encompass not only the physical systems and the services that flow among countries but the creation of international joint ventures on specific projects whose scopes do not cross borders in the strictly physical sense of the word.

Prospects for Regional and Cross-border Infrastructure Networks

A number of possible initiatives are being discussed for enhancing and integrating infrastructure networks in the Mercosur countries. These may well require new technological and regulatory paradigms, and they should also be evaluated for their likely effects on both market and social development. In this section I identify certain areas of concern and specific projects that seem to offer a promising approach for determining how Brazil might best improve international infrastructure networks. It is remarkable that, in fact, most of these projects aim at developing cross-border infrastructures with São Paulo at their core. Not only digital networks, but all other infrastructure networks as well—highways, railways, electric power, waterways—are crucial to the economic development of the Mercosur bloc. Trade hindrances often arise becasue of the lack of interconnected highways within the Mercosur region, for instance; just 25 percent of the total production flow circulating in this area is delivered by surface transport, while 58 percent is transported by ocean. At the beginning of 2001, 27.2 percent of the total volume of products transported among the main cities in this region originated in São Paulo City with Buenos Aires as final destiny; 12.4 percent from Buenos Aires to Valparaiso; and 11.7 percent from São Paulo to Montevideo (GMLA 2001b).

The implementation of all sorts of infrastructure networks are also necessary to guarantee São Paulo as the regional central node, since goods, capital and labor have to flow without hindrance to sustain the city control of the regional articulation.

a) Surface Transport

- A bridge over Rio de la Plata, connecting Buenos Aires (through Punta Lara—Argentina) and Colonia de Sacramento (Uruguay) will solve one of the main historical bottlenecks of road connections between Brazil and Argentina from North to South. The existing systems require either a modal change of transport to cross the water surface or a considerable detour across Argentina's northwestern provinces. The proposed bridge will be the world's largest open-sky bridge, with an extension of 42 kilometers. It is designed as a thirty–year concession to private operators who are expected to raise the money needed to finance its construction (GMLA 1996e). At this time, planning and financing are completed but construction has not yet started.

- The bridge connecting Santo Tomé (Argentina) to São Borja (Brazil) is part of an axis that will link the Chilean ports of Iquipe and Antofagasta on the Pacific Ocean to the Brazilian port of Rio Grande on the Atlantic Ocean. Construction started in 1997 and is to be managed by a consortium that has a twenty-five-year operating concession. The 80-kilometer Victoria-Rosario highway and bridge in Argentina (under construction in

2000) will complete the connection between the Pacific and Atlantic Oceans, also linking the central western region of Argentina to southern Brazil (GMLA 1997a).

- The Mercosur Highway (also called Highway São Paulo)—the modernization of the Brazilian highway that links São Paulo, Curitiba, Florianópolis, and Osorio (near the Uruguay border) is expected to be concluded in the early 2000s, and will represent an important distribution network for São Paulo production to Mercosur countries (GM 1998b).

- Waterways could be crucial to Mercosur trade. The Paraguay-Paraná waterway is navigable from southern Brazil to the port of Nueva Palmira in Uruguay, but needs some heavy engineering to improve the transportation system in the countries involved: Argentina, Bolivia, Brazil, Paraguay, and Uruguay. This project, with the financial support of the Interamerican Development Bank, includes a flapper link-up with the Tietê-Paraná system, one of the major contemporary Brazilian priorities in waterway network infrastructure. Although located within Brazil, some of these projects are of major importance to the entire Mercosur area. This is the case of the Madeira River waterway in Amazonas, which would open an international link to northern Brazil before reaching the main ports of the Southeast, lowering the total costs of international freight to Europe, including long-distance road transport inside Brazil (GM 1998a).

- The need for railway integration should not be overlooked. Despite the incompatibility of gauges, the main problem is that railways in South America suffer from a systematic decline that grew out of and concomitantly with the development of the road network and the automobile industry. The Brazilian Western Rail Network, privatized in March 1996, includes important branches connected to Bolivia and—potentially in conjunction with the Tietê-Paraná waterway—to the Pacific harbor of Antofagasta in Chile.

b) Air Transport

Up to the Mercosur summit of December 1996, air carriers in the region were regulated by the same system that applies to intercontinental air transport. In practice, this means that most of the connections to or from secondary urban centers of neighboring countries had to be mediated by lines connecting major international airports. Only four out of forty-eight commercial airports operating in Brazil in 1999 operated as terminal points to regular international flights. According to studies carried out by the Brazilian Commission for International Air Transport, twenty-three other airports are ready to operate international commercial flights immediately, with minor adaptations. The same is likely to occur in other Mercosur countries, where regional companies operating segments currently considered unprofitable by the large international carriers will probably proliferate.

c) Telecommunications

- The operation of the optic-fiber link joining Brazil, Uruguay, and Argentina—the Unisur—was made possible after a multilateral agreement among Embratel (Brazil), Telintar (Uruguay) and Antel (Argentina). The 1,720-kilometer cable was put into place at the end of 1996, and for optimum performance, a connection has been made within the Brazilian link, between the northeastern city of Fortaleza (terminal of the Americas I cable, departing from Miami) and the southern city of Florianópolis. This link was inaugurated by the Brazilian government in December 1996 and has a total extension of approximately 5,000 kilometers of land and underwater cables (GMLA 1996b).

- The *Brasilsat B4* communications satellite, unlike its predecessor, the *Brasilsat B3*, covers all of Latin America, and some of its twenty-eight channels, on "C" band, are directed at Mercosur countries outside Brazil This satellite, in orbit since mid-2000, and the B2, which covers just part of Argentina and Chile, and all of Paraguay and Uruguay, besides Brazil itself, are designed to serve more than 255 million telephone terminals, besides data transmission, Internet and television; all bands use digital technology (UOL/Infonews/082000).

Maps 1 and 2 show, respectively, how the Brazilian Internet backbone developed during the 1990s and the cross-border digital networks regarding the Mercosur countries in the year 2000.

d) Energy

- Natural gas pipelines connecting Santa Cruz de la Sierra (Bolivia) to São Paulo (Brazil) and the "Mercosur pipeline" connecting Salta (Argentina) to São Paulo (Brazil), will significantly improve the energy base of the state of São Paulo. Traditionally supplied by hydropower generation, this state is undergoing a change in its electricity standards in advance of the enhanced supply of natural gas from both pipelines. By the early 2000s, fourteen thermal generation units will have been built in western São Paulo state and neighboring states, with capacities varying from 60 to 560 megawatts. (GMLA 1997b).

- To make the cross-border exchange of electricity feasible, Brazil and Argentina have agreed to build a frequency conversion station in the vicinity of the Uruguay River that would make the operating standards of the two countries compatible: Brazil's is 60 hertz, whereas Argentina's is 50 hertz (GMLA 1996a).

- Argentina and Paraguay have three hydropower projects on the Paraná River: a) the Yacyretá-Apipé complex (capacity of 3.2 megawatts) was operating seventeen of its twenty turbines at the end of 1998; b) the Corpus Christi Station (capacity of 4.6 megawatts), is under way; and c) the Itati-Itacorá (capacity of 1.7 megawatts) is still under way (GMLA 1997a, e). The second and third projects are not yet completed.

- Argentina, Brazil, and Paraguay have a project of electric-power-generation interconnection among the hydropower plants of Itaipú (Brazil-Paraguay), Corpus Christi, and Yacyretá to enhance the safe supply of electricity in those countries (GMLA 1997a) .

Mercosur regional integration cannot be assessed merely by infrastructure networks, trade freedom, or institutional compatibility, however. Considering that Brazil was colonized by Portugal, and that the other Latin America countries were colonized by Spain, the Mercosur union also has to address multiform cultural trends. This feature has even led to a cooperative project called the Mercocities Network (GMLA 1996c), with nineteen Mercosur cities (ten from Brazil) participating (São Paulo, however, is inexplicably absent). The project aims at connecting the main cities of this region, particularly by forming nine thematic workgroups, including science and technology, culture, and urban management. Later, aspects of this project are to become the basis for political and economic agreements within the bloc. But perhaps most important are the trade data shown in table 6 which also highlights the economic leadership of Brazil—the leading exporting and importing country to trade outside the bloc. Brazil and Argentina expanded their trade relations throughout the 1990s to such an extent that the intra-Mercosur trade between them in 1999 represented about 80 percent of total trade. Brazil was home to more than 33 percent of all foreign affiliate companies in Latin America and the Caribbean in 1999 (UNCTAD, WIR 2000: table I.4). Of the 1,000 largest companies by stockholders' equity in 1999 in Latin America, 783 were in Mercosur countries and Chile, and 511 of those were in Brazil. These 511 companies have a net worth of about U.S.$374 billion—more than three times the corresponding amount for the 209 Argentinian companies on the list (GMLA 1999: 32). Foreign investments in the financial sector in Brazil also reacted quickly to the macroeconomic measures, and in December 1999 Brazil held eighty-four of the hun-

TABLE 6

MERCOSUR TRADE OPERATION (1999)

Country	Total Exports	Exports to Mercosur	Total Imports	Imports from Mercosur
Argentina	23,318	7,043	25,537	6,293
Brazil	48,011	6,778	49,218	6,719
Chile	...	...	...	...
Paraguay	741	545	1,935	1,541
Uruguay	2,245	1,012	3,357	1,463

(Unit: US$ million / ... no data)

Source: CEI, website: Anexo 15, Jan. 2001.

dred largest financial funds (domestic and foreign) of Latin America and the Caribbean, which is especially impressive if compared with the three funds held by Argentina (GMLAa: 40–41).

Considering that the Mercosur expansion of cross-border transactions depends largely on the implementation of specific infrastructure projects, as well as on a coherent and effective regulatory framework, it stands to reason that environmental aspects, social rights, and fair trading should be addressed from a common regional standpoint.

THE RESTRUCTURING OF THE LABOR MARKET AND SOCIOECONOMIC IMPACTS

Despite a decrease in Brazil's population growth rate since the early 1980s, demographic growth is still higher in Brazil than in developed countries. This fact, plus an uneven distribution of wealth and a very inefficient system of social security, makes the availability of jobs (more so than higher salaries) one of the core conditions to fostering social peace.

The gigantic inequality of income distribution in Brazil can be assessed by comparing the poorest 50 percent to the richest 10 percent of the Brazilian economically active population. The former held a 13.5 percent share of the national income in 1976, and 10.9 percent in 1989, and in the same period, the latter increased their national share of income from 50.4 percent to 52.2 percent (Cacciamali 1996: 221). For 1996, the World Bank Development Report (2000/2001) states the figure of 5.5 percent for the poorest 40 percent and 47.6 percent for the richest 10 percent, figures that represent one of the most highly concentrated income distributions among the capitalist countries listed in the report.

The rise in unemployment is one of the well-recognized and generalized upshots of the globalization of Brazil's economy during the 1980s and 1990s. In Brazil's case, this trend has favored a growth in informal jobs,[17] which, albeit a well-known structural historical process,[18] is nonetheless remarkable, especially in the larger cities. According to Baltar and Dedecca (1997), the drop in the number of workers in the formal labor market in Brazil was about 14 percent from 1990 to 1992, representing 4.7 million people living in open unemployment. This fact is partly attributed to the upshot of early economic restructuring. The period from 1992 to 1995 showed a certain recovery in the total employment rate, prompted mostly by the growth in informal jobs, especially those related to domestic services, autonomous work, and startups of small firms with fewer than five employees. Autonomous work represented the largest growth within the informal job sector, but personal income remained low: just 20 percent of autonomous workers over the age of thirty-five earned more than ten times the minimum wage a month, whereas 40 percent earned less than three times the minimum wage, and 10 percent earned less than the minimum wage (about U.S.$100 in 1998).

From the standpoint of the organized labor force, the challenge of maintaining jobs has not yet been effectively taken on. Squeezed by growing unemployment and a flimsy social security system with extremely low provisions for unemployed workers, and subject to an array of bureaucratic conditionings, trade unions have no choice but to accept a de facto informalization of labor relations. In practice, this means losing some basic guarantees and support: health assistance, thirteenth monthly wage bonus, paid holidays, retirement, and compensation at dismissal; these have been in effect since the 1940s for formal jobs and have always been argued to be necessary benefits to compensate poor wages.

The decline of the formal labor market has a clear-cut impact on major Brazilian urban agglomerations, worsening the quality of life, particularly in terms of violence engendered by open and hidden unemployment.[19] Although these factors are not exclusive to Brazil or São Paulo, they are leading to a trend that opposes sustainable policies geared to overcoming poverty. This fact is aggravated by the predatory interregional and interlocal competition for direct incentives, namely infrastructure, financing, and land, and the municipal tax exemption that followed the opening up of the Brazilian economy in 1994. In the context of growing unemployment and a globalized economy, this means that each single locality, in seeking out what job creation businesses they wish to shelter, will try to offer the best competitive advantages to those businesses on a global scale, and will not consider any national compensation system. This competition among states was directed basically at attracting new automobile plants,[20] and was so unbending that it has been called a "tax war."

A deeper assessment of the tax war process indicates that concessions to private companies are usually so far-reaching that city budgets are compromised for several years to come, with no real guarantee of economic or social returns (Piancastelli and Perobelli 1996). This can be disastrous particularly to midsize towns with small municipal budgets, since, in the prospect of enhanced integration in the globalized economy, the regions that offer the best competitive advantages—such as Brazil's Southeast, and particularly São Paulo—will be privileged in receiving new investments to modernize their infrastructure. Needless to say, this process entails the aggravation of an interregional distribution of wealth. This triggers a wide-scale trend toward social degradation, which the Brazilian federal government unwittingly encourages by channeling federal resources to those regions able to enhance the competitiveness of Brazilian firms and to attract new foreign direct investments.

Thus Brazil is faced with a dilemma: establishing international communications and a modernized manufacuring infrastructure are essential if the country is to compete successfully for new industrial investments; but meeting the costs of creating these competitive advantages means draining scarce regional and local resources that would otherwise be invested in direct social needs.

Social Impacts

Because of São Paulo's performance, the city reacts faster than others to shifts in today's world economy. In this sense, two distinct effects can be observed in its urban structure. On the one hand, it accumulates the benefits of greater investments, namely direct and infrastructure investments,[21] it shelters the skilled labor force, and it has an abundant supply of advanced technology and global-market-oriented urban activities, not to mention affiliates of sophisticated international shops. On the other hand, it is also the *locus* of social perversities that result from the side effects of greater globalization. The increase in unemployment and informal jobs, in violence and in urban squatter settlements become more visible on the streets of the city with each passing year.

An official survey in the São Paulo Metropolitan Area indicates that people working in informal jobs constituted almost 15 percent of the working-age population in 1996. The survey also found an overall deterioration in labor market conditions compared to earlier years: some 59 percent of new jobs in São Paulo are attributable to the informal job sector, 13 percent to outsourcing, and 14 percent to workers without any kind of benefits, which is unlawful. The results of the survey indicate that while the salary gap between formal and informal jobs is decreasing, there is a significant decline in both groups in job opportunities for less qualified workers (Montagner and Springer 1997).

The tertiary sector has not created the jobs needed to compensate for manufacuring job losses resulting from decentralization and restructuring processes. As a consequence, the informal job sector has expanded and social problems have become aggravated by a sharp decrease in the supply of housing and infrastructure for low-income groups. The portion of the population living in squatter settlements went up from 476,621 people in 1980 to 1,344,250 in 1996, corresponding to an increase in the total number of squatter homes from 100,318 to 318,021 (FIBGE, Censo Demográfico 1980 and Contagem da População 1996).[22] This growth is even more telling if we consider that the total population growth rate has been decreasing to such an extent in the last decades that in 1980 this metropolis sheltered 15.1 percent of the domestic urban population (21.2 percent of squatters), and in 2000 (according to preliminary census data) about 13 percent of the domestic urban population.

Moreover, the geographical distribution of the population has followed a very exclusionary pattern, with negative rates in the more central and consolidated areas, where the upper-income population lives, and positive rates in the outskirts, where there is much less infrastructure, water sewage, transport, telephones, hospitals and a lower-income population. This urbanization pattern is spreading beyond the city limits, with the poorest population being pushed into the neighboring municipalities within the metropolitan area, having no choice but to invade the reservoir-protected areas to build new squatter settlements.

In addition to the socioeconomic impact on the population, all the economic changes aimed at aggrandizing Brazil's presence in the global economy have interfered in the physical urban structure of the city of São Paulo. The increasing gap between the areas concentrating advanced "global" activities and the peripheral areas demonstrates the dramatic physical impact of this process. The more evident effects show up in the imbalance of infrastructure in the two areas, such as the much higher concentration in the central city of telematics, fiber optics, cable TV, and mobile telephone central stations.

The implementation of these more sophisticated systems of infrastructure has focused either on existing consolidated business districts or on new business developments, creating new centers in the overall urban complex. This parallels the development in Buenos Aires (Ciccolella and Mignaqui, this volume) and Mexico City (Parnreiter, this volume). These centers can be measured by the extent to which they have attracted new commercial buildings, which represented 26.6 percent of the total new construction in the city from 1990 to 1995. The enhancement and shifting of central areas is a typical characteristic of the São Paulo Metropolitan Area that is not to be confused with the American pattern of suburbanization. There is no real autonomy and polycentric structure, but rather, an enhanced—and somewhat deconcentrated—unicentered urban structure. In architectural terms, these renovated districts reproduce an international design pattern very similar to the new central business districts of major cities like New York or Los Angeles.

The gentrification process occurring in most of the modernized districts is the result of urban renewal by private capital, but is based on heavy state and/or municipal investments, set aside not only for telematics and other direct core-business-related infrastructure, but for new access channels such as roads and tunnels, most of which cut the traditional urban fabric. The resulting renovated areas are not a consequence of previous official planning, nor has the population dwelling in these areas ever been consulted on the convenience of these changes. Therefore, the urban result in most cases is a miscellany of modern business land and old dwellings, creating confused transport flows and the connotation that the whole city organization is a makeshift arrangement, despite the high costs of the works involved.

Altogether, the concentration of the communications infrastructure and financial activities in São Paulo has definitely contributed to making it the preferred location for regional headquarters of corporations acting in the Mercosur area. Besides the necessary infrastructure and specialized services for business, São Paulo offers hotels, shopping, and leisure opportunities in line with the demands of a new international elite. Nevertheless, the city's large scale, its growing traffic problems, its environmental depletion, and its social violence have jeopardized the quality of life to such an extent that its functional attractiveness may be marred by its everyday problems. São Paulo's centrality in the Mercosur depends on the removal of infrastructure hindrances to regional integration, especially so with Argentina and Uruguay in the case of surface integration. The cross-border linkages, digital or physical, had to be built in order to assure not just regional integration but also to maximize the connectivity of the Mercosur bloc with all other markets.

CONCLUSIONS

Greater internationalization of the economy, particularly since the early eighties, forced developing countries into institutional restructuring to allow their greater inclusion in global processes. In Brazil, these reforms focused mostly on deregulating specific sectors to encourage cross-border transactions and participation of foreign capital as a direct investor, either in manufacturing or finance. The internal reforms required strong state intervention. A compulsory economic plan was introduced in 1994 to effect monetary stabilization (it was essential to inspire confidence in foreign investment returns) by introducing monetary dollar parity and high annual interest rates. At the same time the economy was radically opened by lifting trade restrictions, which resulted in the reduction of almost all duties on imported goods. Legal and institutional changes designed to spur the privatization process of heavy industries and public services were also introduced. Concerning the latter, two distinct mechanisms were put into place: the first called for the privatization of electric power and telecommunications companies, and the second, for partnerships with the private sector through the concession of services and some operations. Neither process was accompanied by a strict regulatory framework, leading to uncertainties related to quality and price output, and to a lack of concern about whether the lower-income population was being served suitably (Silva 1996).

The economic model established by Brazil in the 1990s abruptly exposed domestic manufacturers to international competition without a transition period that would have allowed them to regroup so as to compete effectively. As a result, unemployment and employment in informal jobs soared, especially for the less skilled labor force, which led to greater social exclusion and a widening of the income gap. The São Paulo Metropolitan Area, as the main Brazilian and Mercosur economic center, experienced the broader—national and regional— inclusion in international trade and business patterns in extreme ways. On the one hand, it developed the most advanced services and financial activities, the largest stock market and commodities exchange in Latin America, as well as sophisticated shopping and leisure activities. On the other hand, social side effects such as urban violence, marginality, and homelessness, have also been on the rise.

The centrality of São Paulo regarding the Mercosur region was reinforced by the construction of a complex digital telecommunications system linking this city (and Brazil) to the main economic world centers, including those in Latin American countries. At the same time highway, energy power, railway, and waterway networks had to be enhanced in order to integrate the Mercosur bloc and to expand its outward articulation with other parts of the world. In broad terms, trends such as the increase in the number of specialized services and finance institutions, and the supply of sophisticated infrastructure used both by business and by high-income groups in São Paulo indicate the sustained leadership of this city, both within Brazil and in South America. Nevertheless, the same conditions which have given São Paulo reasonable comfort and uncontested leadership domestically and regionally, have also led to the social instability inherent to economic change and the accentuation of inequality. This may threaten São Paulo's leadership in the long run. Investments need to address not only global-market-oriented activities, but also the everyday life of this large metropolis and its very exclusionary urban structure.

APPENDIX
JAPAN AND LATIN AMERICA: A CHANGELESS ECONOMIC ARTICULATION

The leading recipient of Japan's foreign direct investment was the United States, which received about 45 percent of the total amount in the 1980s and much of the 1990s. Although this share decreased in the late 1990s, with a simultaneous increase in the European share, the United States continues to be the main destination of Japan's overseas investments (World Bank 1997).

The Latin American share of Japan's FDI began to rise after the 1997 financial crises in Asia. The cumulative share from 1951 to 1994 stood at 11.9 percent compared to 16.5 percent for Asia. This gap broadened to, respectively, 8.0 percent and 14.2 percent in 1991, and 7.6 percent and 22.4 percent in 1995 (table A). The 1999 figures show a sharp fall in the Asian share and a marked increase in the Latin American share, resulting in a similar level of about 11 percent.

A key factor explaining the difference in the earlier period from the 1970s to 1996 was the strong economic development of the Asian "Tigers," particularly South Korea, Taiwan, Hong Kong, and Singapore, in comparison with the economic stagnation of most Latin American countries. The East Asia economic crisis of 1997 and the expansion of investments in the Cayman Islands tax haven (JETRO White Paper 2000: 16) have contributed to rechanneling Japanese foreign direct investments to the developing countries. The Cayman Islands became the largest first recipient of Japan's FDI in Latin America in the 1990s, surpassing Panama's historical leadership.

Brazil has played a distinctive role in Japan's investments in Latin America. While Panama was a key node for shipping activities and the Caymans for financial investments, Brazil was important for agriculture, manufacturing, and new financial services.[23] São Paulo is the key node for these investments. The city also is home to the largest Japanese immigrant community.[24]

The establishment of new Japanese firms, or of joint ventures between Japanese and Brazilian companies in Brazil, has been a response to both the performance of the Brazilian economy and the guidelines laid down to accomplish the specific requirements of Japan's domestic industry. The decline in new start-ups during the 1980s reflects the Brazilian economic crisis. Few new Japanese-Brazilian companies were established in the early 1990s. Most of the ones that were established were small;[25] many were representative offices rather than production plants. This contests Suzuki's thesis[26] of an impressive increase in the late 1990s of Japanese investments in the Brazilian manufacturing sector because of Mercosur's market potential. The 1990s saw some hefty new investments in Japanese manufacturing companies already operating in Brazil. This was especially the case for investments in the Toyota and Honda automobile assembly lines. Although both corporations already had factories in Brazil, neither produced automobiles. Toyota, formerly engaged in producing automobile parts, is investing large amounts to build an automobile assembly line in a new manufacturing plant. Honda started operating a new automobile factory in Brazil in 1997, whereas, previously, its traditional business was motorcycles.[27]

In overall terms, Japan's major investment interests in Brazil have been

TABLE A1
JAPAN'S FOREIGN DIRECT INVESTMENT BY KEY COUNTRIES AND REGION

Selected Countries/Region	1991 amount	1991 share	1993 amount	1993 share	Cumulative Total 1951–1994 amount	Cumulative Total 1951–1994 share	1995 amount	1995 share	1997 amount	1997 share	1999 amount	1999 share
U.S.A	18.026	43.3	14.725	40.9	194.429	41.9	22.193	43.8	20.769	38.5	22.296	33.4
Canada	797	1.9	562	1.6	8.261	1.8	558	1.1	620	1.1	2.474	3.7
North America Total	*18.823*	*45.2*	*15.287*	*42.4*	*202.690*	*43.7*	*22.761*	*44.9*	*21.389*	*39.6*	*24.770*	*37.1*
Panama	1.157	3.7	1.390	3.9	21.784	4.7	1.660	3.3	1.119	2.1	...	
Brazil	171	0.4	419	1.2	8.849	1.9	301	0.6	1.182	2.2	...	
Caymans	158	0.4	841	2.5	9.249	2.0	659	1.3	2.538	4.7	...	
Mexico	193	0.5	53	0.1	2.973	0.6	206	0.4	320	0.6	...	
Chile	75	0.2	3	0.0	430	0.1	137	0.3	23	0.0	...	
Argentina	40	0.1	34	0.1	545	0.1	117	0.2	57	0.1	...	
Latin America Total	*3.337*	*8.0*	*3.370*	*9.4*	*155.148*	*11.9*	*3.877*	*7.6*	*6.336*	*11.7*	*7.437*	*11.1*
Indonesia	1.193	2.9	813	2.3	16.981	3.7	1.596	3.1	2.514	4.7	918	1.4
Hong Kong	925	2.2	1.238	3.4	13.881	3.0	1.125	2.2	695	1.3	917	1.5
Singapore	613	1.5	644	1.8	9.535	2.1	1.152	2.3	1.824	3.4	962	1.4
Korea, Rep. of	260	0.6	245	0.7	5.268	1.1	445	0.9	442	0.8	980	1.5
China, Rep. of	579	1.4	1.691	4.7	8.729	1.9	4.473	8.8	1.987	3.7	751	1.1
Asia Total	*5.944*	*14.2*	*6.637*	*18.4*	*76.216*	*16.4*	*12.264*	*24.2*	*12.181*	*22.6*	*7.162*	*10.7*
Middle East Total	*90*	*0.2*	*217*	*0.6*	*4.737*	*1.0*	*148*	*0.3*	*471*	*0.9*	*213*	*0.2*
United Kingdom	3.588	8.6	2.527	7.0	33.830	7.3	3.445	6.8	4.118	7.6	11.718	17.6
Netherlands	1.960	4.7	2.175	6.0	19.447	4.2	1.509	3.0	3.295	6.1	10.361	15.5
Germany	1.115	2.7	760	2.1	8.061	1.7	547	1.1	732	1.4	649	1.0
Europe Total	*9.372*	*22.3*	*7.940*	*22.0*	*89.867*	*19.4*	*8.470*	*16.7*	*11.204*	*20.8*	*25.804*	*38.7*
Africa Total	*748*	*1.8*	*539*	*1.5*	*7.698*	*1.7*	*379*	*0.7*	*332*	*0.6*	*515*	*0.8*
Australia	3	6.1	1.904	5.3	23.932	5.2	2.635	5.2	...		...	
Oceania Total	*3.278*	*7.8*	*2.035*	*5.6*	*27.250*	*5.9*	*2.795*	*5.5*	*2.058*	*3.8*	*894*	*1.3*
Total	**41.185**	**100**	**36.025**	**100**	**463.606**	**100**	**250.694**	**100**	**53.972**	**100**	**66.694**	**100**

(Unit: amount = US$million/share = %)

... No data

Source: Jetro White Paper on Foreign Direct Investments (after Japan's Ministry of Finance data), several years.

related to iron, steel, and nonferrous metals. Shareholders' equity in the two largest Japanese-Brazilian companies in 1999 (CST and USIMINAS), both in the steel industry, shows sharply higher investments compared with other firms on the list. Japanese imports from Brazil also reflect this primary interest in steel and iron products, considered essential to Japan's domestic industry. Taking the post-1999 data, iron ore as a raw material accounts for 20.8 percent of the total amount exported to Japan, whereas iron and steel, in their final form as semi-manufactured products, represent 0.4 percent. Semimanufactured nonferrous metals, including aluminum, are Brazil's second most exported product, accounting for 13.7 percent of total Brazilian exports to Japan in 1999.

Brazilian imports from Japan in 1999 were dominated by equipment, which accounted for 75.4 percent of the total. There were significant changes in the major items in both imports and exports on the list during the period analyzed (1985 to 1999) (SEPIP, several years). However, some changes can be expected, particularly in view of the above-mentioned establishment of the two big Japanese automobile factories in Brazil.

Brazil and Latin America in general, although considered potential markets for Japanese products and investments, remain far behind Asia, despite the Asian economic and currency crisis of late 1997. Asia is still the strongest economic network among the developing nations for Japanese investments. Economic globalization, however, is triggering unexpected capital flows toward different regions and countries. From this perspective, Brazil may well represent an alternative for Japanese investments rather than a mere continuation of old patterns. Furthermore, the economic choices open to Brazil concerning the development of its own production forces will surely weigh decisively in determining whether ties based on new economic relations are to be fostered between these two countries.

NOTES

1. See GMLA 1996f: 25 concerning the transfer of traditional Argentinean domestic manufacturing capital to foreign capital.

2. Banco Bilbao Vizcaya (Spain) acquired the Banco Francés del Rio de la Plata and the Banco de Crédito Argentino; Banco Santander (Spain) bought the Banco Rio de la Plata; and the Hong Kong and Shanghai Bank (Great Britain) bought Banco Roberts (GMLA 1997d).

3. American Fidelity Investments, Prudential Securities and Alliance Capital Management, and the British Fleming Investment Management; J. P. Morgan Investment and Merrill Lynch, both already installed in São Paulo, Brazil, also stepped up their activities substantially (GM 1997).

4. Latin America vehicle sales, as a whole, increased from 1.2 million in 1990 to almost 3 million in 1999; more than half of these vehicles were produced in Brazil (GMLA, 2001a).

5. The first year it was implemented (1994), the annual interest rate was roughly 45 percent. It declined slowly, dropping to less than 30 percent in 1996, but after the Asian economic crisis in mid-1998, the rate rose to nearly 50 percent.

6. Brazilian foreign reserves were (in billions of U.S.$): 8.7 (1990); 8.5 (1991); 19.1 (1992); 25.9 (1993); 36.7 (1994); 50.5 (1995); 67.5 (August 1998); 44.9 (September 1998); and 33.0 (December 2000). See (GMLA 1996a, 1998; and GM 2001b), as per Brazilian Central Bank data.

7. According to the Brazilian National Bank of Economic Development, the import rate for goods increased 2.5 fold from 1990 to 1995, to 15 percent of domestic consumption by November 1996 (GM 1996d).

8. An example is the automobile industry. The duty on cars was lowered at first from 100 percent to 30 percent, prompting feverish car imports. The negative impact on domestic production was such that the tax was increased to 70 percent after less than a year. However considering that "domestic" automobile companies are all controlled by foreign capital (American and German), another law was introduced that allowed automobile manufacturers established in Brazil to import at a reduced duty of 35 percent, protecting their prices against Asian and French car prices, for instance. The greatest impact however was on the manufacturers of automobile parts. These had to face foreign competition head-on because the duty on car parts was slashed to about 2 percent. Most of these manufacturers operated with national capital, and a large number have since opened themselves to foreign capital, including one of the most traditional and largest automobile parts manufacturers, called "Metal Leve," which has always been a national symbol of advanced technology and efficiency.

9. This law is called Anexo 4 and was introduced by the Brazilian Central Bank.

10. See Pasanezze 1993 for a further assessment of the first cycle of the Brazilian privatization process.

11. Chile has not yet joined the Mercosur bloc as a full member. Nevertheless it has a special free trade agreement with the bloc. Recently, Bolivia entered into a similar free trade agreement as a first step to future membership.

12. Especially some large corporations formerly located in Rio de Janeiro.

13. In 1993, the number of bank agencies in the city of São Paulo represented 32 percent of all agencies statewide, and concentrated 70.7 percent of total state deposits and 81.1 percent of credit operations (FSEADE 1995: 64–68).

14. According to the 1996 *Gazeta Mercantil* Annual Ranking (GM- Balanço Anual, 1996).

15. The number of responses was not considered adequate to draw any definite conclusions.

16. The author thanks Prof. Ricardo Toledo Silva for making data available for this item.

17. Informal jobs classification based on International Labor Organization information: independent workers (not including those who work for just one firm with more than five employees); workers in firms with fewer than five employees); workers with no benefits; owners of a family business with fewer than five employees; members of a family working for no wages in a family business.

18. The agricultural production system, based on large properties and seasonal hiring of labor, has never absorbed the available labor suppply, and regional imbalances have promoted important migratory flows toward the more wealthy Southeast, which is now absorbing most of the structural unemployment associated with the globalization process.

19. According to IBGE methodology that considers those individuals who have not worked in the month preceding the survey unemployed, the official rate of unemployment in October 2000 for the Metropolitan Area of São Paulo was 8 percent while the average of the other five largest metropolitan areas was 7.5 percent (FIBGE: PME).

20. See ESP 1997 and the *Financial Times* 1997.

21. In 1993, all the department stores in the state operating with bar codes were based in the city of São Paulo. And 31.6 percent of the international telephone calls placed or received in Brazil were recorded in the city of São Paulo (FSEADE 1996: 64). The number of helicopters in the city in April 2001 was around five hundred for two hundred heliports (GMLA, 2001).

22. These numbers are largely underestimated, insofar as the FIBGE (state statistical agency) does not consider agglomerations of fewer than fifty-one homes as squatter settlements.

23. All data concerning Brazil and Japan trade relations were compiled from "Japan Annual Trade Reports," organized by the JETRO Office in São Paulo.

24. Massive Japanese immigration to Brazil occurred during the early part of this century, when coffee production in the state of São Paulo lacked a sufficient labor force. From 1908 to 1925, the

São Paulo state government subsidized this immigration. After 1925, the Japanese government subsidized the immigration to Brazil, but this time the Japanese came as small farmers, instead of as a waged labor force.

25. According to the number of employees reported by most, only one company, in the computer industry (Epson), had a substantial head count (100), whereas the other ten had no more than about 150 employees altogether.

26. Takanori Suzuki works for the Deloitte Touche Thomatsu consulting company and wrote the book "Brasil, o despertar de uma nação" ("Brazil, the Waking Up of a Nation") (1997); see, G. M. 1997b.

27. *Financial Times* 1997.

REFERENCES CITED

Baltar, P. E. de A. and C. S. Deddeca. 1997. "O mercado de trabalho no Brasil: o aumento da informalidade dos anos 90." In IPEA, International Workshop: *O setor informal revisitado: novas tendências e perspectivas de políticas públicas.* Brazil.

Cacciamali, M. C. 1996. "The Growing Inequality in Income Distribution in Brazil." Pp. 215–234 in *The Brazilian Economy: Structure and Performance in Recent Decades,* ed. M. J. F. Willunsen and E. G. da Feonseca. University of Miami: North-South Center.

CEI (Centro de Economia Internacional del Ministerio de Relaciones Exteriores, Comercio Internacional y Culto de la Republica Argentina) 2000. "Exportaciones e Importaciones." Buenos Aires, Argentina. (web site cei.mrecic.gov.ar/anexmer)

Chudnovsky, D. 1997. "Beyond Macroeconomic Stability in Latin America." Pp. 125–154 in *The New Globalism and Developing Countries,* ed. J. H. Dunning and K. A. Handani. Tokyo: United Nations University Press.

ESP (O Estado de São Paulo) 1997. "Guerra fiscal abala finanças dos Estados" July 13, p. B-1.

EXAME São Paulo. 2000. *Exame* 273 (December).

FIBGE (Fundação Instituto Brasileiro de Geografia e Estatística). 1980. "Censo demográfico." Rio de Janeiro: IBGE.

———. Various years. "Contagem da população." Rio de Janeiro: IBGE.

———. "Pesquisa Mensal do Emprego (PME)." Rio de Janeiro, IBGE, several years.

Financial Times. 1997. *Motown's New Eldorado.* January 7, pp. 11–12.

FSEADE (Fundação Sistema Estadual de Análise de Dados). 1995. "Estratégias recentes no terciário paulista." São Paulo: SEADE.

———. 1996. "São Paulo." São Paulo, SEADE.

———. 1999. "PAEP—Pesquisa da atividade econômica paulista." São Paulo, SEADE.

GM—*Gazeta Mercantil.* 1996a. "Cresce a presença das importações do mercado." November 13, p. A-8.

———. 1996b. "Investimentos do Brasil duplicam em cinco anos na região." December 12, p. I-6.

———. 1997a. "Estrangeiros chegam para gerir fundos." June 23, p. B-20.

———. 1997b. "Japoneses preferem atuar sozinhos" (Japanese prefer to act alone). October 14, p. C-5.

———. 1998a. "Tietê chega finalmente ao Paraná." January 12, p. A-5.

———. 1998b. "Projetos entregues no prazo" June 29, Report 1.

———. 1998c. "Investimento externo mundial bate recorde em 1998." November 11, p. A-10.

———. 1999. "Atlas do Mercado Brasileiro." São Paulo.

———. "Balanço Anual." São Paulo, several years.

———. 1999. "1000 maiores da empresas da América Latina." September.

———. 2000a. "1000 maiores fundos de investimento da América Latina." April.

———. 2000b. "1000 maiores da América Latina." October.

———. 2001. "Indicadores." January 11, p. 26 Various years. Balanco Anual.

GMLA—Gazeta Mercantil Latino-Americana. 1996a. "Avança a integração energética." April 26, p. 16.

————. 1996b. "Fibra ótica até a fronteira" p. 16.

————. 1996c. "Consolidar metrópoles." September 9, p. 4.

————. 1996d. "Déficit na conta corrente atinge 2,89% do PIB" November 23, p. B-1.

————. 1996e. "Uma velha aspiração" November 24, p. 8.

————. 1996f. "Mudando de mãos. Empresas tradicionais são vendidas na Argentina." December 9, p. 25.

————. 1997a. "Bloco carece de infra-estrutura." March 17, pp. 12–15.

————. 1997b. "Novo gasoduto." March 31, p. 3.

————. 1997c. "Um mundo chamado São Paulo." July 4, pp.17–18.

————. 1997d. "O desafio dos bancos latinos." July 14, p. 20.

————. 1997e. "Caminho aberto para a integração." September 22, p.11.

————. 1998. "Indicadores." November 16, p. 31.

————. 2001a. "Produção de veículos no Mercosul longe dos 3 mi." January 8, p. 21.

————. 2001b. "Falta integração, sobra prejuízo." March 12, p. 14.

————. 2001c. "A São Paulo dos executivos estrangeiros." April 16, p. 4.

JETRO (Japanese External Trade Office) *"Annual Trade Report."* Several years. São Paulo: Jetro Office.

————. 2000. *White Paper on Foreign Direct Investment.* Tokyo: Jetro.

Montagner, P., and P. Springer. 1997. "Evolução das inserções ocupacionais na Região Metropolitana de São Paulo, 1988/96." In: IPEA, International Workshop: *O setor informal revisitado: novas tendências e perspectivas de políticas públicas.* Brazil.

Pasanezze, R. F. 1993. "Porque privatizar a infra-estrutura pública. Da racionalidade do estado à racionalidade de cada setor." In: INFURB, International Seminar: *Infrastructure supply and urban policies in the prospect of privatization.* São Paulo.

Piancastelli, M. and F. Perobelli. 1996. *ICMS: evolução recente e guerra fiscal.* Brazil: IPEA.

Schiffer, S. R. 2001. "Economic Restructuring and Urban Segregation in São Paulo." In P. Marcuse and R. Van Kempen (eds.). *States and Cities; the Partitioning of Urban Space.* Oxford: Oxford University Press

SEPIP (Seleções Econômicas, Publicações, Informações, Pesquisas). 1998. *"Anuário: Empresas Japonesas no Brasil (Japanese Companies in Brazil Annual Report)."* São Paulo: SEPIP.

Silva, R. T. 1996. "Elementos para a regulação e o controle da infra-estrutura regional e urbana em cenário de oferta privada de serviços." Associate Professor thesis. FAUUSP, São Paulo.

UNCTAD—United Nations Conference on Trade and Development. *"World Investment Report."* Geneva: UNCTAD/United Nations, several years.

World Bank. 1997. *"World Investment Report. Transnational Corporations and Competitiveness."* Washington, DC: UNCTAD/ONU.

————. *"World Development Report."* Washington, DC: World Bank, several years.

Chapter 8

BEIRUT: BUILDING REGIONAL CIRCUITS

Eric Huybrechts

After a long civil war Beirut today is being rebuilt as a metropolitan hub for the Near East, which is expected to reinsert Beirut in regional and global economic systems. The reconstruction of the city is taking place in an environment with little social cohesiveness. There are multiple causes for the often sharp social divisions in the city, ranging from past conflicts among religious and political groups to the rapid expansion of the city, and they all exert influence. Alongside common problems raised by economic development processes and the disproportionate concentration of activities in Beirut, more complex dynamics arise from the city's specific role in the prewar period, the real estate development options created by the massive physical destruction of the city's built environment, the role Beirut is expected to play in the global economy by some of its powerful elites, and the fact that all of this is occurring in a context where the social fabric of the city is torn by old and new divisions.

The development of Beirut as a metropole can be seen as representing the territorial form of globalization (Escalier 2000: 207–219). As an actual development it is strongly connected with the global exchange of flows of people, money, goods, and information. The reshaping of Beirut can be understood in terms of the relation between the city itself and the place it is trying to become.

Although this essay will address urban segregation as it has emerged in relation to metropolitanization and the civil war, the main focus is on the economic rebuilding of Beirut and on its role in the Near East and the Gulf. How is the development of Beirut connected with globalization? Is Beirut a relay, with an interface function between the Near East and the global economy? If development is linked with globalization, will this impose new urban forms and functions corresponding to changes within the international economic system?

Must the urban transformations observed in Beirut adhere to and be consistent with these trends? Will the urban forms and the actors supporting these links become apparent?

THE POST–CIVIL WAR YEARS: THE NEED FOR URBAN COHESIVE POLICIES?

During the Lebanese civil war, Beirut was structurally devastated and was thrown into political, social, and economic chaos. The factors responsible for this were numerous, complex, and mainly linked with geopolitical frictions (Corm 1986). Longtime socioreligious (Picaudou 1989) and socioeconomic divisions in Beirut are a microcosm of divisions that exist in Lebanon as a whole, and these partitions have found tangible expression in the city's housing patterns. And so as the country's internal political situation deteriorated into conflict between rival groups, the sociospatial divisions in Beirut allowed the city to become a clearly demarcated battlefield.

The causes of these sociospatial divisions are partly historical. An analysis of the prewar period indicates the presence of extreme poverty in the midst of great wealth, as is clear in the longtime existence of a poverty belt (shantytowns, occupied mainly by Palestinians) in the context of rapid economic development (growth of more than 5 percent over a period of fifteen years). The so-called Lebanon miracle is based on an unbalanced economy, with a deficit in the balance of trade and a surplus in the balance of payments. And this "miracle" is being played out mainly in Beirut; the country's economic development is largely concentrated in that one city. This process of concentrating resources and activities in Beirut began in the middle of the nineteenth century and was strengthened during the French mandate (1920–1943) when Beirut was the capital of the Levant. The city's centrality is the fruit of a cumulative process spanning more than one and a half centuries.

The application of geographic principles to the comparative analysis of the social divisions and urban growth of the postwar era provides a clearer understanding of the current processes of metropolitanization and social collapse. Such a methodology reveals that the causes for social fragmentation in Beirut are more complex than usually considered and cannot be simply attributed to general socioeconomic factors. In fact, the social division of the city was also the result of political divisions concerning the Palestinians. Moreover, during the war the dispersion of the city's centralized activities and the displacement of its population are results of the conflict and the virtual demolition of the city center. Current efforts to make Beirut into an international metropole are reflected in the desire to bring the city center up to internationally recognizable standards. (See also the case of Shanghai, this volume).

The "demetropolitanization" of Beirut in the 1980s, when the city lost its regional status, corresponds to the most important division of the city. In this period, oil prices were low, and the Palestinian leaders were expelled from Lebanon. Christian militiamen held enormous power. The city was a disorganized mosaic of microterritories (Beyhum 1990). The main access to the city, port, airport roads—was controlled by private militiamen. The division of the city weakened the financial and political significance of Beirut in the region. Here metropolitanization and demetropolitanization processes are not causes for the divisions in the city but are rather a result of the divisions in the city.

Today, community-level divisions largely follow religious lines: the Christians live on the east side of the city and the Muslims on the west side. This seems to be the dominant divisive factor, but it is strongly contested by other forms of sociospatial structures (as I'll discuss below) with few or no attempts at social reconciliation (Huybrechts and Douayhi 1999). Housing patterns also reflect socioeconomic divisions. Rent laws protecting tenants have been in effect since 1970. The diminution of the Lebanese pound (which fell to one-thousandth of its prewar value during the war) reduced the annual rent of many apartments to the price of a single dinner in a restaurant. As a result, development of rental housing plunged. This contributed to concentration of the population in the municipality of Beirut; three-quarters of the people living in Beirut rented housing. Running contrary to this was the displacement policy of the government, which after the war expelled tens of thousands of squatters from the central districts, a move that also helped demarcate the suburbs. The property rights of the displaced are the subject of continual political contention for the different governments concerned. The real estate market plays a strong role in the location of people, which in turn has crucial consequences for community solidarity and social control. For example, gated communities, designed mainly before the war (Ghorra-Gobin 1981–1982) and built both during and after the war, have been located in areas that have very little other housing. There are dozens of new commercial malls with luxury shops and security control in every type of neighborhood. (See also chapter on Buenos Aires, this volume).

Thus two important factors in the lack of social cohesion in Beirut can be distinguished: socioeconomic divisions and community polarization. These two factors are interlinked and complex and are seldom contested by current social science research. Community links relate to the political "clientelism" based in the political practices of the country. Economic networks are formed upon this clientelism but in a way that seeks to override socioreligious divisions. Investors from different communities are encouraged to mix their religious networks for commercial promotion. So Shia invest in Christian neighborhoods; Christians sell land to Sunnis; Christians invest with Muslims in various commercial or real estate projects. By contrast, in rural areas it is difficult to buy land for non-local inhabitants. The city allows mixed and open exchanges. Community divisions seem to be more present in the political sphere than in economic activities. However, within this economy, political power plays a strongly protectionist role in the market, so that real estate, import-export, and diaspora investments are all closely interlinked in the economic sphere. The administrative structure appears to be no more than a mechanism used by numerous public-private actors to garner comparative advantages. The state is one of the main links between community and economic dynamics.

Strong contrasts exist in the spatial recompositions of the postwar period: irregular settlements stand close to new residential areas; new residential and industrial buildings are built on agricultural and natural areas or next to ruins; large urban projects are implemented without the underpinnings of adequate government policies. At first glance, the urban chaos is the most prominent feature of this city, followed by the mountainous backdrop. This chaos is a result of a multitude of individual and collective strategies enacted without coordination in the field. But decisions about the rebuilding process and the formulation of urban and regional policies are made at the national level, as are policies governing specific zones or sectors. These two contradictory operational modes have effects at different levels of the redevelopment of Beirut.

Consequently, policies that aim at urban cohesion are now clearly more important than ten years ago, when the war ended. The daily movement of people and traffic, formerly segmented along the East-West divide according to the 1994 findings for the Greater Beirut Transportation Plan, has now been freed up by the rebuilding process. Former battlefield sites now boast public facilities and residential areas. Roads that once were impassable because of the skirmishes being fought on them now carry more traffic than before the war. There has been a recent explosion of cellular telephone lines (four hundred thousand lines in three years), and 1.3 million old land lines have been restored to use; both developments are seen as signs of rapid recovery of communications in the city and beyond. The building of more than twenty commercial malls and the prospects of forthcoming European hypermarkets (Carrefour, Metro, Leclerc, Spinneys) accompanied by cinema complexes, supermarkets, hotels, and foreign brands are all forces of change that will alter the daily mobility of people.

Thus the mobility of people seemingly follows paradoxical trends: on the one hand, increased diversity in the commercial, employment, and leisure sectors reduces the necessity to live further away from the city center; on the other hand, the enhanced transportation system (Huybrechts 1999a) and the disparities at the level of microterritories encourage suburbanization and limit the opportunity to use the agglomeration as a whole.

New public spaces have become more attractive to residents. The Beirut Corniche has become the most popular place in the city for walking, jogging, and swimming. The new Dbaye Corniche, in the northern suburbs, is becoming popular with families. In these public places, Beirut is recovering its hyper-urbanity in a metropolis extended and reshaped by the war and reconstruction. On the other hand, the demolition of the city center during the years of war stimulated the creation and strengthening of secondary centers (Jounieh-Zouk, Borj Hammoud, Furn ech-Chebbak, Ouzai, Jbeil). Many contradictory trends are observable; structure-enhancing elements within communications sectors are paving the way for urban cohesion policies, but their construction is causing delays in the implementation of other projects (mass-transit highways, city center schemes), all of which disturb the rhythm of this change.

AIMING AT REINSERTION IN GLOBAL MARKETS

A short and static analysis of the current economic situation could cast doubt on the likelihood that Beirut will attain the regional role to which it aspires. Beirut has 1.7 millions inhabitants (Huybrechts 1999b) but clearly is not a megapole as defined by international standards; there are 119 cities in the world that are larger in population. In fact, the port area reconstruction in Beirut is less than one-third as large as Haifa (Israel) and only one-twentieth the size of Dubai's container port. The city's airport handles about the same amount of traffic as the airports at Amman, Doha or Damascus, but only half the air traffic in Cyprus and one-third that of Dubai, Cairo, Tel Aviv, or Jeddah. However, the strong economy in Beirut and the development of huge new capacities signal the possibility of its reemergence as a regional center.

The war left three-quarters of the city damaged, 5 percent of it in ruins. This would seem to allow parallels with decayed industrial areas in other countries. But in fact such comparisons are difficult because the remetropolitanization of Beirut is pursuing a process continuous with what happened in the city before, during, and after the war. The war allowed for the opportunity to amplify urban restructuring projects initiated before the war and to develop projects at a scale that would have been impossible in the prewar era. For example, one of the aims of the city center project was to triple its real estate surface by demolishing 80 percent of the dilapidated buildings and reclaiming 64 hectares on the seashore.

Despite the extent of social segregation and spatial division in the city during the war, and despite the constitutional change of repartition of power, there is a strong continuity in urban planning. Much of the major infrastructure and many of the facilities and urban operations are more or less in the former war zones or in the seashore suburbs on reclaimed land (340 hectares of reclaimed land in the northern suburbs and 560 hectares in the southern suburbs), providing ample space for further expansion of the projects. The key political and financial actors within this process are participating collectively by defining and implementing the process of metropolitanization.

Some of these projects aim to relocate Beirut within the international exchange system. The reconstruction of the infrastructure requires expansions of a scale that surpass local economic dimensions: the international airport of Beirut, situated 7 kilometers from the city center, has doubled its passenger traffic in five years, reaching 2.3 million passengers, despite the nearby Israeli military presence and the depressed regional context. Today, fifty-two airline and air-transport companies use the airport. The proposed new terminal would allow the airport to serve 6 million passengers a year, and the "open sky" policy that commenced in February 2001 is expected to increase the opportunity for the Beirut airport to compete as a hub with Cyprus, Tel-Aviv, Cairo, and Dubai. The new extension of the container port of Beirut opened early in the year 2001. The port capacity is four times greater than before, which could allow Beirut to compete with Haifa, Eshkalon, or Damiette and others in the Near East and the Gulf. Beirut may become the main point of entry to the Levantine coast in this region. Large new facilities have been built to accommodate international regional demand: a new stadium of 65,000 seats and a new campus for the university (forty-five thousand students) on 70 hectares.[1]

Large road projects are planned to connect with the regional highway network from Turkey to Egypt, adding Lebanon to the Arab highway system of Syria, Jordan, Iraq, and Saudi Arabia. Communications networks are now at international standards: fiber-optics networks of high capacity connect Beirut with the global network; and satellite communications, cellular phones, and the rapid expansion of Internet service (one hundred thousand users for 3.8 million people in Lebanon) are signs of rapid integration into international exchange networks.

Large urban operations are being designed to be compatible and competitive with the main business, commercial, and leisure industries in the Middle East. The rebuilding of the city center (4.69 million square meters) is the focal point of this reconstruction process. High-quality standards are applied in this "old city of the future," mixing old-style and contemporary architecture in buildings, public spaces, and pedestrian streets. Further, large-scale projects are planned for the southern suburbs (Clerc 2001) and for those vast areas reclaimed from the sea (Ghandour-Atallah 1998). All these ambitious developments have one main goal: to allow Beirut to compete as a prime location for investment and commercial distribution in the Middle East.

Infrastructure construction has contributed to a real estate boom and enormous change in the built environment. More than fifteen thousand buildings went up between 1991 and 1996, matching the volume of new construction in Paris or Moscow. Still, this volume is slightly lower than it was before the war, when one-third of tangible investments were devoted to land and real estate. Reusing the same model from before the war, land speculation is again one of the main pillars of the Lebanese economy.

Beirut is trying to attract the regional convention trade, marketing itself as a Near East center for exhibitions and fairs. It is also promoting itself as a place to live that offers a high quality of life, and it is using its media advantage in the Middle East to that end. The Lebanese TV has strong impact within Gulf countries, and Lebanese media production is in high demand in Arabic nations.

Major Lebanese and international companies are returning to Beirut. Coca-Cola is leaving Cyprus for Beirut; Vivendi chose Beirut over Dubai for its regional office; and Bouygues is undertaking a $230 million reconstruction project there. In addition, the ESCWA, the regional United Nations organization, left Amman in favor of Beirut. Important multilateral stakeholders are strengthening this integration into the mainstream international free market channeled through several regional and global processes, according to EUROMED, WTO, and the Arab League (Compain 1998).

COMPETITION AND COMPLEMENTARITY IN THE MIDDLE EAST

All of this speculative development is taking place in a region that may appear economically marginalized in global terms. The southeastern part of the Mediterranean constitutes less than 2 percent of world financial exchange. Regionally, financial activity is much more concentrated in Egypt and Israel. Income diminished by 2 percent in the Near East between 1980 and 1995. Although Lebanon's gross domestic product of $4,000 per capita is higher than that of other Arab countries of the Near East, it is far less than that of Israel ($16,000) and the Gulf countries ($25,000). Lebanon's manufacturing sector, with $1.7 billion in value added in the year 2000, is not aiming to increase its presence in world production.

Rather, Beirut is orienting its activities around services, media, and commerce. International companies are using Beirut's location to launch their products in the Near East and Gulf countries. These international firms do not require a large labor force to carry out their operations. Thus the effect, while strategic, is small in its impact on the creation of office buildings. Most of these firms have joint ventures. For example, one-third of the seventy-five banks in Beirut are joint-ventures. Some of these banks have aims for regional expansion. Thus Beirut is reclaiming its prewar role of relay in the region for international companies (Paix 1973), but without having any primacy in the region in which it is competing.

Beirut's port is not in competition for shipping traffic with Gulf ports, such as Dubai or Aqaba (Jordan) because of their regional locations on different main traffic networks. Beirut gives better opportunities for ships coming from the Occident that want to avoid the Suez Canal and thus save three or four days on their route to Gulf countries. Here competitive advantage is obvious, thanks to good terrestrial links (highways, rapid crossing of tolls). Thus, port competition is concentrated within the Levantine coast. The main competitors are Haifa (Israel), Eshkalon (Israel), and Lattaquia (Syria). The opening of Iraq and the economic development of Syria are two markets for these four ports. The macroregional political context interferes with Syria, which in turn produces pressures to limit the capacity of Lebanon's competitiveness despite the low capacity of Syria's port. Israel, on the other hand, has political and cultural handicaps that limit its ability to develop exchanges in the region; but Israel also offers more efficiency at its port (it takes no more than a few hours to transit containers in Haifa, as opposed to the week it may take in Beirut before the opening of the new container terminal).

The already weak industrial infrastructure in Beirut sustained further damage during the Israeli attacks. International competition from Egypt, Turkey, and eastern Europe reduces opportunities for Beirut, except in some protected segments. The main areas in which Beirut might become competitive are finance, media, education, health, commercial development, fairs/exhibitions, leisure, and real estate. These sectors are the same in Amman, Kuwait, Abu Dhabi, Bahrain, Dubai, all of which have a thirty-year head start on developing them. Damascus and Aleppo are not competitive because of constraints imposed by the regime in Syria.

Beirut's clearest competitive advantage is that it has solid links with a large diaspora. Overseas Lebanese networks connect Beirut with multiple international business centers. Further, in comparison with other metropolises that import manpower (e.g., 90 percent of Dubai's workers are migrants), Beirut appears more stable, with less dependence on foreign workers and more capacity for long-term economic development.

However, Beirut's development depends in large part on regional development capabilities, currently stymied by deep political crises. Forecasts based on a rapid solution for the regional peace process and OPEC aid indicate the fragility of the strategy. The present period is particularly difficult because of a large national debt (140 percent of the GDP) and slower regional economic development than anticipated. In this context, Beirut is a metropolis that is ready to host a large part of the speculative investment of the next regional economic boom. But the current waiting period, intended to protect domestic markets before the regional openings, has become a period in which the accumulated debt cannot be redressed without rapid, and that means regional, expansion.

CONCLUSION

As indicated above, the success of the strategy for reinserting Beirut in regional and global circuits is closely related to the regional context, and right now there is a lot of uncertainty about the future in the region. The future is dependent on the reduction of divisions in the region, notably closed frontiers and high toll taxes. But if regional differences can be resolved, the Middle East can be promoted as a location for investment, and with the large capacities that Beirut is able to offer after ten years of rebuilding, the city should be a major competitor. Its integration into the global economy will be based on the successful marketing of its services, commerce, tourism, and education, but not on manufacturing. This corresponds to its traditional role of interface between the Mediterranean Sea and the Middle East. The regional opening will be a signal for speculative and volatile investments, and for consumer industries (leisure, tourism). The important investments in land and real estate are linked to the comparative advantages of this sector (low taxes, high density). The accumulation of wealth in this sector before, during, and after the war is a handicap for further development, but it is also a sign of the vitality of the speculative economy. It is one of the motors running the metropolitanization of Beirut.

Integration into the global economic system is focused on the development of communications infrastructures, the use of foreign images and models, and the accumulation of wealth by investments in banking and real estate and growth in the import and export trade. Integration is not centered on world-class innovation systems. Transforming Beirut into a metropole is a cumulative process that began in the middle of the nineteenth century. Today, the effort is to recover a place in the region after fifteen years of war. Beirut's dominant stakeholders are pinning their hopes on an infusion of global investments and trade in the Middle East, and they are reshaping Beirut in the image that those hopes dictate. The city is being shaped not by the reality of its integration in a global economy, but by the expectation that it will happen. The models, and images of its reshaping are those of certain sectors with a strong orientation toward the larger regional and global economies.

NOTES

The author thanks the Institute for Advanced Study, United Nations University (Tokyo) for its support.

1. Beirut has also attracted much media attention recently as the host of the pope's visit to Lebanon (1997), the Asiatic Games (1998), Arab cultural capital (1999), Asia football cup (2000), Francophony Congress (2001), with many more notable events forthcoming, such as the regional environmental exhibition (2003) and annual automobile racing (from 2005).

REFERENCES CITED

Beyhum, N. 1990. "Espaces éclatés, espaces dominés. Étude sur la recomposition des espaces publics centraux de Beyrouth de 1970 à 1990." Master's thesis, sociology department, Lyon II University.

Clerc, V. 2001. "Les principes d'action des acteurs de l'urbanisme sur les quartiers irréguliers: le cas de l'opération urbaine Elyssar à Beyrouth." *Lettre de l'ORBR* 13. Beirut: CERMOC.

Compain, D. 1998. "Regionalisme et multilatéralisme: le cas du Liban." *Document du CERMOC* 1. Beirut: CERMOC.

Corm, G. 1996. *Geopolitique du conflit libanais*. Paris: La Decouverte.

Escallier, R. 2000. "La métropolisation dans le Monde arabe." Pp. 207–219 in *Identité et apparte-nances dans le Monde arabe,* Congress of the AFEMAM, Revue de l'AFEMAM. Tours: L'Astrolabe.

Ghandour-Atallah, J. 1998. "The Northern Sector: Projects and Plans at Sea." In P*rojecting Beirut: Episodes in the Construction and Reconstruction of a Modern City,* ed. P. Rowe and H. Sarkis. New York: Prestel-Verlag.

Ghorra-Gobin, C. 1981–1982. "Le processus de création des centres résidentiels: une greffe de modernité dans l'agglomération de Beyrouth." *Annales de géographie de l'USJ.* Beirut: University of St-Joseph.

Haeringer, P. 1998. "La métropolisation. Un autre monde, un nouvel apprentissage. " In *De la ville à la métropole: essor ou déclin des villes au XXIe siècle?* ed. J.-C. Burdès, M.-J. Roussel, T. Spector, J. Theys. Centre de Prospective et de Veille Scientifique, Paris : METL.

Huybrechts, E. 1999a. "Densités beyrouthines.'" *Lettre de l'ORBR* 9. Beirut: CERMOC.

———. 1999b. "La mise en œuvre du plan de transport de la région métropolitaine de Beyrouth." *Lettre de l'ORBR* 12. Beirut: CERMOC.

Huybrechts, E. and C. Douayhi. 1999. "Reconstruction et réconciliation au Liban: négociations, renouement du lien social, lieux publics." *Cahier du CERMOC* 23. Beirut: CERMOC.

Paix, C. 1973. "La porté e spatiale des activités tertiaires de commandement économique au Liban."

Picaudou, N. 1989. *La déchirure libanaise. Questions du XXe siècle.* Paris: Éditions Complexe.

ERIC HUYBRECHTS

PART THREE

NETWORK
NODES

Chapter 9

HONG KONG: GLOBAL CAPITAL EXCHANGE

David R. Meyer

Advances in telematics—the integration of telecommunications and computer technologies that permit instantaneous transmission of information—raise anew the specter that key actors in finance, commodity exchange, corporate management, and other businesses controlling exchange of capital will disperse from their metropolitan bases. This scenario contrasts with an alternative claim that advances in transportation and information transmission technologies permit more dispersed production and consumption of goods and services, creating demands for greater interaction. The need to control and coordinate increasingly complex exchange requires that actors specialize, thus intensifying the need to communicate sophisticated information, often through face-to-face exchange. These specialized actors and growing complexity of exchange also create demands for production of services to help manage exchange. Service actors, such as lawyers, accountants, and management consultants, need close access to each other and their clients to coordinate strategies. Paradoxically, greater centralization of control and coordination activities results; changes in global cities such as New York, London, and Tokyo epitomize this process (Janelle 1969: 348–364; Pred 1977: 173–182; Sassen 2001).

This debate reflects disagreement over the relation between technology and society. Visions of seamless links among individuals via telematics represents another version of technological determinism; each innovation sets off a new era in human spatial behavior. However, a more fruitful approach examines how individuals and social groups incorporate each new technology into business activities. This does not dismiss the possibility that new social behaviors arise, but it recognizes that people continue or modify previous behaviors (Thrift 1996: 1463–1493). I propose that intermediaries controlling international exchanges of commodity and financial capital employ their social networks to organize and implement exchanges of capital, and they incorporate telematics in their decision-making process. Global cities are agglomerations of these decision makers, and they operate in local and interurban social networks.

This conception of global cities and social networks binding them highlights the critical distinction between physical means of telematic information processing and communication and decisions about capital exchanges; these need not coincide.[1] Telematics has high fixed costs and low variable costs, a trait typical of most transportation and communications technologies, and high infrastructure costs to connect dispersed sites through linkages and nodes contributes to those traits. Teleports—combinations of satellite clusters and local fiber-optics linkages—manifest that characteristic (Warf 1989: 257–271; 1995: 361–378). Global cities with great concentrations of finance and corporate headquarters lead teleport construction, but future innovations might obviate juxtaposition of users of teleports and actual infrastructure. Teleports and linkages radiating from them are merely conduits for information exchange; decisions about control of capital exchanges need not coincide with teleport locations.

This distinction between telematics as a technology to process and communicate information and decisions about capital exchanges has old roots. Before the telegraph, information moved long distances with passengers and as written communications carried by passenger and freight vehicles (horse, wagon, ship), and routes reflected types of transport systems. However, those linkages did not necessarily match connections among decision makers controlling exchanges of commodity and financial capital; their social networks served as those connections. Even after the global telegraph network reached its initial form around the 1870s (Farnie 1969: 185–186), information movement over telegraph lines followed circuitous routes with no necessary correspondence to social network linkages among decision makers. Those controlling decisions about capital exchanges operated from hub positions in the network, and London was the global pivot. Yet, even that was not deterministic, because decision makers controlling capital exchanges made certain their bases were connected to the network. Their social networks comprise the fundamental linkages among global cities; the logic of those networks is examined now.

NETWORKS OF CAPITAL

International trade and financial intermediaries, as well as other intermediaries of global capital, confront the problem of exchanging capital across political boundaries.[2] That introduces potential conflict as competitors appeal to force, that is, request their nation-state to enforce sanctions against external intermediaries. International intermediaries also confront broader problems of malfeasance by exchange partners such as failure to fulfill contracts, theft, and fraud. This forces intermediaries to build transactions on trust in order to minimize risks of exchange across international boundaries; they do that through friendship, family, ethnic, or religious ties.

Networks of capital also build as intermediaries react to competition. Those controlling capital exchanges always face potential competition from less specialized intermediaries taking advantage of economic growth and development to start intermediation at less specialized levels. If growth and development continue, intermediaries use accumulated capital to compete with more highly capitalized intermediaries, who then must react to that competition; they have two options. They can remain at their existing level of specialization and face shrinkage of business, unless growth and development raised total business for all intermediaries at that level of specialization. Alternatively, they may use their larger capitalized position and greater access to information about exchange to follow a specialization strategy, thus maintaining dominance of international exchange at the larger volume and territorial scale. Sometimes these reactions to competition consist of internalizing intermediary functions previously carried out by specialized firms. In either case, greater specialization enlarges complexity of exchange, including exchange up and down a hierarchy of specializations. Intermediaries also may react to competition by investing in transportation and communication improvements; telematics represents one means to alter transaction costs among intermediaries.

They also agglomerate as a means to reduce transaction costs, and that serves multiple purposes. Within the agglomeration, intermediaries build trust through business and social ties, and close proximity enhances sharing complex information face-to-face. They can develop cooperative ties in international exchange permitting them to share risks, thus lowering probability of failure, and they can share high fixed costs of international transportation and communication infrastructure. Once an agglomeration emerges, subsequent intermediaries have incentives to locate with existing ones to exchange information, cooperate, and share in fixed infrastructure costs. Each additional intermediary enhances attractions of an agglomeration to subsequent ones. If producers and consumers of commodity and financial capital in a territory distant from the original agglomeration experience economic growth and development, some intermediaries may form a new agglomeration in or near that territory. However, the new agglomeration forms only if intermediary gains in controlling exchanges of those producers and consumers compensate for substantial benefits to intermediaries of being in the original agglomeration. Therefore, the global system of cities comprises social networks of intermediaries controlling exchanges of capital. The friction of distance impacts their decisions about capital exchanges across political boundaries, such as through their capacity to ship commodities or through delays in accessing information face-to-face over long distances. Nevertheless, their agreements to engage in exchange with each other are direct linkages that, once forged, can be maintained over long distances. The world city system always has had a network foundation; modern telematics, while permitting instantaneous communication of vast amounts of information, has not created a network system where none existed before.

The network structure of today, global urban system comprises one or more cities housing the most specialized and highly capitalized intermediaries; these are the great global metropolises (London, New York).[3] They forge exchange linkages with other intermediary agglomerations operating at less specialized and less capitalized levels. World-regional metropolises (for example, Miami, Frankfurt) and older, leading centers retaining prominent decision makers in capital exchanges (for example, Amsterdam) also have widespread linkages both within their world region and outside it, though not at the scale of great metropolises. Beneath these agglomerations other metropolises may have decision makers controlling capital exchanges over a multicountry territory (for example, Singapore, San Francisco). At the next level national metropolises whose intermediaries have limited capacity to control exchange outside their borders have most of their exchange linkages controlled by more specialized and capitalized intermediaries in other metropolises. Leading global metropolises have intermediaries exchanging capital with most metropolises, but linkages among metropolises also have some territorial basis; intermediaries in world-regional metropolises have extensive influence over exchanges in their world region. And some of these metropolises also house numerous branches of global firms, thus providing linkages with most major cities in the developed world (for example, Hong Kong). Metropolises beneath the world-regional level whose countries are active in import and export markets have widespread global ties with commodity trade partners (for example, Paris, Chicago, Sydney).

Hong Kong offers an intriguing venue to explore the future of global cities and the impact of telematics. As a city-state and British colony, it possessed no national hinterland; decision makers controlling exchanges of capital did the vast majority of business in other political jurisdictions, except for significant local sharing of information, cooperation on deals, and economic exchanges among firms. The return of Hong Kong to Chinese sovereignty in 1997 added a national hinterland, but placed a wealthy "capitalistic" economic system under control of an impoverished "socialist" state (Welsh 1993). Yet, through all these twists and turns, Hong Kong stands as one of the greatest concentrations of decision-makers controlling exchanges of global capital.[4] Explanation of that paradox shifts attention from idiosyncratic factors to generalizations about control of capital exchange. Trade and financial bonds of Hong Kong reach two broad groups—Asian countries and developed countries outside Asia.

RISE OF HONG KONG AS TRADE AND FINANCIAL CENTER

Trade and financial linkages of Hong Kong reveal the position of its intermediaries in global capital exchange. Hong Kong became a British colony following ratification of the Treaty of Nanking between Britain and China in 1842 that opened five "treaty ports," and, from the start, the British viewed it as their great emporium of trade in the Far East. Within three years as many as fourteen hundred oceangoing ships entered and cleared the port, and by 1866 this number had surged to almost seventy-six hundred. Trade and financial patterns established during these years persisted until the First World War. From the start, prominent British and American trade and finance firms of Hong Kong forged direct linkages to leading global metropolises, especially London and New York, through their control of capital exchanges. At a smaller scale, firms from other European countries such as Germany and France forged linkages to London, as well as to metropolises in their home countries (Bard 1993; Tom 1964: 107, appendix 4).

British merchants used Hong Kong as their base to trade throughout Asia, especially with China, and Hong Kong was administrative center for opium imports from elsewhere in the region, principally India, and for re-export to China. This trade loomed large until its suppression around the turn of the century, accounting for close to half of China's imports in some years (Endacott 1973: 194; Miners 1987: 207–210). British merchant houses in Hong Kong, such as Jardine, Matheson & Company and Dent & Company, along with other Western merchant houses, controlled opium imports as part of their China trade. They hired Chinese managers known as compradors to operate from treaty ports and negotiate with local and interior merchants to sell opium and British manufactures and to buy tea and silk, and compradors also arranged payments through local banks and supplied market intelligence to merchant houses (Hao 1970). Chinese merchants in Hong Kong increasingly controlled redistribution of imported British manufactures to China, and this coastal trade often bypassed treaty ports British merchants had to use. However, Hong Kong merchants did not dominate China's export trade to the same extent, because distant merchants in Europe and North America controlled simple trade in leading goods such as tea and silk (Endacott 1973: 194–197). In these trade and financial linkages, they used the telegraph to communicate with London and other major cities in Asia, and shipping provided means to communicate through mails. Nevertheless, social networks of intermediaries comprised the fundamental governing structure of exchange. Hong Kong's agglomeration of foreign and Chinese firms made key decisions about trade and financial exchange in Asia and with the developed world (Meyer 2000).

Hong Kong quickly became a Chinese city with a tiny British superstructure comprising less than 5 percent of the population (Endacott 1973: 183,

252). Many Chinese worked as laborers on docks, in warehouses, and in ship-yards, but a critical minority were entrepot merchants. They made Hong Kong the pivot of the trade and information network in the Far East binding dispersed Chinese merchant communities. On the one hand, Chinese merchants of Hong Kong retained substantial control of export of goods to China, and, on the other hand, they supplied Chinese specialty goods to growing Chinese communities throughout the Far East; but they did not monopolize this trade. Compradors in China also usurped some foreign trade of merchants who originally hired them, such as trade between Chinese ports and Singapore (Hao 1970: 117–120). Because Hong Kong served as a leading final embarkation point for Chinese heading to the Straits, Australia, and North America, its business community could monitor ongoing changes in the Chinese diaspora (Endacott 1973: 121–132, 183–197; Tsai 1993: 23–35). British guarantees of free trade for Chinese and Western merchants made Hong Kong the optimal base to trade throughout the Far East and with Europe and North America.

From 1850 to World War I, Hong Kong was one of the world's greatest ports. In 1866 the seventy-six oceangoing ships entering and clearing the port totaled about 3.8 million tons; and by 1911 the ship total had reached 19,644, comprising 20.5 million tons. Hong Kong's trade with China soared from 1869 to 1911 as exchange rates between Hong Kong dollars and Shanghai taels held steady. Imports from China rose tenfold from $16 million (Hong Kong dollars) to $161 million, and exports to China rose eightfold, from $29 million to $230 million. The British share of China's import and export trade gradually declined, whereas Hong Kong merchants handled a greater share of China's trade. During the 1890s Hong Kong controlled about 50 percent of China's imports and about 40 percent of her exports. As Hong Kong's dependence on British trade declined, trade expanded to other parts of Europe (Germany, France, Russia), Japan, and North America (Endacott 1973: 253; Tom 1964: 107, 151–152, 159–160, appendices 4, 5, 19). Hong Kong had become an international emporium of trade with exchange linkages to most of the leading metropolises of the developed world.

Finance lubricated this trade. The Oriental Bank, based in India, opened a Hong Kong branch in 1845, just two years after the colony's founding, and other banks, principally based in India, followed during the next several decades. These banks focused on financial exchange operations supporting trading companies: accepting deposits; buying and selling currencies, bullion, and bills of exchange; and granting credit for purchasing goods (Endacott 1973: 118; King 1987: 83). Opening of two main offices of the Hong Kong and Shanghai Banking Corporation in the respective cities in 1865 heralded a financial watershed. An international consortium of merchant trading firms from Britain, Germany, Norway, and the United States, with major operations in Asia, joined merchant firms based in Hong Kong to found the bank. From the start, directors guaranteed that Hong Kong served as headquarters and that the bank operated as an exchange bank to finance the trade of Hong Kong, the treaty ports of China, and Japan. Within a year the bank had added two branches outside Hong Kong at Yokohama and London and a worldwide array of agents. Over the next three decades, the Hongkong and Shanghai Bank expanded its branch office network in Asia, in many cases founding branches in cities in which it initially had agents. (King 1987: xl, 53–5, 95, Map 2, Table 3.5). Through its internal organizational structure this bank epitomized the global reach of Hong Kong firms that made it a world-regional metropolis.

This office expansion underscored the growing financial power of the Hongkong and Shanghai Bank in Asia and solidified its access to European capital markets. In 1865, in addition to opening a London branch, the bank forged financial agreements with two of the city's leading banks—London and Westminster Bank and London and County Bank. Following 1874 the Hongkong and Shanghai Bank became dominant lender for loans to the Chinese government, taking a principal position in finance of China's import and export trade. The Bank leveraged its ties to London's financial market to lead the formation of consortiums of lenders to China. By 1885 it had the largest banking presence in China's treaty ports, and by 1895 had attained global importance (King 1987: 6, 100–101, 500–562).

From 1895 to 1918 Hongkong and Shanghai Bank expanded the number of branches and agencies in the Malay states and China. Officers of these units increasingly committed the bank's capital to financing economic activity in their territory of operations, such as natural resource development, imports, exports, and infrastructure (ports, railroads), in addition to handling exchange operations for the bank. During this period the bank also expanded merchant banking and became a leading syndicator of loans for Chinese railways. These loans required a global approach: the London branch handled negotiations with the British government and with London and other European banks, while the Hong Kong and Shanghai offices, as well as Chinese branches in other cities, especially Beijing, handled negotiations with the Chinese government. By the First World War, Hongkong and Shanghai Bank ranked as the foremost exchange bank in Asia, leading merchant bank in the finance of China loans and head of international consortiums, and financial agent for the Chinese government.[5] Hong Kong joined the group of top ten international financial centers, partly due to activities of the Hongkong and Shanghai Bank, but also because prominent banks from around the world placed branch offices in Hong Kong. In 1900 Hong Kong ranked fourth globally, and over the next eighty years fluctuated between third and tenth rank.[6]

From the end of the First World War (1919) to the Communist Party takeover of China (1949), Hong Kong faced an interregnum as emporium of trade and finance. British economic and military power declined, and challenges arose at home to British imperialism. Hong Kong remained a premier financial center and port, but its status grew uncertain as internal disturbances gripped China and the Japanese flexed economic, political, and military muscles in Asia. Japan occupied Hong Kong in December 1941; following 1945 China plunged back into civil war, unleashing a flood of refugees to Hong Kong (Endacott 1973: 285–310).

These refugees transformed Hong Kong; a large number entered from Guangdong province, bordering Hong Kong, providing a reservoir of low-wage labor. A small number arrived from Shanghai, China's industrial heart, bringing capital and entrepreneurial skills in manufacturing. Before 1950, shipbuilding and entrepot manufactures dominated Hong Kong's small industrial sector, but new entrepreneurs diverged from that path. During the mid-1950s they founded numerous small textile and clothing firms, but by 1960 textiles declined relatively and manufactures such as artificial flowers and plastic toys and dolls increased; clothing continued as a major sector, constituting about one-third of all exports until 1970. By the mid-1960s the industrial importance of electrical machinery and appliances began a sharp rise. Growth in number of firms—from 1,050 employing sixty-four hundred workers in 1947 to 17,239 firms—employing 589,505 workers in 1970 mirrored this industrial expansion.[7]

Exports of locally produced manufactures reinvigorated Hong Kong's trade. Total trade (imports and exports) rose from $5.8 billion (Hong Kong dollars) in 1954 to $32.8 billion in 1970. In the early years, developing nations in Southeast Asia took the exports, but they soon envisioned entering the same lines of manufactures as Hong Kong. This competition encouraged factories in Hong Kong to shift to more sophisticated products; by 1970 the United States and Britain took 54 percent of Hong Kong's exports. Exports to China languished because Soviet bloc nations became suppliers of capital goods to China, and food constituted a significant share of imports from China up to 1970 (Endacott 1973: 316–119; Szczepanik 1958: 51–2, 158, table 14).

RECENT TRADE AND FINANCIAL BONDS OF HONG KONG

Since 1970 Hong Kong's trade has continued soaring (see table 1), and it maintains two patterns dating from the nineteenth century—high levels of exchange with developed countries in North America and western Europe, and with other Asian countries. These account for more than 90 percent of the value of all types of trade—domestic exports, reexports, and imports. Domestic exports comprise mostly manufactured goods produced in Hong Kong for sale elsewhere, and their growth reflects post-1945 industrialization of Hong Kong. Exports surged from 1974 to 1984 as North America took the largest share of

TABLE 1

TRADE TIES OF HONG KONG, 1974-1998

Domestic Exports	Millions of Hong Kong Dollars			Percent Distribution		
World Region	1974	1984	1998	1974	1984	1998
North America	$8,042	$65,935	$58,440	35.1	48.0	31.1
Central & South America	428	1,616	2,026	1.9	1.2	1.1
Western Europe	7,757	33,021	37,156	33.9	24.0	19.8
C.I.S. & Eastern Europe	48	430	296	0.2	0.3	0.2
Middle East	630	3,369	1,018	2.8	2.5	0.5
Asia	3,170	26,191	85,705	13.8	19.1	45.6
Africa	1,043	2,200	1,054	4.6	1.6	0.6
Australia & Oceania	1,786	4,628	2,402	7.8	3.4	1.3
Total	$22,904	$137,390	$188,097	100.1%	100.1%	100.2%

Reexports	Millions of Hong Kong Dollars			Percent Distribution		
World Region	1974	1984	1998	1974	1984	1998
North America	$578	$13,068	$277,673	8.1	15.6	24.0
Central & South America	191	947	36,120	2.7	1.1	3.1
Western Europe	765	4,692	190,284	10.7	5.6	16.4
C.I.S. & Eastern Europe	10	217	6,949	0.1	0.3	0.6
Middle East	253	2,837	17,225	3.6	3.4	1.5
Asia	4,745	57,799	596,060	66.6	69.2	51.4
Africa	293	1,991	14,099	4.1	2.4	1.2
Australia & Oceania	290	1,952	20,787	4.1	2.3	1.8
Total	$7,125	$83,503	$1,159,197	100.0%	99.9%	100.0%

Imports	Millions of Hong Kong Dollars			Percent Distribution		
World Region	1974	1984	1998	1974	1984	1998
North America	$4,827	$25,708	$115,784	14.2	11.5	8.1
Central & South America	278	1,863	11,390	0.8	0.8	0.8
Western Europe	6,212	29,983	168,415	18.2	13.4	11.8
C.I.S. & Eastern Europe	235	930	3,893	0.7	0.4	0.3
Middle East	804	1,390	8,227	2.4	0.6	0.6
Asia	20,237	156,986	1,098,357	59.3	70.4	76.9
Africa	609	2,096	4,880	1.8	0.9	0.3
Australia & Oceania	911	4,093	18,015	2.7	1.8	1.3
Total	$34,113	$223,049	$1,428,961	100.1%	99.8%	100.1%

Source: Census and Statistics Department (various years).

the rising tide of output, whereas western Europe's share fell. By 1984 North America accounted for almost half of Hong Kong's domestic exports, and hints of trade reorganization appeared with the jump in share of exports to Asia. Nevertheless, domestic export growth slowed from 1984 to 1998; the share moving to North America and Western Europe plunged, while Asia's share surged.

Increased prominence of re-export trade indicates a reassertion of old activities of Hong Kong traders as collectors and redistributors of commodities; the value of reexports soared from 1974 to 1998 (table 1). The share of reexports moving to North America and Western Europe rose significantly, and their increased share since 1984 suggests they receive increasing shares of manufactured exports via Hong Kong traders rather than direct exports from its factories. Declining share of reexports destined for Asia misleads; their volume soared and still accounted for more than half of all reexports from Hong Kong. Imports to Hong Kong come overwhelmingly from Asian countries, and their share rose dramatically, whereas import shares from North America and western Europe fell (table 1). Their smaller value of imports, compared to the combined value of domestic exports and reexports heading to them, reveal the substantial trade surplus Hong Kong has with Asia. These results by region are the clue to understanding how Hong Kong's trade is centered in Asia.

Trade within Asia soared from 1974 to 1984, but the small base meant expansion during early Asian export industrialization did not impact Hong Kong significantly; major changes came subsequently (see table 2). Domestic exports to Asia restructured in relative terms; the share moving to Japan fell sharply from 1974 to 1998, whereas the share to China soared, making it the overwhelming destination. Value of domestic exports to newly industrializing economies such as Taiwan, Korea, and Malaysia rose, but their share fell; Hong Kong factories are not competitive producers for those economies. Singapore maintains moderate status as destination of domestic exports, because its traders redistribute goods to traditional markets in Malaysia and Indonesia (Huff 1994). Much of Hong Kong's soaring trade with Asia from 1984 to 1998 occurred as reexports and imports (table 2). The rise of China as destination of reexports overwhelms other shifts, and that change has a compensating balance in soaring value of imports from China. Those exchanges reflect the massive move of Hong Kong factories to nearby Guangdong province following opening of China to investment with the reforms of Deng Xiaoping in 1978, but the major shift came in the late 1980s (Ho 1992; Vogel 1989). Hong Kong factories send intermediate goods and other inputs to factories for processing, and factories and traders of Hong Kong reexport products to Asia, North America, and western Europe. Nevertheless, focus on this large bilateral trade with China obscures momentous growth in reexports to, and imports from, other Asian

TABLE 2

TRADE OF HONG KONG WITHIN ASIA, 1974-1998

Domestic Exports	Millions of Hong Kong Dollars			Percent Distribution		
Political Unit	1974	1984	1998	1974	1984	1998
Taiwan	$362	$1,611	$6,505	11.4	6.2	7.6
Indonesia	230	469	676	7.3	1.8	0.8
Philippines	96	1,106	1,991	3.0	4.2	2.3
Korea, South	95	410	1,563	3.0	1.6	1.8
Thailand	176	719	1,598	5.6	2.7	1.9
Japan	1,061	5,151	6,435	33.5	19.7	7.5
China, Mainland	99	11,283	56,066	3.1	43.1	65.4
Vietnam	34	17	749	1.1	0.1	0.9
Malaysia	221	1,021	1,821	7.0	3.9	2.1
Singapore	626	2,627	5,103	19.7	10.0	6.0
Other	170	1,777	3,198	5.4	6.8	3.7
Total	$3,170	$26,191	$85,705	100.1%	100.1%	100.0%

Reexports	Millions of Hong Kong Dollars			Percent Distribution		
Political Unit	1974	1984	1998	1974	1984	1998
Taiwan	$692	$4,868	$27,368	14.6	8.4	4.6
Indonesia	615	3,654	3,357	13.0	6.3	0.6
Philippines	193	1,478	11,081	4.1	2.6	1.9
Korea, South	278	3,440	12,241	5.9	6.0	2.1
Thailand	161	1,202	9,809	3.4	2.1	1.6
Japan	1,023	4,633	64,194	21.6	8.0	10.8
China, Mainland	197	28,064	407,366	4.2	48.6	68.3
Vietnam	81	558	3,198	1.7	1.0	0.5
Malaysia	171	1,082	8,735	3.6	1.9	1.5
Singapore	862	4,511	25,625	18.2	7.8	4.3
Other	472	4,309	23,086	9.9	7.5	3.9
Total	$4,745	$57,799	$596,060	100.2%	100.2%	100.1%

Imports	Millions of Hong Kong Dollars			Percent Distribution		
Political Unit	1974	1984	1998	1974	1984	1998
Taiwan	$1,765	$17,347	$104,075	8.7	11.1	9.5
Indonesia	240	1,195	14,035	1.2	0.8	1.3
Philippines	149	1,886	10,248	0.7	1.2	0.9
Korea, South	864	7,289	68,836	4.3	4.6	6.3
Thailand	809	2,199	22,234	4.0	1.4	2.0
Japan	7,142	52,620	179,947	35.3	33.5	16.4
China, Mainland	5,991	55,753	580,614	29.6	35.5	52.9
Vietnam	129	689	1,803	0.6	0.4	0.2
Malaysia	311	1,585	32,479	1.5	1.0	3.0
Singapore	1,889	12,229	61,457	9.3	7.8	5.6
Other	948	4,194	22,629	4.7	2.7	2.1
Total	$20,237	$156,986	$1,098,357	99.9%	100.0%	100.2%

Source: Census and Statistics Department (various years).

economies, especially after 1984. From the perspective of Hong Kong, Asian economies are becoming more tightly integrated through flows of manufactured goods.

Financial bonds of Hong Kong mirror these trade ties. Large, global banks with major operations in Hong Kong predominantly come from western Europe, North America, and Asia (table 3). The degree of bank oligopoly within countries affects their numbers; nevertheless, the important finding is the sweep of bank representation in Hong Kong from highly developed economies outside Asia. Within Asia, Japanese banks dominate in Hong Kong, as they do among all highly developed economies, but equally significant is the large number from mainland China and wide representation from economies across Asia. Thus, Hong Kong financial institutions maintain tight integration with global financial institutions of economically advanced economies and of Asia. That integration remains consistent with the argument that flows among advanced economies and between those economies and less developed economies dominate global intermediation; direct ties with less developed economies outside Hong Kong's world-regional hinterland remain minor (Meyer 1986: 553–581; 1991). These swelling bonds of trade and finance Hong Kong intermediaries forge, in the face of a seemingly uncertain geopolitical future with China's reacquisition of sovereign control in 1997, raises a paradox requiring resolution.

This resilience of Hong Kong rests on its significant benefits. Intermediaries continue to invest in transportation and communication infrastructure, thus lowering operating costs, but equally as important, Hong Kong houses pivotal intermediaries critical to Asian trade and finance. Because the largest, most highly capitalized intermediaries from Europe and North America chose Hong Kong as an operational base at the start, it continued to attract subsequent intermediaries. Furthermore, Chinese intermediaries also made Hong Kong their operational base for trade in Asia, and they agglomerated there to be with foreign intermediaries; those Chinese intermediaries provide intra-Asian links so critical to making Hong Kong the pivot of capital exchange in Asia (Enright, Scott and Dodwell 1997; Le Fevour 1970; Lockwood 1971; Meyer 2000). Development of Hong Kong's telematics poses profound implications for its future, because telematics is critical to intermediary capacity to control exchanges of commodity and financial capital.

TELEMATICS AND INTERMEDIARY BEHAVIOR

Greater integration of telecommunications and computer technologies raises the volume and complexity of information that businesses transmit. This telematics expansion has two contradictory, yet related, consequences for how intermediaries conduct business. Enhanced capacity to transmit information

TABLE 3

POLITICAL UNIT/REGION OF OWNERSHIP OF LICENSED BANKS IN HONG KONG, 1998

Political Unit/Region		Number	Percent of Total
Europe	Austria	3	1.7
	Belgium/Luxembourg	4	2.3
	Denmark	2	1.2
	France	8	4.7
	Germany	10	5.8
	Italy	6	3.5
	Netherlands	3	1.7
	Spain	3	1.7
	Sweden	2	1.2
	Switzerland	2	1.2
	United Kingdom	7	4.1
	Subtotal	50	29.1
Middle East		2	1.2
North America	Canada	6	3.5
	United States	14	8.1
	Subtotal	20	11.6
Asia & Pacific	Hong Kong	16	9.3
	Australia	4	2.3
	China, Mainland	18	10.5
	India	4	2.3
	Indonesia	3	1.7
	Japan	36	20.9
	Korea, South	3	1.7
	Malaysia	3	1.7
	Pakistan	1	0.6
	Philippines	2	1.2
	Singapore	5	2.9
	Taiwan	4	2.3
	Thailand	1	0.6
	Subtotal	100	58.1
Grand Total		**172**	**100.0%**

Source: Hong Kong Monetary Authority 1998: 140–141, table C.

permits increased separation between exchange of assets in physical form, such as commodities and pieces of paper, and exchange of assets in symbolic form, representing only claims on assets.[8] These claims include options to buy and sell, credits and debits, and securities representing ownership of properties. On the one hand, processing this information may transform from nonroutine, where sophisticated individuals make decisions about allocating capital and computing values, to routine, where sophisticated software processes information that semiskilled workers input. This transformation also undergirds the long-term trend of separation of back-office white-collar jobs from corporate headquarters. Before innovations in information processing, corporate headquarters staff directly monitored most information processing, but innovations routinized processing; this permitted firms to locate back-office jobs in places with lower wage and land costs. Therefore, advances in telematics that transform information processing from nonroutine to routine continue a process under way for more than a century.

Telematics advances also permit intermediaries to collect, process, and analyze larger volumes of information and greater complexity of types of information. This contributes to centralization of sophisticated decision making, counterbalancing transformation of nonroutine to routine information processing. In the labor process, this may appear as new, specialized intermediary activities. For example, emergence of specialized units in large commercial and investment banks focusing on creating sophisticated financial instruments, such as derivatives or elaborate packages of currencies, became possible with the advent of high-powered computers and software built on complex mathematical algorithms. At the same time, trading in these derivatives and currencies required global transmission of vast amounts of information to continually price these financial products. Senior executives must closely monitor units creating these products, and these units engage in extensive face-to-face exchanges of information as they design them (Meyer 1998).

Once products are created they trade like other financial products, including stocks, bonds, and raw material commodity contracts. Advances in telematics boost capacity to handle products with greater complexity at higher volumes and speeds of trading. This raises the possibility that traders do not need to physically meet in exchanges because telematics allows computerized exchange; that type of trading has commenced and residual physical exchanges may decline. Emergence of this type of intermediary exchange suggests that traders could operate from dispersed sites rather than in an intermediary agglomeration. For individuals and members of firms who are allocated fixed amounts of capital to exchange based on credits established at a financial institution, such dispersed trading already is feasible. However, extrapolation from that form to all intermediary exchange of these symbolic assets dismisses the role of trust and problems of monitoring malfeasance. Whenever risk-taking in trading places firms' equity in jeopardy, they need to closely supervise traders. That places social construction of trust at the core of firms' activities, and face-to-face meetings remain a key means to build and monitor trustworthy behavior. Trading sophisticated symbolic assets may remain centralized within firms because complicated strategy discussions are needed to gain advantages. That pits groups of individuals collectively developing strategies against sole practitioners (Meyer 1998). And, the production of, and trading in, some complex, risky financial products, such as interest-rate swaps, require intense personal interaction within and among firms, sharing highly confidential information, and building trust. Participants prefer to keep track of each other through face-to-face contact to maintain a sense of the market and have trustworthy partners to exchange with in other firms, and even though they operate in a global market place, they agglomerate in only selected global cities (Agnes 2000: 347–366).

Advances in telematics also provide complex information used for exchange of assets whose values are based on future economic activity—floating stocks and bonds, forming new firms such as joint ventures, and loans to firms. Intermediaries require face-to-face exchange to acquire this information from other intermediaries, develop strategies, and acquire trustworthy partners. This remains essential because these exchanges entail substantial risk that intermediaries cannot adjust easily by selling assets instantaneously as traders of symbolic assets can do.

TELEMATICS IN HONG KONG

Hong Kong, along with other global metropolises, witnesses an ongoing shift of back-office jobs to sites away from the agglomeration, especially in nearby Guangdong province; thus, telematics maintains this traditional impact of innovations in transportation and communication (Meyer 2000: 227). These shifts signify that the size of Hong Kong's intermediary agglomeration always remains problematic. Removal of numerous back-office workers opens vast amounts of space that new, highly specialized intermediaries may not fill. With continued specialization and sophistication of Hong Kong's intermediaries, the number of them may not change much.

Telematic expansion within Hong Kong provides its intermediaries greater capacity to compete. Its number of leased circuits—high-capacity lines that firms use to transmit global communications among units within the firm—more than quadrupled from 297 in 1972 to 1,205 in 1979; they rose an additional 50 percent during the 1980s, and by 1999 approached 2,300. Outward volume of international telephone calls in minutes soared: it grew at compound annual rates of 18 percent from 1972 to 1980, jumped to annual rates of 34 percent during the 1980s, and slowed to annual rates of 11 percent during the 1990s (Langdale 1989: 501–522).[9] Greater bonds between China and Hong Kong contribute substantially to this volume growth, but increasing use of other forms of telematics retards growth of older forms of long-distance communication.

Hong Kong continues to rapidly upgrade telematics infrastructure. Fiber-optic cables link all telephone exchanges and major commercial buildings, and the internal system has reached 100 percent digital format. It has the greatest array of fiber-optic international cables of any metropolis in Asia; numerous submarine cable systems link it with Asia, Oceania, North America, and Europe, and its satellite contacts permit global reach. A communications center in Hong Kong serves as the switching node for thirty-five hundred international leased circuits and local extension lines, and Hong Kong operates the largest teleport in Asia. When the local market was deregulated in 1995 telematics capacity surged. As of 2000 it had eleven mobile phone networks reaching 70 percent of the population, around 4.7 million people. Internet use exploded, with almost two hundred Internet service providers, and about 50 percent of the population with Internet access by 2000. Businesses rapidly moved into the internet domain, with forty thousand companies registered under HK.com, and more than fifteen hundred dotcom companies started in Hong Kong in a fifteen-month period preceding 2001.[10]

Hong Kong's government proactively encourages telematics while maintaining its traditional role of facilitator of development rather than formal director of it. Sophisticated agency leaders and highly competent civil servants leverage their extraordinary ability to respond to new challenges of upgrading telematics capacity. In 1998 the government announced its Digital 21 IT (information technology) strategy that presented a vision and goals, with efforts directed to developing high-capacity telecommunications networks, building information infrastructure, promoting IT education, and cultivating a culture encouraging use of new technologies. The government also draws on the non-profit sector and businesses to place this Digital 21 strategy into a broader framework; the Strategic Development Commission of Hong Kong—a high-level advisory group of leaders from the SAR (Special Administrative Region) government, business, academia, and other sectors—promulgated a broad development proposal aiming to make Hong Kong the global city of Asia. Government units implemented direct changes: the Hong Kong Post established a public certification authority to address security concerns in cyberspace, and the government passed an Electronic Transactions Ordinance in 2000 to enhance certainty and security of electronic transactions. And the entire government aims to move many services on-line, instituting a major effort to bring educational institutions from elementary through colleges and universities fully into Internet use. Restructured government departments support the new strategy; for example, the venerable Industry Department, a fixture of the government during manufacturing growth following 1950, was reorganized in 2000. Its technology section was separated to operate as a single entity under the commissioner of innovation and technology, and to recognize the power of this unit, the former director general of the old Industry Department was appointed commissioner of the new entity. The government draws on rich contact networks that businesses maintain globally, especially with the United States, and specifically, Silicon Valley in California; these networks provide sophisticated information and advice that are used in decision making about telematics strategies.[11]

The Cyber-Port project at Telegraph Bay on the west end of Hong Kong Island may indicate greater government meddling. In May 2000 this technology park and residential development, estimated to cost $1.7 billion, was awarded without bidding to Richard Li, leading local tycoon and son of legendary tycoon Li Ka-shing. The project will be completed in phases from 2001 to 2003, and IT companies will be offered below-market rental space because the government gave the land free of charge. However, property developers, Internet and e-commerce companies, politicians, and the media vigorously criticized the government's decision to provide prime waterfront without bidding. They argued that although the government would own the office complex after completions Richard Li's potential profits from the residential development and the credibility he gained from this high-profile product counterbalanced risks he took as developer. Nevertheless, Cyber-Port may be an exception to government policy minimizing direct intervention in guiding business; private developers demonstrated government intervention was not needed. While Cyber-Port was awarded in 2000, office developers opened extensive space with the latest infrastructure IT companies for fiber-optic cables and specially designed offices to accommodate machinery, air-conditioning, and room for cables. Even Richard Li's father, Li Ka-shing, attracted forty technology companies to his eighty-story building—the Center; and nearby a twenty-two-story outdated building was transformed into Dotcom House with the latest IT infrastructure, which did attract Internet firms. These buildings near Central, Hong Kong's core retail and office area, are only a portion of numerous buildings IT firms occupy; they extend east to the Wan Chai office district and to other office districts along the harbor. Across the harbor in the New Territories, a cluster of IT firms has emerged in Sai Kung, near Hong Kong University of Science and Technology (Crisp and Chung 2000: 65; *Hong Kong Imail* 2000; Jacob 2000b: 6).

Demand from global businesses based in Hong Kong powers dramatic expansion of telematics, and international firms supplying this capacity explicitly cite demand in Hong Kong as the reason they are boosting construction of undersea fiber-optic lines. Asia Global Crossing completed its Hong Kong link first, according to John Legere, head of the firm, "because of the demand for broadband capacity and its [Hong Kong] emerging role as a leading telecommunication hub in the region" (*Asia Pulse* 2001). This link connects Hong Kong to more than two hundred business centers in twenty-seven countries, and all major countries in Asia will be connected in future expansion, but it is only one component of surging investment in undersea fiber-optic cables; as many as forty ships were laying cables in the Pacific and South China Sea during late 2000. Singapore Telecom finished linking Hong Kong to its pan-Asian fiber-optic network during 2001, and its motivation was growth of broadband demand from international businesses in Hong Kong and its position as gateway to China. Local firms such as Hutchison Global Crossing continue expanding fiber-optic lines in Hong Kong to link with growing external telematics capacity, and specialized services emerge to support swelling telematics demand from global businesses. PSINet chose Hong Kong for its center to manage its Asia-Pacific network, and its local Global Internet Hosting Center will provide advanced hosting and application outsourcing services to Internet content and applications companies for reaching a global market. Developers upgrade large amounts of old industrial space to provide facilities for data service centers, and some firms supply computer engineers to support clients who lease space. As WorldCom expanded data centers it chose Hong Kong as the site for Asian launch of voice-over Internet protocol (VOIP) services. And Dubai-based International Telecommunications Clearing Corporation (ITCC) selected Hong Kong as the Asian Internet trading floor, with other global floors that located in London, New York, Los Angeles, and Miami.[12]

As the Asian metropolis with the most sophisticated global financial intermediaries, Hong Kong generates demand for continual upgrading of telematics to service firms. The Hong Kong Monetary Authority often leads in increasing capacity of Hong Kong institutions to provide premier financial services to global firms. By the start of 2001 the authority had a state-of-the-art U.S. dollar clearing system, the first in Asia; this permits businesses to have real-time clearing of holdings of U.S. dollars, significantly lowering costs and reducing settlement risks to businesses in Asia. To service growing Asian bond markets three international banks—Citigroup, Deutsche Bank, and the Hongkong and Shanghai Banking Corporation—in 2000 formed a joint venture called BondsinAsia, a company that will provide an electronic trading system of bonds on-line; they chose Hong Kong and Singapore as initial places to operate platforms. And East West Trade Center (EWETC), a Hong Kong–based company, in 2000 created an Internet-based global trading system to allow traders to operate through International Trade & Banking Facility (iTBF). This Internet facility, designed initially for Asia, is a globally integrated system connecting bankers, importers, exporters, manufacturers, shippers, and buyers and sellers.[13]

Because Hong Kong is China's international metropolis, soaring business links between them spur continual transformation of Hong Kong's telematics capacity, and accession of China to the World Trade Organization (WTO) will stimulate greater demand for Hong Kong's sophisticated business services. China's own telematics capacity grows at prodigious rates as mainland companies such as China Telecom, China Netcom, and China Railway Telecom connect cities nationwide with fiber-optic lines. And Hong Kong's Citic Pacific, whose parent is China International Trust & Investment (Citic Beijing), plans a fiber-optic network to connect all important mainland cities. Equally as significant, Hong Kong is the regional metropolis of southern China, and nearby Guangdong province houses the mainland's wealthiest population. Hong Kong's government explicitly aims to deepen integration of Hong Kong and southern China, and China's leading telecommunication firms such as China Telecom and China Netcom continue expanding high-capacity fiber-optic lines between Hong Kong and all major cities (including Guangzhou and Shenzhen) of Guangdong province; and these lines connect with Hong Kong's global networks. This swelling telematics capacity serves the vast industrial development of its hinterland, many of whose firms are based in Hong Kong. It also supports the white-collar back-office expansion in Guangdong province of Hong Kong–based firms and regional headquarters of global firms.[14]

TELEMATICS REINFORCES HONG KONG AS A GLOBAL METROPOLIS

Continued agglomeration of Asian and global intermediaries in Hong Kong and improvements in Hong Kong telematics capacity operate circularly and cumulatively to maintain its dominance as a global telematics hub. Other Asian metropolises might use heavy government subsidies to attempt to keep up with Hong Kong's telematics capacity, but their locally based intermediaries do not generate equivalent demand for the most sophisticated telematics infrastructure and services. As global metropolis for Asia, Hong Kong continues attracting the most highly capitalized and specialized intermediaries of commodity and financial capital with the greatest span of control for exchanging capital in Asia and between Asia and the global economy. They generate prodigious demands for telematics infrastructure and services, and possess capital to fund them. As China's international metropolis, Hong Kong requires enormous telematics infrastructure to integrate it with the mainland economy; the capacity of large Chinese and Hong Kong firms to supply infrastructure supports it as a pivotal hub in global telematics. However, Hong Kong's telematics capacity has more significance than physical infrastructure and services; foreign and Chinese intermediaries use telematics to enhance control of global and Asian capital exchanges. That control rests on their social networks of capital that meet in Hong Kong; these networks root in long-standing relationships and bonds of trust linking firms locally, throughout Asia, and across the globe. Other Asian metropolises do not have that concentration of capital networks, and construction and improvements of telematics cannot substitute for social networks. Therefore, Hong Kong's pivotal position in global exchanges of capital rests on networks of capital uniting foreign and Chinese intermediaries; rapidly improving telematics capacity strengthens their dominance.

NOTES

The author thanks the Institute for Advanced Study, United Nations University (Tokyo) for its support, and the Center for Advanced Study in the Behavioral Sciences (Palo Alto, CA), for hosting one of the meetings of the research network.

1. For a discussion of the distinction between physical exchange and decisions about control of exchange, see Meyer 1980: 120–140.

2. For further elaboration of these points, see Meyer 1991: 393–416.

3. This synthesis draws on Meyer 1991: 406–409.

4. See Centre for Asian Pacific Studies 1993 and Meyer 1997: 257–263. For a full discussion of Hong Kong as the pivotal center of decision making about capital in Asia from the 1840s to the present, see Meyer 2000. For a focus on finance, see Jao 1997.

5. See King 1988a: 92, 90–146, 258–520, table 2.1; King 1988b: 66; Lim, Nooi, and Boh 1983: 356–358.

6. See Reed 1981: 131–138, table A.11. The data measure numbers of locally based international banks and numbers of offices of non-locally based international banks, as well as numbers of indirect bank links. These data are consistent for the period from 1900 to 1980. On a measure that also includes total foreign financial assets and liabilities held in a center, Hong Kong ranked between fourth and ninth from 1955 to 1980, and in two years, 1970 and 1980, it did not rank in the top ten centers. Also see Reed 1981: 139–141, table A.12.

7. For various figures, see Endacott 1973: 316; Henderson 1989: 85, table 5.3; Riedel 1974: 36, table 7; Szczepanik 1958: 4–6.

8. For more discussion of the exchange of assets and their relation to telematics, see Meyer 1998: 410–432.

9. Data and calculations in this paragraph come from Census and Statistics Department (various issues).

10. For figures, see Burn and Martinsons 1997; Crew 1993: 93–100; Enright, Scott, and Dodwell 1997: 91–92, 157–158; *Xinhua* 2000c, Hong Kong Trade Development Council, n.d.; Ure 1995: 22–29.

11. For various analyses, see Chong 2000; *Xinhua* 2000a, 2000e; *Asia Pulse* 2000; Martinsons 1997; Petrazzini and Ure 1997.

12. See Kwok 2000: 4; Li and Woo 2000; Onag 2000; *Economist* 2000; Whai 2000; Yeung 2000; Yuk-min 2000.

13. See *Deutsche Presse-Agentur* 2000; *BusinessWorld* 2000; *Xinhua* 2000d.

14. See Chan, Ng, and Sito 2000; *ChinaOnline* 2000b; *Xinhua* 2000b: 4; *ChinaOnline,* 2000a; Ng 2001; *BBC Summary of World Broadcasts* 2000; Sito 2000; Jacob 2000a.

REFERENCES CITED

Agnes, P. 2000. "The End of Geography in Financial Services? Local Embeddedness and Territorialization in the Interest Rate Swaps Industry." *Economic Geography* 76: 347–366.

Asia Pulse 2000. "Hong Kong to Launch Major E-Government Measure by End of 2000." October 20.

———. 2001. "Asia Global Crossing Celebrates the Landing of East Asia Crossing." January 11.

Bard, Solomon. 1993. *Traders of Hong Kong: Some Foreign Merchant Houses, 1841–1899*. Hong Kong: Urban Council.

BBC Summary of World Broadcasts. 2000. "Optical Line to Link Shenzhen With Hong Kong." December 13.

Burn, J. M., and M. G. Martinsons, eds. 1997. *Information Technology and the Challenge for Hong Kong*. Hong Kong: Hong Kong University Press.

BusinessWorld. 2000. "An Internet Platform to Link Banks, Clients for Trading." August 22.

Census and Statistics Department. Various years. *Annual Review of Hong Kong External Trade*. Government of the Hong Kong Special Administrative Region, Hong Kong.

Census and Statistics Department. Various years. *Hong Kong Annual Digest of Statistics*. Hong Kong Special Administrative Region, Hong Kong.

Centre for Asian Pacific Studies. 1993. *Hong Kong's Role in the Asian Pacific Region in the 21st Century*. Proceedings and papers of the ASEAN-China Hong Kong Forum 1992. Hong Kong: Centre for Asian Pacific Studies, Lingnan College.

Chan, C., E. Ng, and P. Sito. 2000. "Operators Set to Scramble for Slice of Lucrative Telecoms Pie." *South China Morning Post*, December 5, Business Post, p. 8.

ChinaOnline. 2000a. "New Fiber-Optic Cable Network Connects Mainland, Hong Kong." July 14.

———. 2000b. "Fiber-Optic Cable Links Southern China." October 19.

Chong, F. 2000. "All Aboard the Internet: Hong Kong's Property Companies Discover There's More to Business than Bricks and Mortar." *Asia Today*, April.

Crew, G. L. 1993. "Hong Kong as a Telecommunication Centre." Pp. 93–100 in *Hong Kong's Role in the Asian Pacific Region in the 21st Century*, Proceedings and Papers of the ASEAN-China Hong Kong Forum 1992. Hong Kong: Centre for Asian Pacific Studies, Lingnan College.

Crisp, P., and Y. Chung. 2000. "Connect the Dots: Is Cyber-Port Still Indispensable to Hong Kong's High-Tech Future?" *Asiaweek*, June 9, p. 65.

Deutsche Presse-Agentur. 2000. "Asian Electronic Bond Trading Network Planned." July 21.

Economist. 2000. "Waves under Water." December 16.

Endacott, G. B. 1973. *A History of Hong Kong*. Hong Kong: Oxford University Press.

Enright, M., E. Scott, and D. Dodwell. 1997. *The Hong Kong Advantage*. Hong Kong: Oxford University Press.

Farnie, D. A. 1969. *East and West of Suez: The Suez Canal in History, 1854–1956*, Oxford, England: Clarendon Press.

Hao, Yen-P'ing. 1970. *The Comprador in Nineteenth Century China: Bridge between East and West*. Cambridge, MA: Harvard University Press.

Henderson, J. 1989. *The Globalisation of High Technology Production: Society, Space and Semiconductors in the Restructuring of the Modern World*. London: Routledge.

Ho, Yin-Ping. 1992. *Trade, Industrial Restructuring and Development in Hong Kong*. Honolulu: University of Hawaii Press.

Hong Kong Imail. 2000. "Cyberport Project in First Stages of Work." August 21.

Hong Kong Monetary Authority. 1998. *1998 Annual Report*. Hong Kong: Hong Kong Monetary Authority.

Hong Kong Trade Development Council. n.d. *A Global Reach*. Hong Kong: Hong Kong Trade Development Council.

Huff, W. G. 1994. *The Economic Growth of Singapore: Trade and Development in the Twentieth Century*. Cambridge: Cambridge University Press.

Jacob, R. 2000a. "Hong Kong to Plan to Become Regional Hub." *Financial Times*. February 22.

———. 2000b. "Hong Kong to Subsidize IT Offices." *Financial Times*, May 18.

Janelle, D. G. 1969. "Spatial Reorganization: A Model and Concept." *Annals of the Association of American Geographers* 59: 348–364.

Jao, Y. C. 1997. *Hong Kong as an International Financial Center: Evolution, Prospects and Policies.* Hong Kong: City University of Hong Kong Press.

King, F. H. H. 1987. *The Hongkong Bank in Late Imperial China, 1864–1902: On an Even Keel.* Vol. 1 of, *The History of the Hongkong and Shanghai Banking Corporation.* Cambridge: Cambridge University Press.

———. 1988a. *The Hongkong Bank in the Period of Imperialism and War, 1895–1918: Wayfoong, the Focus of Wealth.* Vol. 2 of *The History of the Hongkong and Shanghai Banking Corporation.* Cambridge: Cambridge University Press.

———. 1988b. *The Hongkong Bank between the Wars and the Bank Interned, 1919–1945: Return from Grandeur.* Vol. 3 of *The History of the Hongkong and Shanghai Banking Corporation.* Cambridge: Cambridge University Press.

Kwok, B. 2000. "WorldCom Lines Up Data Hub, Voice Option in Asian Drive." *South China Morning Post,* October 17, Business Post, p. 4.

Langdale, J. V. 1989. "The Geography of International Business Telecommunications: The Role of Leased Networks." *Annals of the Association of American Geographers* 79: 501–22.

Le Fevour, E. 1970. *Western Enterprise in Late Ch'ing China: A Selective Survey of Jardine, Matheson & Company's Operations, 1842–1895.* Cambridge, MA: Harvard University Press.

Li, S. and R. Woo. 2000. "Data Centers Lift Hope; Upgrades Ease Space Dilemma as Developers Cash in on Hi-Tech and Telecoms." *South China Morning Post,* May 24, Property Post, p. 1.

Lim, C. P., P. S. Nooi and M. Boh. 1983. "The History and Development of the Hongkong and Shanghai Banking Corporation in Peninsular Malaysia." Pp. 350–391 in *Eastern Banking: Essays in the History of the Hongkong and Shanghai Banking Corporation,* ed. F. H. K. King. London: Athlone.

Lockwood, S. C. 1971. *Augustine Heard and Company, 1858–1862: American Merchants in China.* Cambridge, MA: Harvard University Press.

Martinsons, M. G. 1997. "IT Policies and Information Infrastructures: Comparing Hong Kong to the Singapore Model." Pp. 27–59 in *Information Technology and the Challenge for Hong Kong,* ed. J. M. Burn and M. G. Martinsons. Hong Kong: Hong Kong University Press.

Meyer, D. R. 1980. "A Dynamic Model of the Integration of Frontier Urban Places into the United States System of Cities." *Economic Geography* 56: 120–140.

———. 1986. "The World System of Cities: Relations Between International Financial Metropolises and South American Cities." *Social Forces* 64: 553–81.

———. 1991. "Change in the World System of Metropolises: The Role of Business Intermediaries." *Urban Geography* 12: 393–416.

———. 1997. "Expert Managers of Uncertainty: Intermediaries of Capital in Hong Kong." *Cities* 14 (5): 257–263.

———. 1998. "World Cities as Financial Centres." Pp. 410–432 in *Globalization and the World of Large Cities,* ed. Fu-chen Lo and Yue-man Yeung. Tokyo: United Nations University Press.

———. 2000) *Hong Kong as a Global Metropolis,* Cambridge: Cambridge University Press.

Miners, N. 1987. *Hong Kong under Imperial Rule, 1912–1941.* Hong Kong: Oxford University Press.

Ng, E. 2001. "Telecommunications Seen Following Path of IT Revolution." *South China Morning Post,* January 2, Business Post, p. 3.

Onag, G. 2000. "Network Hub: PSINet Ups Investments in Hong Kong." *Asia Computer Weekly,* February 28.

Petrazzini, B., and J. Ure. 1997. "Hong Kong's Communication Infrastructure: The Evolving Role of a Regional Information Hub." Pp. 61–90 in *Information Technology and the Challenge for Hong Kong.* ed J. M. Burn and M. G. Martinsons. Hong Kong: Hong Kong University Press.

Pred, A. 1977. *City-Systems in Advanced Economies.* New York: Wiley.

Reed, H. C. 1981. *The Preeminence of International Financial Centers.* New York: Praeger.

Riedel, J. 1974. *The Industrialization of Hong Kong.* Tubingen, Germany: J. C. B. Mohr.

Sassen, S. 2001. *The Global City: New York, London, Tokyo.* 2nd ed. Princeton, NJ: Princeton University Press.

Sito, P. 2000. "Citic Pacific Unit in Talks on Mainland Telecoms Service." *South China Morning Post*, December 16, Business Post, p. 1.

Szczepanik, E. 1958. *The Economic Growth of Hong Kong.* London: Oxford University Press.

Thrift, N. 1996. "New Urban Eras and Old Technological Fears: Reconfiguring the Goodwill of Electronic Things." *Urban Studies* 33: 1463–1493.

Tom, C. F. J. 1964. *The Entrepot Trade and the Monetary Standards of Hong Kong, 1842–1941.* Hong Kong: K. Weiss.

Tsai, Jung-Fang. 1993. *Hong Kong in Chinese History: Community and Social Unrest in the British Colony, 1842–1913.* New York: Columbia University Press.

Ure, J. 1995. "Telecommunications in China and the Four Dragons." Pp. 11–48 in *Telecommunications in Asia: Policy, Planning and Development.* Hong Kong: Hong Kong University Press.

Vogel, E. F. 1989. *One Step Ahead in China: Guangdong under Reform.* Cambridge, MA: Harvard University Press.

Warf, B. 1989. "Telecommunications and the Globalization of Financial Services.' *Professional Geographer* 41: 257–271.

———. 1995. "Telecommunications and the Changing Geographies of Knowledge Transmission in the Late 20th Century." *Urban Studies* 32: 361–378.

Welsh, F. A. 1993. *A Borrowed Place: The History of Hong Kong.* New York: Kodansha International.

Whai, Q. H. 2000. "C2C Submarine Cable System to Land in Hong Kong Next May." *Business Times, Singapore,* December 1, p. 8.

Xinhua. 2000a. "Hong Kong Aims to Become World City in Asia." February 21.

———. 2000b. "Hong Kong to Make Most of China Advantages, Financial Secretary." March 8.

———. 2000c. "Submarine Cables to Be Laid to Connect Hong Kong and Japan." September 8.

———. 2000d. "U.S. Dollar Clearing System to Enhance." December 19.

———. 2000e. "Hong Kong Gives Spur to IT Development." December 21.

Yeung, S. 2000. "ITCC to Launch Net Exchange." *South China Morning Post.* December 12, Business Post, p. 3.

Yuk-min, H. 2000. "Hutchison Unit Eyes HK$5 Billion Link Expansion." *South China Morning Post*, October 13, Business Post, 4.

Chapter 10

SHANGHAI: RECONNECTING TO THE GLOBAL ECONOMY

Felicity Rose Gu and Zilai Tang

With the intensification of globalization, the 1990s witnessed increasingly explicit competition among major cities in the Asia-Pacific region in claiming economic dominance. As well as marketing their places as business hubs for the regional headquarters of multinationals, and for the specialized corporate services associated with them, local governments in these cities have been actively involved in a new round of development of urban and regional infrastructure. This comprises telematics infrastructure in addition to conventional infrastructure such as that related to transportation (Warf 1995). This chapter considers these trends in relation to one Asian-Pacific megacity: Shanghai.

Compared with its East Asian competitors, Shanghai is a latecomer in telematics development. In the pre-Reform era, Shanghai, like other Chinese cities, was developed in isolation from the rest of the world. It was not until the beginning of this decade—when Pudong was designated as a special development zone at the forefront of the country's economic reform—that Shanghai regained its central status in the Chinese economy. Together with Hong Kong, which has now returned to Chinese sovereignty,[1] Shanghai is expected to play a leading role as one of the control centers of Chinese economic development, particularly over the Yangtse River Delta as well as the whole eastern part of China.[2]

The primary aim of this chapter is to present a case study of the effects of global and regional economic pressures and opportunities on one emerging regional or global city. In particular, it is a case study of the role of infrastructure developments, especially telematics, in the development of the city, and in (re)defining the city's role in regional and global urban-economic systems. Shanghai has made major efforts to internationalize and modernize itself, the initiative coming from the municipal and national governments via extensive reform programs in place since 1978. This chapter therefore offers insights into the role, or potential role, of the state in telematics and conventional infrastructure development. It also illustrates how cities in developing and transition economies are reacting to the demands of the global economy, and how telematics developments are being regarded as crucial in the development of the city and its economy. Finally, the chapter illustrates the importance of modern infrastructure for the functional transformation of the city, especially efforts to raise competitiveness and participation in financial and related services industries: infrastructure has to keep pace with functional change in the city, and, at the same time, provide the framework for such change.

The chapter is structured as follows. The first section provides an overview of economic and urban development in Shanghai in the postreform period. It considers Shanghai's connections into global and regional urban-economic systems, focusing on the role of foreign direct investment (FDI), trade, sociopolitical linkages, transport, telecommunications, and transnational corporations (TNCs). The importance of the Chinese political economy and public policy in influencing the pace and pattern of development outcomes is also discussed. The second section discusses in detail the development of telematics infrastructure in Shanghai. The impacts of the combined processes of modernization and internationalization on urban spatial and functional structure, and interurban relations—including Shanghai's relations with Hong Kong—are discussed in the third and fourth sections. The final section summarizes the findings and concludes the chapter.

SHANGHAI IN THE GLOBAL AND REGIONAL ECONOMIES
Postreform Urban and Economic Development Patterns
Throughout its history, the urban development of Shanghai has revolved around its role as an economic center. Initially a seaport and trading and fishing town of only local importance, its designation as a treaty port in 1842 produced a turnaround in Shanghai's economic fortunes and allowed it to develop into the country's leading industrial and commercial center.[3] Between 1860 and 1930, 68 percent of the total value of Chinese trade passed through Shanghai, while by 1936 it handled half of China's foreign trade (Ning 1995). The financial sector was developed in Shanghai under foreign management during this period, and by 1947 the city had fourteen foreign banks, thirteen trust companies, and seventy-nine money exchanges. This represented a massive concentration of capital in the city. Shanghai also grew into a strong industrial center, producing textiles (especially cotton and silk), flour and tobacco, and its first shipyard was established by the British in 1851. By the 1930s, Shanghai's industrial development was of national significance, accounting for half of total

national capital investment and total value of production (Ning 1995). This in effect gave China two capitals: the political and administrative capital in Beijing, and the economic capital in Shanghai. Although the degree of concentration of industrial, financial, and trading capacity in treaty port Shanghai was dissipated in the post-Liberation period,[4] Shanghai remained China's leading metropolis through 1978. At the start of the 1980s, Shanghai produced one-eighth of gross national industrial output value, and one-sixth of national financial income. One-third of the volume of freight was also handled by Shanghai's port. Since Reform began in 1978, and especially since 1990, Shanghai has been leading development in the dynamic Yangtse Delta region, the emerging Yangtse River Valley, and coastal China; tertiary sector functions especially have expanded rapidly (see Liu, Song, and Wu 1998). Shanghai recorded GDP growth of 13 percent in 1996, with the tertiary sector accounting for 43 percent of GDP (SMSB 1997).

Shanghai's growth and development since 1978 divides into two phases: the period up to 1990, when growth was below the national average, and the urban and economic transition was held back both by a cautious government approach to Shanghai and by the policy and investment focus on southern China; and the period since 1990, when Shanghai's growth rate has led national figures and urban change has been far reaching, following the opening of Pudong New Area and government backing to foreign investment–based development. Table 1 illustrates Shanghai's GDP growth over the past two decades.

China's initial experiments with the open and market economy were made in the Special Economic Zones (SEZs) of Guangdong and Fujian. This was a risk-averse strategy; the distance of these provinces from Beijing would mitigate any negative social or political consequences of this market-oriented development, and their prior industrial development had been of lower economic significance than that of the eastern and northeastern provinces. At the same time, it was hoped that proximity to Hong Kong, Macau, and Taiwan would assist in the rapid development of the SEZs and their hinterlands. Given Shanghai's dominance of the urban economic hierarchy, it was considered too great a risk to allow the experiments to take place in Shanghai. This served to hold back Shanghai's development throughout the 1980s, despite the fact that the city was one of fourteen Open Coastal Cities designated in 1984. The Chinese government's focus on Guangdong coincided with that of overseas investors. This was especially the case for Hong Kong and Taiwanese industrialists looking for lower-cost production sites, following the restructuring of both their own and global economies, and changes in the spatial divisions of labor and production. Shanghai, lacking the locational proximity to overseas Chinese and the incentive structures of the Special Economic Zones (SEZs)

TABLE 1

SHANGHAI'S GDP GROWTH, 1978-1999

Year	GDP (100 m yuan)	GDP Index (1952=100)	GDP/Capita (yuan)
1978	272.81	888.0	2,498
1980	311.89	1033.8	2,738
1985	466.75	1596.6	3,855
1990	756.45	2103.2	5,910
1995	2462.57	3875.0	18,943
1999	4034.96	5987.5	30,803

Source: Shanghai Municipal Statistics Bureau 1997; 2000.

U.S.$ is equal to approximately 8.3 RMB yuan.

became marginalized in the new race for investment and growth. Shanghai was further disadvantaged by its heavy contributions to national revenues. The average annual GDP growth rate for Guangdong over the same period was 11.4 percent, compared with 8.1 percent for Shanghai; the national average was 9.3 percent (SSB 1996). Nevertheless, Shanghai retained the largest share of urban population throughout this twelve-year period, and remained one of China's largest heavy industrial centers. Development in south China relied, in contrast, on light industrial activity, especially assembly and export processing for Hong Kong and Taiwanese enterprises.

The 1990 opening of Pudong as, in effect, China's sixth SEZ proved to be the catalyst for Shanghai's rapid urban and economic transformation. Map 1 illustrates the location of Pudong in relation to the original urban core in Puxi. In addition, since the late 1980s, Shanghai has been able to retain a larger portion of revenues, which have been reinvested in the city's urban and economic development (Ning 1995). Some analysts argue that the central government misjudged the impact of the delay in promoting the development of Shanghai, and that competition with the now very strong Pearl River Delta continues to hamper Shanghai's development. However, while the delay undoubtedly did slow Shanghai's modernization, the diversified nature of the Shanghai economy, as well as the metropolis' strategic location on the eastern seaboard and as the heart of the Yangtse River Delta, have allowed it to overcome many of the hindrances of competition and earlier marginalization.

Shanghai's GDP reached 290.22 billion yuan in 1996 (SMSB 1997). This represented 4.3 percent of total national GDP (SSB 1997). GDP growth in 1995–1996 was 13.0 percent; this compared with a national average growth rate of 9.7 percent, and a growth rate for the eastern region of 11.5 percent. Average

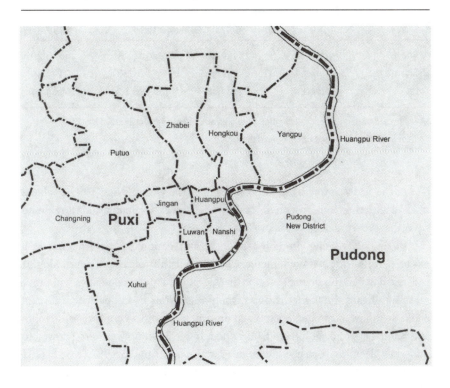

growth between 1978 and 1995 was 9.5 percent (SSB 1996). GDP per capita rose from 2,498 yuan in 1978 to 5,910 in 1990 and 30,803 in 1999 (SMSB 1997; 2000). Industrial output value was 506.657 billion yuan in 1996, 5.1 percent of the national total (SSB 1997). Since 1978, the Shanghai economy has restructured, with a reemergence of light industry and services as significant sectors of the economy, and a growth in high-technology activity; the finance and banking sector has grown rapidly in terms of contribution to GDP. The real estate sector has also grown rapidly since the early 1990s. The contribution of the tertiary sector to GDP rose from 18.6 percent in 1978, to 26.1 percent in 1985, to 37.9 percent in 1993, and to 43.0 percent in 1996 (SMSB 1997). However, the secondary sector remains Shanghai's leading sector in terms of both contribution to GDP and speed of growth.

Shanghai's strength has always been in its dynamic, broad-based economy. In the reemergence of its tertiary sector, Shanghai has resurrected its historical "dual-function" economy, with importance as both a national manufacturing and service center. In 1989, China established two stock exchanges, one in Shanghai and the other in Shenzhen; the Shanghai stock exchange has become

TABLE 2

TRANSACTION VOLUME OF MARKETABLE STOCKS IN SHANGHAI STOCK EXCHANGE (100 MILLION YUAN)

	1996	1997	1998	1999
A-Shares	9020.24	13550.24	12304.23	16826.20
B-Shares	94.57	212.94	81.88	139.59
Total	9114.82	13763.18	12386.11	16965.79

*A-shares are traded domestically in RMB, B-shares are traded overseas in U.S.$.

Source: *Statistical Yearbook of Shanghai* (2000)

one of the fastest-growing stock exchanges in the world (Ning 1995). Table 2 tracks the tremendous growth of the Shanghai Stock Exchange and its rebound from the 1997 financial crises in Asia.

Shanghai is being promoted by local and national policy rhetoric as a national, if not international, financial center, but this role is still developing. It is particularly in the financial sector that developments in telematics will prove most significant. Shanghai is one of only four cities in China where foreign banks are allowed to open operational branches; the others are Dalian, Tianjin, and Shenzhen. Several foreign banks operating in Pudong were also allowed to undertake Renminbi yuan transactions for the first time in 1997 (e.g., HSBC [United Kingdom], Citibank [United States], Bank of Tokyo-Mitsubishi [Japan]). Overall, Shanghai is the leading center for the Chinese headquarters of overseas banks, although the number of representative offices in Beijing continues to exceed that of Shanghai. Japanese banks dominate, reflecting investment and trade patterns in which Japanese firms play a major role. The majority of Chinese state banks have their headquarters in Beijing; the exception is the Bank of Telecommunications which moved its headquarters to Shanghai in 1997. Additionally, Pudong Development Bank has headquarters in its mother city.[5] Various reforms have also been introduced to enhance Shanghai's role as a major domestic trading center, including the establishment of futures markets and wholesale markets for industrial and agricultural products. These changes represent the central government's commitment to the development of Shanghai as a national financial and manufacturing center.

Table 1 summarizes Shanghai's position as China's leading metropolis. In terms of per capita GDP, investment and so on, Shanghai leads China. As a city, Shanghai has China's largest urban and nonagricultural populations as shares of provincial population and in national totals. Share of the tertiary sector in GDP and employment is the highest in the country, while Shanghai also has a strong manufacturing sector. The real estate sector is among the most active in China, leading to massive redevelopment of the central city. The total value of retail sales is the highest in the country.

These static development indicators, however, need to be considered in conjunction with indicators of Shanghai's role in the international urban and economic systems in order to fully appreciate the forces for, and extent of, change in the city, and its potential position in the global and regional economies. The next section therefore analyzes the internationalization of Shanghai—its economic and sociopolitical linkages with external cities, and the infrastructure supporting Shanghai's growing global and, especially, regional interaction. This process of integration is promoted by national and local policy rhetoric, and by proactive urban planning and political activity designed especially to attract inward investment. This policy response and the political economy underlying it are discussed in the following section.

The Internationalization of Shanghai

Shanghai has since the nineteenth century been China's largest and most economically advanced city. It has arguably also been the most open Chinese city and the one most influenced by international interests. As mentioned above, Shanghai was one of fourteen Open Coastal Cities designated in 1984, but it was the opening of Pudong New Area in 1990 that provided the main impetus for Shanghai's reintegration into the global and regional economies. Since 1990, and especially since Deng Xiao Ping's "tour of the south" in 1992, foreign investment and trade have expanded rapidly, and sociopolitical ties, including twinning, exchange visits, trade fairs, and official delegations, have also grown. These links have been supported by a growing transportation and telecommunications infrastructure, and the expansive networks of multinational corporations and firm-firm and firm-state relations.

Foreign Investment

Foreign investment to Shanghai, especially foreign direct investment (FDI), has risen rapidly since 1978, and especially during the 1990s. A total of U.S.$108.8 million in foreign capital was utilized in Shanghai in 1985, a figure that rose to U.S.$4.7 billion by 1996. The cumulative total to the end of 1999 was U.S.$27.7 billion (Statistical Yearbook 2000). FDI amounted to 31 percent of Shanghai's total investment capital during the Eighth Five-Year Plan period (1991–1995); this figure was expected to rise to one-third or one-half by 2000.

FDI to Shanghai has to date been dominated by flows from within East Asia; 73 percent of FDI to Shanghai comes from seven East Asian countries (Hong Kong, Japan, Macau, Taiwan, South Korea, Singapore, and Thailand). Of these, Hong Kong and Japan are the principal investors; in 1996, Hong Kong provided 47 percent, and Japan 13 percent. The second-largest investor

TABLE 3

FOREIGN DIRECT INVESTMENT IN SHANGHAI

Year	Million US$
1995	325.0
1996	471.6
1997	480.8
1998	363.8
1999	304.8
Total by end of 1999	27.73 Billion US$

Source: Statistical Yearbook of Shanghai (2000)

to Shanghai in 1996 was the United States, which contributed more than 14 percent of total FDI. Non-Asian investors are mostly involved in industrial projects and show a reluctance to become involved in real estate. Table 3 shows the extent of foreign investment in Shanghai for the last five years of the century. As in table 2, the harmful effects of the 1997 financial crises in Asia are evident in the numbers.

More than 52 percent of foreign capital used in 1996 went to the industrial sector, and 46 percent went to tertiary industry, of which 48 percent was in real estate. Reflecting this focus on industry and real estate, 23 percent of FDI was utilized in Pudong, primarily an industrial district, but also incorporating the new central business district area, Lujiazui, where real estate development has been intense and large scale. Meanwhile, more than 16 percent went to Minhang, an industrial district, and around 29 percent went to the districts of Huangpu, Nanshi, Luwan, Xuhui, Jingan, and Changning in central Puxi (West Shanghai), where overseas real estate companies have been active in developing high-rise commercial complexes. This pattern of FDI distribution within Shanghai also reflects national, municipal, and district government policies, including various locational incentives and directives, which push foreign economic activity to certain parts of the municipality.

Shanghai firms have also started to invest abroad, and a process of two-way interaction is beginning to emerge. However, such transactions are embryonic, and the outflows of capital from Shanghai are marginal as compared with the inflows. By the end of 1996, 452 Shanghai enterprises had established operations abroad, and total accumulated investment value was U.S.$ 246.08 million (SMSB 1997). These figures may be underestimates, however, due to the registration of a large number of mainland companies in Hong Kong in order to take advantage of tax breaks and other incentives when they reinvest in China. This practice is well known, but no figures are available for its extent.

Foreign Trade

Shanghai's foreign trade has risen rapidly since 1978, its total value reaching almost U.S.$52.9 billion in 1996 (SMSB 1997). Exports from Shanghai amounted to 8.7 percent of national exports in 1996; Shanghai accounted for 9.6 percent of total trade (SSB 1997). Domestic consumption, especially of household consumer goods, is high; this demand, accompanied by demand for raw materials and components (including those for export-processing activities) accounts for high and rising import values. Import values reached almost U.S.$25.6 billion in 1996 (SMSB 1997). Export values are also rising, but not as quickly as import values. As with investment, Shanghai's trade is dominated by linkages within East Asia, especially in the case of exports. Japan is China's largest trading partner; nearly the same percentage of its imports and its exports (26.8) were to/from Japan. The balance of trade is, however, shifting; between 1993 and 1996, the shares of North and South America in export trade rose from 21 percent to 22 percent, and Europe from 15 percent to 18 percent, matched by a 2 percent fall in exports to Asia. The Shanghai municipal government is actively encouraging an expansion of trade outside East Asia, in the wake of the regional financial crisis.

Sociopolitical Linkages

Tourism, educational visits, twinning arrangements, political and cultural exchanges, and government-sponsored trade fairs are increasing in number and frequency, providing an additional means of linkage between Shanghai and other cities and countries regionally and globally. While often not specifically economic in nature, such activities assist in the exchange of information on Shanghai's cultural, social, political, and economic affairs, and enhance an understanding of Shanghai, and China, in the external marketplace: they assist in the marketing of the city for investment, trade, and other economic activity, and in the development of local capacities in business affairs.

Several examples of such sociopolitical linkages may be cited. Most city and district government officials travel abroad at least once per year for training and/or to review development practices overseas; they also participate in the dissemination of information on business opportunities in Shanghai, both informally and formally through such events as trade fairs. Trade fairs, held both overseas and in Shanghai, promote relationships among governments, private firms (especially TNCs) and Chinese government-owned/backed corporations. Shanghai regularly receives diplomatic missions from overseas; in 1996, thirteen cultural delegations from the governments of ten countries made official visits to Shanghai. "Twin city" arrangements also contribute to sociocultural and economic exchange. Shanghai had established such relations with thirty-nine cities worldwide by the end of 1996; sixteen twin cities are in

Europe and eight are in East Asia, including three cities in Japan and two in South Korea. Shanghai is a major consular center, and at the end of 1996, thirty countries had consulates in Shanghai. Considerable consular activity is aimed at developing commercial relations with local authorities and firms in Shanghai and surrounding provinces in the Yangtse Delta (Zhejiang, Jiangsu, Anhui). The growth of consular representation in Shanghai indicates both a growing expatriate population in and around Shanghai, and, more important, the perception of Shanghai as a key center within China for overseas business.

Tourists are an important source of foreign exchange for Shanghai and China, as well as assisting in deepening sociocultural relations. Shanghai received 1.4 million international tourists in 1996, a sixfold increase since 1978 (SMSB 1997). Of these, 39 percent were from Japan, and 7 percent from the United States. In contrast with Guangdong and Fujian, where Hong Kong, Macanese, and Taiwanese tourists account for the vast majority of total tourist arrivals, and a national average of 87 percent, only 29 percent of tourists visiting Shanghai are from these territories. Though there are tight links between the southern Chinese provinces and clusters of overseas Chinese in Southeast Asia (especially Hong Kong and Taiwan), Shanghai does not have any specific links with overseas Chinese communities, which may account for the different tourist patterns. Location, proximity to Japan, and the availability of transpacific flights also help determine the distribution of tourist arrivals. The expatriate population in Shanghai is small but growing, and its workforce places particular demands on urban space, especially for high-quality, Western-style housing and recreational facilities. These various social, cultural, and political linkages contribute to Shanghai's integration into regional and global systems, and strengthen the underlying trends for trade and investment linkages.

The Infrastructure of International Connections

Improved transportation links, telecommunications networks, and a web of international firms, including many large multinationals, are providing the infrastructure for Shanghai's interface with global and regional systems. These are discussed in turn below.

Transportation. Transportation networks form the underlying infrastructure for most forms of interaction across space. Shanghai has extensive sea and air linkages with cities internationally, and especially with South Korea and Japan. With the increasing demand from business and domestic travelers, and growing foreign trade, these links are expanding. Shanghai was linked by air with seven cities in 1985; this had risen to twelve by 1990 and fifteen by 1995 (ICAO 1985, 1990, 1995c). The majority of links are within the East Asian region, although links with North America, Europe, and Australasia have been established. The density of links is also important. For example, nine airlines fly between Shanghai and Japan; China Eastern Airlines alone flies to seven cities in Japan. Shanghai is China's second-largest airport for passenger traffic, and the largest in terms of freight transported. Only Beijing has more international connections, and only Shanghai and Beijing fly to all continents. Guangzhou is important for Southeast Asian connections and also has a link with Australia. In 1995, 1.7 million passengers disembarked in Shanghai, equal to 53 percent of Beijing's passenger volume, but 463 percent of Guangzhou's (ICAO 1995a). In 1993, Shanghai loaded and unloaded 118,900 tons of freight, compared with 117,500 tons in Beijing (ICAO 1995b). A new airport is currently under construction in Pudong as part of a plan to enhance Shanghai's "triple-port" (airport, seaport, and information port) functions for the twenty-first century.

Shanghai is not, however, an *international* transportation hub. Rather, East Asian air transport functions are concentrated in Tokyo, Hong Kong, Bangkok, and Singapore (e.g., Hong Kong was linked with ninety-six cities worldwide in 1995 (ICAO 1995c) and acts as a transfer point for, *inter alia*, passengers from Taiwan and overseas to China). Shanghai's principal role is as the gateway to eastern China and, especially, the Yangtse Delta, with Beijing serving as both a gateway to the north and, since it is the national capital, the national airline center, and with Hong Kong and Guangzhou serving as gateways to the south. Shanghai is nevertheless a *national* air, rail, and road hub, and as such allows passengers and freight using its international airport easy access to the Yangtse Delta, Shandong, Jiangsu, Zhejiang, and Anhui provinces, and cities nationwide. It is also linked with Hong Kong via a high-speed rail service, and indirectly with the Russian rail links via Beijing and Urumqi. Shanghai is therefore important to the national-international distribution systems, acting as a gateway or coupling point.

Shanghai is also linked by sea with 440 ports in 160 countries (Zhuang 1996). Again, links within Northeast Asia are particularly strong: direct shipping routes link Shanghai with Japan (Yokohama, Kobe, Kitakyushu, and Nagasaki) South and North Korea, Taipei, and Vladivostok. In 1995, Shanghai's seaports handled 165.7 million tons of import-export cargo, and 96 percent of all freight containers handled in Shanghai were international (SMSB 1997). Due to its location at the mouth of the Yangtse River and its rail links, Shanghai is East China's principal trans-shipment point for international cargo being transported to and from inland cities, including Nanjing, Wuhan, and Chongqing. Scheduled passenger services also travel between Shanghai and the Yangtse ports, Hong Kong, and Japan.

Telecommunications. Rimmer (1996) has argued that telecommunications developments have become the key means for the development of the global urban system, by bringing down barriers of space and time in international interaction. This section briefly reviews telecommunications infrastructure developments in Shanghai; further details on these developments, planning for their enhancement, and their implications are given in the next section.

More than three million telephones had been installed in the urban area of Shanghai by the end of 1996 (SMSB 1997), an increase of forty times the number installed by the end of 1978, and 36 percent above the 1995 figure. In 1996, 39.9 million international calls were made from Shanghai (SMSB 1997), of which approximately half were to Hong Kong and Macau. This compares with 4.4 billion domestic long-distance calls. Both figures have increased rapidly in recent years, from 4.7 million and 31.3 million respectively in 1990, and only 29,700 and 6.3 million in 1978. Ownership of telephones, mobile telephones, pagers, computers (with Internet and e-mail connections), and fax machines is now commonplace among businesses and households in the urban area. Figures for information exchange are limited for China and for Shanghai. However, it is known that 472,000 pieces of express international mail were exchanged with Shanghai in 1996 (SMSB 1997), and that 4,600 tons of international mail was loaded and unloaded at Shanghai airport in 1993, the highest in the country and exceeding Beijing by 900 tons.

Business dynamism and the role of MNCs. Multinational and transnational corporations of all sizes play a significant role in the integration of the global and regional urban-economic systems through their own cross-national activities (intrafirm linkages between headquarters and branches), and, more important, through their relations with local governments and firms in host cities. The behavior of companies in the global marketplace has served to link cities through their role as business centers. Since 1990, Shanghai has seen an influx of overseas firms. Forty-six of the world's top 100 industrial corporations had operations in Shanghai at the end of 1996. There were 15,927 registered overseas enterprises (6.6 percent of the national total), and a further 4,147 representative offices of foreign-invested ventures. Almost half of the representative offices are those of Hong Kong or Macanese companies, and 20 percent from Japan, indicating a strong regional bias in participation in the Shanghai and Chinese economies, and hence the degree of the city's exposure to the East Asian financial crisis. While the majority of overseas enterprises are engaged in industrial or real estate projects, two other types of firm are also becoming involved in Shanghai's economy—financial and banking sector firms, and architectural and design consultants. The activities of both groups are important for the development of the city. Foreign banks, if located in Pudong, can engage in Renminbi transactions and create the facilities to service the growing number of overseas productive enterprises in the city. Architectural and design firms are being engaged by city and district governments, as well as individual developers, often through international competitions. These firms are introducing international styles and standards in the development of the city. Such "soft" internationalization is as much a part of Shanghai's global and regional integration as the "hard" internationalization through investment, trade, business activity and infrastructure.

Peculiarities of the Local Political Economy and Public Policy Responses to Globalization

Shanghai has, over the past decade, become increasingly integrated into global, and, especially, regional urban-economic systems, as described above. Foreign trade with and investment in Shanghai have, in particular, expanded rapidly, supported by falling cost barriers and enhanced transport and telecommunications. The Chinese development process is capital driven, and as such the inflows of FDI via TNCs have been important in initiating and sustaining the pace of economic and urban transformation in the municipality. Social, cultural, and political exchange has also been important in the interaction between Shanghai and the global and regional economies.

However, development in Shanghai is not *controlled* solely, or even largely, by the global system; there has been only very limited reduction in the control of the state over urban and economic development processes and patterns. But there have been significant alterations to state policy and practice as a result of the extensive Reform program initiated in 1978 and deepened since. Following gradual political and administrative decentralization that began in the early 1980s, governments at the city, district, and county levels have seen their powers in urban and economic decision-making increase within legal and policy frameworks set nationally and provincially. Development outcomes are therefore the result of the *interaction* of state behavior with external economic forces for development and change, forces controlled not at the national level, but internationally, through, *inter alia*, the activities of TNCs. In other words, development in Shanghai represents the results of a global-local nexus in decision making. This section considers briefly the attributes of the political economy of local development in China and Shanghai, and how the actions taken by local governments are manipulating global and regional forces for change and hence the locality's competitive position in the international system.

The Chinese political economy has been in transition since 1978. While dramatic changes have been seen in the transformation of economic organization, especially in the coastal region, political change has been less forthcoming. Today the situation is one of a partially market-oriented economy operating within a social and political system controlled by the Chinese Communist Party dictatorship. Even in the economic sphere, continued state ownership of much industry, all Chinese banks and all land, strict regulations in the financial sector, stock exchange dictates, macroeconomic controls, and so on shape business practice and limit the scope of free-markets practice, and of the participation of foreign companies in the Chinese economy. At the same time, the state is burdened by continued responsibility for employee welfare and for failing state industries, by severe urban construction and infrastructure problems, and, partly as a consequence of these factors, by constrained public revenues. China is a developing country, and, despite rapid development in some coastal megacities, this continues to set the underlying conditions and constraints for government and business activity. In such circumstances, the attraction of FDI is viewed by state organs as vital to economic or urban development.

In the sphere of global and regional interaction, government intervention has primarily been threefold: intervention to direct or guide the location of foreign-investment and other economic enterprises within the city; competitive place-marketing activities to attract investment to Shanghai over other cities in China, the region of globally; and development activities to improve internal infrastructure to support Shanghai's functions as a multifunctional city, and external infrastructure connections, in order to ensure ease of access between Shanghai and external business centers. These are considered in turn below.

Direction and Guidance of the Location of Economic Activity

Through a mixture of regulation and incentive, the Shanghai municipal government has attempted to direct the location of economic activity, especially foreign economic activity, within Shanghai. For example, restrictions on the operations of firms, particularly in the financial sector, whose addresses are not in Pudong has ensured the concentration of tertiary-sector activities in the Lujiazui Finance and Trade Zone, a central-level project designed as a key part of Shanghai and China's strategy for the 21st century functional development of the city. Only foreign banks that are located in the zone can engage in Renminbi transactions. Business licenses are granted only to firms in any sector that are located in Pudong. However, in the current transition property market and business environment, and while Lujiazui remains under construction, many firms have established front offices only in Pudong, while continuing their principal business activities closer to client bases in Puxi. Special development zones have been established across Shanghai, by national, city, or district/county governments. These include: Hongqiao Economic and Technological Development Zone (primarily a location for office function referred to as Business Park), Caohejing High Technology Development Zone (mainly for 'clean' industrial or processing activities referred to as a Technology Park), Waigaoqiao Free Port (for trading activities), Jinqiao Export-Processing Zone, and Zhangjiang Science Park (see map 2). Each zone carries various

MAP 2
LOCATION OF DEVELOPMNET ZONES

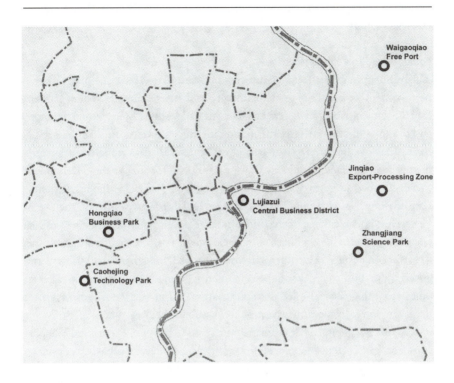

incentives for inward investors, including tax breaks; essential infrastructure is also already provided on-site, and the leasing or construction of factories in the industrial zones is relatively straightforward. Industrial development in general is not permitted within the urban area, unless it is within one of the special development zones; however, efforts to integrate nonpolluting "urban industry" into the urban core are emerging. These means effectively give the government very strong control over industrial and commercial location within Shanghai, although the choice for investors is increasing as infrastructure improves throughout the municipality, and as individual districts and counties within Shanghai, and cities elsewhere in the Yangtse Delta, improve their local investment environments and open further sites for development and use by overseas corporations. In some circumstances, this is increasing the bargaining power of overseas capital to obtain concessions and incentives, and permission to locate on particular sites, as cities and counties play competitive games to attract investment.

The municipal government and district authorities have attempted to direct the location of foreign investment through not only regulatory and financial measures but also physical measures in terms of the concentration of infra-structure provision in certain areas, most likely those development zones or prominent locations such as Lujiazui, Hongqiao and Huaihai Road central business centers.

Competitive Place-marketing

The municipal and district governments in Shanghai perceive the need to com-pete with other localities both nationally and internationally for investment capital, and measure themselves against other localities by economic strength and progress in urban development and renewal.[6] In China, this competition is intensified by the government and party structures. In a nonelected govern-mental system, leaders are judged for promotion according to the development success of their current localities. This competition has led to the implementa-tion of extensive place-marketing strategies. Such practices include the use of incentives, image enhancement (including the development of prestige projects and environmental upgrading), the development of office buildings and infra-structure, trade fairs and other activities to foster links between business and government, and so on. Though such activities generally have a positive effect on the city, they have also led to duplications in infrastructure and office center development, a neglect of investment in public facilities, such as parks, for which private capital is less forthcoming, and, because of the individualist approach of districts coupled with a project-by-project approach to develop-ment, a fragmentation of the overall city form. Immense public investment has centered on prestige projects, such as Lujiazui and the renewal of People's Square (including a new concert hall), often designed by international archi-tects, while the road system is operating beyond capacity, subway and light rail construction is incomplete, and the basic housing needs of a large majority of the population are not being met.

Infrastructure Development Activities

As part of its goal to develop Shanghai into a leading, international, and mul-tifunctional city, the government has actively engaged in large-scale infrastruc-ture projects. These plans include high-speed road links with suburban areas and adjacent provinces, an inner and an outer ring road, four subway lines, two light-rail lines, river tunnels, river bridges, a new airport, a new seaport, and a teleport. To date, these plans have been only partially realized in practice. Two river bridges, a river tunnel, two subway lines, the inner ring road and suburban and intercity highways are operational. The various projects are designed to service Shanghai's business activities in both the tertiary and industrial sectors, and to improve Shanghai's connections with external cities and regions, reduc-ing spatial and time distances and enhancing the transmission of information.

In the long run, the goal is not only for overseas companies to operate with ease and low cost in Shanghai, but also to offer Chinese companies ready access to overseas markets and allow them to engage in multinational business from a Shanghai headquarters. The location of particular infrastructure projects within Shanghai is reinforcing other locational trends and directives; government policy is in particular attempting to support the development of Pudong as a national and local focus for economic activity and foreign industrial and commercial corporations by concentrating advanced infrastructure in the new area, including the new airport, seaport, and Infoport.

The development of Shanghai is therefore highly planned and state controlled. TNCs and other foreign economic agents are encouraged to provide capital, technical expertise, and so forth for Shanghai's development, but there has been no transfer of decision-making power in terms of the *pattern* of urban development from the state to the global community. The development of advanced telematics infrastructure is one aspect of Shanghai's efforts to improve the local environment for investment and business activity, to exchange information and to integrate further with the global economy. This latest state-sponsored initiative is designed under the assumption that the city and its districts *have* to join the global market, and *have* to respond to the forces of competition unleashed thereby. Telematics developments are analyzed in detail in the next section.

THE PLANNING, DEVELOPMENT, AND USAGE OF TELEMATICS INFRASTRUCTURE

A New Round of Development: From Conventional to Telematics Infrastructure

The advancement of urban and regional infrastructure has long been regarded as a necessary condition for a city claiming to be a business hub—defined as the concentration of regional headquarters of multinationals and specialized corporate services associated with them. Following the resumption of its central status in the national economy, Shanghai was quickly involved in the current round of competition with other major cities in the region in terms of the advancement of urban and regional infrastructure. The first half of the 1990s saw massive development and redevelopment of the city's built environment, as indicated by a significant increase in investment in fixed assets and infrastructure as percentage of GDP from 30.0 percent and 6.2 percent in 1990 to 67.3 percent and 13.1 percent, in 1996 respectively (see table 4). One estimate gave Shanghai twenty-one thousand building sites in 1996 (China Daily 1996) and another, 44.7 million square meters of buildings under construction (Shanghai Star 1996).

In the current round of urban and regional restructuring, the competitiveness of a place as a business hub is reinforced by not only the centrality of the place in the geography of the built environment, which is supported by trans-

TABLE 4

CHANGE IN INVESTMENT IN FIXED ASSETS AND INFRASTRUCTURE AS THE PERCENTAGE OF GDP IN SHANGHAI (1990–1999)

Year	Fixed Assets (%)	Infrastructure (%)
1990	30.0	6.2
1995	65.0	11.1
1996	67.3	13.1
1997	58.9	12.3
1998	53.3	14.4
1999	46.0	12.4

TABLE 5

CHANGE IN COMPOSITION OF INFRASTRUCTURE INVESTMENT IN SHANGHAI IN 100 MILLION YUAN (MY) AND % (1990-1999)

Year	Transportation		Postal and Telecommunications			Total
1990	7.16my	15.2%	2.90my	6.1%	47.22my	100%
1995	25.94	9.5	53.42	19.5	273.78	100%
1996	69.66	18.4	77.55	20.5	378.78	100
1997	85.06	20.6	61.04	14.8	412.85	100
1998	108.79	20.5	72.68	13.7	531.38	100
1999	102.24	18.4	63.92	12.7	501.39	100

Source: Statistical Yearbook of Shanghai 2000.

portation-related infrastructure, but also, perhaps more important, the centrality of the place in electronic space, which is supported by telematics infrastructure (Sassen 1996). In the case of Shanghai, while transportation-related infrastructure is still a significant component in the development of urban and regional infrastructure, it has recently been overshadowed by a sharp increase in the investment in telematics infrastructure (table 5). Since 1995, investment in postal and telecommunications-related infrastructure as a percentage of total investment in infrastructure compared with those in transportation-related infrastructure. This is significant considering the massive development of mass transit, highway, and bridge and tunnel systems since the early 1990s. It is also in line with national trends, and Shanghai is one of the key focal points of national investment in telecommunications infrastructure. Between 1991 and 1995, U.S.$7 billion was spent by China on telecommunications infrastructure, especially optic fiber cabling and digital switching. It is estimated that more than U.S.$20 billion will be needed to meet the goals of the Eighth and Ninth Five-Year Plans. Attracting FDI to the telecommunications sector is therefore a major government goal.

In Shanghai, the municipal government has actively promoted a strategy of telematics development, consisting of three major initiatives, namely the Infoport Program, Intelligent Buildings, and Electronic Business Systems. These are considered in turn below.

Infoport Program

Shanghai is one of three nodes (the others being Beijing and Guangzhou) of telecommunications and computer networks within China; these three cities are also China's only entry and exit points for international information highways. Shanghai is the junction of three transnational fiber-optic cable systems, including the Sino-Japan, the around-the-world submarine lines, and the Asia-Europe land line, and several nationwide linkages such as the southern and the northern coastal lines, together with satellite earth stations, Shanghai is one of the very few teleports in China through which digital information can be transmitted to the outside world.

Based on the city's centrality in electronic space in terms of the junction of transnational and national electronic networks, as well as its key position in terms of industrial and especially service-sector business functions, including finance, a strategy of telematics development for the next fifteen years, called the Infoport program, was initiated in 1996. This strategy comprises the following policy measures (Shanghai Municipal Government 1997):

- provision of information for public, business, and scientific users;

- development and integration of electronic networks for various users, including a citywide Internet service called Shanghai Information Interchange (SHIINet), an electronic network for information service related to social security (SSSNet), an electronic data interchange network for business-related information services (EDINet), and communitywide information networks (SCSNet);

- development of high-speed, mass-volume and multi-medium information transmission systems;

- development of information technology and industry;

- development of information-related legislation and standards.

In the period from 1996 to 2000, an investment of about U.S.$5 billion from both public and private sectors would be devoted to the Infoport Program

(Shanghai Municipal Government 1997). While a considerable amount of progress has been made in the development of telematics infrastructure, the most strategic development in recent years has been the completion of a city-wide information highway, comprising a circular line of 75 kilometers, a central line of 32 kilometers and several suburban lines of 300 kilometers in total. There have also been a number of Internet service providers (ISPs), such as Shanghai Online, through which a large number of information services on both global and local scales can be obtained. Exact figures for Internet usage are unavailable, and the number of users is thought to increase daily; an estimated 150,000 users held internet accounts nationwide in mid-1997, but this figure is likely to have risen dramatically since. Shanghai is expected to account for a large percentage of this usage, both for business and domestic purposes, because of the higher-than-average incomes and computer ownership in the city. One of the most frequently accessed websites is the Shanghai Stock Exchange, given the large numbers of individual investors.

It should be mentioned that the development of telematics infrastructure in Shanghai is closely related to the requirements of multinationals and the specialized corporate services associated with them. In recent years, with the rapid growth of their business in China, an increasing number of multinational corporations and banks have either newly set up their China business headquarters in Shanghai or, in a few cases, relocated them from Hong Kong or Beijing to Shanghai, with a control function in terms of management and investment for the whole Chinese market. According to the latest statistics, forty multinationals have their China headquarters in Shanghai, and 80 percent of the top fifty banks in the world have offices in the city. For example, with eleven joint-venture enterprises and an investment of U.S.$ 640 million in different parts of China, Unilever has newly located its China business headquarters in Shanghai with the responsibility for its businesses not only in the mainland, but also Hong Kong and Taiwan. The local government is also encouraging Chinese corporations of nationwide significance to locate or relocate their headquarters in Shanghai.

Related to the development of telematics infrastructure is the geographical concentration of multinationals and specialized corporate services in a few areas in Shanghai, namely Lujiazui Finance and Trade Zone, Hongqiao Economic and Technological Development Zone, and Huaihai Road Central (in the central-western part of Shanghai; see map 3), forming what Sassen (1996) has called a headquarters-corporate services complex. These concentrations are partly the result of planning and other policy mechanisms of the local government. As these industries are among the most intensive users of telematics infrastructure, the geographical concentration of telematics infrastructure in these locations is also justified on the technical ground that telematics infrastructure

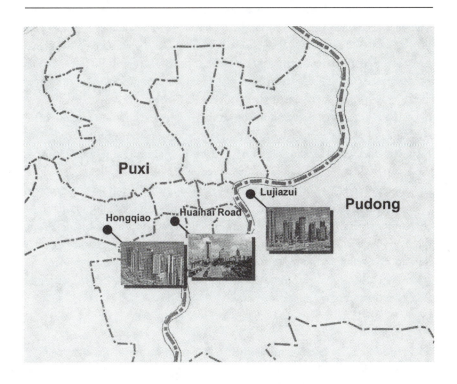

of higher than normal standards, which is extremely expensive, can be provided only in a few designated areas where the most intensive users are expected to locate, rather than spreading over the whole city. It was originally proposed that one Infoport center would be located in the Jinqiao processing zone in Pudong, to aid overseas producers in this key industrial area; however, it was found that demand for the highest standard of information technology in the zone was low—simple electronic means of communication, with no particular demands on speed or security, were found to be sufficient for such a location. When the system is complete, stations will be located in each district and development zone, and individual landholders will be able to pay to make the connection from that local center to their sites. It should be remembered that, in terms of timing, the geographic concentration of top office functions occurred *prior to* the development of telematics infrastructure in Shanghai. Real estate analysts in Shanghai report that, up to now, most foreign firms have been unwilling to pay the higher rents commanded by the "intelligent buildings" in the three nodes, but that developers are now keen to connect their buildings to telematics networks to give them marketing advantages in conditions of severe office oversupply.[7]

The same justification can also be applied to the concentrations of headquarters corporate services complexes in a few major cities. According to Sassen (1996), economic globalization has increased the scale and complexity, and therefore reinforced the association between headquarters and specialized corporate services management functionally even if not always geographically, as well as raised their requirements for telematics infrastructure of higher than normal standards. This in turn results in their concentrations in some nodal localities in a global or regional grid, which are articulated through cyber-routes or digital highways, in addition to conventional forms of communication infrastructure. In a new geography of centralization, telematics infrastructure adds to, rather than replaces, conventional forms of communication infrastructure, as shown by the case of Shanghai where three nodal places are all located along the underground lines or expressways, either completed or under construction and connecting to airports. Shanghai is building its telematics infrastructure—the Infoport—in order to enhance its function as a center of financial and advanced service activities in China, East Asia, and the Pacific Rim. It is thus an important part of the city's competitive strategy, and is being adopted at a relatively early stage of economic development, reflecting the active participation of the state in urban decision making.

Intelligent Buildings

The potential of telematics infrastructure has to be realized through facilities within individual buildings, where the end users, such as multinationals and corporate services, are situated. Associated with the Infoport, an Intelligent Buildings construction program has been initiated by the Shanghai municipal government. In 1996, a design guideline—Design Standards for intelligent buildings—was produced by the relevant authority (Construction Committee of Shanghai Municipal Government 1996). A set of design standards are applied to the electronic systems of various services and facilities within buildings, such as telecommunications, supply of power and water, air conditioning, fire detention, transportation (elevators and escalators) and security, as well as the integration of these subsystems. Buildings are graded into three categories according to the standard of electronic services and other facilities. In Pudong Development Zone, where the presence of multinationals and the corporate services associated with them has been increasing, the local government produced, in 1997, a regulation on the construction of intelligent buildings (Bureau of Urban Construction and Bureau of Environmental Protection, Pudong District Government 1997).

Shanghai's municipal government has been actively involved in promoting the development of intelligent office buildings, especially in the above-mentioned three locales, through the granting of intelligent building certificates of different categories to office buildings that reach standards set by the design guidelines. Many developers believe that with the intelligent building certificate, the competitiveness of an office building in the local property market might be improved. The local government is currently considering the possibility of using urban planning mechanisms (such as zoning) to designate certain areas where office buildings are required to meet intelligent building design standards.

The concept of the intelligent building is not confined to the development of office buildings. There have been similar experiments in two state-run housing estates, both of which are governed and funded by the Post and Telecommunications Bureau. The authors were invited to visit a housing estate where an electronic information system is being applied to community services (such as teleclinic and telelibrary), estate management (such as security supervision) and utility provision (such as telemetering). A number of private-sector housing developers have shown interest in the electronic information system HomeNet, which was developed for the experimental estates. However, the financial feasibility of applying such systems to all developments, especially in the private sector, would seem limited, at least given present income levels and household purchasing power in relation to property. Nonetheless, these experiments illustrate the forward-thinking approach current in Shanghai to adapting the latest communications technologies in both the business and household sectors, despite the relatively low overall development of the local economy.

Electronic Business Systems

Telematics infrastructure has been developed in Shanghai and China not only to satisfy the requirements of multinationals, but also to improve the competitiveness of small local enterprises by providing them with easy access to the global market through a technological innovation called electronic business systems. These are designed for enterprises to conduct their businesses through electronic networks (such as the Internet), instead of conventional forms of communication. This can therefore improve the competitiveness of small enterprises by enabling them to enter the global market at much lower costs. A case study of the local branch of a multinational trading company revealed that the cost of using electronic services is marginal compared with that of conventional means like mail, fax and telephone communication systems. As a result, its business transactions are conducted increasingly by electronic means.

The local government has encouraged small enterprises to capitalize on the opportunity provided by electronic business systems to enlarge their share in the global market. Recently, a number of exhibitions have been organized by the local government to promote the application of electronic business systems, with the involvement of multinational producers. Hewlett Packard and Intel have both signed agreements with the local government to develop electronic business systems for local enterprises (*Wenhui* 1998). However, there is a long way to go before electronic business systems are routine for small enterprises in China. This is not just a technical issue, but demands a full-scale change in enterprise culture and other nontechnical elements.

Thus Shanghai has made significant efforts to improve its telematics infrastructure in the mid-1990s. Compared with cities such as Hong Kong and Tokyo, however, there is a wide gap in provision. Although many developments remain under planning, usage of computerized communications systems is increasing rapidly. Developments in this sector are being driven by state actors—primarily the Shanghai Post and Telecommunications Bureau, which owns and controls all infrastructural hardware and Internet services—supported by some private-sector investment. Within government, however, there is some evidence of a lack of coordination; interviews with district and municipal urban planners, for example, revealed a general awareness of telematics strategies, but little knowledge of the geographic distribution of nodes and district stations within the city. Nonetheless, we can say that although still undergoing major functional and socioeconomic transition and still being in the early stages of development, Shanghai is making significant efforts to link into global communications networks. This strategy, part of an overall goal of rapid modernization and internationalization that also includes developing conventional infrastructure and forging business and government linkages internationally, is helping transform Shanghai functionally and spatially, and in particular supports its attractiveness as a site for business in the financial sector.

IMPACTS: CHANGING SPATIAL PATTERNS AND URBAN FUNCTION
Changing Spatial Structure
Since 1978, and particularly since 1990, the spatial structure of Shanghai has undergone significant development and restructuring. The urban area has expanded following the development of Minhang, Caohejing, Baoshan, Pudong, and other areas as industrial zones and satellite/suburban residential areas. In the central city, land use structure has been transformed through the expulsion of industry to peripheral areas; the relocation of large numbers of residents from substandard housing to new, peripheral estates; the construction of large-scale infrastructure projects (especially high-speed roads); the conversion of industrial, residential, and other land to commercial uses (especially high-rise offices and comprehensive developments); and, most recently, the injection of public open space and general efforts to "green" the city.

However, it should be remembered that China and Chinese cities remain *in transition* with regard to their political economy and urban development. China is also a developing country, and the cities, especially megacities like

Shanghai, have severe developmental problems (housing shortages, overcrowding, sewerage inadequacies, water supply shortages, etc.) with which to contend. Urban spatial planning and development in Shanghai over the past two decades have therefore been a function of meeting these basic developmental challenges, while, *at the same time*, attempting to meet the demands placed on urban space and urban buildings by the opening of the economy, the influx of foreign investors, and the local government's strategy of attracting FDI and boosting global interaction to assist in the functional as well as physical development of the city. The time-period for development has been dramatically compressed, as Shanghai Municipal Government attempts to meet *both* basic needs in housing, public infrastructure, etc., *and* the advanced needs of a modern, international business city. The developments in telematics discussed above have been one result of the latter.

The spatial structure of Shanghai is therefore changing as a result not only of global pressures and imperatives, but also in response to underlying development needs and conditions and the priorities of local government. Nevertheless, certain changes in the spatial development of Shanghai can be attributed primarily to globalization, and the activities of international corporations: (1) prestige projects and high-rise commercial developments; (2) special development zones; (3) villa and other high-class housing estates; and (4) triple port development strategy.

Prestige Projects and High-rise Commercial Developments

Following from a globalization of property markets and the increasing participation of a small group of international architects in design competitions and projects worldwide (what Olds [1995] has termed the "global intelligence corps"), Shanghai has since the early 1990s been witnessing the rapid development of high-rise commercial (mostly office) buildings in the downtown area. Particular concentrations of these new, international-style, construction projects are to be found in the state-level finance and trade zone, Lujiazui, and the city-level economic and technological development zone, Hongqiao. However, all central-city districts have approved such projects, especially Luwan (Huaihai Road Central), Xuhui (Xujiahui), Huangpu and Jingan (Nanjing Road West) districts. The Shanghai Center, on Nanjing Road West, was the earliest of the new generation of comprehensive (office, retail, hotel, and residential) developments, opened in 1990, and built by a consortium of American, Hong Kong, and Japanese developers in conjunction with the Shanghai Exhibition Center, the original landholders. The surrounding area in Jingan district has now become a popular location for new commercial development, especially by Hong Kong development groups. However, this area may be marginalized as the new generation of intelligent buildings come on stream elsewhere in the city. While some national banks have become active developers, most of the new construction is being carried out by overseas developers, primarily from East Asia, often in joint venture with a local organization which is usually the original landholder.

In addition, public prestige projects are being developed in key locations in Shanghai with both public and private funds; these projects are all initiated by the government at the national, city, or district level. Examples include Lujiazui Finance and Trade Zone, the Bund renewal and waterfront projects, and the redevelopment of People's Square (including a new concert hall). Olds (1995) reports that the development of Lujiazui is part of a global trend of urban megaproject development, planned by governments, designed by international architects, and executed by developers who operate regionally or globally. In Shanghai, individual districts are also concerned with urban image and place marketing, and therefore are planning smaller-scale prestige projects, especially office commercial centers, as well as other image-enhancement programs, such as the removal of slum housing, and the development of public open space and street-side landscaping.

Special Development Zones

In order to meet the demands set by the globalization of industrial production, Shanghai has a number of function-specific development zones (e.g., Jinqiao, Caohejing, Zhanjiang, Waigaoqiao, Minhang). These provide high-quality infrastructure, factory units or land for their construction, and so on, plus various investment incentives, within a bounded area. Mostly located in Pudong and suburban districts and counties, these zones concentrate foreign-based manufacturing activity in specific areas; spatially there is often a sharp visual boundary between the zone and its neighboring land areas. Similarly, Hongqiao Economic and Technological Development Zone and Lujiazui Finance and Trade Zone have been established in the city to meet the needs of international business, including banks, for representative and operational offices.

Villa and Other High-class Housing Estates

In order to meet the real or perceived demand for expatriate housing (as well as for housing the small but growing class of wealthy Chinese), a large number of villa and other high-class housing developments have been built in Shanghai, mostly in peripheral or suburban areas. Given the limited market and the fact that the quality of the developments is often poor, many of these buildings remain empty. One of the best established of the new housing areas is Gubei New Area in Changning District, which is adjacent to the Hongqiao Economic and Technological Development Zone and close to Hongqiao airport.

Triple Port Development Strategy

As discussed above, Shanghai has adopted a triple port development strategy in order to tap into global communications networks. This forms part of a wider infrastructure development program to build Shanghai's internal and external connections. A new seaport and airport in Pudong are designed to service Shanghai's industrial and business communities, tourism sector, and the distribution of industrial products and raw materials (imports and exports). The Infoport, with its three principal nodes in Lujiazui, Hongqiao, and Huaihai Road Central, will reinforce the strength of these three office concentrations. Although telematics developments can theoretically allow a dispersal of office space, as well as home working, these dispersal factors are likely to be outweighed by the forces of other government policies (especially locational policies, discussed above), the need for face-to-face transactions, the scarcity of computer networks in other parts of the city, even in the medium term, and the need for certain types of businesses (especially banks and finance houses) to have immediate access to the highest-quality, highest-speed, and highest-security telematics resources, which can be provided only in a limited number of locations. Telematics developments, while allowing greater connectivity between individuals and businesses within the city, therefore appear to be reinforcing government plans and development trends vis-à-vis office location. Branch connections to residential, industrial, and noncentral commercial areas will also assist business and personal communication within the city, but it is unlikely to have a major impact on the spatial configuration of the city.

These four trends, working alongside more general development processes in Shanghai, are producing spatial-functional divisions in urban form. While local-level anomalies may occur because of developers negotiations with district governments on a particular project, the city is essentially evolving according to a predetermined strategy and plan. Spatial and functional change are intimately related, both within government strategy and in the development trends observable to date. Functional changes are analysed in the next section.

Changing Urban Function

Shanghai is a dual function economy, with both a strong industrial sector and an expanding tertiary sector which now accounts for 43 percent of the GDP. Central government strategy promotes Shanghai as China's leading financial and banking center, and Lujiazui has been developed at least in part to aid these functions. Under the strict government planning discussed above, industry has largely been relocated to suburban areas, while central areas concentrate on commercial and residential functions. Telematics developments are assisting in the development of Shanghai as an international business center, but the impacts have to date been limited because so much telematics infrastructure remains under planning or construction. Once the principal intelligent buildings have been completed and the infrastructure is in place, Shanghai should be able to fully service the demands of international businesses with offices in the city for capital transfers, business transactions, information exchange, and so forth. The existence of such infrastructure will also enhance Shanghai's reputation as a city with the capacity for international-standard business activities, theoretically attracting more business and leading to an expansion of infrastructure in response to growing demand.

Shanghai, as the gateway to eastern China, therefore has the *potential* and *capacity* to develop as a key service city; government backing, at both the central and local levels, supports such functional development. At the same time, however, Shanghai's twin functions of services and industry are likely to persist in parallel, although the urban-industrial boundaries between suburban Shanghai and neighboring districts in Jiangsu and Zhejiang provinces may dissolve, despite continuing administrative boundaries. These functional shifts, and the improving telematics and other infrastructure to support them, have an impact on Shanghai's relations and potential relations with other cities nationally, regionally and globally. These interurban dynamics are considered in the next section.

Impacts: Interurban Relations and Shanghai's Competitive Position

The *Comprehensive Urban Plan for Shanghai (CUPS)* promotes Shanghai as the bridgehead between China and the global economy, and as a city that will play a pivotal role in regional and national development. The plan is ambitious: "Shanghai must be built into one of the greatest centers along the west Pacific coast" (*CUPS* 1986: 8). Pudong is seen as key to Shanghai's externally oriented development strategy, its role being to act as the "dragon's head" of urban and economic development, not only for Shanghai's metropolitan area, but also for the Yangtse River Delta and Valley regions, and for eastern China, if not the country as a whole. Pudong and Shanghai are promoted nationally and locally as the engine of regional development, by linking the hinterland to the global economy, via FDI, trade, and international communications networks: Shanghai is China's eastern gateway to the regional and global marketplace.

This section considers how far Shanghai has already moved to becoming a key urban center in China, in East Asia, and globally since 1978, in the light of earlier discussions on its national and international linkages, its urban and economic development status, and, in particular, telematics developments. The relationship between Hong Kong and Shanghai is also discussed.

Shanghai in China

Shanghai is the key city in eastern China, and as such serves local, regional, and national functions, as the focal point for inward investment, and as a center of economic management and control. It is strategically located at the mouth of the Yangtse River, and at the midpoint on the coast between Beijing, Guangdong, and Hong Kong. As a seaport, it has links to the urban-industrial centers in northeast China, Tianjin, Shandong, south China, and, internationally, to Korea, Japan, and the rest of the world. As a riverport, Shanghai is linked with central and western China; this river connection is important given China's poor east-west rail and road links. Shanghai is also an important railway hub along China's east coast, linked directly to Beijing by a new high-speed track, and to cities in southeastern China. New road and rail links have been especially important in creating spatial cohesion within the Yangtse River Delta, and Shanghai is now connected by superhighway and high-speed train to Suzhou, Wuxi, and Nanjing to the north, and Hangzhou to the south. This strategic location, supported by infrastructural developments, has historically been a key factor in Shanghai's development, and ensures the city's continued role as China's leading economic center.

Under the centrally planned economic system of the pre-Reform period, the scope of direct horizontal linkages between cities was severely curtailed. The growth of economic regions that crossed administrative boundaries therefore became impossible. Since 1978, however, local autonomy has gradually increased, and region-based urban development has become possible. However, at the same time, decentralization has increased *competitive* relations between cities. Intraregional *cooperation*, which would contribute to efficiency in resource use, and enhance the position of each region in the external economy, has not been forthcoming.

Shanghai forms the core of four overlapping regional spaces:

- The Yangtse River Delta EMR, spanning southern Jiangsu province and northern Zhejiang province;

- Shanghai Economic Zone, officially designated in 1982, and covering ten cities in the Yangtse River Delta, plus parts of Anhui and Jiangxi provinces;

- The Yangtse River Valley, stretching inland as far as Chongqing and eastern Sichuan Province;

- The central-east China region, incorporating the provinces of Hebei (southern part), Shandong, Henan (eastern part), Jiangsu, Anhui, Jiangxi (northern part), Zhejiang and Fujian (northern part).

All four regions conform to the concept of divorcing administrative and economic boundaries in an integrating global economy. There is evidence of growing economic and spatial linkages between the cities and towns, and urban and rural areas, within these regions. Shanghai's role is as the regional financial, industrial, trade, service, and distribution center, and a location for the management offices of manufacturing firms with factories located elsewhere in these regions.

Of the four, the Yangtse Delta represents the tightest consolidation of urban space within one economic area. The region has an area of 99,610 square kilometers, with a total population of 73.7 million, and an urban population of 30 million (Chan 1997). The urban hierarchy comprises three very large cities (Shanghai, Nanjing, and Hangzhou), four large cities (Wuxi, Suzhou, Changzhou, and Ningbo), seventeen medium-size cities, and thirty small cities (Chan 1997). Linkages between Shanghai and cities in southern Jiangsu are particularly strong, and detract from the lead-city functions of Nanjing as provincial capital. Although cities in this region, including Shanghai itself, are still undergoing economic and urban transition, there is an emerging pattern of firms (especially multinationals) locating their management and sales offices in Shanghai city, while their manufacturing plants are located either in suburban Shanghai or in a neighboring province. While cost and local incentives are cited as important factors in this relocation from Shanghai, however, international manufacturing firms have reported differences in technical and professional expertise, infrastructure, living standards for expatriate staff, distribution facilities, and market size between Shanghai and other cities in the region, which are making them as yet reluctant to relocate within the Delta region. Shanghai's municipal and district governments are prioritizing the attraction of high-caliber multinational companies prepared to pay Shanghai's higher labor costs, and are therefore pushing small and medium-size firms, to whom cost differentials can be significant, to peripheral areas and neighboring provinces.

Linkages within the Delta region as they have developed in the 1990s are therefore more horizontal than vertical. A large number of cities and localities, taking advantage of decentralization to manage their own economic and urban development, are developing rapidly on the basis of localized industrialization and, wherever possible, foreign investment. Rural industrialization, through township and village enterprises (TVEs), has been very important in this growth since the 1980s, while the main cities have focused on attracting foreign investment as the catalyst for industrial modernization and urban redevelopment. This has detracted from Shanghai's function as a regional center, and has contributed to Shanghai's continued strength as a manufacturing city in its own right. There has been no coordinated regional planning for the Delta, and this has enhanced the individualist approach of localities. Competition is encouraging local infrastructure and environmental developments, but not necessarily producing net positive additions in economic activity, regional or nationwide. There is evidence of small and medium-size firms "phasing incentives"—once period concessions (e.g., tax breaks) have expired, they relocate to other areas where they can obtain preferential treatment as if they were first-time investors. This competition and lack of coordination have also led to inefficiency and wastage in the allocation of resources, especially for infrastructure development; the duplication of airport development in several cities in the Yangtse Delta, as in the Pearl River Delta in southern China, is a commonly cited example here.

Shanghai's links with the Yangtse River Valley and the wider eastern region are less concrete. However, as a transportation hub and seaport and riverport, Shanghai has an important role in both regions. Shanghai is a market for, and consumer of, products and raw materials from China's interior, and an entrepot and distribution center for goods and resources to national and international markets. At the same time, regional cities and provinces are also consumers of Shanghai's finished products. Migration from other provinces, especially Anhui and Sichuan provinces, further produces strong human and economic links between Shanghai and its hinterland regions. Although the southern regional block (Pearl River Delta, Hong Kong, Macau, Guangdong, and spurs to Fujian, Guangxi, and Hainan) is currently stronger than the eastern block centered on Shanghai, the growth *potential* in the Yangtse Basin and coastal region is far higher, and its urban centers (e.g., Chongqing, Wuhan, Nanjing, Qingdao, Hangzhou, etc.) are well established for industrial and/or tertiary activities.

Shanghai–Hong Kong Relations

There has been much discussion of growing competition between Hong Kong and Shanghai, and of the potential for cooperation between the two megacities now that they are part of one country. There is little competition as of yet, however, because the two cities have different levels of development and functional structures. Hong Kong's infrastructure, advanced postindustrial economy, and concentrations of MNC regional headquarters make it considerably stronger than Shanghai in serving both the East Asian and Chinese economies. Shanghai's urban and economic development, although rapid, still lags far behind that of Hong Kong. Location is also a key factor and may allow the long-run development of Shanghai and Hong Kong in parallel, with each serving separate subnational and international economies. Shanghai, in east China, is a node in the Yangtse Delta and Valley, eastern coastal China, and Northeast Asia, while Hong Kong, in the south, forms the core of the Pearl River Delta and southern coastal China and links strongly with economies in Southeast Asia. Cooperation between the two megacities can assist Shanghai's catch-up and allow both to contribute to China's national development. Geographic differences should allow both cities sufficiently large markets, investment networks, and manufacturing hinterlands to coexist as key national and international urban and economic centers within China and East Asia, and globally.

Shanghai Regionally and Globally

As one of China's most important economic centers, as the central city for the Yangtse region and a site of advanced infrastructure, Shanghai acts as the crossroads in linking China to the global and regional economies. In Northeast Asia in particular, Shanghai is an important node in the regional system, and has strong connections with Japan and Korea. Shanghai has the underlying economic strength to develop as both a locus for inward industrial investment and as a "control center" for the activities of service-sector corporations and firms with manufacturing operations elsewhere in eastern China. However, Shanghai's role in the regional and global urban-economic systems is in its earliest stages. Today, Shanghai is simply a gateway between eastern China, East Asia, and world markets.

This limited regional and global role can be illustrated by two indicators: (1) the number of multinational firms whose regional or global headquarters are located in Shanghai, and (2) the degree to which Shanghai is a hub of international transport and telecommunications networks, rather than a branch or gateway. Several thousand MNCs and TNCs have operations in Shanghai, including some China business headquarters, but there are no international headquarters in the city. Shanghai served only sixteen airline routes in 1995, compared with ninety-six in Hong Kong and seventy-six in Tokyo.[8] International passengers transfer in Shanghai to domestic routes, but not to other international ones. Shanghai's developing financial and service-sector functions serve the needs of international investors *in China*, rather than the regional or global marketplace as a whole. This contrasts with Hong Kong or Tokyo, which have financial markets and tertiary functions that are international in scope. Therefore, although Shanghai acts as a transportation, telecommunications, and business gateway to China, in the absence of control and hub functions it cannot be classified as a "regional" or "global city," although it does have global city functions.

CONCLUSIONS

Since 1978, and especially since 1990, Shanghai has made rapid progress toward internationalization and modernization. Telematics developments have been just one aspect of multiple efforts embraced by the local government, with the assistance of private, often global, capital to improve Shanghai's connections to the global economy, and to serve its emergent functions as a national and, potentially, international financial and business center. Developments in conventional telecommunications and transportation infrastructure, along with the increasing participation of MNCs in the Shanghai economy, growing trade and investment flows into the city, a strengthening and widening of sociopolitical linkages, and the improvements in telematics, have allowed Shanghai increasingly to integrate into global and regional economic-urban systems. In this context, the city has been planned and managed to further enhance international connectivity, competitiveness, and economic development. These trends have had important implications for both the internal spatial and functional structures of Shanghai, and for Shanghai's relations with other cities in the national, regional, and global urban spheres, as discussed above.

These findings demonstrate the continued role of the state, particularly the municipal government, in guiding and producing urban change. Urban planning strategy in Shanghai prioritizes developments in international communications as part of the goal to turn the city into a key economic center on the Pacific Rim. This has, *inter alia*, allowed Shanghai to adopt advanced telematics technologies and infrastructure at a relatively low level of economic development. The municipal government has been key in identifying the needs of the city in terms of both conventional and state-of-the-art infrastructure, and has taken action to provide for them. Although Shanghai's telematics infrastructure is very limited by the standards of cities such as Hong Kong and Tokyo, it can be expected that, given the current level of effort in this field, Shanghai will make significant short-run inroads into catching up.

Despite being a city in a developing country and transition economy, Shanghai is paying explicit attention to its place in global systems, and, especially, the need to develop advanced infrastructure as the support framework for various economic activities, particularly in the service sector. These developments are occurring despite multiple urban and economic development challenges and a relatively low current level of development. This could have implications for other low-income cities facing similar economic and urban development challenges even as they are being required to compete globally.

Telematics developments form only a part of the overall strategic development package for a city, but their provision can have an important role to play in defining the role and potential role of a city in the global and regional economies—that is, in defining urban function, especially with regard to financial and service-sector activities and as the headquarters location of multinational corporations. In the case of Shanghai, state-sponsored telematics developments are supporting the development of the city as a financial and service center in east China, and potentially regionally and even globally, and in doing so are reinforcing the concentration of the highest-quality real estate development and advanced, globally oriented business functions in certain key downtown locales. As the Infoport program and other projects move from plan to implementation, these spatial and functional effects are likely to increase. In conjunction with other factors (including location, human resources, etc.), the economic centrality of Shanghai within China is being enhanced by telematics developments, as are its key office areas for advanced service functions. These developments will also bind Shanghai increasingly into international urban networks, as one of several key functional nodes spanning East Asia and the Pacific Rim. For the present, however, the level of infrastructure, industrial, and other developments allows Shanghai a role principally as a gateway between the Chinese and global and regional economies, rather than as an equal player in a network of regional cities.

NOTES

The authors thank the Institute for Advanced Studies, United Nations University (Tokyo) for its support, and the Center for Advanced Study in the Behavioral Sciences (Palo Alto, CA), for hosting one of the meetings of the research network.

1. China regained sovereignty over Hong Kong from the United Kingdom on 1 July 1997.

2. For further discussion on the role of Shanghai in China and East Asia, and Hong Kong–Shanghai relations, see Liu, Song, and Wu 1998; Ning and Jiang 1998; and Rose Gu 1999.

3. Following defeat in the Opium Wars, China signed a series of peace treaties allowing foreign powers extraterritorial and trading rights in settlements in several coastal and Yangtse River port cities, including Shanghai, Tianjin, Guangzhou (Canton), and Chongqing. The foreign colonial presence in these "treaty ports" lasted from the mid-nineteenth century to the Second World War. Interested readers are referred to Hsü 1995 and Rose 1996, which give further details.

4. See, for example, Chan, Hsuen, and Luk 1996 and Ma and Hanten 1981 for discussion of Maoist economic and regional development policy.

5. Pudong Development Bank was founded by the Shanghai municipal government in the early 1990s, but is a shareholding bank, owned by SMG and private business.

6. In-depth analysis of competitive government behavior in Shanghai is provided in Rose Gu 1999.

7. Vacancy rates of 20 percent were reported for Grade A offices in mid-1998, and up to 50 percent for lower-quality space. These rates are expected to persist for two to five years.

8. Where one airline route is one city-city link; this may be flown by more than one airline.

REFERENCES CITED

Bureau of Urban Construction and Bureau of Environmental Protection of Pudong District Government. 1997. *Regulation on Construction of Intelligent Buildings*. Shanghai: Bureau of Urban Construction and Bureau of Environmental Protection, Pudong District Government.

Chan, R. C. K. 1997. "Regional Development in the Yangtze and Pearl River Delta Regions. " Paper presented at the 5th Asian Urbanisation Conference, SOAS, London, August.

Chan, R. C. K., T. T. Hsueh and C. M. Luk, eds. 1996. *China's Regional Economic Development*. Hong Kong: Chinese University Press.

China Daily. 1996. November 12.

Comprehensive Urban Plan for Shanghai (*CUPS*). 1986.

Construction Committee of Shanghai Municipal Government. 1996. *Design Standards for Intelligent Buildings*. Shanghai: Construction Committee of Shanghai Municipal Government.

Hsü, I. C. Y. 1995. *The Rise of Modern China*. 5th ed. New York: Oxford University Press.

ICAO. 1985. *Traffic by flight stage, 1985*. Quebec: ICAO.

———. 1990. *Traffic by flight stage, 1990*. Quebec: ICAO.

———. 1995a. *Airport traffic, 1995*. Quebec: ICAO.

———. 1995b. *Civil aviation statistics of the world*. Quebec: ICAO.

———. 1995c. *Traffic by flight stage, 1995*. Quebec: ICAO.

Liu, D., Y. C. Song and W. Wu. 1998. "Jiuqi huigui: Hu-Gang jingji jingzheng yu hezuo" (Return to the motherland: Economic competition and cooperation between Hong Kong and Shanghai). Unpublished paper, East China Normal University, Shanghai (in Chinese).

Ma, L. J. C. and E. W. Hanten, eds. 1981. *Urban Development in Modern China.* Boulder, CO: Westview.

Ning, Y. M. 1995. "Case Study of Shanghai, China." In HABITAT, *Metropolitan Areas: Management and Planning in Developing Countries.* Nairobi: UNCHS.

Ning, Y. M., and L. Jiang. 1998. *Zhongguo guojixing zhongxin chengshi fazhan de zhanlue wenti yanjiu* (On strategic issues of developing international central metropolises in China). *Urban Planning Forum* 2 (in Chinese).

Olds, K. 1995. "Globalization and the Production of New Urban Spaces: Pacific Rim Megaprojects in the Late 20th Century." *Environment and Planning A* 27: 1713–1743.

Rimmer, P. 1996. "Transport and Telecommunications among World Cities." UNU/IAS working paper, Tokyo: United Nations University, Institute of Advanced Studies.

Rose, F. C. 1996. "Historical Legacy or Global Economy? Urban Design in the Former Treaty Ports of China." University of Cambridge, Department of Land Economy, Discussion Paper Number 71.

———. 1998. "Globalisation, Regionalisation and Chinese Cities: A Case Study of Shanghai's Integration into Regional and Global Urban-Economic Systems." UNU/IAS working paper. Tokyo: United Nations University, Institute of Advanced Studies.

———. 1999. "Globalisation, Governance and Growth: A Study of Urban Planning and Development in China, with Special Reference to Shanghai." Ph.D. dissertation, Cambridge University, United Kingdom.

Sassen, S. 1996. "The Spatial Organization of Information Industries: Implications for the Role of the State." In *Globalization: Critical Reflections*, ed. J. H. Mittelman. London: Lynne Rienner.

Shanghai Municipal Government. 1997. "The Ninth Five-Year Plan for Infoport Program and Development Targets by the Year 2010." Shanghai: Shanghai Municipal Government.

SMSB Shanghai Municipal Statistics Bureau. (SMSB). 1997. *Statistical Yearbook of Shanghai, 1997.*

———. 2000. Shanghai: *Statistical Yearbook of Shanghai, 2000.*

Shanghai Star. 1996. November 15.

State Statistics Bureau (SSB). 1996. *The Gross Domestic Product of China, 1952–1995.* Dalian: Dongbei University of Finance and Economics Press.

———. 1997. *China Statistical Yearbook, 1997.* Beijing: State Statistics Bureau.

Warf, B. 1995. "Telecommunications and the Changing Geographies of Knowledge Transmission in the Late 20th Century." *Urban Studies* 32 (2): 361–378.

Wenhui Newspaper. 1998. "Electronic Business Is No Longer a Remote Phenomenon." April 4.

Zhuang, L. Q., ed. 1996. *International Trade Ports.* Beijing: Renmin Jiaotong Chubanshe (in Chinese).

Chapter 11

BUENOS AIRES: SOCIOSPATIAL IMPACTS OF THE DEVELOPMENT OF GLOBAL CITY FUNCTIONS

Pablo Ciccolella and Iliana Mignaqui

Structural changes at the end of the century tend to concentrate particularly in large metropolitan spaces, turning them into the main scenes of the struggle between emerging global trends and the revival of local identities. In the 1990s, the restructuring of those spaces—within the context of privatization, deregulation, and economic liberalization—has meant that factors external to the metropolis and its country have tended to supercede domestic factors, potentially causing considerable loss of control over the economic, social, and territorial processes that develop in these urban spaces. For instance, fragmentation and urban segregation do not develop only because of social divisions or urban planning, but because urban spaces are unevenly incorporated into the global network. Poorly integrated sectors, neighborhoods, or municipalities coexist with modern, globalized, specialized, and competitive urban fragments.

One key aspect in the struggle for dominance between the local and global, and domestic and external influences in Buenos Aires, can be represented by the characteristics and trends of new investment activities. Of particular significance are the ways in which these activities affect or induce the revaluation of the building process, private management, and consumption, as well as the intensification of territorial segregation between residential areas of different income levels. The return of the suburb together with different types of "private urbanization" has altered the form of urbanization prevalent until the mid-1980s. Change has occurred not only in zoning and the use of space (from public neighborhoods to gated communities), but in social appropriation (from the lower and lower-middle socioeconomic classes to the upper and upper-middle classes). In some Latin American countries (Argentina, Brazil, Mexico, etc), during the import-substitution industrialization (ISI) model followed during the 1940s and 1950s, the industrial sector was more closely related than other sectors to the processes of metropolitanization, inducing either directly or indirectly a substantial growth in the residential space of popular and marginal sectors. In contrast, in the last quarter-century, these processes have appeared to be more related to the rise and spatial diffusion of large sites of consumption (e.g., shopping centers, supermarkets, entertainment and performance centers), the formation and regeneration of state-of-the-art office districts that concentrate command functions, and the promotion of new types of residential space for the middle- and upper-income population—gated communities within the city or isolated in the outskirts or along waterfronts and so on. In this way, a Taylorist-Fordist spatial order is apparently being replaced by one that is post-Fordist, postsocial, and postmodern.

Apart from the transformations in technology and production—extensively studied in recent years and biased toward new investments—sociocultural changes and political/institutional transformations seem to have had considerable relevance in the formation of new trends in the structuring of metropolitan space. The suburbanization process taking place also reveals changes in consumption patterns. The tendencies toward privatization of space are not exclusive to residential areas, but also manifest themselves in commercial and recreational areas that can be reached only by private cars via the highway network. The withdrawal of the state from explicit territorial policy making in the face of the growing role of the private sector is one of the distinctive features of the 1990s in Buenos Aires.[1]

The central effort in this chapter is to relate the new urbanization processes in Buenos Aires to the significant increase in investment, much of it foreign, during the 1990s. Buenos Aires is one of the ten largest urban agglomerations in the world, located in the second hierarchical level of global cities together with São Paulo and Mexico City, with more weight in its national economy than these cities in theirs and in this regard more like Greater London with respect to the United Kingdom or Ile de France with respect to France. It concentrates close to 35 percent of the national population but almost 53 percent of the GNP, and the central city by itself accounts for 8.3 percent of the national population and 25.5 percent of national GNP (equivalent to Chile's GNP). Average individual income in the center is similar to that of France ($25,000). In contrast, the rest of the metropolitan and national population have an income of $6,000, an amount only slightly higher than the per capita income in Brazil. The reform of the state, the privatization of public sector firms and services, the reactivation of economic growth, monetary stability, and the implementation of Mercosur, among other factors, have established a new macroeconomic scenario that attracts certain types of investments. However, these factors have also deepened social polarization in Argentina and Buenos Aires. This work hopes to contribute to the reflection and debate about the duality and contradictions of these processes that tend toward modernization and globalization, on the one hand, and toward deepening social exclusion on the other.

METROPOLITAN RESTRUCTURING TRENDS IN THE 1990S

The development alluded to above signals the emergence of a new phase of capitalism, in which the shift in the accumulation regime contributes to new territorial dynamics and urbanization patterns. However, although these changes seem deeply connected to the new production, technological, and macroeconomic conditions of global capitalism, they might also be explained in terms of local influences that are more political, institutional, and sociocultural. Yet, the weakening of state social policies, particularly land policies, and the lack or obsolescence of legal-administrative frameworks and urban planning instruments in many cases render local governments defenseless against the pressure of the private sector's use and appropriation of land located in high-value urban or protected areas (which are mostly rural).

The selectivity of capital in its spatial location strategies will produce various effects in a metropolitan area. In several counties within metropolitan Buenos Aires, where urban density is low, the diffusion of "private urbanization" developments involves risks that are still difficult to evaluate in terms of social integration and land use. The establishment of fences and walls repels, expulses, and excludes others. This urbanization pattern solidifies an exclusive model of the city (Mignaqui 1997). In contrast, in central Buenos Aires high-density, high-rise housing is proliferating, altering the older urban fabric.

These changes, combined with a historically unequal socioeconomic structure, may be deepening preexisting inequalities. The European city model, more physically compact and equitable from the point of view of social appropriation, is giving way to the American city model, more dispersed and structured as islands connected through highway networks. These new urban enclaves combine residence in gated communities with a shift in consumption to shopping malls, supermarkets, and mega-recreation centers, along with privatized education, health, and security services.

These "new urban objects" that underlie the spatial fragmentation are characterized by additive, heterogeneous, ephemeral, and *excluding* architectures, responding to specialized processes embedded in the new urban culture. They alter the urban morphology, fabric, and landscape, as well as the land uses and functions, the predominant economic activities, and the labor market of each urban segment (neighborhood, county, etc.), in many cases jeopardizing its identity. Housing and spaces designated for recreation, leisure, commerce, or transport are developed with new guidelines and criteria for developers that can no longer be understood as a simple extension of previously tested solutions.

The shift from the "traditional city" to the "alienated city," typical of the urban peripheries referred to by Kevin Lynch, could imply a breakdown of cognitive maps, the maps that allow an individual to orient and reconstruct his trajectories and represent his physical position with respect to the city as a whole. The loss of these global cognitive maps is one of the risks of the current process of urbanization. This is closely related to the breakdown of identities, which would no longer be defined territorially but rather by the new guidelines of using and consuming space.

In contrast to the idea of urban identity as constructed through multiple interactions with others, the identity of private urbanization in the metropolitan suburb is strengthened through maximizing the otherness of the outsider (Arizaga 1999). This solidifies the myth of "the purified community" that Sennett (1975) criticizes as perceiving a common identity, a pleasure in recognizing ourselves and what we are and the disappearance of the conflict that otherness reserves. And this voluntary exclusion transcends the limits of gated communities and incorporates a growing range of social practices (commerce, leisure, and recreation) and the spaces in which these practices take place. The suburb manages to simplify the social environment by making social life more elementary as one searches for the mythical solidarity of the old village at a time when technological resources for social structures are becoming more complex (Sennett 1975).

The city becomes a space for the upgrading of the logistics of consumption and advanced services.[2] The city's industrial role, living environment, and atmosphere of encounter and sociability decline at the same time that the city assumes a larger role as a competitive locus, a space for capital valorization, and a spatial form and condition for accumulation for large investors and local and nonlocal businesspeople. As a result, the relation between public and private space is put at risk. Quite apart from its substantial effects on structure, form, and territorial organization, the deepening of the flexible accumulation regime has also generated a selective model of incorporation/exclusion of areas, determining the decline of some and the rise of others (Benko and Lipietz 1994). This process has provoked a strong competition among regions and among cities—all at the global level—to attract investments, generating interterritorial competitiveness (Ciccolella and Mignaqui 1994).

The contradiction between the development of telecommunications—often interpreted as leading to the end of space, geography, and local specificities—and a new era of metropolitan concentration can be explained by the fact that although a company may be distant from its clients, it requires proximity to advanced services more than ever. Indeed, authors such as Pierre Veltz and Saskia Sassen concur that the expansion in the market for specialized or advanced services is responsible for the new urban boom, as the most dizzying amounts of development have occurred in the past few years in precisely those areas. Furthermore, these sectors of growth represent in themselves attractions for large investments and large firms, and consequently for the remetropolitanization process. The companies can locate far from their clients, and in fact far from their suppliers of raw materials, parts, assemblies and industrial components in general, but they do need to be close to specialized services and the centers of knowledge and innovation, and these are normally found in sufficient quantity and quality only in large metropolises (Veltz 1994a; Sassen 1999). What for some authors seems to be the remetropolitanization process as "expanded concentration," either amplified or as overflow (de Mattos 1997), constitutes for Sassen (1999) and Castells (1995) a trend of more complex characteristics that results from the dialectic between centralization and decentralization, in which the main role is played by services and information. In any case, these arguments are not contradictory, but are perceptions and interpretations of the same phenomenon: the transformation of metropolitan territorial structures.

The relation of contiguity means very little in the new processes of production and articulation of space. The way in which space is articulated in flexible capitalism is not primarily horizontal. The "verticalities," in the terminology of Milton Santos (1996), play an important role as articulators in a space that tends to structure itself from vertical and pyramidal relations that are superimposed on horizontal, contiguous, and hegemonizing relations. Although local conditions can potentially present a more "fertile"[3] territorial scenario than others, there is nothing that prevents one city or company from prospering in the middle of a declining region, so long as it is able to inscribe itself in the multiscalar functional, organizational, and informational relations that arise out of the transition from a space of zones or places to a space of networks or flows (Veltz 1994b). The complexity of structures and territorial contents seems to be the key factor in this process.

The renewal of growth in large urban spaces, the return of territorial inequities, the formation of networked territorial structures, the decline of territorial neighboring relations, the predominance of fluidity over place, the valorization of specificities, and the multiplication of microterritories in contrast to past continuities, homogeneities, and macroterritorial differences—all these trends synthesize the economic-territorial dynamics. They signal a new economic geography and one in which power is organized through the *global control* exercised in a complex and hierarchical network constituted through thirty or forty global cities, including cities like São Paulo, Mexico City, and Buenos Aires. These appear toward the end of the century as specialized spaces for the economic management of the global operations of firms and markets. The leading cities in this network exert influence not only locally and nationally, but globally. It is in these cities that the most advanced production, services, and even cultural innovation and political management sectors are concentrated. Metropolitan economies are displacing the territorial economies that laid the foundations of the nation-state; interterritorial transborder interactions are replacing old interactions formed within the framed protection of the welfare state, bringing an end to territorial subsidies. From this remarkable territorial selectivity of global capital, a new map of winner and loser[4] regions emerges, one in which only the "best" spaces will participate in the new dynamism of accumulation.

The growth of foreign direct investment (FDI) in Buenos Aires since the beginning of the 1990s has altered the economic base and the social and territorial structure in a very short period. It has done so in a way that differs from what Sassen found in New York, London, and Tokyo, where the axis of dynamism was developed around the so-called advanced services or producer services (Sassen 1999). In the case of the Latin American megacities, the economic, social, and territorial restructuring seems to be more related to what we can call *banal services*, basically involving consumption and not production (for instance, shopping centers, supermarkets and megashops, entertainment centers, the international hotel industry, restaurants, parks, construction and marketing of gated communities, and the services associated with gentrified areas). There was at the same time a considerable expansion and restructuring of industrial and financial activity, of producer services, computing and insurance, and pension funds. But the first group of activities seem to have more impact and to be the leaders of growth in the city and the larger metropolitan area. These activities are strongly related to FDI in the 1990s, while the new urbanization of the outer metropolitan area (gated communities, marinas, etc.) and the construction of roads and highways have been more related to local investments.

CHANGES IN THE METROPOLITAN STRUCTURE OF BUENOS AIRES

Here we examine several macro-tendencies in the restructuring process of Buenos Aires, particularly the new forms of suburbanization, the evolution of centrality and the patterns of increasing gentrification and social polarization.

The growth of private urbanization in the larger metropolitan area introduced a network pattern with low population density. The older metropolitan geography was compacted and marked by a gradual expansion of the urban fabric. Now it is a city-region with diffuse borders and polycentric, a *megalopolis*. In other words, structured territories based on the horizontal and contiguous articulation of places and regions became tridimensional territories structured vertically through networks. The first transformations of this type, in the form of country clubs, appeared in the 1960s and 1970s, mainly along the axis interconnected by different roads of the Northern Access or the Pan-American Highway. Until the beginning of the 1990s, these were mainly used as a second residence. In the 1990s the development of multiple types of private urbanizations accelerated.[5] With the exception of the farm clubs, these generally are permanent residences. Even the old and new country clubs changed into permanent residences in the 1990s. Another real estate trend in the 1990s, evident in Buenos Aires and in the most consolidated areas in the metropolitan area, was the development of exclusive high-rise residential communities (commonly known as *countries verticales* or *en altura*) with a variety of services, sports infrastructure, and private security. The territorial dispersion of these has also been very restricted and selective, favoring more central areas of the city and some of the wealthiest metropolitan counties.

Some of these are large-scale transformations that actually create self-sufficient private cities, such as Nordelta, which will have approximately 15,000 hectares, and Puerto Trinidad, with 350 hectares. These suburban communities, accommodating between three hundred thousand and five hundred thousand residents altogether, along with shopping and entertainment centers, constitute the first massive examples of North American–type suburbanization in a metropolis that had maintained until the end of the 1970s a more European pattern of urbanization.

These new residential configurations generate tremendous changes in the landscape and in the urban metropolitan fabric, jeopardizing the classical conception of the functional unity of the urban fabric. One configuration expands the area of construction, densifying in vertical terms but with a visual impression of openness, as in the case of high-rise fully serviced complexes. Other configurations extend the space constructed from the metropolis in radical extensions of very low density, with green areas predominating in the outskirts (Mignaqui 1998). The social implications of these physical configurations are unavoidable: isolation and the de facto exclusion of populations that do not have high or medium-high incomes, an effect readily seen in the offerings of sports infrastructure and security that characterize many of these residential spaces (Mignaqui 1999).

The urban center underwent a triple process of transformation (Ciccolella 1998):

- The existing central districts became denser in a process of increasing verticalization and modernization

- Spillover or extension of the central districts area occurs to the east and southeast. There is a massive recovery and expensive renovation of what had been often neglected and low-value areas of the city such as old Puerto Madero. A similar process of renovation in Retiro will likely lead to expansion of this central district toward the north. From the morphological point of view, the restructuring of centrality in Buenos Aires has drawn a *lineal district,* or one in the form of a corporate *corridor* that connects Puerto Madero through the center and on to Retiro to form a new space of centrality. This contrasts with the previous space of the center, which was compact.

- *Subcenters* appear in the periphery of the agglomeration. The strength of the process is clear. The construction of "smart buildings" alone increased from 100,000 square meters in 1995 to 1 million square meters in 1999, and 700,000 square meters more is under construction. More than 80 percent of the existing office parks were built between 1997 and 1999, and their construction is expected to increase by 70 percent in the next two years. The share of these that are "smart"—designed, wired, and equipped with computer capabilities in mind—has grown tremendously over the years, from less than 10 percent of the office parks built in 1995 to 28 percent in 1999. Close to 40 percent of the office parks currently under construction are "smart," which means that such buildings now, in 2001, constitute 35 percent of the total number of office parks built since 1995. However, this phenomenon does not topple the hegemony of the earlier cited *corridor* extending the old center. This dense and continuous corridor will maintain about two-thirds of the business areas and advanced services, and the rest will be spatially dispersed in the new areas being developed.

The territorial displacement of the poor by affluent people is known in the Anglo-Saxon literature as *gentrification.* As an extension, the residential, cultural, or commercial appropriation by the privileged classes of central spaces occupied by the poor are also denominated in this way. The paradigmatic cases of gentrification have developed from the rehabilitation of old port areas, as in the Docklands in London or the Villa Olimpica in Barcelona. In Buenos Aires, these processes, have been played out at the old Puerto Madero and the Abasto (previously a working-class whole-sale, produce market). What has happened at the Abasto is a case of gentrification in a strict sense, with the physical displacement of the poor.[6]

The development of the outer metropolitan area has brought with it a relative decrease in the flows to and from the center. The new industrial parks, commercial and entertainment centers, and university campuses of the periphery greatly reduce the need for residents to travel to the center to meet their everyday needs. Commutes have been shortened or changed and are much more likely to take residents to the center of their county or to other counties in the area. At least three sociodemographic groups can be identified as having little mobility: the poor, because of unemployment or lack of resources; the young and homemakers, because they can meet their needs locally; and the residents of the gated communities, who make far less frequent trips to the city center than do the people from regular neighborhoods.

These transformations of the last decade of the twentieth century are deepening territorial forms of exclusion associated with Fordist urbanization. Among these are poor settlements, the deterioration of the inner city and the popular habitat created in the Fordist accumulation era, and the growth of shanty towns (*villas miseria*). The territorial segmentation produced by these transformative processes indicates strong dynamism and modernization in some areas, and the deterioration and desertion of others, producing a geography of winners and losers. These transformations and changes in land use are accompanied and allowed by the multiple changes in the institutional frameworks and regulation.[7] More significant, they are allowed by changes at the conceptual and instrumental level of planning and urban management, in which context the state begins to act as a promoter of the large property or private urban transformations (Mignaqui 1997b).

THE NEW GUIDELINES FOR METROPOLITAN DEVELOPMENT

The developments described above can be thought of as *new urban objects* (NUO). These NUO will foster the simultaneous introduction of new construction materials and technologies, and new aesthetic patterns in design and architecture. Thereby they emerge as the main agents in the constitution of new landscapes and urban morphologies. Increasingly, foreign models are taken and followed, especially regarding the construction process and metropolitan urban management, beyond the origin of capital and global control of the new metropolitan economy. The design and upgrading of metropolitan space increasingly originates outside the city and the country in which it is located. In other words, the logic, mechanisms, factors, and actors that preside over the transformation of Buenos Aires increasingly belong to the realm of the global strategies of international capital.

Within the macrotendencies described, the new logic for metropolitan development can be synthesized as follows:

- The different variants of private urbanization described earlier and their associated services (shopping centers, schools, private universities, cinemas, restaurants, and recreational areas) are articulated with the modernization and growth of the roads network and with changes in the guidelines dictated by metropolitan elites.

- The new spaces of entrepreneurial management and production (the proliferation of smart buildings, shopping centers, and businesses, along with international hotel industry expansion) have contributed to strengthening the space of the center in Buenos Aires and to expanding the central business district. Apart from this, the regeneration and consolidation of industrial parks constitutes one of the main guidelines for investment and metropolitan modernization.

Transport and traffic infrastructure have been among the most important investment sectors during the 1990s, with a great impact over the metropolitan restructuring process. Around 150 kilometers of new highway has been constructed, and many preexisting roads have been upgraded and extended. An additional 300 kilometers of highway is under construction and is expected to be finished soon. The estimated total investment in roads in the metro region from 1990 through the end of the decade is estimated at $2 billion. The main beneficiaries of the new or upgraded roads are the new production, consumption, and residential spaces. Built through concessions and toll schemes, these roads are generating new processes of urbanization and metropolitanization[8] because they favor usage of private cars over public transport (trains and buses) and therefore increase car ownership and sharpen socioeconomic differences.

In the 1990s around $4.5 billion[9] was invested in approximately three hundred private urbanizations with an average of 100 hecters and 5 million square meters of built space. Together they cover an urbanized area of 30,000 hectares and have 300 square kilometers of constructed space (one and a half times the area occupied by the city of Buenos Aires); in ten years these types of developments expanded the urbanized area of Metropolitan Buenos Aires by 10 percent. Investments in high-rise residential complexes reached close to $8 billion, distributed among some five hundred projects.

The group of commercial centers in the metro area represents a total investment of approximately $4 billion. Shopping centers have a strong impact because in one site they concentrate a variety of interconnected consumer outlets (megastores, boutiques, department stores, food courts, cinemas, services, photo shops, dry cleaners, etc). They contribute simultaneously to a strong destructuring of previous commercial location patterns and introduce sharp changes in urban land value, traffic patterns, and forms of urbanization. These centers tend to locate near places that are central to other activities and land uses. Of forty shopping centers currently existing in Argentina, twenty-five are located in the Buenos Aires metro area, with more than half of these in the city. Further, the metro area has around two-thirds of the 900,000 square meters of total land area covered and around 2 million square meters of total built area of the country's total. The vast majority of these were developed during the 1990s, especially after 1995. The impact of the concentration of these large shopping centers is especially noticeable in the city of Buenos Aires, which has about a third of the shopping centers (but only 8.5 percent of the national population)

(*Shopping Centers Today* 1999). More than half of the megastores of the country are located in the metro area.

The modernization of retail, and in particular megastores, tends to contribute simultaneously to the generalization and dualization of urban space by helping to define new metropolitan scenarios; by generating new forms of urban fabric that compete with the original urban fabric, fracturing it and isolating the poverty areas, habits that contribute to deepening ruptures in the social fabric; and, finally, by introducing a new labor market structure in which new types of jobs are created and a good part of the preexisting labor and commercial structure is destroyed, increasing marginalization and unemployment levels.

The modernization of entrepreneurial management space with the construction of hypermodern office buildings, smart buildings, and business centers, constitutes yet another relevant investment sector ($2.5 billion) and metropolitan restructuring element. In the second half of the 1990s, around forty office buildings and business centers were built (or are still under construction) with partial or total computer wiring. The expansion and increasing density of these projects within the Buenos Aires center city or over the northern access to the city has led to the formation of specialized areas for business activities that can be defined as command districts. Closely related to this phenomenon is the expansion of hotel capacity, given increased demand by business people and investors. Since 1995, the amount of hotel space has doubled. The new international hotels are concentrated in the center of Buenos Aires, despite the fact that some less central areas have been developed, and even the international hotel industry has, for the very first time, branched out of Buenos Aires with several projects. Similarly, the tourism industry has grown, especially in areas related to science and the arts, and that has also attracted several international hotel franchises. The total investment for this sector—with the historic international hotels (four and five stars) acquired recently by international firms, the new hotels built during the 1990s, and the extensions and upgrading of existing hotels—has been estimated at $1 billion.

The new command districts and international hotels are strengthening the historical patterns of centrality and generating new ones in some privileged peripheries within the metropolitan region. These NUO are changing the overall landscape and the distinctive features of the city, generating new emblematic images of economic power. The loss of the territorial roots of national economic groups seems to be materially related to the adoption of corporate images that reproduce, at a different scale, the architecture and urban expression of the economic power of global centers like Wall Street, La Defense, or Docklands.

Successive restructuring of the industrial sector since the mid-1970s has also modified the landscape and the structure of some metro areas both visually

Investment Sector	U.S.$ Million	Value per Unit U.S.$	Total Area	Investment Source
Roads	2,000	4,440,000/km	450 km	Local 70 percent
Business Centers	2,500	1,470/m2	1.7 million m2	Local 50 percent
Shoppings Centers**	1,400	1,000/m2	1.4 million m2	Foreign 75 percent
Hypermarkets**	2,250	1,125/m2	2 million m2	Foreign 75 percent
Entertainment Centers	150	1,500/m2	100,000 m2	Local 75 percent
Thematic parks	130	—	15 ha	Local 50 percent
Private Neighborhoods	4,500	—	300 km2	Local 70 percent
Vertical Communities***	8,000	800/m2	10 million m2	Local 80 percent
New industrial plants	6,500			Foreign 80 percent
International Hotels	1,000	2,000/m2	500,000 m2	Foreign 75 percent
TOTAL	28,430	—	—	Local 50 percent

* Includes advanced projects

** Total covered area

*** Total area (including the noncovered area) is about twice as big.

Source: based on authors' calculations from data from Fundación Invertir and news media.

and functionally. The regeneration or decline of industrial parks and infrastructure in areas that have traditionally been industrial shows a trend of disarticulation and social and spatial decay. At the same time, the inner metropolitan ring is undergoing a revitalizing and consolidating of new industrial spaces, such as in the Industrial Parks in Pilar, Garin, and Zarate. These include configurations related to IT and organizational technologies of flexible capitalism; the influence of "just in time" technologies; and in the association between Argentinean and Brazilian holding companies as part of Mercosur. Approximately $6.5 billion was invested in new industrial plants,[10] of which 55 percent is concentrated in ten out of forty counties of the northern axis of the metro area.

TOWARD THE DUAL CITY

The patterns of real estate and infrastructure development in Buenos Aires can perhaps best be described as a kind of institutional gentrification rather than gentrification in its most restrictive conception. Between the 1940s and the beginning of the 1980s state-subsidized housing as well as private developments targeted the middle class. This changed sharply in the latter 1980s and 1990s. Today a fractured and dual organization of urban space is evident in Buenos Aires. Spaces formed under the Fordist regime are declining, and in the process socioterritorial destructuring has set in. On the other hand, new central and peripheral spaces that respond to post-Fordist, postmodern, and postindustrial logics are restructuring both the city and the larger metro area. Until the mid-1980s the urban transformation was labor intensive, while during the last fifteen years, it has tended to be more capital intensive. Development has become increasingly autonomous from the size of the population, the demand by people, and from mass consumption. Development today is geared toward the effective and enhanced demand of privileged sectors.

This process has produced an effect very similar to one discussed extensively by Sassen in *The Global City* for the case of New York, London, and Tokyo. In Buenos Aires we see: (1) growth of high- and low-wage jobs, along with the destruction of a much larger number of middle-range skilled jobs held by workers in production and commerce; (2) a growing incidence of precariousness in sectors of new employment compared to older employment patterns; and (3) a fall in real earnings for the large majority of workers. In this new phase, unemployment rates increased from 6 percent to 8 percent in the 1980s and soared to 15 percent in the last years of the 1990s, with a decrease of between 15 percent and 20 percent in purchase power. Temporary employment increased from 27 percent in 1990 to 35 percent in 1998, and 75 percent of the jobs created during 1998 were temporary or informal.

Entire areas in the city of Buenos Aires and entire communities in the metro area have barely registered metropolitan globalization. Nor have they obtained any benefits from it from a social perspective. In the city of Buenos Aires, with only 5.2 percent of the population living below the poverty level, compared to 71 percent in Gran Buenos Aires, the resident population in shanty towns increased 65 percent between 1991 and 1998. Curiously, although there are opulent areas (Recoleta, Palermo, Belgrano) and modest ones (almost all the southern part of the city of Buenos Aires), marginalization measured in absolute terms is as present if not more so in those opulent areas as in the southern barrios of the city.

A trialectic seems to shape the spatial reorganization of metropolitan Buenos Aires at the end of the century, one that combines European virtues, North American corruption, and Latin American contrasts. European origins are evident in architecture, urbanism, urban fabric, and quality of public space. Characteristic of the large Latin American cities, and some of their suburbs, as well as North American slums are the ruptures of the urban fabric of some central areas—postmetropolitan urbanization, disorder, and a mix of urban conditions. Buenos Aires is a city in three different speeds: a just-in-time city, on line and in real global time, inhabited by 10 or 15 percent of its population that moves rapidly by computer networks and state-of-the-art highways; a second city constituted by the majority of the population, that still moves slowly through avenues and streets; and a motionless city of those who are not able even to displace themselves, the city of between 25 and 30 percent of the population.

OPEN END: BUENOS AIRES GLOBAL OR DUAL?

After fifteen years of low growth and little change, Buenos Aires underwent accelerated transformation in the 1990s. Key components are foreign capital flows and the development of new types of urban projects that are materially and symbolically related to economic globalization and to the sociocultural postmodernist paradigm. The boom of the 1990s is profoundly disassociated from its population. The increased prosperity of the 10 percent of households with incomes higher than $2,000 per month is not enough to compensate for the impoverishment of most of the strata left behind. As in the cities described by Sassen, the explanation lies partly in the growing importance of intermediate consumption in the economy rather than household consumption. In this way, Buenos Aires seems to follow from a distance—and probably with a worsening of the most perverse aspects—the changes in the urban economy that Saskia Sassen documents for New York, London, and Tokyo.

What is the meaning of the mostly foreign control over the development of urban space in Buenos Aires and the weakening of the nation-state's control over its main city? On the one hand, it could be argued that Buenos Aires is experiencing a process of material expansion of its globalized space and that the city proper has growing visibility among global investors. The increase in business trips, business centers, financial activities and corporate services, the proliferation of "common places" of globalization (international hotels, shopping centers, megastores, private suburbs, restaurants, exclusive boutiques, city verticalization, gentrification, and designer-shaped urban lifestyles), all suggest that Buenos Aires undoubtedly is living the symptoms of a peripheral megacity strongly marked by the penetration of the global economy. However, another process, less spectacular, is also taking place in the form of a deepening of social polarization, exclusion, and socioterritorial metropolitan fragmentation. The slums and marginal areas of the 1990s, without demanding as much space as that used by gated communities, have not stopped growing or spreading.

The profound dualization of Buenos Aires advances through processes of social exclusion and territorial fragmentation. The marked territorial selectivity of investments at the end of the century is a key factor in development and the strengthening of this new metropolitan map. Dualization is growing rapidly because there is no resistance or containment via direct state intervention, neither through investment or the large-scale generation of low-income housing programs and social infrastructure. There is now also a new map of public and private spaces in Buenos Aires, not only in terms of social use, but even more because it demarcates spaces for different types of social actors depending on investment. This has produced tensions between strengthening classic forms of urban centrality and the formation of new centralities, illustrated by the concentration of almost 80 percent of investments in the northern axis of Buenos Aires. High-income sectors have emerged as subjects of this type of metropolitan expansion and as its promoting agents.

The facts described in this chapter raise a final question, one present in an important part of the literature about urban transformation: Is there a contradiction between globalization and dualization processes in Buenos Aires? Is Buenos Aires becoming a global city or a dual city? Is the dualization of cities a contradiction or *an essential characteristic* of the new post-Fordist, postmodern, and postindustrial metropolitan space of both Sassen's global cities and peripheral megacities?

NOTES

The author thanks the Institute for Advanced Study, United Nations University (Tokyo) for its support. This chapter is based on the first results of the research program PROREMBA (Programa de Estudios sobre Reestructuracion Metropolitana in Buenos Aires), which includes several research projects financed by the University of Buenos Aires.

1. The Metropolitan Region of Buenos Aires includes the city of Buenos Aires (200 square kilometers and 3.1 millions residents), the inner metropolitan region with twenty-five counties in an area of 3,680 square kilometers and with a population of about 9 million, and the outer region with an area of about 15,800 square kilometers and a population of 1.6 million residents. Together they

comprise an area of 19,680 square kilometers and a population of about 13.7 million. The focus in this chapter is mostly on the first two.

2. This refers to activities such as production management, project engineering, information control, research and development, technological innovation, financial consultancy, accounting, information technologies, etc.

3. According to the meaning given by Kamppeter (1995) when he talks about *fertility* as a collection of attractive conditions for capital (95–97).

4. In some cases it can be observed that the condition of winners and losers of certain subspaces and regions is ephemeral. There are many examples of winner regions in the 1980s that became losers in the 1990s. In Argentina, such regions include Ushuaia, Rio Grande, San Luis, and La Rioja, while Buenos Aires and Cordoba are two metropolitan regions that lost in the 1980s but became winners in the 1990s.

5. Among these are *barrios cerrados,* marinas, farm clubs, pueblos, and *ciudades privadas.*

6. In the case of London, Dublin, New York, Paris, and Barcelona, these operations have tended to worsen social problems, by displacing a large number of people who subsequently became part of the homeless population.

7. Among these are the overall state reform, Convertibility Law, privatization, concessions, decentralization of governmental functions, Law of Economic Emergency, Conurbano Bonaerense Fund, Reforms to the Law 8912 of Ordenamiento and Land Use of the Buenos Aires Province, multiple exceptions to the Urban Planning Code of the City of Buenos Aires, etc.

8. Commuting times from the outer metro area have been reduced. Realtors and developers are using the (alleged) easy commute as a marketing ploy. Advertisements for gated communities in the southeast zone, for instance emphasize the fact that they are only 15 minutes from Puerto Madero in the center.

9. Taking into account the initial land purchase investment in the development of infrastructure and an estimate of investment in the construction of about 24,600 houses (*Prensa Economica* 1999).

10. Adding the extension of existing plants, the investment figure jumps to approximately $17 billion. Adding the purchase of goods, the total reaches $ 23 billion.

REFERENCES CITED

Arizaga, M. C. 1999. "Los barrios cerrados y el mito de la comunidad purificada," *Reviste de Arquitectura de la Sociedad Central de Arquitectos* 193. Buenos Aires.

Benko, G., and A. Lipietz. 1994. "El nuevo debate regional." In *Las regiones que ganan,* ed. G. Benko and A. Lipietz. Valencia, Spain: Edición Alfons el Magnanim.

Caprón, G. 1996. "La ville privée: les shopping centers à Buenos Aires." Doctoral dissertation, University of Toulouse.

Castells, M. 1995. *La ciudad informacional. Tecnologías de información, reestructuración económica y el proceso urbano-regional.* Madrid: Alianza Editorial.

Centro de Estudios para la Producción. 1998. *Síntesis de la Economía* Real 16. CEP, Secretaría de Industria y Minería-Ministerio de Economía y Obras y Servicios Públicos, Buenos Aires.

Chudnovsky, D., and A. López. 1998. "Las estrategias de las empresas transnacionales en la Argentina y Brasil ¿Qué hay de nuevo en los años noventa?" *Desarrollo Económico,* Número Especial, vol. 38. Buenos Aires: IDES.

Ciccolella, P. 1995. "Reestructuración global, transformaciones económicas en la Argentina y reterritorialización de la Región Metropolitana de Buenos Aires. Hacia una ciudad competitiva, globalizada y excluyente," *Revista de Estudios Regionales* 43. Málaga: University of Andalucía Press.

———. 1998. "Territorio de Consumo. Redefinición del espacio en Buenos Aires en el fin de siglo." In *Ciudades y Regiones frente al avance de la Globalización,* comp. S. Gorenstein and C. R. Bustos. Bahía Blanca: Press of the National University of the South.

Ciccolella, P., and I. Mignaqui. 1994. "Territorios integrados y reestructurados. Un nuevo contexto para el debate sobre el Estado y la Planificación," *Revista Interamericana de Planificación* 106. Cuenca, Ecuador: SIAP.

de Mattos, C. 1995. *Globalización, territorio y ciudad: el caso de Chile.* Documentos, Instituto de Estudios Urbanos, Santiago de Chile: PUCCH.

———. 1997. "Globalización, movimientos del capital, mercados de trabajo y concentración territorial expandida." In *Fronteiras na América Latina,* org. I. Castello, et al. (Org.) Porto Alegre, Brasil. FEE-Editora da Universidade, Universidade Federal de Río Grande do Sul.

Featherstone, M. 1995. *Cultura de consumo e Pós-Modernismo:* Studio Nobel, São Paulo.

Fernandez, D. R. 1993. "La metrópolis como espacio de la crisis global," *Espacio y Sociedad* 8, Madrid.

Ferreira, F. R. 1996. *Centres Commerciaux: Îles Urbaines de la Post-Modernité.* Paris: L'Harmattan.

García, C. N. 1995. *Consumidores y ciudadanos. Conflictos multiculturales de la globalización.* Buenos Aires: Edit Grijalbo.

Indec. 1994 and 1997. *Edificación. Permisos de construcción privada en Argentina.* Buenos Aires: Indec.

Jameson, F. 1992. *El posmodernismo o la lógica cultural del capitalismo avanzado.* Buenos Aires: Paidós.

Kamppeter, Werner. 1995. "Fertilidad Nacional, Estado—Nación y Sistema Economico Mundial." *Nueva Sociedad.* Caracas, Nro. 137.

Kralich, S. 1998. "Accesibilidad y exclusión social en el Gran Buenos Aires." In *Globalización y territorio: mercados de trabajo y nuevas formas de exclusion,* ed. I. Caravaca. Huelva: University of Huelva.

Méndez, R. 1997. *Geografía Económica. La lógica espacial del capitalismo global.* Madrid: Ariel.

Mignaqui, I. 1997. "Barrios cerrados y fragmentación espacial." *Revista Distrito 2* (34). La Plata, Colegio de arquitectos de la provincia de Buenos Aires.

———. 1998. "Dinámica inmobiliaria y transformaciones metropolitanas. La producción del espacio residencial en la RMBA en los '90: una aproximación a la geografía de la riqueza." In *Actas del IV Seminario Internacional sobre globalización y Territorio, Red Iberoamericana de Investigaciones sobre Globalización y Territorio.* CIDER–Universidad de Los Andes, Bogotá, Colombia, 1998.

———. 1999. "De falansterios, garden cities y barrios cerrados," *Revista de Arquitectura de la Sociedad Central de Arquitectos* 193, Buenos Aires.

———. 1997b. "Reforma del estado y práctica urbanística. Las intervenciones urbanas recientes en Capital Federal: entre la ciudad global y la ciudad excluyente." In *Postales urbanas del fin del milenio. Una construcción de muchos,* comp. H. Herzer. Buenos Aires: Ediciones del CBC, Instituto de Investigaciones Gino Germani, Fac. de Ciencias Sociales, UBA.

Precedo Ledo, A. 1996. *Ciudad y desarrollo Urbano.* Madrid: Edit. Síntesis.

Prensa Económica. 1999. Special edition, April, Buenos Aires.

Sack, R. 1992. *Place, Modernity, and the Consumer's World.* Baltimore: Johns Hopkins University Press.

Santos, M. 1996. *A naturaleza do espaço. Técica e tempo. Razao e emoçao.* São Paulo, Brazil: HUCITEC.

Sassen, S. 1994. "La ville globale. Elements pour une lecture de Paris." *Débat* 80. Paris: Gallimard.

———. 1999 *La ciudad global. Nueva York, Londres, Tokio.* Buenos Aires: Eudeba.

Sennett, R. 1975. *Vida urbana e identidad personal. Los usos del desorden.* Barcelona: Colección Homosociologicus. Editorial Península.

Shopping Centers Today. 1999. April. Buenos Aires.

Veltz, P. 1994a. "Jerarquías y redes en la organización de la producción y el territorio." In *Las regiones que ganan,* ed. G. Benko and A. Lipietz. Valencia, Spain: Edicion Alfons el Magnanim.

———. 1994b. *Des territoires pour apprendre et innover.* Paris: Editions de l'aube.

Chapter 12

LOCAL NETWORKS: DIGITAL CITY AMSTERDAM

Patrice Riemens and Geert Lovink

This essay is part of an ongoing participatory action research endeavor into the Digital City (DDS De Digitale Stad), an Amsterdam-based free community network and the most famous of the initiatives that became known collectively as the Amsterdam Public Digital Culture. Launched in January 1994, the DDS quickly attracted tens of thousands of users, making it the largest "freenet" in the world. Thanks to the publicity it generated, it was instrumental in the introduction of the Internet to the general public in the Netherlands. The aim of its founders was to democratize the use of the Net and create a digital public domain.

In the first part of this essay we will look at the local roots and the premises underlying the Digital City project within the broader new media culture that existed in Amsterdam in the early 1990s. The second part focuses on internal developments within DDS in the late 1990s, since they exemplify the changes that occurred in the local media culture with the tremendous growth of the Internet. Finally, since DDS is a work in progress, we will devote an afterword to the most recent developments, including DDS's buyout and privatization, the determination of the new owners to discontinue the public domain functions of the Digital City, and the resistance that decision provoked among users, former DDS employees, and various concerned groups.

THE IMPORTANCE OF BROAD PUBLIC MEDIA CULTURES

By the early 1990s, the (in)famous Amsterdam squatters movement, which had dominated the sociocultural and political (law-and-order) agenda in the previous decade, had petered out in the city's streets. But its autonomous yet pragmatic mode of operation had spread to the more progressive cultural institutions. It was a time when cultural centers like Paradiso and De Balie, which were at the vanguard of local cultural politics, embraced the theme of "technological culture" in their programming. In the beginning this took the shape of a critical, if somewhat passive, observation of the new technologies, their risks and opportunities. This lectures-based approach was soon replaced, however, by more broadly based efforts whereby various Amsterdam groups and the public joined in making an event happen.

The shift, which reflects a shift in generations, came when (information) technology was no longer seen as the preserve of science, big business, or the government, but as a venue for the handiwork of average groups or individuals. Mass availability of cheap electronic hardware and components had created a broad user base for decidedly low-tech applications, which in turn spawned a profusion of video art, pirate radio, public access television initiatives, and well-attended festivals at which technology was put to creative, playful uses. It was a time when the self-appointed vanguards of Amsterdam's progressive cultural sector did not want to merely reflect on the impact of technologies on society but wanted active involvement by society. In this post-Thatcherite, but pre–Third Way era of deregulation and privatization, with brutal and repeated budget cuts in the arts and culture sectors, the expectation that the state would become the architect and caretaker of a public domain in cyberspace ceased to make sense. Its creation and management were going to be matters for the public itself. And the time to act was then and there—before major media corporations had a chance to move in and, in close collaboration with governments, seal off the new electronic spaces to gain control of what they saw primarily as an economic opportunity presented by the accessibility of a broad consumer base.

Originally, of course, computer networks were adopted by the military, financial institutions, and academia, but their usage was restricted to a few well-defined activities. In just a few years, however, a number of grass-roots computer enthusiasts built up a patchwork of bulletin board systems, and it was the hackers' repeated and much-publicized intrusions in the Internet that put electronic communications for the general public on the political agenda. Thus was the demand for public access born, in the Netherlands at least.

What made the Amsterdam situation even more special, however, was the degree of organization among the hackers and their willingness to structure themselves as a new, open social movement. This enabled them to communicate with a wide audience and to negotiate their acceptance in society at large through scribes, cultural mediators, some politicians, and even a few enlightened members of the police force. After a whirlwind performance in Paradiso by the already notorious German Chaos Computer Club in the fall of 1988, the stage was set for the Galactic Hackers Party, the first open, public, and international convention of hackers in Europe. This took place in August 1989, again with Paradiso as venue. From then on, hackers deftly positioned themselves in a cultural landscape dominated by artists, intellectuals, political activists, and cultural workers in general. They even received praise from some parts of the computer industry. The concept of public media was already familiar in Amsterdam, thanks to the uniquely deep penetration of cable broadcasting: cable radio and television reached more than 90 percent of households in the city by the mid-1980s. The cable operation was run by the KTA Corporation, a corporation set up, operated, and owned by the city. It was run as part of the public utilities provision, and the choice of channels it transmitted and its tariff rates were set by the city council. The council had also legislated that one or two channels were to be made available to various constituencies, such as minority and artist groups. This was intended to curb the wild experiments of TV pirates, and so various programs that were broadcast on the local channel had a bill of fare that, to put it mildly, deviated distinctively from mainstream television.[1] Aside from the radio and television shows, a number of small, specialized, noncommercial outfits, proliferated, such as Steim in the realm of electronic music, Montevideo and Time Based Arts in the arts—the former devoted to general art, and the latter to more political video art—and technoculture magazines such as *Mediamatic*.

THE CREATION OF PUBLIC DIGITAL SPACE

All this resulted in a politically (self-)conscious, technically fearless, yet financially modest and hence unassailable atmosphere and constituency, which went a long way in fostering a media culture in Amsterdam that was neither shaped by market-oriented populism nor informed by highbrow cultural elitism. The various players and the institutions in the field did obtain some support from the usual funding bodies and government agencies, but they managed to retain their independence, thanks to a mostly volunteer-based mode of operation and a low-tech—actually, an "in-house tech"—and low-budget approach. In keeping with the ruling market conformist ideology of the time, the shifts in funding practice, moving from recurrent subsidies to project-linked disbursements, left their marks on the format of these activities. Many small-scale productions had thus seen the light, but the establishment of more permanent structures remained constrained. This in turn led to the prevalence of a hands-on, innovative attitude, an ingrained spirit of temporariness, and the deployment of quick-and-dirty aesthetics by groups such as TV 3000, Hoeksteen, Park TV, Rabotnik, and Bellissima (all active in the public broadcasting space provided by the cable channel SALTO). This "edgy" climate also resulted in a dearth of direct linkage with, and hence influence by, the political establishment. Such a media culture was therefore seen as a buffer, an in-between, and not an expression of or an appendage to representative democracy. It reflected what the

Adilkno collective has termed "sovereign media," liberated from the statutory obligation to serve an audience and benefit shareholders (Adilkno 1998).[2]

Thus in late-twentieth-century Amsterdam, noncommercial, public access media were not an instrument of the political class. This does not mean, of course, that they were nonpolitical. The hackers movement, operating under the banner of the Hacktic group (which published a magazine by the same name that was full of technical disclosures, annoying the Telecom managers to no end), threw up a coup by obtaining permission from the Dutch academic network officially to hook up to the Internet and resell the connectivity. What no one had anticipated, least of all the budding hackers-turned-entrepreneurs, was that all five hundred accounts that formed the starting base of Hacktic Network would be snapped up the first day. Access to the Internet through nontraditional service providers was henceforth established as a norm of sorts in the Netherlands. Combined with the technological savvy of the hackers, this created a situation in which commercial enterprise would follow. The latter benefited from the existing creative diversity rather than riding the waves of the Internet hype and making quick money without any incentive to innovate or any concern for public participation.[3]

These developments did not escape the smarter elements in the government who were on the lookout for ways to modernize the social and economic infrastructure of the country in the wake of a global economy. Since electronic communication was at the same time perceived to pose all sorts of threats on the law-and-order front, a two-pronged approach obtained, meant to contain the "menace" on the one hand, and to co-opt the "whiz kids" on the other. Comprehensive and fairly harsh laws targeting computer crime were approved by Parliament in 1993. The second big hackers convention in the Netherlands, Hacking at the End of the Universe, in the summer of 1993, responded to this potentially repressive climate with a public relations offensive. By stressing the public liberties aspect, the convention formed a coalition among computer activists and various media, culture, and business players who did not want to be reduced to being mere consumers of the agenda set by big corporations. The idea was that programmers, artists, and other concerned parties could—if they moved early enough—shape, or at least influence, the architecture and the content of the networks. This was also the characteristic stance of the earliest Internet users since it enables one to gain ideological ascendance when influential projects are taking shape, a move suitably, if somewhat cryptically, called in German *Die Definition der Lage in die Hand nemen* (to take the definition of the situation in one's own hands). It was a form of citizens' activism which in the late 1990s would be identified and relabeled as the "spirit of entrepreneurial leadership."

Elected politicians meanwhile struggled with another "situational" prob-

PATRICE RIEMENS AND GEERT LOVINK

lem: that of their very own position amid dwindling public support and sagging credibility. This was blamed on a "communication deficit" for which a substantial application of new media suddenly appeared to be an instant antidote. The cue was not lost on De Balie cultural center, which approached City Hall with a freenet-based proposal to link up the town's inhabitants through the Internet so that they could engage in dialogue with their representatives and with policy makers. The system itself was to be set up by the members of Hacktic Network, the only group of "technologists" that was readily available—or affordable—at that time. The Digital City of Amsterdam was launched as a ten-week experiment in electronic democracy to coincide with campaigns for municipal elections to be held in mid-March 1994. In no time, "everybody" was communicating with everybody else—with one exception: the politicians themselves never made it to the new medium.

Even though the DDS did not bridge the gap between politicians and the electorate, it soon grew to be Europe's largest and most famous public computer network, or freenet. In practice, this meant scores of dial-in phone lines, a free e-mail address for every user (and, later, disk space for a home page), lots of opportunity to make contact and gather or disseminate information, and, above all, freedom from censorship and surveillance. The Digital City also grew rapidly into an international symbol of the public domain in cyberspace. It is unquestionable that the DDS functioned as a catalyst for Internet acquaintance and usage in the Netherlands. For many it represented their first contact with the world of electronic networks, either because they participated themselves or because they read or watched television programs about it.

The central interface played a key role in the evolution of the community identity of the Digital City. It was originally designed to provide within a fully text-based environment an overview of the mass of information on offer. In keeping with the metaphor implied in the system's name, the DDS interface is built around the notions of "squares," "buildings," "homes," "streets," and "side streets." But it does not show pictures of or simulate the actual Amsterdam cityscape, as many people had expected. Rather, the arrangement is intended to be thematic, such as to attract communities of (shared) interests. There are, for instance, squares devoted to the environment, death, sports, books, tourism, social activism, government and administration, and so on. But the interface was never able to give a full representation of the underlying activities. News features and the DDS newspaper, *The Digital Citizen*, attempted to fill this gap.

By mid-1998 DDS had more than seventy thousand "inhabitants"—that is, registered users—and many more visitors, or "tourists." Even more people wanted to join, but the limits of the system's capacity had been reached long before. The Amsterdam Digital City had spawned a diverse and lively Internet culture. Most European community Internet and web projects that tried to match DDS's initial success remained fairly empty and virtual indeed. For example, Berlin's Internationale Stadt initiative, the DDS's closest clone, never had more than about three hundred users, and it closed down in early 1998.

The DDS system came to be so big and intricate that hardly anybody—least of all the people managing it—had an overview of it. The Digital City had become a huge networked community center without becoming a community in itself. One of the main reasons for this peculiar state of affairs is that DDS never attempted to resolve or even properly address the contradictions in objectives and methods of operation that resulted from the friction between the local and the global that is inherent to the digital age. As Steve Cisler contends (2000: 1), within the DDS and many other freenet-inspired initiatives, "the driving interest in the organizing group was divided between those who wanted a focus on local information, communication, and networking, and those who wanted access to the global Internet." Apart from the decision to stick to the Dutch language in external communication and all administrative matters, the DDS simply let itself be overrun by the onslaught of the Internet (especially in its "World Wide Web" manifestation). But the image of a virtual community, as Howard Rheingold calls it in his book by that name, was never really appropriate here. DDS had rather grown into a multifaceted amalgam of small communities, which shared among themselves the intention to perpetuate the DDS system as an "open city." Out of that, a somewhat Faustian, and in any case unwritten deal was hatched between the inhabitants and the management of the Digital City, whereby the DDS would keep facilitating the activities of the users free of charge and leave them alone for the remainder. Users, in their turn, would allow the management to manage and would not interfere in the daily operations of the DDS "business," thereby acquiescing in the "democracy deficit." From then on, most "inhabitants" used the DDS as a free-of-charge way to roam cyberspace and could hardly be bothered by the alleged Amsterdam stamp of their provider.

In its first few years, however, the Digital City was an enormous success, primarily because of the freedom granted to its users from the beginning. The importance of this factor is perhaps clearest when contrasted with the tight control that universities and businesses exert over Net use, especially outside the Netherlands. The Digital City had quickly rejected the option to become a public relations channel for City Hall under the usual pretense of bringing politics closer to the common people. The DDS system was not the property of the municipal corporation, though many people assumed this to be the case. In fact, apart from the initial grant, the DDS never received any direct subsidy from the local (or national) authorities, and the mundane fact that politics constitutes only a small fragment of our daily lives has proved to be true on the Net as well. Besides, it became apparent rather quickly that politicians were unwilling to familiarize themselves with the new medium and that citizens were far more interested in communicating among themselves.

But the independence that was so crucial to DDS's character ended up costing it a high price. DDS increasingly grew into a business, albeit by default rather than by design, while striving at the same time to retain its not-for-profit character. The DDS organization came to be divided into three components: a commercial department going out for the money, an innovation wing that developed new technologies for paying customers, and the community of users itself, which DDS wished to represent as a social laboratory of sorts. The management courted a handful of major potential customers in hopes they would infuse significant financing into the Digital City. The challenge was to attract projects that fit into DDS's terms of reference, however vague, and that was not a totally frictionless process.

PARTICIPATION IN PUBLIC DIGITAL SPACE

Nina Meilof was hired in 1995 as director of community relations and of the local broadcasting and "streaming media" (combining Internet with radio and TV) wing of DDS operations. Her first task was to organize discussions about local political issues. A number of issues pressed upon the city of Amsterdam at the time, including an attempt to restructure the municipality into an "urban province," a controversial house-building drive into the Y-lake at IJburg, an even more controversial north-south underground railway project, and a proposed expansion of Schiphol Airport, which had the whole environmental community up in arms. The DDS appeared to be a promising tool to stimulate discussion between residents and the city council, and indeed the opinions expressed, which were mainly against the proposals, gained wide publicity and support. But the exchange never led to the kind of sustained discussion that had been hoped for—in many cases, people expressed opinions, then disappeared without trace—and in the end the city council endorsed the projects.

The DDS was more successful in general interest sites, and a broad diversity of "neighborhoods" sprang up in the Digital City. Meilof said in 1996, "A major advantage of DDS remains its anarchic character. There are a lot of secret nooks and crannies." The sites' subject matter varied widely and wildly, ranging from the esoteric and academic to the earthy and mundane. "I was getting the log stats of the most popular houses [home pages], so I would go and look into them from time to time. We had, for instance, a network of male homosexual houses springing up at some juncture. . . . Cars, substances, advice on how to grow your own weed [marijuana], music sites with extensive libraries, and those sorts of things were on offer. There was also a extensive circuit where you could obtain or exchange software, and some of these 'warez-houses' would be up for one or two days only and vanish again. And of course, you had Internet games. . . . But it may also have been a home page on some very rare bird, becoming an internationally famous site attracting ornithologists from all over the planet."

Thus there was a gigantic alternative and underground world that existed "beneath" the official Digital City as it appeared on the surface and in the public eye. The DDS's policy was to look for a balance between the two worlds, between private group interests and general public issues, whereby the subcultures could grow optimally, but without "politics" being discarded altogether. The political subject matter most often brought to the public face of the DDS was of the "Democracy and the Internet" variety. For six months in 1996 and 1997 an experiment was conducted with a Digital Square on Traffic and Transport Issues, sponsored by the Dutch Ministry of Public Works, Roads, and Waterways and paid for by the government. The experiment even boasted the luxury of a professional moderator, journalist Kees van den Bosch, who invited a different high-profile politician each month to stir up discussion. Although van den Bosch expressed satisfaction with the forum, its success— quantitatively and qualitatively—is arguable. The forum generated an impressive number of statements, but these came mostly from a handful of people, and genuinely new ideas and arguments were few and far between. A report evaluating the forum stated that little use had been made of the opportunity to obtain background information on the problems discussed. A large majority of participants (perhaps as many as 75 percent) made one contribution and disappeared, and the remainder soldiered on until the end. The report also mentioned the high occurrence of very personal traffic experiences being recounted.

Issues arising from DDS's experience as a political tool remain unresolved throughout the industry. It is still not clear whether the Net is really a good place, let alone the premier place, to conduct a meaningful, in-depth discussion of political matters. And in DDS's case, its performance as a political medium was compromised by unclarities about its own identity. Was the DDS to be a medium like others with editors who would organize and edit (and hence, censor) the discussion? Or would it be a digital remake of the corner soapbox?

Meilof put more faith in the new media influencing opinion indirectly. A good example was the dressing-down of the referendum instrument by the local body politic. A few weeks before our interview with Meilof in 1996, Amsterdam had introduced the concept of' a "corrective referendum" in matters of local decisions by the municipal council. The idea had not really taken off, because City Hall embarked almost immediately in restricting its scope and upping its threshold at the same time. Meilof said, "Every referendum was getting comprehensive coverage in the DDS, but it was clear every time that politicians did not want to be bothered (with responding)." Although the Internet's growth had been exponential, the institutions and rituals in Amsterdam (as was the case elsewhere) were slow to adapt to the situation.

A completely different political practice was embodied by hackers and kindred groups. They represent a culture of confronting immediate issues and of on-the-spot decision making. Call this activism in a very literal sense, a translation of the "hands-on imperative" in political terms. Potentially explosive issues such as those related to privacy, copyright, sabotage, and the exposure of official secrets are defused in a mix of piecemeal pragmatism, immediatist intensity, and radicalism. This approach enabled the hackers' commercial ventures, to which, unlike the "culture people," they were not at all averse, to grow and prosper against all odds. They published an incredibly popular magazine, *Hacktic*, that kept them financially afloat for years, and they started Hacktic Network, transforming it in short time into a major Internet provider (XS4ALL). Thanks to them the fledging Digital City survived continual bouts of technical glitches and lapses in conceptual guidance at the top. But these type of activities are of course far removed from the grand narrative track, and the traditional media spoke of the movement as if it was a mostly apolitical affair.

Indeed, a tremendous amount has happened over the past few years in the field of ITC development. And ever since its hackers' days, DDS has given entirely free reign in computer-related matters to the technical people. As DDS was also a relatively big but underfunded network growing fast, technical crises were a permanent feature for those handling system operations. Technical problems and glitches were an everyday occurrence as the system's hardware and software were constantly pushed to their operational limits and beyond. Added to this was an overriding ambition to be on the cutting edge in innovative technology, and to take a pole position on the knowledge frontier— which DDS has been remarkably successful at until recently. Many of the innovations took place when Meilof was at DDS. "At some point," she said, "we got heavily into real audio and video [streaming media]. It would be great if we would be able to provide for home-page TV for our users. In order to achieve this, you must be well aware of the latest technical developments, and one must also nurture a good relationship with the owners of bandwidth who are going to carry this fancywork. We wanted to prevent the situation in which normal citizens have to go to big corporate players if they want to put television on the Net—and pay their price. We felt that streaming media too should be readily available to the greatest number, so that any private person could start web-TV at home."[4]

This technical innovation push did not always square well with some users' expectations regarding content and the quality of public discussions. In the early days of DDS, the Digital City was conceived to be an empty shell that would be filled up by users and customers, without much intervention from the DDS organization itself. But that formula resulted in a very static system. Not very much changed in the content structure of DDS over the years.

The Digital Citizen, DDS's online newspaper, was designed in part to put more structure and coherence in the presentation of the system's content. It also carried a line of supplements that users had the option of receiving. This made for an interesting spot for users' contributions, which were filtered by an editorial board. In addition, "webring" technology was made available, whereby sites were automatically beaded together, and visitors could be taken on an organized tour by the editors. As usual, two models competed here. One might be called anarchistic, where things fall into place only after some time, if ever. The other is a more organized one, with editors surfing the place on the lookout for those really interesting sites. A webring was seen as a nice compromise between the two. However, DDS never implemented all the models discussed here, nor did it change its interface very much. In fact, a few years after its inception, and while it was still growing at a fast pace, it became obvious that the Digital City had come to a conceptual standstill.

THE CITY IN PUBLIC DIGITAL SPACE

The fate of DDS as a "city" seemed precarious. Would the city idea die at some point, and with it the DDS, having achieved its emancipatory task? What about its strictly local role? Would that dwindle into insignificance also? Around 1998 no more than a quarter of the "inhabitants" were actually living in the town of Amsterdam.[5]

One of the very few policy decisions that the DDS management took was to retain Dutch as the official language of the Digital City. Many users, for instance, were unwilling or found it difficult to express themselves in English. Generally it was felt that sticking to the tongue of its founding city was one of the few areas where the Digital City could claim some local anchorage. In itself, however, this said very little about the local or global character of the system. That was something for the users to decide, and for their Internet usage to show. Hence, successful home pages usually ended up having international exposure, thus making at least some use of English. But at the same time, the Internet was being increasingly used in a local or regional context. One could now go online to check out the program of the culture club next door. On a more practical level, the question arose of how much longer such typical metaphors as "houses" and the "post office," which had been the hallmark of DDS, would retain any relevance. But then, the Digital City never tried to impose its own metaphors onto the users. It was mostly outsiders, not the inhabitants themselves, who took the Digital City name literally, and then dismissed the city metaphor as inadequate.

But perhaps the city metaphor is not simply inadequate but misleading. After all, the Digital City certainly was not all-inclusive in the way that a real city is. Clearly, the "public" that constitutes a public digital culture is not the same constituency as that of the traditional media, the occupants of the public domain in real space, or the franchised electorate in general. Even if some of the basic tenets of the public domain (and especially its ethics) can be transferred to cyberspace, their mode of implementation is for a large part yet to be invented or put into practice. The barrier of computer literacy is very much operative, and this has a great deal of influence both on which actors are involved and what their actions are. Thus, the digital culture of the late 1990s remained to a large extent the preserve of geeks/hackers, students, media professionals, and of a smattering of people who had the resources and the interest required to become conversant with computers.

Contrast this to the state that seems assumed by the "founding myths" of the network. That refers to a rumored Golden Age when "everybody" was an active participant, and "everything" was public domain. Freeware and shareware were the rules then, a near-perfect gift economy obtained, and the absence of authority was in itself a safeguard to privacy and a guarantee of the upholding of morals. This lore naturally glosses over the fact that users at that time had by necessity an extremely high level of computer competence, and were even less representative of the general population than their counterparts are now. Such an Athenian democracy model automatically generates its own story of inevitable decline. It cannot deal in a positive way with the consolidation of the user base, even though that was the very thing it had propagated in the first place.

Most Amsterdam digital initiatives had, more or less consciously, tried to escape this predicament. This policy was successful insofar as it built upon a well-entrenched pragmatism in matters organizational and connected with a media environment that was traditionally run on a nonprofit basis. In keeping with Dutch values, pluriformity was taken for granted, high expectations were conspicuous by their absence, and benign neglect by the powers that be was the rule. These are still the basic premises of the current situation.

THE CHALLENGES OF CREATING A PUBLIC DIGITAL DOMAIN
Clearly, creating a digital public domain has never been a priority with officials in the Netherlands. Up to now, the state has declined to administrate, design, let alone finance anything looking like a public domain in cyberspace. Even universal access is not seen by the Dutch government as a specific task for the authorities to intervene in. One significant example can be found in the proposal to install public terminals at a large number of locations to provide cheap mass Internet access, an idea that died for want of funding. The total indifference of the body politic to these sorts of issues may be the single most important reason why Internet use has remained relatively exclusive in the Netherlands. Such an approach only reinforces the notion of the public being some kind of indeterminate, and ultimately irrelevant, third space that floats

between participation in the market, where it take cares of itself, and control by the state, the modalities of which are none of its business. To mitigate things on the other hand local customs ensure that as long as you put your requests in the right context—that is, suggesting the possibility of a conflict while at the same time showing an inclination to dialogue—the planning of structures, including those of cyberspace, always remains open to negotiations.

Yet a thorny problem remains. We have left the 1970s far behind, with its well-circumscribed constituencies and the idea of an ordered dialogue by proxies between the public and the political decision makers, and we need to look into the new forms taken by the distribution of influence. The public itself has become much more layered and demands more diversity. Local decision making, on the other hand, has become a virtual process, and this not only in a technical sense. The new media are attractive to politicians only insofar as they allow the politicians to continue their model of "representative" democracy, while modernizing or upgrading it. And so the political establishment, which has never been good at envisioning itself in terms of media (unless it is to abjectly surrender to their whims), is almost totally at loss when it comes to understanding the technological culture. The traditional figure of the "alternative" political activist also had trouble adjusting to the new dispensation obtaining in the Information Age. Nowhere is the love-hate relationship with technology so pronounced as among this group. But split personality, rather than splinter groups, has been the outcome, in a possibly classic case of painful tension between "the Self and the Net" (Manuel Castells). Their deep ambivalence about the nature and the consequences of the new media has for a long time prevented political activists from staking a substantial claim for themselves in the digital revolution. A majority joined the networks only when it became unavoidable. A few embraced bulletin board systems in the 1980s, but most of them were later unable to relate to the higher scale, or speed, of the cyber economy that was coming into being. Hence they found it difficult to bring their practice to the required level of technicality. This failure to use cyberspace as a venue for political change does not, however, reflect on the medium. In fact, quite a few activists have very effectively fought new issues (on animal rights, on gene technology, against road building, etc.), and Amsterdam has witnessed a number of radical projects run by grass-root outfits that have a commendable level of Internet presence.

Despite the obvious limitations, the Amsterdam digital culture has thrived—and still is thriving, in a certain sense. One of the least publicized off-shoots of the digital culture in the city is the number of jobs that have been created: more than ten thousand in the areas of design, software engineering, and services, most in small and medium-size businesses and ventures. Experience in the realm of theater, the visual arts, and music are easily transferred into one-off projects, commercial or not. What is called elsewhere the process of modernization or adjustment to globalization has in Amsterdam frequently taken the shape of a big subcultural work-in-progress in which not everything has been from the very start subjected to the dictates of hype, commodification, or both. This has to some extent put brakes on the ongoing process of institutionalization of social initiatives.

By the late 1990s, Amsterdam, hitherto better known for its large and diverse alternative social movements, saw some spectacular shifts taking place in its urban landscape. After decades of relative economic stagnation, with inhabitants and jobs departing, investments suddenly started flowing back. In just a couple of years, real estate prices rose sharply and exclusive designer shops and gourmet restaurants multiplied. People who had once been unconventional activists followed the trend and reinvented themselves in large numbers as creators and managers in ITC and new media culture.[6]

Meanwhile, DDS too was reinventing itself, at least internally. Hapee de Groot, who worked with the DDS as an editor and content manager from 1997 to 1999, said in an interview with the authors in 2000 that when DDS started up, there was no distinction between the public, external side of DDS and its internal mode of operation. "The DDS was one big collective, and everybody was doing everything," said de Groot. "There were no bosses or functionaries for specific tasks. It was a tight group of people who were interested in working for a good cause. . . . The internal workings of the DDS slowly changed, but the external picture of it did not." The opportunity to turn the Digital City into a truly self-governed networked community was put aside in favor of an executive model of governance, with Joost Flint, coordinator of the organization, at its head. When de Groot joined DDS, a division of labor was already in place, with a sales department, a programming department, a separate section for the technical people, the public domain division, and an administrative branch. Because the DDS was still a foundation, de Groot said, "it was not expected to turn a profit, yet internally it had grown into a top-down organization. Nothing could be done without Joost's fiat. Joost was also the only person reporting to the board of the foundation. And it was the board, in collaboration with Joost, which charted out the future of the Digital City. An organizational structure based on a division of labor may have been inevitable. But in combination with a more open internal structure (such division) could have worked perfectly well. But there was no such open structure. There were no general staff meetings, for instance." Sometime after the foundation's board appointed Joost as director,[7] a management team of sorts came into being. From then on, all employees had to meet preset targets. Even then, complaints were few. In these exciting years, when everyone seemed to be participating in the construction of the Internet, few people involved in the work raised questions about ownership, power relations, and work conditions; it was considered bad form, when it was considered at all. Critiques of the management and demands for more participation, or even for better pay, were rarely expressed.

In league with internal changes at DDS were intrusions of the market ideology that dashed Amsterdam's early hopes of extending the notion of a public sphere in the media, so important to the city in the early 1980s, to the new technologies. This would have lent Internet access the (potential) character of a public utility provision. As we saw, the Digital City was conceived as a temporary experiment. When the decision was made for permanent status, investments in hardware and bandwidth together with increasing staff numbers necessitated ever larger disbursements which were not handled well. Such monies were not easily obtained within a structure characterized by a hybrid and often somewhat uncomfortable mix of community service, technology research and development, and increasingly commercial activities. Neither the city of Amsterdam nor the Dutch state were prepared to provide for recurrent subsidies after their initial disbursements; the European Union, which was approached later, declined to do so. This left as the only remaining avenue of raising money contract work for and sponsorship by the corporate sector, together with consultancy and hosting jobs for various public and semipublic bodies. This mode of operation, besides not sitting very well with community building and community service in general, gave rise to an increasingly obfuscating rhetoric of public-private partnership masquerading as policy. As could be expected, both concepts proved elusive in the end and this lack of direction left the DDS both politically vulnerable and gravely, and permanently, underfinanced.

The growing number of users, with individual requirements and little patience for "idealistically" induced technical deficiencies, as well as the need to deliver a better performance to the paying (institutional) customers, made this predicament even more acute. The lack of substantive political, and hence financial, support compelled the DDS to turn even more to the market, but its status as a foundation precluded it from attracting investors' money.

The final stage in the Digital City's evolution from an amateur, low-tech, nonbudget and grass-roots initiative into a fully professionalized, technology- and business-driven organization came with its corporatization in December 1999. DDS shed its foundation status and became a private enterprise as a result of management buyout. Incorporation took place with the assent of the Digital City Foundation's board, which discharged a number of enabling conditions under which this privatization by DDS's two directors was deemed permissible, while acknowledging at the same time that it was "inevitable."

As it turned out, the inevitable arrived belatedly. By the end of the 1990s, complimentary access and other services that DDS had pioneered became much more generally available. Scores of commercial free access providers and hosting services had entered the market, some offering more and better services than DDS was able to provide. They had mounted massive advertising campaigns, and they addressed a potential customer base that was far removed from the idealistic concerns that had informed the original Digital City. This almost immediately resulted in a substantial erosion, quantitative and qualitative, of the DDS's own user base. Though the number of accounts had risen to an alleged all-time high of 160,000 in early 2000, an analysis of the use patterns shows that most of these could no longer in any way be related to the concept of community building or even to sociopolitically relevant information exchange. Home-page building and upkeep, for instance, no longer attract much interest. And DDS's once-valuable real estate, its web space, has turned into empty lots as fewer inhabitants claimed ownership of an electronic homestead. Most clients in fact saw DDS as a convenient, free funnel for one-to-many, Dutch language interchange, and cared little for the "community" as a whole.

Hundreds of thousands of new users may have debarked on the scene over these past two years, but few have any aspiration to be part of an online culture or a public sphere as such. Their usage is limited to just a few applications (usually provided in a Microsoft OS environment), and they perceive the Internet as a mere component—and probably not the most important one—of a gadget-filled, playful telecommunication sphere.[8] This, by the way, is not meant as a moral judgment. In order to create on-line communities, skills and practices other than the mere possession of a device are necessary; Internet use and new media literacy are not the same.

Aside from France, almost all the European states have declined to administrate, design, let alone finance the public part of cyberspace (the exceptions include Bayern Online, Bologna's Iperbole, and a few others). Rather, we now have a narrow, but, from the political point of view, comfortable economic approach to the opportunities offered by the Information Age. At the street level, we witness the explosion, both in number and size, of Internet cafes catering to the need for connectivity that public utilities have declined to provide. In fact, and completely in tune with the prevalent ideology of market conformism, even universal access is not seen as something for the authorities to intervene in, as one can readily infer from the very limited, usually fruitless efforts to make public access terminals generally available.

In the Dutch new media cultural scene, the Polder model ("the society of dialogue and consensus") has engendered its own digital clone, and it goes under the name of the Virtual Platform. This partnership of sorts between various new media-related cultural institutions was founded in 1997 to build up and maintain a working consensus among its members, thereby avoiding harmful competition. By enforcing a modicum of corporatist discipline—brought about the Dutch way, by endless rounds of meetings—it ensures that the fledgling institutions do not go at each other's throats over such (financial) support as is provided in homeopathic doses by the largely indifferent national and European governmental bodies. The practical outcome of this model is that a limited number of organizations (V2, De Balie, Society for Old and New Media, Steim, Paradiso, Montevideo, and a few others) have shed their startup/experimental/anarchistic avant-garde status and consolidated themselves into new mainstream institutions without being forced to merge or to disappear. The shadow side is that since the Virtual Platform is not a truly open body, its very existence substantially raises the threshold for those newcomers who, for whatever reasons, are not yet members. This then begs the question whether a limited number of not necessarily representative organizations can claim to embody the public digital realm. In the meanwhile, and as could have been foretold, the Virtual Platform has mainly turned into a convenient intermediate for the Ministry of Culture to "outsource" its administrative burden and its policy-making headaches and thus retain patronage without responsibility. For better or worse, this concept has proven a successful formula, and its format, already adopted and adapted by Belgium and (pre-Haider) Austria, is poised for further export.

These "mean and lean" state policies and attitudes have had a surprising outcome: as creative spirits moved out of the limitations and frustrations of the not-for-profit cultural sphere, they went to create their own (ad)ventures on the commercial front. These days, doing business is being experienced as challenging, rewarding, and fun. But it should not hide the fact that the current enthusiasm for entrepreneurial drive was basically the sole option open in those circumstances. The Digital City remains of course the prime example of this flight into capital—as a belief system. But it is far from the only one, and having now all but foundered, it is far from the most successful one.

The commercial analogue of the Virtual Platform has meanwhile come into existence as the Amsterdam New Media Association (ANMA), modeled after the New York original. It has something of the "first Tuesday" format, with less emphasis on networking for venture capital and more emphasis on social networking, debating, and even policy making. Oddly enough, the municipality's Economics Department has awakened to this development and shows itself an enthusiastic supporter, maybe too much so. And with this the circle has been closed. The allegedly receding state turns out to be very present and manages to participate without applying governance. Under this new dispensation, a ubiquitous yet absentee state portrays itself as just another partner in business. Within this depoliticized framework, representation and accountability have been instrumentalized away in favor of convoluted yet subtle "networked" procedures, responding in the mandatory flexible manner to the requirements of the all-powerful and, to culture at least and digital culture in particular, benevolent markets. Alain Minc said it all before: "Democracy is not the natural state of society—but the market is."

POSTSCRIPT: 2001

The buyout of DDS by Joost Flint and his business partner (and DDS co-director) Chris Gödel was finalized on March 1, 2000, when the Digital City was formally incorporated as a limited company. DDS as a whole was vested in a holding company, DDS Holding BV, and its operations were split among four limited companies: DDS Ventures for research, DDS Services for hosting, DDS Projects, the web-design bureau, and DDS City, the community. This setup was merely formalizing the practice that had developed over the years. However, in a commercial environment, it intensified the difference between earning and spending departments, this time, to the detriment of the latter. In the original business plan, the DDS community was seen as a potential breeding ground for all sorts of value-adding activities, which, even though not commercial in themselves, would reflect positively on the balance sheet of the other DDS companies. Unfortunately, the "dot-com" craze was sinking fast at the time, and the community began to be seen as a drag on the holding's resources. In November 2000 the DDS content staff were fired, and the provision of news at the opening pages of the portal was discontinued. Meanwhile, Internet College, a high school students portal site that was the sole component of DDS Ventures, had been sold to an educational publisher, promptly followed by the sale of the hosting company, DDS Services, which was bought by the English electricity utility Energis. This left DDS Projects, the web-design bureau, as the sole revenue-earning company in the holding, further undermining the community's financial base. At that time Flint and Gödel let it known that they were seriously considering dismantling the Digital City as we knew it.

In January 2001 a group of Digital City users decided to forestall, if possible, the likely demise of the public domain section of DDS. An initiative launched by Reinder Rustema in the columns of the online magazine *Smallzine* attracted more than four hundred to the Save the Digital City association, now registered as the Open Domain Association (http://www.opendomein.nl) (the name was changed because of an almost immediate conflict with the holding company about "DDS" as a protected brand name). The association's goal is to take from the holding company as much of the old networked community as possible, with the aim of preserving its spirit as a public domain in cyberspace. The association has initiated talks with the current owners of DDS, but for the moment, finding common ground appears to be an uphill task. Quite apart from the fairly deep distrust both parties harbor about each other's agenda and actions, there is a conflict of interest with regard to the domain name ('dds.nl'), and the value that should be ascribed to the individual, private accounts themselves (now believed to number seventy thousand at the most, half of them active). This also because the mere coming into being of the association has suddenly revived the market's valuation of the DDS, while its subsequent activities have even given credence to the feasibility of transforming it into a fee-earning Internet service provider. For now however, the DDS Holding cannot finance the upkeep of the free service much longer and will have to find a solution in keeping with its commercial interests—including its public relations component. Only the future will tell whether the users association will be part of that solution.[9]

NOTES

The authors thank the Institute for Advanced Study, United Nations University (Tokyo) for its support, and the Center for Advanced Study in the Behavioral Sciences (Palo Alto, CA), for hosting one of the meetings of the research network.

1. The TV pirates were thus taken out, but the radio freebooters stayed on. Three nonprofit "cultural pirate" radio stations continue to be tolerated till the present day.

2. Adilkno, which describes itself as a "foundation for the dissemination of illegal knowledge," an intellectual collective originally based in Amsterdam, described the process in these terms: "Sovereign media insulate themselves against hyper-culture. They seek no connection; they disconnect. . . . Once sovereign, media are no longer attacked, but tolerated and, of course, ignored."

3. Hacktic Network, renamed XS4ALL (Access for All) for obvious marketing reasons, became a profitable, albeit always very tricky, business venture. After protracted negotiations, which ensured complete policy independence for a period of three years, it was sold to KPN Telecom, the former state monopoly, for an undisclosed but significant amount of money. Both its six owners (key members of the original Hacktic group and some associates), and permanent staffers can look at the process with satisfaction. Parts of the proceeds of the sale have also gone to worthy causes, such as the Dutch Branch of the EFF (Electronic Frontier Foundation) and the digital liberties watchdog Bytes of Freedom.

4. It has turned out in the meanwhile that this option was deliberately turned down by the management, which wanted to make it available to a number of selected and paying customers only.

5. Peter van den Besselaar commenced a comprehensive research program in 1996 on DDS in general and its users' profile in particular. In the beginning, these quantitative inquiries were made with permission of and in collaboration with the DDS management. Permission was withdrawn, however, when the DDS's privatization drive transformed these data into "commercially sensitive information."

6. Cheap housing has again become an intractable issue, but yesteryear's activists have few successors.

7. Telling for the state of affairs in the later days of DDS is that the membership of the foundation's board, though not exactly an official secret, was never very much publicized.

8. There are in fact ominous signs that the mobile telephone is going to constitute the main "immersive communication environment" of the larger population, and that, for the moment at least, Internet applications will be a mere, and probably klunky, add-on, Japan seeming to be the exception.

9. Those who had hoped for a change of mind of the authorities on the subject of fostering the public domain in cyberspace are in for yet another disappointment. The city and national governments have let it be known that saving the DDS is not on their agenda.

REFERENCES CITED

CISLER, Steve, "Will Internet Serve Citizens?' (2001)
http://home.inreach.com/cisler/citizens.html
URL list of sites mentioned, or otherwise useful:
http://www.dds.nl

PATRICE RIEMENS AND GEERT LOVINK

(Digital City Amsterdam)
http://www.opendomein.nl
(Newly founded DDS users association)
http://www.xs4all.nl
(Hackers-originated ISP)
http://www.waag.org
(Society for Old and New Media in "de Waag," Amsterdam)
http://www.desk.nl
(cultural/commercial content provider)
http://www.desk.org
(The purely cultural spinoff of the above)
http://www.tv3000.nl
(Cultural/commercial service provider and television producer)
http://www.montevideo.nl
(Dutch Institute for New Media Arts, Amsterdam)
http://www.contrast.org
(Political content provider, sponsored by XS4ALL)
http://www.steim.nl
(Laboratory for Electronic Music)
http://www.bellisima.net
(Experimental cable TV group)
http://www.desk.nl/~hksteen
(Live cable program on politics and the arts)
http://www.radio100.nl/_eng/index.html
(Independent music pirate radio station)
http://www.v2.nl
(V2 Organization for electronic arts, Rotterdam)
http://www.balie.nl
(Center for culture and politics, Amsterdam)
http://www.paradiso.nl
(Cultural center, mostly famous as a pop venue)
http://www.mediamatic.nl
(Design company, magazine for new media arts and theory)
http://www.doorsofperception.com
(Conference organization on design issues, spinoff of the Netherlands design Institute, now closed down)
http://www.anma.nl
(Amsterdam New Media Association)
http://www.dds.nl/~virtplat
(Dutch Virtual Platform)
http://www.balie.nl/tulipomania
("Tulipomania dotcom" conference on the New Economy, Amsterdam, June 2000)
http://www.nettime.org/nettime-nl.w3archive/
(Dutch-language mailing list on [Dutch] new media culture)
http://www.n5m.org
(Conference organization on "tactical media" issues for activists and artists)
http://net.congestion.org
(Streaming media conference)
http://www.squat.net
(International squatters information site)
http://squat.net/ascii/
(Squatters Internet workplace/cybercafe)

Notes on the Contributors

Jon Beaverstock is reader in economic geography at Loughborough University and co-director of GaWC. His research has focused upon London as an international financial center, currently in terms of comparisons with Frankfurt, and elite migration of service professionals between world cities.

Pablo Ciccolella is professor of economic and urban geography, director of the geography department, and director of the Research Program on Metropolitan Restructuring in Buenos Aires at the Institute of Geography of the University of Buenos Aires. He has served on several scientific juries and various advisory panels, including the Economic Development Secretariat of Buenos Aires City Government. He is the author of several books and numerous journal articles.

D. Linda García is director of academic affairs of Georgetown University's Communication, Culture and Technology program. Previously, she was project director and senior associate at the Office of Technology Assessment, U.S. Congress, where she directed studies on electronic commerce, intellectual property rights, telecommunications policy, standards development, and telecommunication and economic development.

Stephen Graham is professor of urban studies in the Centre for Urban Technology in Newcastle University's School of Architecture, Planning and Landscape in the United Kingdom. His books include *Telecommunications and the City: Electronic Spaces, Urban Places* (1996) and *Splintering Urbanism: Networked Infrastructures, Technological Mobilities, and the Urban Condition* (2001).

Eric Huybrechts is the director of a regional research center at METROPO-LIS and CERMOC, in Beirut, Lebanon. He has studied regional and urban planning, urban design, and architecture at several research institutes in France. He has also conducted studies and field work in several countries.

Ramin Keivani worked for several years as a planner and development specialist in Iran. He is currently a researcher at South Bank University, London, oversee-ing projects on globalization and urban competitiveness in Central Europe and the Middle East. He has published a number of journal articles on globalization and urban development. He is a member of Iran's Society of Urban Planners. He worked in the Ministry of Housing from 1993 to 1996 where he supervised the master plans to several cities, iincluding Bandar Abbas and the Horning Strait.

Geert Lovink is a media theorist and activist. He is the founder of numerous Internet initiatives, including the Digital City; former editor of *Mediamatic,* a new media arts magazine; author of *Cracking the Movement, The Media Archive,* and two forthcoming collections of essays and interviews. He also organizes on-line forums and media laboratories.

Iliana Mignaqui is adjunct professor in the faculty of Architecture, Design, and Urban Planning and Director of the Research Program in Urbanization and the City at the University of Buenos Aires. She also is an urban planning consult-ant to the Buenos Aires city government.

David R. Meyer is professor of sociology and urban studies at Brown University in Providence, Rhode Island. He studies international financial intermediaries, their social networks of capital, and their activities in global cities, especially in Asia and Hong Kong. He is the author of *Hong Kong as a Global Metropolis* (2000).

Christof Parnreiter is a researcher at the Institute for Urban and Regional Studies at the Austrian Academy of Sciences and a lecturer at the University of Vienna. His research focuses on the effects of globalization on Latin America, in particular on migration and the development of cities in Mexico.

Ali Parsa is currently reader in planning and director of real estate research at South Bank University, London. He has worked as a consultant for a number of agencies in Iran, the UAE, Japan, and Europe and has written widely on comparative planning policy, urban development, and real estate markets in the emerging markets of central Europe, Asia, and the Middle East. He is co-founder and Chair of the Slaijah Urban Planning Symposium.

Patrice Riemens is a geographer and associate research fellow with the Amsterdam Institute for Globalization Issues and Development Studies of the University of Amsterdam. He is a cultural and Internet activist and works with new media activists worldwide.

Felicity Rose Gu received a Ph.D. in Land Economics from Cambridge University in 2000. Her dissertation was on "Global Economic Change and Urban Development in People's Republic of China." She was a doctoral fellow at the Institute for Advanced Studies, United Nations University (Tokyo) from 1997 to 1998. She has held several positions in international organizations. Most recently with Urban Management as Associate Expert in the Regional Office for Latin America and the Caribbean, she is currently on assignment on behalf of the British Government in several countries in Africa.

Saskia Sassen is Ralph Lewis Professor of Sociology at the University of Chicago and Centennial Visiting Professor at the London School of Economics. Her most recent books are *Guests and Aliens* (1999), *Globalization and Its Discontents* (1998), and a new edition of *The Global City* (2001). Her books have been translated into ten languages. She is currently completing *De-Nationalization* based on her five-year research project titled Governance and Accountability in the Global Economy. She is chair of the newly formed Information Technology, International Cooperation and Global Security Committee of the SSRC.

Sueli Ramos Schiffer is professor of urban planning and head of the Department of Technology in the faculty of architecture and urban planning at the University of São Paulo. She is the author of *The Process of Urbanization in Brazil* (1999) and numerous journal articles.

David Smith is a professor of sociology and urban and regional planning at the University of California, Irvine. He is the author of *Third World Cities in Global Perspective* (1996) and numerous journal articles, coeditor of *A New World Order* (1995) and *States and Sovereignty in the Global Economy,* and editor of the journal *Social Problems.*

Zilai Tang is professor of planning and deputy head of the Department of Urban Planning at Tongji University, Shanghai. He has been involved extensively in academic research on urban spatial transformation and in planning urban land and property development, with a specific focus on the effects of globalization.

Peter J. Taylor is professor of geography at Loughborough University in the United Kingdom and founder of the Globalization and World Cities Study Group and Network. He is founding editor of *Political Geography* and *Review of International Political Geography* and the author of eighteen books and more than two hundred articles.

Michael Timberlake is professor of sociology at the University of Utah. His research interests include urbanization in the world economy, cross-national patterns of socioeconomic development and inequality, and the community context of rural poverty in the United States. His chapter with David Smith in this book is part of a larger project on global cities, their location in urban networks, and their relations.

David Walker is a senior lecturer at Loughborough University. His research has focused upon using geographical information systems to study environmental problems, and his current work involves quantitative analyses of world cities as global service centers.

Index

14, 20–21, 31n. 5, 32n. 9; impacts of new technologies on, 13; of global cities, 74–78, 119, 175, 314; spaces of, 14

centralization, 3, 4, 294, 313

CESP, 214–15

Chen, X., 185

Chicago, 5, 6, 14, 82, 96, 100, 101, 104, 106, 107, 108, 111, 112, 113, 124, 127, 128, 129, 130, 131, 132, 133, 134, 138, 167, 170, 171, 252

Chile (*see also* Santiago), 214, 215, 221, 222, 224, 225, 232, 234n. 11, 310

China (*see also* Fujian; Guangdong; Guangzhou; Hong Kong; Shanghai), 19, 25, 30, 33n. 15, 134, 136, 160, 190, 232, 253, 255–56, 259, 261, 266, 267, 275, 277, 281, 283, 284, 288, 290, 291, 292, 294, 300, 304, 306n. 3; British imperialism and, 256, 306n. 3; businesses in, 292, 304; coastal, 275, 279, 286, 303; Communist Party in, 256, 285; decentralization in, 285, 301–302; eastern, 273, 283, 300, 301, 303, 304, 305; Eastern Airlines, 283; export trade of, 253, 255; financial sector, 274; foreign banks in, 274, 278, 292; foreign investment in, 278–79, 286, 300, 302, 304; imports, 253, 255; industrial sector, 302; infrastructure development, 274, 278, 301; International Trust & Investment, 267; investment in, 280, 300, 303; local governments in, 285; modernization in, 302, 304; Netcom, 267; Pearl River Delta, 276, 303; postreform development patterns in, 274–89, 301; Railway Telecom, 267; reacquisition of sovereign control, 252, 260, 273, 306n. 3; southern, 134, 267, 275, 282, 301, 303; Special Economic Zones in, 275–76; state ownership in, 285–86; Telecom, 267; telecommunications infrastructure in, 290–92, 300; telematics development in, 274, 289–96, 304; Yangtse Delta region, 273, 275, 282, 283, 287, 300, 301–302, 303; Yangtse River Valley, 275, 300, 303

Chinese: banks, 278, 286, 298, 299; capital, 188; cities, 273, 278, 296–97, 301–303, 306n. 3; communities, 254; companies, 289, 292, 295–96, 302; economic development, 273, 279; economy, 273, 284, 285–86, 289, 303; financial sector, 286; government, 255, 275, 281, 286; government corporations, 281, 302; gross domestic product, 289; hinterlands, 275, 303; industry, 276, 303; labor, 187, 302; manu-

facturing, 301–303; merchant communities, 254; migration, 303; Open Coastal Cities, 275, 279; open-door policy, 186; overseas communities, 19, 282; political economy, 274, 285, 296; public policy, 274; railways, 255, 283, 301; sovereignty, 252, 273, 306n. 3; stock markets, 277–78, 286; trade, 253, 274, 279, 281, 300; urban development, 285, 296–97, 300, 303

Ciccolella, Pablo, and Iliana Mignaqui, 31, 347

Cintra, 174

Cisler, Steve, 332

Citibank, 278

Citic Pacific, 267

cities, 9, 17, 312; Arabic, 205n. 3 (*see also* Abu Dhabi; Dubai); Asian, 134, 136, 139, 146, 167; business, 87; Chinese, 273, 278 (*see also* Fujian; Guangdong; Guangzhou; Hong Kong; Shanghai); collaborations between, 27; dedicated networks of, 87; economic sectors of, 27; economies of, 48; European, 122, 134, 139, 167, 170, 171 (*see also* individual city names); galactic, 61; in global south, 2; industrial, 61, 165, 312; information-producing, 78; infrastructures of, 27, 71–91; Iranian, 193–94, 198–99, 204; Latin American, 146, 166, 171 (*see also* Buenos Aires; Santiago; São Paulo); local digital, 27; Mexican, 158, 168–69 (*see also* Mexico City); networks of, 94, 117, 146, 165–72, 183; new technologies and, 4; Pacific Asian, 273–305; smaller, 76; Third World, 146; U.S., 113, 123, 126, 139, 157, 167, 170, 171, 172 (*see also* individual city names); United Arab Emirates (UAE), 191, 203, 204 (*see also* Abu Dhabi; Dubai); wiring of, 71

Citigroup, 266

city: -regions, 72–73, 96; -states, 102, 186, 187; -to-city connections, 87; models, 311

Cleveland, 100

Coca-Cola, 243

Cologne, 100

Colombo, 100

colonialism, 146, 193, 224, 253, 256

COLT (City of London Telecommunications), 80, 84–85, 85

Columbus, Ohio, 100

command and control functions. *See* control and command functions

commodity: chains, 121; exchange, 249–50, 252, 260; flows, 121

communication technologies, 19–20, 52, 250; computer, 93; spatial impact of, 39

Japan (*see also* Tokyo), 10, 12, 23, 88, 102, 103, 186, 187, 209, 233, 254, 255, 256, 258, 259, 261, 279, 281, 282, 283, 284, 301, 304, 344n. 8; foreign direct investment of, 230–33, 297; government of, 25; imports of, 233; Latin America and, 24, 230–33, 234n. 23; NTT, 65n. 40
Jebel Ali, 195, 196, 197
Jeddah, 194, 241
Johannesburg, 6, 7, 34n. 24, 82, 83, 100, 101, 102, 103, 106, 107, 108, 166
Johor state, 186
Jordan, 242, 243

Kansas City, 100
Katz, Daniel, and Robert L. Kahn, 62n. 7
Keeling, David J., 121, 122
Keivani, Ramin, 348
Kellerman, A., 72
Khor Fakkan, 195, 197
Kiev, 100
Kish Island, 189, 191, 192, 193, 194, 195, 196, 197, 198–99, 204
Klang Valley, 186
knowledge, 22, 55–56, 65n. 35, 313; intrafirm, 110; local, 60, 66n. 44
Knox, Paul L., 174
KTA Corporation, 329
Kuala Lumpur, 6, 7, 82, 83, 88, 99, 100, 101, 106, 107, 108
Kuwait, 203, 244

labor, 29, 221; -capital relations, 145; costs of, 187, 196, 199, 256; farm, 51; international divisions of, 18, 24, 66n. 44, 93, 102, 145, 147, 160, 176, 187, 203, 204; low-skilled, 157, 178n. 14, 199, 210, 213; markets, 3, 147, 311; migration, 120–21, 172; regional divisions of, 156–57, 158, 160, 162; skilled, 210, 227; spatial divisions of, 275; supply, 63n. 16
Labuan, 107
Laos, 186
Latin America (*see also* South America), 10, 12, 16, 18, 30, 102, 103, 109, 110, 168, 172–73, 209–12, 213, 215–16, 224, 225, 230, 233, 233n. 4, 309; cities in, 146, 166, 209–33, 309–23 (*see also* Buenos Aires; Santiago; São Paulo); economic restructuring of, 210; foreign direct investment in, 11, 209–11, 231; Japan and, 230–33; privatization process, 210; telecommunications in, 168–69; trade, 173; U.S. firms in, 167

law, 94, 107, 108; firms, 4, 19, 21, 22, 23, 29, 98–99, 102, 110, 162, 166, 167, 249
leased lines, 79, 85
Lebanese: economy, 242; gross domestic product, 243; manufacturing, 243, 245; television, 243
Lebanon (*see also* Beirut), 190, 237–45; balance of trade, 238; Christian militiamen in, 239; diaspora investments in, 240, 244; domestic markets, 244
Leeds, 100
Legere, John, 266
Lehman Brothers, 33n. 22
Li Ka-Shing, 265
Li, Richard, 265
liberalization, 72–74; economic, 74, 309; telecommunications (*see* telecommunications, liberalization)
Lille, 100
Lima, 100
links, 40, 44, 249, 250, 252; Asia-Europe, 291; Asia-U.S., 136; between world cities, 73, 112, 119, 120–22, 174; China-U.S. cable networks, 88; command-and-control, 162; European Union, United States, and Canada, 10; financial, 253; Hong Kong-Asia, 266; Hong Kong-China, 264; Hong Kong-London, 109; Hong Kong-Shanghai, 274, 300–301, 303; intercity, 14, 24, 28–29, 75, 97; intra-Asian, 260; Japan-Brazil, 209; Japan-U.S., 230–31; London-Mexico, 166–67; London-New York, 109; London-Paris, 109; Mexico-U.S., 172; Persian Gulf-central Asia, 195; trade, 199, 253; U.S.-Latin America, 173
Lisbon, 48, 99, 100, 106
local: assets, 94; communities, 139; governments, 311; identities, 309; loop connections, 81
local-global: connections, 74
London (*see also* United Kingdom), 6, 7, 10, 14, 17, 18, 19, 20, 24, 32n. 9, 48, 63n. 13, 74, 75, 76, 81, 82, 83–86, 87, 96, 97, 99, 100, 101, 103, 110, 111, 112, 113, 120, 123, 124, 125, 126, 127, 128, 129, 130, 131, 132, 133, 135, 139, 166, 167, 174, 249, 250, 252, 253, 255, 266, 310, 314, 321, 324n. 6; -located global firms (LLGFs), 104–109, 166–67, 172; and County Bank, 255; and Westminster Bank, 255; City Research Project, 84; Stock Exchange, 23
Longcore, T., and P. Rees, 77
Los Angeles, 6, 7, 14, 82, 100, 101, 105, 106,

Fordist, 317, 321; private, 309, 311–12, 317; Third World, 146
Uruguay, 214, 215, 217, 221, 223, 225, 229
US West, 60
Utrecht, 100

value added, 22, 77, 178n. 14; consultancy firms, 85; functions, 204
van den Besselaar, Peter, 344n. 5
van den Bosch, Kees, 333
Vancouver, 100, 106, 134
Veltz, Pierre, 312
Venice, 48, 49, 63n. 17
vertical integration, 64n. 31, 65n. 32, 65n. 42, 323
verticalities, 313, 315
Vienna, 100
Vietnam, 88, 186, 259
virtual: environments, 60, 332; industrial districts, 60; private networks, 79; studios, 86
Virtual Platform, 341–42
Vivendi, 243
Vodafone, 65n. 40
Volkswagen, 12, 160

Walker, David, 350
Wall Street. *See* New York, stock exchange
Walton, John, 177n. 3
Warf, Barney, 71, 72
Warsaw, 7, 100, 101, 106, 107, 108
Washington, D.C., 6, 7, 100, 101, 106, 107, 108, 166, 167
Wellington, 99, 100
Western: Hemisphere, 12; standards and norms, 32n. 7

World: Bank, 225; Economic Forum, 25; Trade Organization (WTO), 79, 147, 267; Wide Web, 332
world cities (*see also* global cities), 102, 103, 107–111, 117–20, 137, 139, 166–67, 170, 172, 175; alpha, 100, 101, 104, 111, 113, 133, 134, 140n. 1, 166, 175; beta, 100, 101, 133, 139, 166, 170; dominance of, 117–41; firms in, 110–11; formation of, 100–102; gamma, 100, 101, 133; hierarchies of, 103, 117–41; hypothesis, 123, 140n. 1; networks, 102, 110–13, 121, 124, 139; office connections between, 112–13; research, 113, 146; system, 122, 252
world regions, 101, 103, 109, 172
world systems, 117, 119, 147, 174; capitalist, 156; geography of, 146; hierarchies, 175
World War: I, 205n. 3, 253, 254, 255; II, 156
WorldCom/MCI, 65n. 40, 80, 84, 86, 87, 88, 266

Yamaichi: International Capital Management, 33n. 22; Sercurities, 33n. 22
Yankee Group, 76, 81, 84
Yeung, Yue-man, and Fu-chen Lo, 184, 187
Yugoslavia, 32n. 9

Zilai Tang, 349
Zurich (*see also* Switzerland), 6, 7, 11, 14, 20, 32n. 9, 82, 100, 101, 106, 107, 108, 120, 124, 125, 126, 127, 128, 129, 130, 131, 132, 133, 134, 137, 138, 166, 168, 170